Peachtree® Complete Accounting 2006

Errol F. Osteraa, A.B.A.
Heald College

Janet Horne, M.S.
Los Angeles Pierce College

PEARSON

Prentice
Hall

UPPER SADDLE RIVER, NJ 07458

Cataloging data for this publication can be obtained from the Library of Congress.

AVP/Executive Editor: Wendy Craven
VP/Editorial Director: Jeff Shelstad
Product Development Manager: Pamela Hersperger
Project Manager: Kerri Tomasso
Media Product Development Manager: Nancy Welcher
AVP/Executive Marketing Manager: John Wannemacher
Associate Director, Production Editorial: Judy Leale
Senior Managing Editor, Production: Cynthia Regan
Production Editor: Denise Culhane
Permissions Coordinator: Charles Morris
Associate Director, Manufacturing: Vinnie Scelta
Manufacturing Buyer: Michelle Klein
Design/Composition Manager: Christy Mahon
Cover Design: Nancy Thompson
Cover Illustration/Photo: Photodisc
Printer/Binder: Command Web

Pearson Education LTD.
Pearson Education Singapore, Pte. Ltd
Pearson Education, Canada, Ltd
Pearson Education–Japan

Pearson Education Australia PTY, Limited
Pearson Education North Asia Ltd
Pearson Educación de Mexico, S.A. de C.V.
Pearson Education Malaysia, Pte. Ltd.

10 9 8 7 6 5 4 3 2 1
ISBN: 0-13-173537-3

Table of Contents

	Page
Preface	xi

Chapter 1–Introduction to Computers and Peachtree® Complete Accounting 2006

Computers Have Become a Way of Life	1
Introduction to Computer Hardware	1
Introduction to Software	3
Manual Versus Computerized Accounting	5
System Requirements for Peachtree® Complete Accounting 2006	5
How to Open Peachtree® Complete Accounting 2006	6
How to Open a Company	7
Verify an Open Company	8
Introduction to Peachtree® Complete Accounting 2006 Desktop Features	9
Peachtree® Complete Accounting 2006 Navigation Aids	10
Peachtree® Complete Accounting 2006 Custom Toolbar	12
Menu Commands	13
Keyboard Shortcuts	14
Keyboard Conventions	15
On-Screen Help	16
Peachtree® Complete Accounting 2006 Entry Windows	18
Installation Default Settings	21
Peachtree® Complete Accounting 2006 Lists	24
Peachtree® Complete Accounting 2006 Reports	25
Drill Down	25
Peachtree® Complete Accounting 2006 Analysis Graphs	26
How to Use Windows® Calculator	28
How to Close a Company	28
How to Copy a File	29
How to Create a Peachtree® Complete Accounting 2006 Backup File	30
How to Exit Peachtree® Complete Accounting 2006 and End you Work Session	31
Summary	32
End-of-Chapter Questions	33

Chapter 2–Sales and Receivables: Service Business

Accounting for Sales and Receivables	37
Training Tutorial	38
Training Procedures	38
Company Profile: Comprehensive Computer Consulting	39
Begin Training in Peachtree® Complete Accounting 2006	39
How to Open Peachtree® Complete Accounting 2006	39
Open a Company–Comprehensive Computer Consulting	40
Verifying an Open Company	41
Closing the Peachtree® Today Screen	41
Add Your Initials to the Company Name	42

Peachtree® Complete Accounting 2006 Navigation Aids 43
Beginning the Tutorial 43
Enter Sales on Account 47
Edit and Correct Errors 49
Print an Invoice 50
Enter Transactions Using Two Sales Items 52
Printing the Invoice 53
Adding a Note to an Invoice 54
Prepare Invoices Without Step-by-Step Instructions 55
Print A/R Reports 56
Use the Drill Down Feature 58
Correct an Invoice and Print the Corrected Form 58
Void and Delete Sales Forms 60
Prepare Credit Memos 65
View Customer Ledgers Report 67
Add a New Account to the Chart of Accounts 68
Add New Items to List 69
Verify the Additions on the Item List 70
Add a New Customer 70
Modify Customer Records 74
Record Cash Sales 75
Enter Cash Sales Transactions Without Step-by-Step Instructions 77
Print Items Sold to Customers Report 78
Correct a Sales Receipt and Print the Correct Form 79
Analysis Sales 81
Record Customer Payments on Account 83
Record Customer Partial Payments on Account 84
Record Additional Payments on Account Without Step-by-Step Instructions 86
View Customer Ledgers Report 86
View and Print Sales Journal 87
Print the Trial Balance 89
Back Up and Close Company 89
Summary 90
End-of-Chapter Questions 91
End-of-Chapter Problem: SunCare Lawn and Pool Services 95

Chapter 3–Payables and Purchases: Service Business
Accounting for Payables and Purchases 99
Training Tutorial and Procedures 100
Open Peachtree® Complete Accounting 2006 and Comprehensive Computer
   Consulting 100
Beginning the Tutorial 101
Enter a Bill 102
Edit and Correct Records 103
Prepare a Bill Using More Than One Expense Account 104
Print Vendor Ledger Report 105

Use the Drill Down Feature 106

Prepare Bills Without Step-by-Step Instructions 107

Edit a Posted Transaction From the Vendor Ledger Report 109

Preview and Print a Purchases Journal 111

Prepare Cash Requirements Report 112

Change Report Options 113

Delete a Bill 114

Add a New Vendor While Recording a Bill 115

Modify Vendor Records 118

Enter a Credit from a Vendor 119

View Credit in the Vendor Ledgers Report 120

Paying Bills with Select for Payment 121

Printing Checks for Bills 124

Review Bills That Have Been Paid 125

Petty Cash 126

Add Petty Cash Account to the Chart of Accounts 127

Establish Petty Cash Fund by Using Write Checks 127

Record Replenishment of Petty Cash 128

Pay Bills by Using the Payments Window 130

Edit Payment Transaction 133

Prepare a Check Register Report 134

Delete Payment Transaction 135

Print Checks 136

Void Checks 138

Print Post Printing Check Register 138

Print Aged Payables Report 140

Print Vendor Ledger Report 141

View a Single Vendor Ledger 142

View and Print a Cash Disbursements Journal 142

Back Up CCC Data and Close Company 143

Summary 143

End-of-Chapter Questions 144

End-of-Chapter Problem: SunCare Lawn and Pool Services 149

Chapter 4–General Accounting and End-of-Period Procedures: Service Business

General Accounting and End-of-Period Procedures 152

Training Tutorial and Procedures 153

Open Peachtree® Complete Accounting 2006 and Comprehensive Compute
    Consulting 153

Beginning the Tutorial 154

Change the Name of Existing Accounts in the Chart of Accounts 154

Making an Account Inactive 155

Delete and Existing Account from the Chart of Accounts 156

Adjustments for Accrual-Basis Accounting 157

Adjusting Entries–Prepaid Expenses 158

Adjusting Entries–Depreciation 160

View General Journal 161

Owner Withdrawals 162

Additional Cash Investment by Owner... 163

Non-Cash Investment by Owner... 164

View Balance Sheet 165

Bank Reconciliation 167

Open Account Reconciliation 167

Enter Bank Statement Information 169

Adjusting and Correcting Entries–Bank Reconciliation..................................... 170

Print an Account Reconciliation Report 173

View the Account Register for Checking 174

View the General Journal.. 175

The Working Trial Balance 175

Print the General Ledger Trial Balance 177

Prepare and Print Cash Flow Forecast 178

Statement of Cash Flow 179

Print Standard Income Statement... 180

Print Standard Balance Sheet... 181

Exporting Reports to Excel 182

End-of-Period Backup 184

Passwords... 184

Advance to the Next Period 185

Access Transaction for Previous Period 187

Edit Transaction from Previous Period... 189

Post-Closing Trial Balance 191

End-of-Chapter Backup and Close Company.. 192

Summary 192

End-of-Chapter Questions 193

End-of-Chapter Problem: SunCare Lawn and Pool Services 197

End-of-Section 1–Handy Helpers Practice Set: Service Business 202

Chapter 5–Sales and Receivables: Merchandising Business

Accounting for Sales and Receivables in a Merchandising Business.................... 211

Training Tutorial.. 212

Company Profile:High Ridge Ski Shoppe 212

Open a Company–High Ridge Ski Shoppe 212

Verifying an Open Company... 213

Close Opening Messages 213

Add Your Name to the Company Name.. 213

Beginning the Tutorial 213

Enter Sales on Account 216

Edit and Correct Errors 217

Print an Invoice.. 218

Enter Transaction Using More Than One Item and Sales Tax 219

Prepare Invoices Without Step-by-Step Instructions... 220

Enter a Transaction Exceeding a Customer's Credit Limit.. 222
Prepare a Customer Ledgers Report 224
Use the Drilldown Feature 225
Correct an Invoice and Print the Corrected Form 225
Adding New Accounts to the Chart of Accounts.. 227
Add New Items to List 227
Correct an Invoice to Include Discount Pricing... 228
View and Customer Ledgers Report... 229
Add a New Customer 230
Record a Sale to a New Customer 232
Modify Customer Records.. 233
Void and Delete Sales Forms.. 234
Prepare Credit Memos 236
View and Print an Aged Receivables Report.. 238
Record Cash Sales With Sales Tax 239
Accepting Credit Cards 241
Entering a Credit Card Sales... 243
Record Sales Paid by Check 244
Enter Cash Sales Transactions Without Step-by-Step Instructions 245
Print Items Sold to Customers Report 247
Correct a Cash Receipt and Print the Corrected Form... 249
View and Print Taxable/Exempt Sales Report.. 251
Record Customer Payments on Account 251
Record Customer Payment on Account with Credit.. 253
Record Payment on Account from a Customer Qualifying for an Early-Payment
    Discount 254
Record Additional Payments on Account Without Step-by-Step Instructions................. 256
Record Payment on Account from a Customer Losing an Early-Payment Discount 258
View and Print Customer Ledgers Report 259
Print Aged Receivables Report 260
Prepare and Print a Deposits in Transit Report.. 261
Record the Return of a Check Because of Non-sufficient Funds 262
Issue a Credit Memo and a Refund Check.. 265
Print Journals 267
Print the General Ledger Trial Balance 268
Customer Event Log 269
Customer Analysis... 270
Back Up High Ridge Ski Shoppe Data 271
Summary 271
End-of-Chapter Questions 272
End-of-Chapter Problem: Aloha Sun Clothing Co. 278

Chapter 6–Payables and Purchases: Merchandising Business

Accounting for Payables and Purchases 283
Training Tutorial and Procedures 284
Open Peachtree® Complete Accounting 2006 and High Ridge Ski Shoppe 284

Beginning the Tutorial 284
View and Print the Inventory Reorder Worksheet... 285
Purchase Orders 286
Prepare Purchase Orders for New Items.. 286
Prepare a Purchase Order for New Items... 288
Enter Purchase Orders Without Step-by-Step Instructions 291
View and Print Purchase Order Register 292
Change Minimum Stock Level and Reorder Quantity for an Item............................... 292
View and Print the Purchase Order Report.. 293
Receiving Items Ordered 294
Record Receipt of Items Not Accompanied by an Invoice.. 295
Enter Receipt of an Invoice for Items Already Received 296
Verify That Purchase Order is Marked Closed.. 297
Record Receipt of Items and an Invoice 298
Edit a Purchase Order 299
Record a Partial Receipt of Merchandise Ordered 300
Close Purchase Order Manually 301
Enter a Credit from a Vendor.. 302
Verify Vendor Account Balance.. 303
Enter a Bill 303
Edit Existing Vendors 305
Recording Bills Without Step-by-Step Instructions 306
Edit a Transaction from the Purchases Journal.. 307
Prepare and Print Cash Requirements Report.. 308
Paying Bills With Select for Payment 309
Printing Checks for Bills.. 311
Print Taxable/Exempt Sales Report 312
Paying Sales Tax.. 312
Voiding and Deleting Purchase Orders, Invoices and Checks 313
Vendor Event Log... 314
View and Print an Aged Payables Report.. 314
Backup High Ridge Ski Shoppe Data... 315
Summary 316
End-of-Chapter Questions 316
End-of-Chapter Problem: Aloha Sun Clothing Co. 320

Chapter 7–General Accounting and End-of-Period Procedures: Merchandising Business
General Accounting and End-of-Period Procedures... 324
Training Tutorial and Procedures 325
Open Peachtree® Complete Accounting 2006 and High Ridge Ski Shoppe 325
Beginning the Tutorial.. 325
Change the Name of Existing Accounts in the Chart of Accounts............................... 326
Make an Account Inactive 327
Delete an Existing Account from the Chart of Accounts 328
Adjustments for Accrual-Based Accounting 328
Adjusting Entries–Prepaid Expenses... 329

Adjusting Entries–Depreciation.. 331
Prepare and Print Standard Income Statement... 333
View General Journal 334
Definition of a Partnership... 334
Owner Withdrawals 335
A Note About Net Income/Retained Earnings... 336
Bank Reconciliation 338
Open Account Reconciliation... 339
Enter Bank Statement Information 340
Adjusting and Correcting Entries–Bank Reconciliation.................................. 342
Print and Account Reconciliation Report 344
View the Account Register for Checking 345
View the General Journal.. 346
Print the General Ledger Trial Balance 347
Print Standard Income Statement... 348
Print Standard Balance Sheet 349
Exporting Reports to Excel 350
End-of-Period Backup 353
Passwords.. 353
Advance to the Next Period 354
Access Transaction For Pervious Period 356
Edit Transaction From Previous Period.. 356
Verify the Correction to the Supplies Accounts 358
Footnote for Inventory Adjustments... 359
Back Up 360
Summary.. 360
End-of-Chapter Questions 362
End-of-Chapter Problem: Aloha Sun Clothing Co. 367

End-of-Section 2–Planet Golf Practice Set: Merchandising Business 371

Chapter 8–Payroll
Payroll... 383
Training Tutorial 384
Open Peachtree® Complete Accounting 2006 and Brekners Co. 384
Create Pay Checks 384
Printing Pay Checks 391
Change Employee Information 391
Add a New Employee 392
Create and Print Pay Checks for the Next Pay Period..................................... 395
Voiding and Deleting Checks 400
Payroll Reports.. 402
Print Current Earnings Report 403
Payroll Tax Liability Report 404
Pay Tax Liabilities 405
Pay Other Payroll Liabilities.. 407

Filing Payroll Tax Forms 410

Prepare and Print Form 941 410

Prepare and Print Form 940 412

Prepare and Print Employee's W-2 Forms 413

Backup 415

Summary 415

End-of-Chapter Questions 416

End-of-Chapter Problem: Aqua Ski Manufacturing 420

Chapter 9–Computerizing a Manual Accounting System

Computerizing a Manual Accounting System 424

Training Tutorial 424

Company Profile: Ike's Bikes 424

Create a New Company 425

General Ledger Setup 433

Accounts Payables Setup 436

Tax Tables Setup 440

Accounts Receivable Setup 442

Payroll Setup 445

Inventory Items Setup 452

Jobs Setup 456

Print Lists and Reports 456

Backup 457

Summary 457

End-of-Chapter Questions 458

End-of-Chapter Problem: Gotta Dance 463

End-of-Section 3–The Paint Can Practice Set: Merchandising Business 470

Appendix 489

Index 501

Preface

Peachtree® Complete Accounting 2006 is a comprehensive instructional learning resource. This text has been designed to respond to the growing trend toward adopting Windows® applications and computerizing accounting systems. As a result of this trend, the text provides training using *Windows® 95/98/2000/XP* and the popular Peachtree® Complete Accounting 2006 accounting program.

ORGANIZATIONAL FEATURES

Peachtree® Complete Accounting 2006 is organized into three sections. Accounting concepts and their relationship to Peachtree® Complete Accounting 2006 are presented in each chapter. In addition to accounting concepts, students use a fictitious company and receive hands-on training in the use of Peachtree® Complete Accounting 2006 within each chapter. At the end of every chapter, the concepts and applications learned are reinforced by the completion of true/false, multiple-choice, fill-in and essay questions plus an application problem using a different fictitious company. At the end of each section, there is a comprehensive practice set that reviews all the concepts and applications presented within the section. The final practice set is a comprehensive problem utilizing all of the major concepts and transactions presented within the textbook.

The first section introduces students to the computer, Windows® and Peachtree® Complete Accounting 2006 for a service business. The second section of the text focuses on merchandising businesses. The third section of the book concentrates on payroll and setting up a new company using Peachtree®Complete Accounting 2006.

DISTINGUISHING FEATURES

Throughout the text, emphasis has been placed on the use of Peachtree® Complete Accounting 2006's innovative approach to recording accounting transactions based on a business form rather than using the traditional journal format. This approach, however, has been correlated to traditional accounting through adjusting entries, end-of-period procedures, and use of the "behind the scenes" journals.

Unlike many other computerized accounting programs, Peachtree® Complete Accounting 2006 is user-friendly when corrections and adjustments are required. The ease of corrections and the ramifications as a result of this ease are explored thoroughly.

The text provides extensive assignment material in the form of tutorials, end-of-chapter questions (true/false, multiple-choice, fill-in and essay), and comprehensive practice sets.

Students develop confidence in recording business transactions using an up-to-date commercial software program designed for small to mid-size businesses. With thorough exploration of the program in the text, students should be able to use Peachtree® Complete Accounting 2006 in the "real world" at the completion of the textbook training.

Students will explore and use many of the features of Peachtree® Complete Accounting 2006, including recording transactions, applying customer and vendor discounts, tracking inventory, ordering merchandise, preparing a multitude of reports and closing an accounting period. Peachtree® Complete Accounting 2006 features integration with Microsoft Excel is explored.

In the last practice set, students will have an opportunity to create the computerized records for a company. They will then record transactions, print reports….et al.

COURSES

Peachtree® Complete Accounting 2006 is designed for a one-term course in microcomputer accounting or for use in any accounting course requiring introductory work on a integrated computerized accounting package. Students should be familiar with the accounting cycle and how it is related to service and merchandising businesses. No prior knowledge of or experience with computers, Windows, or Peachtree® Complete Accounting 2006 is required.

SUPPLEMENTS FOR THE INSTRUCTOR

The instructor resources, including the Solutions Manual, Teaching Guide and Tests that also contains a comprehensive answer key to all questions, exercises and practice sets are available at www.prenhall.com/compaccounting. In addition to answers to text assignments, the Teaching Guide and Tests for Peachtree Complete Accounting 2006 contains master data files for all the companies in the text, a sample course outline, lectures for each chapter, written exams for each section, and suggestions for grading. Included are back up positions for the companies at the end of each chapter. Lecture materials include a lecture outline for each chapter and a hands-on demonstration lecture.

SUPPLEMENTS FOR THE STUDENT

The data files for this text are available for download at www.prenhall.com/compaccounting.

WHAT'S NEW FROM PEACHTREE FOR 2006?

Each year, Peachtree adds new or enhances existing features in it's program. The following are the significant items for 2006:

- Online Bank Reconciliation

    Reduce the time that it takes to reconcile bank accounts by downloading bank statements into Peachtree. Items that have cleared the bank are matched up with existing entries in Peachtree for faster reconciliation. Transactions that are missing from Peachtree can easily be created from information supplied from the bank.

- Peachtree Bill Pay

    The Peachtree Bill Pay Service allows you to quickly and easily pay your vendor bills and invoices electronically right from within Peachtree. Your payments, including remittance advice, are electronically transmitted to the Peachtree Payment Center where your payments are processed and delivered to the appropriate vendor.

- Customer Management (A/R) Detail Report

  This new report will report the number of days it takes to pay each invoice along with the average number of days it takes a customer to pay overall.

- Customer Transaction History Report

  All the detail associated with a customer's invoice is now available. See what the customer owes and drill down to the detail from one place.

- Vendor Management (A/P) Detail Report

  This new report will let you see how long it takes to pay each invoice plus the average number of days it takes you to pay your vendors overall.

- Vendor Transaction History Report

  All the detail associated with a vendor's invoice is now available. See what you owe and drill down to the detail from one place.

- More Professional Looking Forms

  More and enhanced forms options provided including the ability to create custom forms. This feature will improve the way forms are designed, improving layout and giving the forms a more professional look.

- Duplicate Reference Number Warning

  Peachtree will now warn you when a duplicate reference number is being used on a quote, invoice, credit memo or purchase order.

- Sort for IDs

  IDs on lookup lists are now sorted alphabetically making data entry fast and easy.

- Auto Complete Text Fields

  With Auto Complete Text Fields, you can complete your data entry faster and with greater accuracy. Peachtree will automatically fill in key fields based on past entries and store info in drop down menus for future use in similar situations.

- Internal Accounting Review

    Use the Internal Accounting Review to look for suspicious transactions and common accounting mistakes such as duplicate transactions and cash receipts that do not debit the correct cash account. The Internal Accounting Review can be run at any time and provides a measure of internal auditing.

- New "Find Transaction" Report

    This new transaction report allows you to save "Find Transaction" results and print them from the screen.

Introduction To Computers and Peachtree® Complete Accounting 2006

1

LEARNING OBJECTIVES

At the completion of this chapter, you will be able to:

1. Turn on your computer, open and close Windows, and open and close Peachtree Complete.
2. Recognize system requirements for using Peachtree Complete and Windows.
3. Use a mouse.
4. Identify Peachtree Complete desktop features and understand the Peachtree® Complete Accounting 2006 navigation aids and custom toolbar.
5. Recognize menu commands and keyboard shortcuts.
6. Open, copy, back up, and close company files.
7. Recognize Peachtree Complete forms and understand the use of lists and registers in Peachtree Complete.
8. Access reports in Peachtree Complete and become familiar with the drill down feature.
9. Use Peachtree Complete Analysis including graphing.
10. Use the Windows Calculator.

COMPUTERS HAVE BECOME A WAY OF LIFE

In today's world, computers are appearing in many different places—from the desktop in the home or office to someone's lap on an airplane or at a sporting event. No longer is a computer simply a large, bulky piece of equipment used for "crunching numbers." Computers are used to process documents such as letters, memos, and reports; to perform financial planning and forecasting; to draw pictures and design equipment; to play games; and, of course, to keep the financial records of a company. A computer system is actually a group of hardware components that work together with software to perform a specific task. The steps involved in the processing cycle are input, processing, output, and storage.

INTRODUCTION TO COMPUTER HARDWARE

"Computer hardware" refers to the equipment used as part of a computer system. While there are several computer classifications, this text will focus on the personal computer and it's use in computerized accounting applications.

The hardware components used in today's computer system are as follows:

Input Devices

Input devices are used to enter data or commands into the computer. Essentially, during the input process the computer receives information coded in electrical pulses that indicate an on or an off state. The electrical pulses are called bits, which stands for binary digit, indicating either the on or off electrical pulse. The bits are grouped into a series of eight pulses to form a byte. In essence, one byte is equal to one character typed on the keyboard.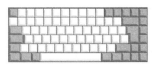

As information is input, it is temporarily stored in the random access memory (RAM) of the computer. Program instructions are also stored temporarily in RAM. Even though it is a temporary storage area, RAM storage is measured in bytes (remember, one byte is equal to one keyboard character). Because of the graphics used in today's software programs, RAM storage must also be quite large and is usually in the range of 128 megabytes (a megabyte equals 1 million bytes and is abbreviated MB) or greater.

The most common input devices are the keyboard, the mouse, and a scanner. Of all the input devices, the keyboard is used most frequently. The keyboard allows the user to key in text, numbers, and other characters for use by the computer to process the data and provide information. Often times software commands or instructions are given via the keyboard.

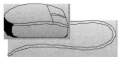 Another popular input device, primarily used to give software commands, is the mouse. Many program instructions can be given by pointing to an icon (picture) and clicking the primary (usually left) mouse button.

To input entire documents at once, a scanner can be used to scan the document and insert an image of the document into the computer.

Processing Devices

The data that have been input into the computer and the necessary program instructions are sent to the central processing unit (CPU) for processing by the computer. The control unit of the CPU directs the transfer of information from RAM into the ALU (Arithmetic/Logic Unit). Using program instructions, the ALU performs the necessary mathematical and logical computations on the data and formulae entered. The results of processing are sent to RAM, and the control unit of the computer sends these results to output or storage devices.

Output Devices

As indicated, the result of processing is output. Output can be shown on the monitor, it can be printed on paper, and/or it can be stored on disk or other media. The most common output device is a monitor. Monitors can be monochrome or color. Today, most computer systems use color monitors to display output.

Output is frequently in the form of a printed or "hard" copy. Several types of printers are available for printing output. The three most common types of printers used are dot matrix, which form characters in groups of dots; ink jet, which spray small droplets of ink on paper to create characters; and laser, which use a combination of a laser beam, static electricity, and ink toner to produce high-quality text.

Storage Devices

The most common storage device is a disk. The most common disk is a removable floppy disk that is 3½ inches wide. The amount of storage space is measured in bytes. Remember that one byte is equal to one keyboard character. Storage space is calculated exponentially, so 1 kilobyte (abbreviated K) of memory is 1,024 bytes. For ease in calculations, the storage capacity is rounded to the nearest thousand. A double-density 3½-inch disk holds a little over 720K, and a high-density 3½-inch disk holds more than 1.44MB. Zip disk drives that hold 100MB, 250MB or more are currently on the market as are USB Flash Memory Keys (Jump Drives) in 64, 128, 256 MB or more. These devices are becoming more popular due to their larger storage capabilities.

3½-inch disk

Most computers have storage available on a hard disk in the local machine or available on a network. These permanent disks hold a great deal of information for the computer. The hard disk is used to store both software programs and data. In a classroom environment data are usually stored on the removable floppy disks or on a user assigned partition on a network. Storage space on a hard drive is also measured in bytes. Because of the ever-increasing size of the programs residing on it, the storage capability of the hard drive is becoming larger and larger. Hard drives are usually measured in gigabytes. (A gigabyte is approximately 1 billion bytes. The abbreviation for gigabyte is GB.) New computers generally come with 80 to 250 GB hard drives and may have more than one hard drive in the system.

INTRODUCTION TO SOFTWARE

Data can be entered on the keyboard and sent to RAM, but the central processing unit will not know what to do with the data unless it is given instructions via a computer program. The computer programs are called software and are divided into two different categories—operating system software and application software.

Operating System Software

System software gives the computer basic operating instructions and is required no matter what application software is used. The operating system software allows data to be input using a keyboard. The operating system software sends the data and program instructions to the CPU for processing, and it allows the results of that processing to be shown on the monitor, sent to the printer, or stored on a disk. In addition to being the controlling program for the computer, the operating system software is used for disk and file management and organization.

When IBM-PC microcomputers started to appear in the office in the early 1980s, the operating system for these personal computers used a text-based command structure and was called PC-DOS. One popular version of a DOS (Disk Operating System) was developed by Microsoft, and IBM eventually adopted this version of DOS for IBM-clone computers. The software was renamed MS-DOS; however, PC-DOS and MS-DOS are almost identical as were several other DOS systems developed by third parties. Apple computers, which actually started the microcomputer revolution, had a user-friendly operating system that used icons (pictures) to give commands. In order to compete with the Apple computers in ease of use, Microsoft developed an operating environment used in conjunction with DOS. This operating environment was Windows. It uses the principle of a graphical user interface (GUI) with pictures or icons representing software programs, hardware, and commands. Rather than rely on typed-in commands, as is done in DOS, Windows receives instructions or commands when the user points to and clicks on an icon or menu selection with a mouse. There are several versions of the Windows operating system in use today. Newer versions have eliminated the need for DOS completely.

There are other operating systems on the market today. Most of the time you are working, you will not have much direct contact with the operating system; however, it is always important to know which system you are using.

Application Software

Application software is task-specific software. In other words, if you want to keep the books for a company, you use a program such as Peachtree Complete to enter information regarding your business transactions and to produce your financial reports. If you want to type a term paper, a word processing program such as Word or WordPerfect will be the application program to use. To do financial forecasting and perform "what if" scenarios, a spreadsheet program such as Excel or Lotus 1-2-3 can be used although many of today's computerized accounting programs will allow you to perform these tasks from within the program. If you want to play a game of solitaire using the computer, a computer game will be the application. Each application program is designed to respond to the commands you give. In some programs the use of a function key will give a completely different result than the use of the same function key in another program.

In the Windows operating system, program commands may be given by pointing to an icon or menu option and clicking the primary (usually left) mouse button. For example, no matter what Windows program or application software you use, clicking on the picture of a printer sends a copy of your document to the printer, or it may take you to another screen on which you can set printing options.

MANUAL VERSUS COMPUTERIZED ACCOUNTING

The work to be performed to keep the books for a business is the same whether you use a manual or a computerized accounting system. Transactions need to be analyzed, recorded in a journal, and posted to a ledger. Business documents such as invoices, checks, bank deposits, and credit/debit memos need to be prepared and distributed. Reports to management and owners for information and decision-making purposes need to be prepared. Records for one business period need to be closed before one moves to the next business period.

In a manual system, each transaction that is analyzed must be entered by hand into the appropriate journal and posted to the proper ledger. A separate business document such as an invoice or a check must be prepared and distributed when required. In order to prepare a report, the accountant/bookkeeper must go through the journal or ledger and look for the correct amounts to include in the report. Closing the books must be done item by item via closing entries, which are recorded in the journal and posted to the ledger accounts. After the closing entries are recorded, the ledger accounts must be ruled and balance sheet accounts must be reopened with Brought Forward Balances being entered. All of this is extremely time consuming.

In a computerized system, the transactions must still be analyzed and recorded; however, posting is done automatically or by giving the command to post. Reports are generated based on an instruction given to the computer—for example, by clicking on a menu item: "Report—Trial Balance." Some computerized accounting systems require the accountant/bookkeeper to enter both the debit and credit portions of each transaction in a General Journal. Other programs allow the use of special journals such as Cash Disbursements or Cash Receipts, Sales, and Purchases journals. Peachtree Complete, however, operates from a business document perspective. As a transaction occurs, the necessary business document (an invoice or a check, for example) is prepared. Based on the information entered from the business document, Peachtree Complete records the necessary debits and credits behind the scenes. If an error is made when entering a transaction, Peachtree Complete allows the user to return to the business document and make the correction. Peachtree can be configured to record all such corrections for auditing purposes. All recording of debits and credits is automatically performed behind the scenes. If you want to see or make a correction using the actual debit/credit entries, Peachtree Complete allows you to view the transaction register and make corrections directly in the register or use the traditional Journal. Reports are prepared by simply selecting the desired report from the report menu.

SYSTEM REQUIREMENTS FOR PEACHTREE® COMPLETE ACCOUNTING 2006

The hardware requirements are an IBM-compatible Pentium II , with a minimum 300 MHz computer (450 MHz or higher recommended); 64 MB RAM (128 MB recommended); 110-250 MB of hard-disk space available for Peachtree Complete, an additional 70 MB of hard-disk space for Microsoft® Internet Explorer 6.0 or newer, 2x CD-ROM drive, mouse, high color 16 bit SVGA or better monitor; Internet access with a connection speed of 56K or higher (for optional services), printer supported by Windows. Either Windows NT 4.0 (or higher) with Service Pack 6 or Windows 98 (or higher), Microsoft® Excel 97 (or higher) if you plan to use the Excel report feature of Peachtree Complete.

HOW TO OPEN PEACHTREE® COMPLETE ACCOUNTING 2006

Once you are in Windows, opening Peachtree Complete is as easy as point and click.

 DO: Click **Start**
Point to **Programs**
Point to **Peachtree Complete Accounting Educational Version 2006** (or the
   program name given to you by your instructor)
Click **Peachtree Complete Accounting Educational Version 2006**

Alternatively, one can enter Peachtree Complete Accounting by double clicking on the Peachtree icon that is placed on the Desktop during the installation process.

 DO: Double click **Peachtree 2006** icon

Names and even icons will vary depending on how the program was installed on your particular machine. If you are operating on a network, you may need to contact your IT department to determine how to access the program.

Regardless of how you access the program, the first screen you should see briefly is the Sage Software screen:

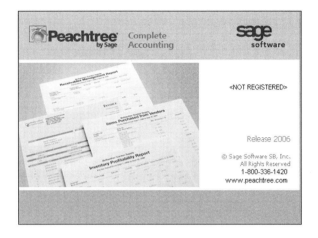

HOW TO OPEN A COMPANY

To explore some of the features of Peachtree Complete, you will work with one of the sample companies that come with the program. The company is Bellwether Garden Supply and is stored on the hard disk (C:) inside the computer. Peachtree presents the user with an opening screen from which a company can be opened.

 DO: Enter Peachtree Complete
Click **Open an existing company.**

Point to Bellwether Garden Supply
Click on **OK** (alternatively double click on the company name)

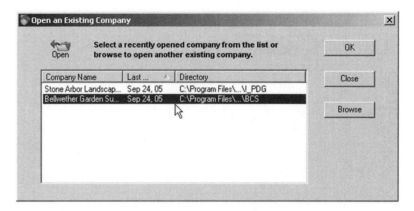

If Bellwether Garden Supply does not appear in the list provided, you must click on Browse to call up the Open Company dialog box. From here you can see all Peachtree companies contained in the default directory rather than just those most recently opened. You can also change your disk drive, your folder or even access network resources for your data files. Ask your instructor for the proper location of the sample company files, should they not appear in the default settings. The Open Company dialog box can also be accessed at anytime while you are in the program by selecting Open from the File menu option.

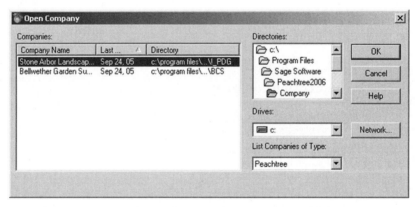

Please note that any changes you make to the sample company will be permanent. Do not make entries into the sample company unless instructed to do so by the textbook or your instructor. A backup to the start position is provided with your sample company files if you should need to restore.

VERIFY AN OPEN COMPANY

It is important to make sure you have opened the data for the correct company. Always verify the company name in the title bar. Note in the example below that Bellwether Garden Supply is the current company. Lack of a name in the title bar indicates no company is open and consequently many of Peachtree's features will not be available.

INTRODUCTION TO PEACHTREE® COMPLETE ACCOUNTING 2006 DESKTOP FEATURES

Once the computer has been turned on, Windows has been accessed, and Peachtree Complete has been started, you will see Peachtree Complete on the desktop. Peachtree Complete displays a title bar. If a company is open, the title bar displays **Peachtree Accounting** followed by the company name. The Windows minimize, maximize, close, and control buttons are available in Peachtree Complete and appear on the screen as will many of the common Windows keyboard commands such as Copy and Paste (Ctrl+C, Ctrl+V). Beneath the title bar is the menu bar. By pointing and clicking on a menu item or using the keyboard shortcut of Alt+ the underlined letter in the menu item will give Peachtree Complete the command to display the drop-down menu. For example, the File menu is used to open and close a company and may also be used to exit Peachtree Complete. Menu items can be selected by pointing and left mouse clicking on the desired item.

Below the menu bar, Peachtree® Complete Accounting 2006 displays the Peachtree Today window. While using Peachtree Today is optional, it is a quick and easy way to give commands to Peachtree Complete based on the type of transaction being entered into the program. This window will appear each time you open a company. If you choose to not use this window for entering commands, you may close it the same as you would any other window. It may be reopened by clicking on the **Today** button that will appear in the toolbar at the bottom of your screen. If you do not want the window to appear when you open your company file, you may set this option by using the Customize Peachtree Today link in the Peachtree Today window.

Remove the checkmark from the box in front of Display Peachtree Today each time this company is opened by left mouse clicking on the checkmark and clicking Save at the bottom of the screen.

Below the Peachtree Today window are the custom toolbar and Peachtree Navigation Aids, consisting of grouping of tasks by function. As an example, the first grouping is Sales and will contain all tasks and reports related to sales, such as invoicing, receipt of payments, customer lists and various sales reports.

This text will primarily use the Peachtree Navigation Aids feature when giving instructions. The student may find it more desirable to use one of the other command options to access the different features of Peachtree Complete Accounting.

PEACHTREE® COMPLETE ACCOUNTING 2006 NAVIGATION AIDS

Peachtree® Complete Accounting 2006 Navigation Aids allows you to access the various tasks, reports and maintenance features of Peachtree Complete according to the type of transaction being entered. Peachtree® Complete Accounting 2006 Navigation Aids will appear as a series of buttons at the bottom of the main Peachtree Complete window when you open the program unless the feature has been turned off. If this is the case with your machine, you must turn it back on by using the View Navigation Aid selection from the Options menu. You may toggle this feature off and on in this manner.

 DO: Open Bellwether Garden Supply
Click **Options**
Click **View Navigation Aid**
Click **Options** again
    Note: The checkmark does not appear next to Navigation Aid
Click **View Navigation Aid** again
Leave **View Navigation Aid** turned on (checkmark to the left)

⊙ Sales	⊙ Purchases	⊙ Payroll	⊙ General Ledger	⊙ Inventory	⊙ Time & Billing	⊙ Analysis	⊙ Company

Let us examine what each of the eight navigation aid groupings contains. They are grouped by accounting function. Most are broken into sections for maintenance, tasks and reports.

Sales	Allows you to maintain your customers, your sales representatives, sales tax authorities and sales tax codes. You can generate sales quotes, sales orders, enter sales, generate sales invoices, age receivables, show cash receipts and print customer statements. Reports that are available include those related to sales as well as general ledger reports.
Purchases	Allows you to maintain your vendors and your inventory items. You can generate purchase orders, show the purchase/receipt of inventory as well as record other goods and services purchased on account. You may also make payments on account and generate checks as needed. In addition, you may access purchases related reports as well as general ledger reports.
Payroll	Allows you to maintain employees, edit company tax tables and access the payroll set up wizard. You can enter payroll data and generate payroll checks. You may also void payroll checks. Reports include payroll related reports as well as general ledger reports.

General Ledger	Allows you to maintain your chart of accounts. Provides access to the general journal, to Peachtree's account reconciliation feature and allows the user to change the current accounting period. You may also access general ledger reports, account reconciliation reports, general journal reports as well as financial statements.
Inventory	Allows you to maintain inventory items and items selling prices. You can show the purchase/receipt of inventory, make inventory adjustments and for a manufacturing firm, build and unbuild assemblies. Reports include those related to inventory and assemblies as well as general ledger reports.
Time & Billing	Allows you to track expenses and time in a job costing system. This is an advanced feature that will not be covered in this text.
Analysis	Allows you to access Peachtree's four Manager Series options: • Cash Manager—analyzes projected cash flow for a specified period of time. • Collection Manager—analyzes accounts receivable. • Payment Manager—analyzes money owed to vendors. • Financial Manager—provides an overall financial picture of business performance.
Company	Allows you to set up a new company, edit existing company information, backup and restore data, import and export data, list important events, create a To Do list, set alerts, close both the fiscal and payroll years and set up job costing.

To demonstrate how easily this feature can be used, let us look at some sales related reports in the sales Navigation Aid.

 DO: If necessary, open Bellwether Garden Supply
Click on the **Sales** button at bottom left of screen
Click Sales Journal in the Report area
Click **OK**
Note: Peachtree instantly created a sales journal showing all of the sales transactions recorded in the current accounting period. You may close the report window when you are finished examining it.
Click the **Close** button.

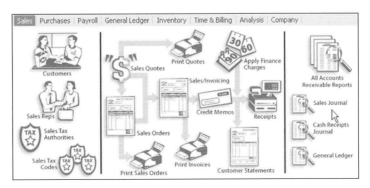

PEACHTREE® COMPLETE ACCOUNTING 2006 CUSTOM TOOLBAR

This new feature added into the 2006 version of the program allows the user to create a custom toolbar containing his/her most commonly used commands. It differs from the Navigation Aids in that each icon represents a specific task rather than a grouping of tasks. Buttons can be added or deleted using the toolbar editor. The toolbar is located immediately above the Navigation Aid buttons.

Every feature available from Peachtree's menu system can be added to your custom toolbar. By clicking on the blue up arrows at the left of the toolbar (see toolbar above), you are presented with a Toolbar Components dialogue box from which you can add icons to the toolbar. Note that the major categories match Peachtree's menu. Each can be opened to reveal the individual tasks within that menu item. One must simply drag and drop the desired icon to the toolbar positioning it where desired. When the toolbar is filled, a second row will be added allowing any number of icons to be added.

MENU COMMANDS

Menu commands can be the starting point for issuing commands in Peachtree Complete. The following menus are available for use in Peachtree® Complete Accounting 2006:

File	Allows you to open an existing company, create a new company, perform print functions, back up and restore company data, import/export files, edit payroll tax tables, and exit Peachtree Accounting.
Edit	Allows you to cut, copy, and paste objects. You can change record ID's, find transactions, edit or delete records, select or save memorized transactions, etc. In addition, you can add or remove lines within transaction fields. The options on this menu vary, depending on which area of Peachtree you are using.
Maintain	Allows you to enter, view or edit required information for your company's customers, vendors, employees, sales reps., chart of accounts, and inventory items. You can also edit company information, use the company setup checklist, set up memorized transactions, enter sales tax codes, add users/passwords and default parameters for how you want your accounting handled.
Tasks	Allows you to enter quotes, sales orders, sales invoices, receipts, purchase orders, purchase invoices, payments, write checks, time and expense tickets, payroll transactions, and General Journal entries. You can also calculate financial charges, select bills to pay, select employees to pay, make inventory adjustments, reconcile bank statements, void checks, enter action items, post and unpost information to the general ledger, change the accounting period, close the fiscal and payroll years, and purge inactive items and old transactions.
Analysis	Allows you to view customized graphical overviews of the entire company to analyze cash flow, collections of amount due from customers, payments due to vendors, and financial status.
Options	Allows you to set certain global options for a company and for Action Items and to change the system date. You can turn on (or off) the Status Bar, Navigation Aid, and Startup Screen.
Reports	Allows you to create a list of reports for printing or viewing. You can also create and edit the format for reports, forms, and financial statements.
Services	This feature is not available in the Educational version of the software. The contents of this menu will be displayed at the end of this table.
Window	Allows you to arrange the displayed windows on your desktop, arrange the buttons on your desktop, and close all open windows on your desktop.
Help	Allows you to open windows of relevant help, run an online tutorial for Peachtree Accounting, display data files statistics for the currently open company, and identify which version of Peachtree Accounting is currently installed. You can access technical support from here as well.

The services menu contains the following items:

KEYBOARD SHORTCUTS

Frequently, it is faster to give Peachtree Complete a command by using a keyboard shortcut than it is to point and click the mouse through several layers of menus or Navigation Aids. The following chart lists common keyboard shortcuts available for use in Peachtree Complete.

General	Key	Help Window	Key
Cancel	Esc	Next day	+ (plus key)
Record (when black border is around OK, Next, or Prev button)	← (press Enter key)	Select next option or topic	Tab
		Select previous option or topic	Shift+Tab
Record (always)	Ctrl+←	Display selected topic	←
Dates	**Key**	Close pop up box	Esc
Next day	+ (plus key)	Close Help window	Alt+F4
Previous day	- (minus key)		
Editing	**Key**	**Moving Around A Window**	**Key**
Edit transaction in selected register	Ctrl+E	Next field	Tab
Delete character to right of insertion point	Del	Previous field	Shift+Tab
Delete character to left of insertion point	Backspace	Toggle between form and navigation bar	Ctrl+0 (zero)
Delete line from detail area	Ctrl+Del	Report column to the right	→ (Right arrow)
Insert line in detail area	Ctrl+Ins	Report column to the left	← (Left arrow)
Cut selected characters	Ctrl+X	Beginning of current field or report row	Home
Copy selected characters	Ctrl+C	End of current field or report row	End
Paste cut or copied characters	Ctrl+V	Line below in detail area or on report	Down arrow
Activity	**Key**	Line above in detail area or on report	Up arrow
New Company	Ctrl+N	Down one screen	Page Down
Open Company	Ctrl+O	Up one screen	Page Up
Back up Company	Ctrl+B	Next word in field	Ctrl+→
Restore Company	Ctrl+R	Previous word in field	Ctrl+←
Find	Ctrl+F	First item on list or previous month in register	Ctrl+Page Up
Find Next	Ctrl+D	Last item on list or next month in register	Ctrl+Page Down
Cut	Ctrl+X	Close active window	Esc or Alt+F4
Copy	Ctrl+C	**Functions**	**Key**
Paste	Ctrl+V	Displays the online Help	F1
Delete	Ctrl+E	Closes the current document window	Ctrl+F4
Print Purchase Orders, Quotes, Invoices, Payments, or Reports	Ctrl+P	Saves the current record in maintenance windows	F5
		Moves to the next window	Ctrl+F6
		Moves to the previous window	Shift+Ctrl+6
		Toggles the menu bar	F10

KEYBOARD CONVENTIONS

When using Windows, there are standard keyboard conventions for the use of certain keys. These keyboard conventions also apply to Peachtree Complete and include the following.

Alt key is used to access the drop-down menus on the menu bar. Rather than click on a menu item, hold down the Alt key and type the underlined letter in the menu item name. Close the menu by simply pressing the Alt or Esc key.

DO: Open Bellwether Garden Supply

Access the **File** menu: **Alt+F**, view the menu choices, close **File** menu: **Alt**

Access the **Edit** menu: **Alt+E**, view the menu choices, close **Edit** menu: **Alt**

Access the **Maintain** menu: **Alt+M**, view the menu choices, close **Maintain** menu:**Alt**

Access the **Tasks** menu: **Alt+K**, view the menu choices, close **Task** menu: **Alt**

Access the **Analysis** menu: **Alt+Y**, view the menu choices, close **Analysis** menu: **Alt**

Access the **Options** menu: **Alt+O**, view the menu choices, close **Options** menu: **Alt**

Access the **Reports** menu: **Alt+R**, view the menu choices, close **Reports** menu: **Alt**

Access the **Window** menu: **Alt+W**, view the menu choices, close **Window** menu: **Alt**

Access the **Help** menu: **Alt+H**, view the menu choices, close **Help** menu: **Alt**

Tab key is used to move to the next field or, if a button is selected, to the next button.

Shift+Tab is used to move back to the previous field.

Esc key is used to cancel an active window without saving anything that has been entered. Depending on what has been entered, you may be prompted to confirm the cancellation of the action.

DO: Access **Tasks** menu **Alt+K**

Select **Sales/Invoicing**

Press **Tab** key to move forward through the invoice

Press **Shift+Tab** to move back through the invoice

Press **Esc** to close the invoice

ON-SCREEN HELP

Peachtree Complete has on-screen help, which is similar to having the Peachtree Complete reference manual available on the computer screen. Help can give you assistance with a particular function you are performing. Peachtree Complete help also gives you information about the program using an on-screen index.

Help may be used to obtain information on a variety of topics. It may be accessed in a number of different ways. When the help menu is selected from the menu bar you are presented with the following options:

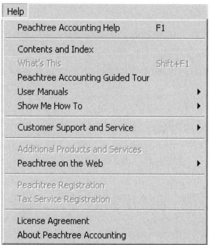

Peachtree Accounting Help	Displays the Help topic associated with the current open window. Pressing F1 achieves the same effect.
Contents and Index	Displays the Help viewer, which allows you to browse Help topics or search for information about the Peachtree program.
What's This?	Changes your mouse pointer to the What's This Help question mark pointer for use in an active window. Click the field or object you want information about, and a pop-up definition will appear. Pressing Shift+F1 achieves the same effect.
Peachtree Accounting Guided Tour	Opens Peachtree's online tutorial. The tutorial has a number of chapters to help you learn Peachtree. If you are new to Peachtree, you will probably want to go through this tutorial.
User Manuals	This option provides for a Getting Started Guide, a User's Guide and a One-Write Plus Conversion Guide.
Show Me How To	Contains demonstrations of Peachtree's most common tasks.
Customer Support and Service	Mainly provides access to Peachtree's support services most of which require a subscription. Some are not available in the educational version. There is also a Files Statistics option that displays file and record information about your company data.

Additional Products and Services	Displays information about additional products and services that Peachtree Software provides.
Peachtree on the Web	Displays links to common Web sites related to Peachtree Accounting products and Peachtree Software. When you choose one of these links, your default Web browser will open and display the corresponding page if you have a Web browser installed and Internet access.
Peachtree Registration	Allows you to examine or update your product serial number and registration information in the full version of the program.
Tax Service Registration	Allows you to register annual payroll tax tables provided by the Peachtree Tax Service in the full version of the program.
License Agreement	Your license to use this Peachtree product
About Peachtree Accounting	Provides the version and product number of Peachtree, as well as copyright information.

When the Peachtree Help window is accessed, either from the Help Menu or by pressing F1 a number of options are presented to the user. The general layout of the Help window includes a series of four tabs, each of which allows you to seek information.

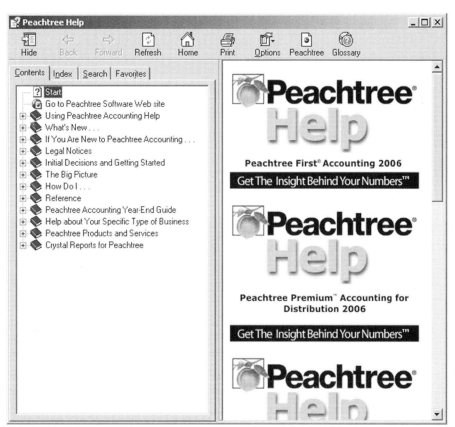

Contents	Provides Peachtree Help information in a book-like table of contents format.
Index	Provides an on-screen index. There is a text box where you may type the first few letters of the name of the item with which you need help. As you key in the item name, Peachtree Complete index displays items alphabetically. When the topic you need appears on the screen, double-click the topic to display it.
Search	Used to search for every occurrence of a word or a phrase. This option will search the entire Help database for any occurrence of the search term. It is a very thorough search, but it may provide topics that are not as relevant as those that appear in the index.
Favorites	Allows the user to select the search results that appear in the right-hand side of the window and place them in a list for easy access.

When the topic for help has been located, information about the topic is provided in the Help window. If there is more information than can be shown on the screen, scroll bars will appear on the right side of the help screen. A scroll bar is used to show or go through information. As you scroll through help, information at the top of the help screen disappears from view while new information appears at the bottom of the screen.

Sometimes words appear in blue underline in the Peachtree Complete Help screen. Clicking on the blue words will take you to other related topics in much the same manner as an HTML page on the Web would work. That is, you are taken to various points in the Help database via links that allow you to move backwards and forwards just as you would through a Web page.

  DO: If necessary, open Bellwether Garden Supply
Click **Help**
Click on **Contents and Index**
Click the **Index** tab
Key in cha
Double click on Change System Date
Read the procedure provided in the right side of the window
Close Help using one of the following methods:
  Click **Alt+F4**
  Click the **Close** button in the upper right corner of the screen

PEACHTREE® COMPLETE ACCOUNTING 2006 ENTRY WINDOWS

In Peachtree® Complete Accounting 2006, transactions are entered directly onto the business form that is prepared as a result of the transaction. For example, a sale on account is recorded by completing the invoice for the sale. Behind the scenes, Peachtree Complete enters the debit and credit to the Journal and posts to the individual general ledger accounts as well as to the subsidiary accounts.

Peachtree Complete has several types of entry windows that are used to record your daily business transactions. They are divided into two categories: documents you want to send or give to people and documents that you have received. Documents to send or give to people include sales invoices, cash sales receipts, credit memos, checks, deposit slips, and purchase orders. Documents you have received include the receipt of payments from customers, bills, credits received from a vendor, and credit card charge receipts.

Most transaction windows within Peachtree Complete will allow the user to select from a variety of different document formats by using the template feature. You may use one of the formats provided by Peachtree Complete or you may change or modify them, or you may create your own custom format for use in the program.

When entering a transaction, you move from one field to the next to enter the information needed. To move from one field to the next, press the Tab key or position the mouse pointer within a field and click the primary (left) mouse button. In most entry windows the return key will also allow you to move from one field to the next. While each window does require different types of information based on the transaction, there are several common features within windows. Examine the invoice that follows.

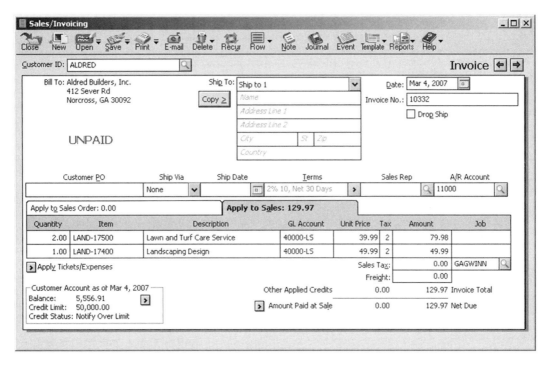

This sales/invoicing window is typical of most windows used for routine tasks. Many of the same fields will be used in other windows while still others will be used with slight modifications. If your invoice does not look like this, see the next section. You may need to change your default settings in order to have the same view as this. In general we can describe the components as follows:

- **Field** is an area on a form requiring information. Customer ID: is a field.

- **Text box** is the area within a field where information may be typed or inserted freely. The area to be filled in to identify the Customer PO is a text box.

- **Drop-down list button** appears next to a field when there is a list of options available. This may take the form of a magnifying glass or an arrow. In some fields the list button does not appear until the field is selected such as Item or Unit Price. On the displayed invoice, clicking the drop-down list magnifying glass for Customer ID: will display the names of all customers who have accounts with the company. Clicking a customer's name will insert the name into the text box for the field.

- **Title bar** at the top of the window indicates the task you are completing. In this case, it indicates **Sales/Invoicing**. The title bar also contains the standard Windows buttons. They include:
  - **Minimize button** allows you to keep the invoice (or form) open but not displayed on the screen.
  - **Maximize/Restore button** enlarges the window to display on the full screen or restores the window to its previous size.
  - **Close button** closes the current screen.

- **Toolbar** at the top of the invoice has icons that are used to give commands to Peachtree Complete or to get information regarding linked or related transactions. Note that many of the Peachtree icons have pull-down arrows that provide multiple options for the button.
  - **Close** is used to close the current screen. You will be prompted to save the transaction if any data has been entered.
  - **New** is used to clear the displayed transaction in order to enter a new one.
  - **Open** will open a previously entered transaction or allow the selection of a memorized transaction.
  - **Save** will save the current invoice or allow the memorizing of an invoice which can then be accessed through the Open icon.
  - **Print** allows the user to preview and/or print the invoice.
  - **E-mail** allows the user to e-mail the invoice to the customer.
  - **Delete** allows the user to delete or void the invoice.
  - **Recur** allows the user to set up a recurring transaction for future accounting periods.
  - **Row** allows the user to add or delete rows in the invoice.
  - **Note** allows the user to add a comment to the invoice. You are provided the option to have the comment printed on the invoice or kept internal to the program.
  - **Journal** allows the user to see the journal entries that will be created from this invoice. This is a behind the scenes look at how Peachtree processes transactions.
  - **Event** allows the user to access Peachtree's Create Event feature from within the sales/invoicing module.
  - **Template** allows the user to select from a list of Peachtree designed input windows or create a customized window.
  - **Reports** allows the user to see a variety of customer related reports at the click of a button.

- **Help** allows the user to receive help on the window in use.

INSTALLATION DEFAULT SETTINGS

In the 2006 version of Peachtree Complete Accounting, you may encounter some differences in your screens to the screen captures contained in this book. This is due in part to the fact that Peachtree may install to one set of settings on a machine that has contained a previous version of Peachtree and to a second set of setting on a machine to which you are installing Peachtree for the first time. See the next page for examples of each. In order to ensure that your screens will be the same as those in this book, make or confirm the following selections from the Options menu item:

1. Open any company within Peachtree Complete Accounting 2006.
2. Select Global from the Options menu.
3. Select the Accounting tab.
4. In the section entitled Hide General Ledger Accounts, remove any checkmarks from the three boxes in that section by left clicking on the checkmark.

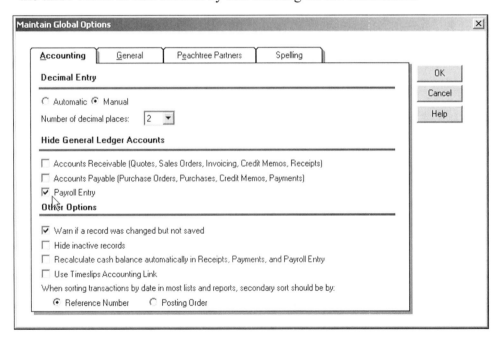

5. Click on the General tab of this same screen.
6. In the Color Scheme section, click on the radio button next to Classic.

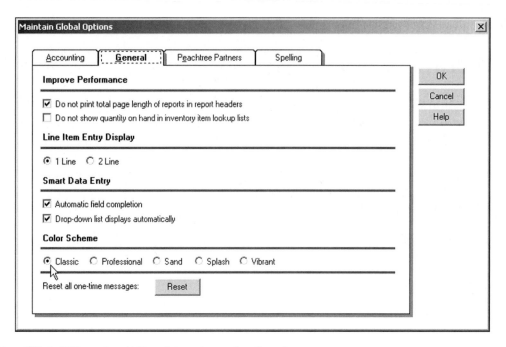

7. Click OK and exit Peachtree to make the changes permanent.

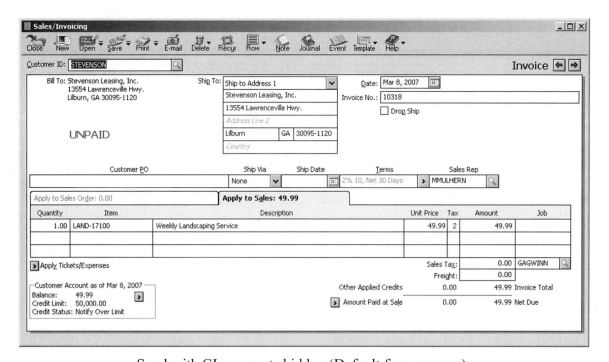

Sand with GL accounts hidden (Default for new user).

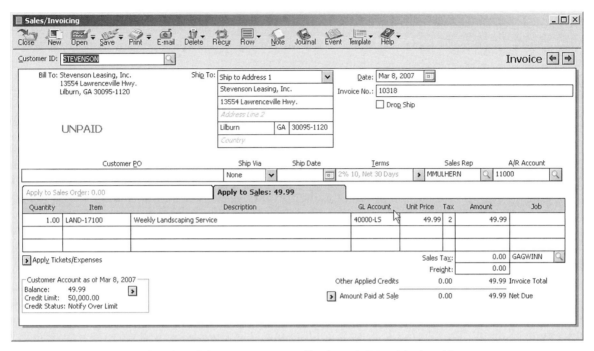

Classic with GL accounts displayed (Used in book).

Let us take a look at some of the different windows Peachtree uses to input transactions. We will open these windows by using the Navigation Aid buttons at the bottom of the screen. Be sure that they are displayed before starting this activity.

 DO: If necessary, open Bellwether Garden Supply

Click **Sales** button

Click **Sales/Invoicing**

Examine the invoice form provided. Explore the features described earlier.

Click the **Open** icon to view a list of invoices that have been completed.

Click the **Cancel** button to close the Select Invoice screen.

Click the **Close** icon

Look at some of the other forms used in Peachtree Complete:

    Click **Purchases** button

    Click **Purchases/Receive Inventory**. Explore and close when finished.

    Click **Purchases** button

    Click **Write Checks**. Explore and close when finished.

    Click **General Ledger** button

    Click **General Journal Entry**. Explore and close when finished.

    Click **Payroll** button

    Click **Payroll Entry**. Explore and close when finished.

As you explored these Peachtree entry windows you should have noticed that many of the features were the same despite some differences that were specific to the task.

PEACHTREE® COMPLETE ACCOUNTING 2006 LISTS

In order to expedite entering transactions, Peachtree Complete uses lists as an integral part of the program. Customers, vendors, sales items, and accounts are organized as lists. Frequently, information can be entered on a form by clicking on a list item. For example, a customer name as well as related customer information, can be entered on an invoice by selecting a customer from the drop-down list created by clicking on the magnifying glass next to the Customer ID: field.

The lists can be created from the Maintain features within the Navigation Aids. Lists can be printed via the use of the Report features within the Navigation Aids. Peachtree Complete allows items to be added to lists "on the fly." This means that if you are preparing an invoice for a new customer, Peachtree Complete allows you to add the new customer to the Customer ID: list while you are filling in the customer invoice.

Let us take a look at some of the lists available within Peachtree.

DO: If necessary, open Bellwether Garden Supply
Click **Sales** button.
Click **All Accounts Receivables Reports** to open a Select a Report window.
Double click on the Customer List option in the Report List area of the Select a Report
      window.
    Note: Peachtree has provided a list of customers currently entered into the system.
Click **Close** to exit this list
The Select a Report window should still be open. From the Report Area: section of this
      window click on Accounts Payable.
Double click on the Vendor List option in the Report List area of the Select a Report
      window.
    Note: Peachtree has provided a list of vendors currently entered into the system.
Click **Close** to exit this list
From the Report Area: section of this window click on Payroll.
Double click on the Employee List option in the Report List area of the Select a Report
      window.
    Note: Peachtree has provided a list of employees currently entered into the system.
Click **Close** to exit this list

Other lists may be accessed in this same manner.

PEACHTREE® COMPLETE ACCOUNTING 2006 REPORTS

Reports are an integral part of a business. Reports enable owners and managers to determine how the business is doing and to make decisions affecting the future of the company. Reports can be prepared showing the profit and loss for the period, the status of the Balance Sheet (assets equal liabilities plus owner's equity), information regarding accounts receivable and accounts payable, and the amount of sales for each item. Peachtree Complete has a wide range of reports and reporting options available. Reports may be customized to better reflect the information needs of a company. Reports may be generated in a variety of ways.

- **Reports menu** includes a complete listing of the reports available in Peachtree Complete. It can be used to access all of the reports available within Peachtree including income statements, balance sheets, accounts receivable reports, sales reports, accounts payable reports, budget reports, various transaction reports, transaction detail reports, payroll reports, list reports, and various custom reports.

- **Navigation Aids** each have a section for reports as well. Selecting a report from here accomplishes the same thing as selecting from the Reports menu.

Let us take a look at two reports that are important to any business, the income statement and the balance sheet.

 DO: If necessary, open Bellwether Garden Supply
　　　　　　　Click **General Ledger** button
　　　　　　　Click **All Financial Statements**
　　　　　　　Double click <Standard> Income Stmnt
　　　　　　　Click **OK** to accept the defaults
　　　　　　　Scroll through the Income Statement for Bellwether Garden Supply
　　　　　　　Click the **Close** button to exit the income statement
　　　　　　　Double click <Standard> Balance Sheet
　　　　　　　Click **OK** to accept the defaults
　　　　　　　Scroll through the balance sheet for Bellwether Garden Supply
　　　　　　　Click the **Close** button

As you close each report you are brought back to the Select A Report window. From here, you may select any report available within Peachtree. You can click on any category in the Report Area to bring up a list of the available reports in that area.

DRILL DOWN

Drill Down allows you to view the transactions that contribute to the data on Peachtree's various detailed reports. When viewing a report, place the mouse pointer over any line and the pointer will turn into a magnifying glass with a Z inside. To see detailed information about the transaction, double-click the mouse. For example, double clicking on a sales transaction shown on a sales report will bring up the original transaction for viewing, editing or even deletion. Drill down does not work with reports displaying cumulative data such as financial statements or a trial balance.

 DO: If necessary, open Bellwether Garden Supply
Click **Sales** button
Click **All Accounts Receivable Reports** from the Reports Area
Double click Aged Receivables
Position the cursor over the first line until it changes into a magnifying glass
Double click while positioned over the first line and note that you are taken to the Sales/Invoicing input screen where the transaction was originally recorded.
Note: You can tab through the various fields for editing. Do not change any of the data.
Click the **Close** button to exit the sales invoice
Click the **Close** button to exit the Select A Report window

PEACHTREE® COMPLETE ACCOUNTING 2006 ANALYSIS GRAPHS

Peachtree Analysis allows the user to view data within the Cash, Collection and Payment Managers in either numeric or graphic (column or bar) formats. This provides the user with an instant visual analysis of different elements within the business. For example, selecting the Payment Manager and choosing graphic format allows the user to see a visual representation of the aging of the company's payables using column, bar or pie charts as follows.

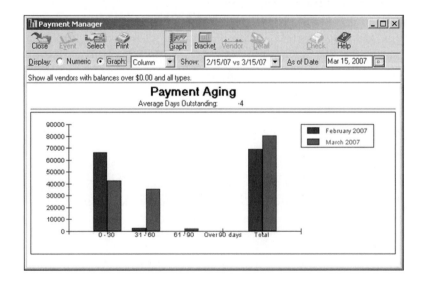

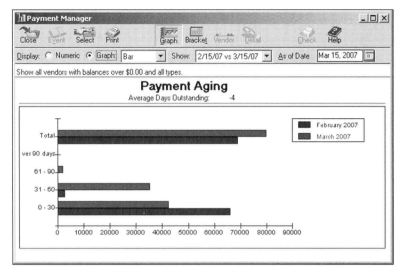

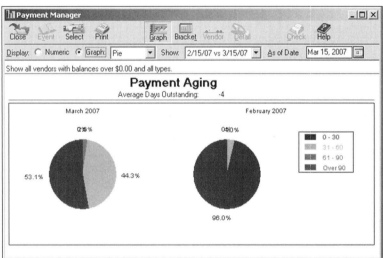

 DO: If necessary, open Bellwether Garden Supply
        Click **Analysis** button
        Click **Collection Manager**
        If not selected, select the **Graph** radio button.
        Using the pull-down arrow for the **Show:** field, select 2/15/07 vs 3/15/07 to
        compare this month with last month.
        Using the pull-down arrow for the **Graph:** field, explore the different graph types
            available.
        Click the **Close** button to close the Collection Manager window

Various charts can also be accessed from the Peachtree Today window. They can be accessed in the My Business choice of this window. Many Peachtree reports can also be exported to Excel from where they can be converted to charts using the Chart Wizard feature.

HOW TO USE WINDOWS® CALCULATOR

Windows includes accessory programs that may be used when working. One of these accessory programs is Calculator. Using this program gives you an on-screen calculator. To use the Calculator in Windows, we must do the following:

 DO: Click **Start**
Point to **Progams**
Point to **Accessories**
Click **Calculator**
Change from a standard calculator to a scientific calculator, click **View** menu, click
     Scientific.
Change back to a standard calculator, click **View** menu, click **Standar**d
Numbers may be entered by:
     Clicking the number on the calculator
     Keying the number using the numeric keypad
     Typing the keyboard numbers
     Enter the numbers: 123+456+789+
     The amount is added after each entry
     After typing 789+, the answer 1368 appears automatically
     To clear the answer, click the **C** button on the calculator
     Enter: 55*6
Press **Enter** or click = to get the answer
Click the **Close** button on the Calculator title bar

The Windows calculator can now also be accessed from within Peachtree on the custom toolbar at the bottom of the screen. Simply click on the icon that resembles a small calculator.

HOW TO CLOSE A COMPANY

In Peachtree a company is closed whenever we exit the program. All changes made to the data were automatically saved as you worked. You may also exit a company by opening a new company from the File menu option. You will be presented with a confirmation box telling you that the current company will be closed if you proceed.

DO: From within Bellwether Garden Supply, click **File**
Click **Open Company**
Click **OK**
Double click Stone Arbor Landscaping
Repeat the process to reopen Bellwether Garden Supply

HOW TO COPY A FILE

A copy of the company files should be kept as a master. Since your data files were furnished on a CD ROM, this will serve as your master copy. To create your working files, the companies contained on the CD ROM must be copied to the working drive. This can be either the local drive or an assigned network drive (your instructor will provide you with details). To copy the data files needed to complete the activities in this book, you must copy the folder for each company along with its contents to a specified location. By default, Peachtree creates new companies with folders within the Company folder of the main Peachtree folder.

Name ▲	Size	Type
!_PDG		File Folder
BCS		File Folder
Forms		File Folder
Letters		File Folder
Reports		File Folder
ERRORLOG	4 KB	Text Document
OPTIONS	8 KB	DAT File
OPTIONS.LCK	0 KB	LCK File
OPTIONS.PTL	0 KB	PTL File
PchSpell	18 KB	Help File
Readme	58 KB	Help File
RPTDATAI	2,059 KB	DAT File
RPTDATAI.LCK	0 KB	LCK File
rptdatai.PTL	0 KB	PTL File
STATUS	996 KB	DAT File
STATUS.PTL	0 KB	PTL File
Taxinfo	25 KB	DAT File
Taxtable	744 KB	DAT File

Two of the folders in the Company folder contain the data files for Stone Arbor Landscaping (!_PDG) and Bellwether Garden Supply (BCS). Although it is not necessary to place your data files in the default Peachtree Company folder, it would be easier to work with your various files if they were all kept in the same location. A master file is never used. It is set aside in case something happens to the company files you are using to do your work. Work within the text will always be performed on a duplicate copy of the company data. Should you wish to make a copy of these files to archive the starting position, you would copy the entire folder to another location. The size of the files being copied and the capacity of the location to which the files are being copied, must be considered when choosing where to back up your files. As an example, Bellwether Garden Supply will require over 12 MB of space in order to copy the files. As such, you would not be able to use a floppy disk for this purpose. A better alternative is to create a backup from within Peachtree.

HOW TO CREATE A PEACHTREE® COMPLETE ACCOUNTING 2006 BACKUP FILE

As you work with a company and record transactions, it is important to back up your work. This allows you to keep the information for a particular period separate from current information. A backup also allows you to restore information in case your data disk becomes damaged or in the event there is a need to return the company to a prior accounting period. There are two different ways in which you can make a backup of your data. If you use Windows Explorer you can make a copy of the folder containing your company's files and store it elsewhere on your local drive, a network drive or a removable disk. In Windows, this is called making a backup.

If you use Peachtree Complete to make a backup, you are actually asking Peachtree Complete to create a condensed file that contains the essential transaction and account information. This file has a **.ptb** extension and is not usable unless it is restored to a set of working company files. Let us back up Bellwether Garden Supply to show how easy this process is.

   DO: If necessary, open Bellwether Garden Supply
Click **Company** button
Click **Backup**

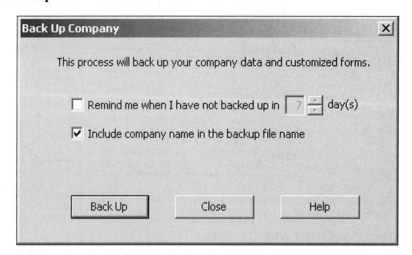

Click in the box next to Include company name in the backup file name
Click **Back Up**

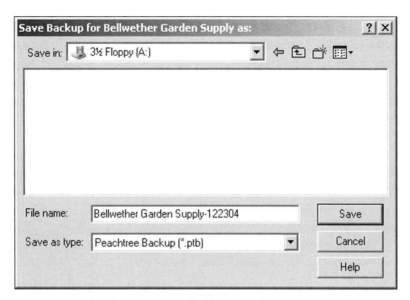

Pull down the menu in the **Save in:** field using the arrow
With a formatted disk in your [A:] drive, click 3½ Floppy [A:]
Click **Save**

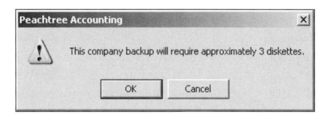

Note: Peachtree is telling you the storage space required for the backup. Make sure the location to which you are backing up has sufficient capacity. If so, click **OK**. If you backup to the hard drive, a zip drive or a USB storage device, space should be no problem.

After Peachtree has completed the backup, you are returned to the main screen to continue working if you so desire. By selecting the option to include the company name, we instructed Peachtree to use the name of our company in the file name followed by the date. Had we not selected this option, Peachtree would have used the date only. Should you desire something other than these options, you can change the file name to whatever is desired. As an example, you may wish to create a backup at the end of each accounting period prior to closing and use the month or year followed by the word end as your file name. e.g. March End.ptb

HOW TO EXIT PEACHTREE® COMPLETE ACCOUNTING 2006 AND END YOUR WORK SESSION

When you complete your work, you need to exit the Peachtree Complete program. If you are saving work on a separate data disk (in A:), you must not remove your disk until you exit the program. Following the appropriate steps to close and exit a program is extremely important.

There are program and data files that must be closed in order to leave the program and company data so that they are ready to be used again. It is common for a beginning computer user to turn off the computer without exiting a program. This can cause corrupt program and data files and can make a disk or program unusable. Always close the company as indicated below before exiting Peachtree Complete. Once Peachtree Complete has been closed, remove your data disk from A: and shut down Windows in the manner you have been instructed to use by your instructor.

  DO: There are several ways to exit Peachtree Complete properly. Select the method of choice and close/exit Peachtree Complete:

Click the **Control menu box** or **Peachtree** icon the upper left corner of title bar, click **Close**

Double-click the Control menu box or Peachtree icon in the upper left corner of title bar

Click the **Close** button in upper right corner of title bar

Click **File** (or Alt+F) and then click **Exit** (or type X)

Click **Alt+F4**

SUMMARY

Chapter 1 provides general information regarding Peachtree Complete. In this chapter, the mouse was used, the computer was turned on, different menus/toolbars were accessed, a company was opened and closed, reports were examined, and a backup file was made.

END-OF-CHAPTER QUESTIONS

TRUE/FALSE

ENTER TRUE/FALSE IN THE SPACE PROVIDED BEFORE THE QUESTION NUMBER.

_____ 1. There are various methods of giving Peachtree Complete commands, including use of Peachtree® Complete Accounting 2006 Navigation Aids, menu bar, and keyboard shortcuts.

_____ 2. In Peachtree Complete, the Window menu is used to switch between documents that have been opened, to arrange icons, and to show more than one open window.

_____ 3. RAM storage is measured in bytes.

_____ 4. If an error is made when entering a transaction, Peachtree Complete will not allow the user to return to the business document and make the correction.

_____ 5. In a computerized accounting system, each transaction that is analyzed must be entered by hand into the appropriate journal and posted to the appropriate ledger.

_____ 6. Peachtree® Complete Accounting 2006 Navigation Aids appear beneath the title bar and have drop-down menus.

_____ 7. If you use Peachtree Complete to make a backup, you are actually asking Peachtree Complete to create a condensed file that contains the essential transaction and account information.

_____ 8. The Alt key + a letter may be used to access the drop-down menus on the menu bar.

_____ 9. When you have exited your application programs and are ready to close Windows, you need to follow proper exit/closing procedures.

_____ 10. Customers, vendors, sales items, and accounts may be added only after the end of the period has been closed.

MULTIPLE CHOICE

WRITE THE LETTER OF THE CORRECT ANSWER IN THE SPACE PROVIDED BEFORE THE QUESTION NUMBER.

_____ 1. Peachtree Complete gives you an instant visual analysis of different elements of your business using ___.
A. line graphs
B. pie charts
C. bar charts
D. both B and C

_____ 2. Windows Calculator is used to ___.
A. calculate ledger balances
B. calculate cash availability
C. make calculations outside the program
D. none of the above

_____ 3. Peachtree Complete keyboard conventions ___.
A. are keyboard command shortcuts
B. use the mouse
C. use certain keys in a manner consistent with Windows
D. incorporate the use of Peachtree® Complete Accounting 2006 Navigation Aids

_____ 4. Buttons on an entry screen toolbar are used to ___.
A. give commands to Peachtree Complete
B. exit Peachtree Complete
C. prepare reports
D. show graphs of invoices prepared

_____ 5. The Help Index tab provides ___.
A. step-by-step instructions for using Help
B. an on-screen index used for finding Help topics
C. a search of all occurrences of a word or a phrase
D. all of the above

_____ 6. Peachtree® Complete Accounting 2006 Navigation Aids ___.
A. is a set of buttons to access frequently used windows within Peachtree Complete
B. is the same thing as the Peachtree® Complete Accounting 2006 Navigator
C. appear above the menu bar
D. appear at the right of the screen

_____ 7. An icon is ___.
   A. a document
   B. a graphic
   C. a chart
   D. a type of software

_____ 8. The Peachtree Complete program is a type of ___ software.
   A. operating system
   B. forecasting
   C. application
   D. word processing

_____ 9. There are ___ buttons or categories available on the Navigation Aids.
   A. 5
   B. 7
   C. 8
   D. 4

_____ 10. To verify the name of the open company, look at ___.
   A. the icon bar
   B. Peachtree® Complete Accounting 2006 Navigator
   C. the menu bar
   D. the title bar

FILL-IN

IN THE SPACE PROVIDED, WRITE THE ANSWER THAT MOST APPROPRIATELY COMPLETES THE SENTENCE.

1. The most common input devices are _____, _____, and _____.

2. The work to be performed to maintain a set of books for any company regardless if they are computerized or manual comprises _____, _____, and _____.

3. Two types of software used are _____ software and _____ software.

4. The Help window can be opened using the keyboard shortcut _____.

5. Peachtree backups use a(n) _____extension.

SHORT ESSAY

Describe the term "on the fly" and tell how it is used in Peachtree Complete.

_____

_____

_____

_____

_____

_____

_____

Sales and Receivables: Service Business

2

LEARNING OBJECTIVES

At the completion of this chapter, you will be able to:

1. Create invoices and record sales transactions on account.
2. Create sales receipts to record cash sales.
3. Edit, void, and delete invoices/sales receipts.
4. Create credit memos/refunds.
5. Add new customers and modify customer records.
6. Record cash receipts.
7. Enter partial cash payments.
8. Display and print invoices, sales receipts, and credit memos.
9. Display and print Customer Ledger reports.
10. Display and print Sales reports.
11. Display and print Sales Journal and General Ledger Trial Balance.
12. Back up data.

ACCOUNTING FOR SALES AND RECEIVABLES

Peachtree® Complete Accounting 2006 uses an invoice created in the Sales/Invoicing module to record credit sales transactions rather than a traditional Sales Journal with debits and credits and special columns. All entries will, nevertheless, be automatically recorded in a Sales Journal by Peachtree to be subsequently posted to the General Ledger. Peachtree will frequently create journals in the background. Entries made through this module will also be entered into the Subsidiary Accounts Receivable ledger. A new customer can be added "on the fly" as transactions are entered should the need arise.

Cash sales do not involve accounts receivable and are recorded in the Receipts module of Peachtree® Complete Accounting 2006. The program allows us to apply cash receipts either to sales or to existing invoices. By choosing to apply cash to sales, we are recording a cash sale. By choosing to apply cash receipts to existing invoices, we are recording a payment on account.

Unlike many computerized accounting programs, Peachtree® Complete Accounting 2006 error correction is quick and easy. Sales invoices, posted or unposted, may be edited, voided, or deleted in the same window where they were created. Customer information may be edited by entering the Maintain Customer window directly from the Sales/Invoice window. Numerous reports relating to sales are available when using Peachtree® Complete Accounting 2006. These reports include Cash Receipts Journal, Customer List, Invoice Register and Sales Journal.

TRAINING TUTORIAL

The following tutorial is a step-by-step guide to recording sales (both cash and credit) and cash receipts for a fictitious company with fictitious employees. This company is called Comprehensive Computer Consulting and is sometimes referred to as "CCC." In addition to recording transactions using Peachtree® Complete Accounting 2006, we will prepare several reports for CCC. The tutorial for Comprehensive Computer Consulting will continue in Chapters 3 and 4, where accounting for payables, bank reconciliations, financial statement preparation, and closing an accounting period will be addressed.

TRAINING PROCEDURES

To maximize the training benefits, you should:

1. Read the entire chapter *before* starting the tutorial within the chapter.
2. Answer the end-of-chapter questions.
3. Each transaction to be entered will be described with a **MEMO**. Read the memos carefully.
4. Complete all the steps listed in the **DO:** that follows the **MEMO**. Skipping a step could result in an incorrect solution for the tutorial in this chapter.
5. When you have completed a section, put an **X** on the computer next to the **DO:**.
6. As you complete your work, proofread carefully and check for accuracy. Double-check each numeric amount entered prior to posting.
7. If you find an error while preparing a transaction, correct it. If you find the error after the transaction has been posted, follow the steps indicated in this chapter to correct, void, or delete the transaction.
8. Print as directed within the chapter or as directed by your instructor.
9. You may not finish the entire chapter in one computer session. Always back up your work at the end of your work session as described in Chapter 1.
10. When you complete your computer session, exit the program. When you begin your new session, restore your data from the backup created in step 9 to eliminate problems created by others making entries in the company in between sessions. You may not need to do this if you are working from a network drive that provides for individual logons. Check with your instructor if you are unsure.

COMPANY PROFILE: COMPREHENSIVE COMPUTER CONSULTING

As the name indicates, Comprehensive Computer Consulting is a company specializing in computer consulting. CCC provides program installation, training, and technical support for today's business software as well as getting clients "online" and providing training in Internet use. In addition, Comprehensive Computer Consultants will set up customer furnished computer systems and will install basic computer components, such as memory, modems, sound cards, disk drives, and CD-ROM drives.

Comprehensive Computer Consulting is located in Southern California. It is a sole proprietorship owned by Roger Alan. Mr. Alan is involved in all aspects of the business and has the responsibility of obtaining clients in addition to performing technical tasks. CCC bills by the hour for training and hardware installation with a minimum charge of $95 for the first hour and $80 per hour thereafter. Clients with contracts for technical support are charged a monthly rate for service.

BEGIN TRAINING IN PEACHTREE® COMPLETE ACCOUNTING 2006

As you continue this chapter, you will be instructed to enter transactions for Comprehensive Computer Consulting. The first thing you must do in order to work is "boot up" or start your computer.

DO: Turn on computer and monitor, if not already on
Allow the computer to "boot up" and show the Windows desktop

HOW TO OPEN PEACHTREE® COMPLETE ACCOUNTING 2006

As you learned in Chapter 1, once you are in Windows, opening Peachtree® Complete Accounting 2006 is as easy as pointing and clicking.

DO: Insert Comprehensive Data Disk in A: (if your files are on a floppy)
Click **Start**
Point to **Programs**
Point to **Peachtree® Complete Accounting 2006**
Click **Peachtree® Complete Accounting 2006**
Note: You may also double click on the **Peachtree** icon on your desktop. If the name of the program does not show as Peachtree® Complete Accounting 2006, check with your instructor to ensure it is the correct program.

OPEN A COMPANY—COMPREHENSIVE COMPUTER CONSULTING

One method of opening Comprehensive Computer Consulting, the company for this work session, is to click on Open an Existing Company from the initial opening screen.

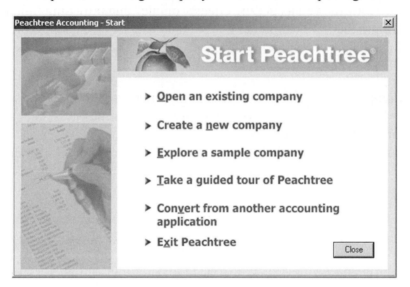

Select Comprehensive Computer Consulting from the **Open an Existing Company** window and click on **OK**.

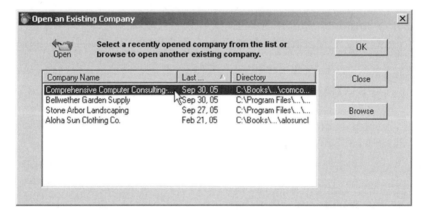

Verify this action by checking the title bar. You should see the name of the company you just opened in the title bar. Peachtree will only show recently opened companies in this screen. If Comprehensive Computer Consulting does not appear as an option, we must "look" for it first. This method of opening the company is illustrated in the following steps.

DO: Click **Open an existing company**
Click the **Browse** button
Click the drop down arrow for **Drives:**
Select the drive where your data files are kept

Note: You may need additional instructions from your instructor to be able to complete this step.

Locate and double click on the Directory (folder) where Comprehensive Computer Consulting is stored

Locate and double click on Comprehensive Computer Consulting (under the **Companies:** text box)

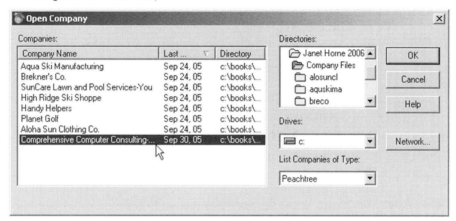

VERIFYING AN OPEN COMPANY

 DO: Verify the title bar heading:

CLOSING THE PEACHTREE TODAY SCREEN

The Peachtree Today screen is on by default when you open Peachtree® Complete Accounting 2006. This screen provides easy access to a number of Peachtree features; however, we will be focusing on accessing the different areas of Peachtree through the use of Peachtree Navigation Aids. As such, you can close this window prior to completing your assignments. As mentioned in Chapter 1, you may turn this screen off permanently.

 DO: If it is showing, close **Peachtree Today** by clicking the close button in the upper right corner of the **Peachtree Today** screen.

ADD YOUR INITIALS TO THE COMPANY NAME

Because each student in the course will be working for the same companies and printing the same documents, personalizing the company name to include your name will help identify many of the documents you print during your training.

  DO: Add your name to the company name
Click on the **Maintain** menu option at the top of your screen
Click **Company Information**…
Click to the right of Comprehensive Computer Consulting-You
Delete the word You by backspacing through it
Type your three letter initials after the dash. For example, Alex P. Smith would type APS
Click **OK**
The change will not show until the company has been opened again.
Click on the **File** menu option
Click on **Open Company**
When prompted for confirmation that you wish to close the current company, answer yes.
Double click on Comprehensive Computer Consulting.

– The title bar now shows Comprehensive Computing Consultants–APS

PEACHTREE® COMPLETE ACCOUNTING 2006 NAVIGATION AIDS

Peachtree® Complete Accounting 2006 Navigation Aids allow the user to access various types of information in Peachtree® Complete Accounting 2006. You may also choose to use the menu bar, custom toolbar or use keyboard commands to access various areas of Peachtree® Complete Accounting 2006. For more detailed information regarding Peachtree® Complete Accounting 2006 Navigation Aids and other access methods, refer to Chapter 1. Instructions in this text will be given primarily for Peachtree® Complete Accounting 2006 Navigation Aids; however, the menu bar, custom toolbar and/or keyboard commands may be used as well.

When you first enter Peachtree® Complete Accounting 2006, you will see the Navigation Aids at the bottom of your screen. As you click on the Navigation buttons, you will open a Peachtree® Complete Accounting 2006 window that allows you to access a variety of tasks related to that button. For example, when you clicked Company Information inside the Company Navigation Aid button, you opened the Peachtree® Complete Accounting 2006 Maintain Company Information window. The Company button contains access to features that relate to the whole company, such as, setting up a new company, backing up and restoring data from an existing company, importing and exporting data, etc. All of these features are presented as graphical links as you can see in the following illustration. Generally formatting for Navigation Aid windows is that the first section will contain maintenance activities, the second will have transaction tasks while the third will have reports.

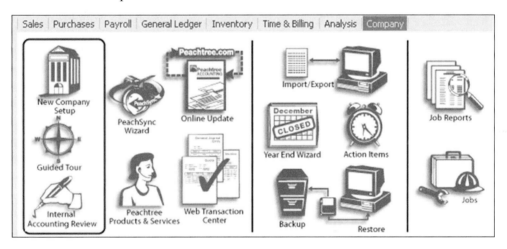

You may open other Peachtree® Complete Accounting 2006 Navigation Aids by clicking the appropriate button (e.g. General Ledger (G/L)) where you will be presented other selections. We will look at these other buttons as we study the activities contained within them.

BEGINNING THE TUTORIAL

In this chapter you will be entering both accounts receivable transactions and cash sales transactions. Much of the organization of Peachtree® Complete Accounting 2006 is dependent on lists. The three primary types of lists you will use in the tutorial for receivables are a Customer List, Chart of Accounts and Inventory Item list.

The names, addresses, telephone numbers, credit terms, credit limits, and balances for all established credit customers are contained in the Customer List. The Customer List can also be referred to as the Accounts Receivable Ledger. Peachtree® Complete Accounting 2006 does not use this term; however, this list contains the detailed information one would find in an Accounts Receivable Ledger. A transaction entry for an individual customer is created first in the appropriate journal, such as the Sales Journal or Cash Receipts Journal. It is then posted to a Customer Log within the customer's account in the Customer List just as it would be posted to the customer's individual account in an Accounts Receivable Ledger. Although the Customer Event Log is not generally accessed in our day to day work, it is interesting to view an example of the log from the sample company to better understand the internal workings of the program. The following is a screen capture from one customer of Bellwether Garden Supply. The log contains a record of all transactions between Bellwether and this customer including sales, receipts and credit memos. The log is accessed through the Maintain Customer menu option.

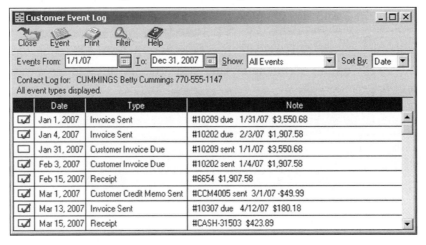

If we total the balances owed by each of the customers, this will be equal to the balance of the Accounts Receivable account in the General Ledger. You will be using the following Customer List for established credit customers. You will be adding customers to this list as you progress through the tutorial.

Comprehensive Computer Consulting-APS Customer List

Filter Criteria includes: 1) Customers only. Report order is by ID.

Customer ID	Customer	Contact	Telephone 1
AND01	Andrews Research Corp.	Eric Andrews	818-555-9825
BAC01	Bachoffer & Sons	Constance Carrero	310-555-8877
BAR01	Barnes, Rachel, CPA	Rachel Barnes	310-555-5782
CRE01	Creative Innovations	Delilah Jones	818-555-0753
CRE02	Creative Design Institute	Stephen Zimmer	310-555-1195
GOL01	Gold, Bradley, CPA	Bernadette Feldman	310-555-4729
HAC01	Hacene Nahid Imports	Ali Nahid	310-555-9825
JEN01	Jensen Ranch	Phyllis Chaing	310-555-8256
JUN01	Jung, Yu	Chai Jung	818-555-0925
KAT01	Kati's Illustrations	Jeffrey Rogers	310-555-7834
MAN01	Mandano, Jose, Esq.	Jose Mandano	818-555-1305
MAT01	Matthews, Thomas, CPA	Hsui Chi	818-555-9127
SHU01	Shultz & Kaufman	Esther Kinoshita	818-555-3967
VIC01	Victor Productions	Morris Williams	310-555-2897
WAL01	Walter, Yancheski, and Yi	Jefferson Jones	310-555-1142
WHI01	White's Design	Marcia White	310-555-3489

Peachtree allows the user to use any format desired when assigning the customer ID numbers. We have elected to use the first three letters of the company name followed by a sequence number. The number allows us to have more than one company whose name begins the same. An example from the above customer list would be CRE01 and CRE02. Both of these company names begin with Creative. The 01 and 02 allows our system to work with both names.

Various tasks performed by Comprehensive Computer Consulting are considered to be sales. In CCC, there are several income accounts in which to record these sales. The specific account required is dependent upon the nature of the work performed. In addition, Peachtree has the capability of setting up service tasks within the Inventory module for quick and easy access when preparing sales invoices. For example, CCC uses Training Income in which to record revenues earned by providing on-site training. There are a number of classifications for the revenue earned in this manner. For example, Training 1 is for the first hour of on-site training and Training 2 is for all additional hours of on-site training. As you look at the Item List, you will observe that the rates for both items are different. Using an Item List allows for speed and provides flexibility in billing and a more accurate representation of the way in which income is earned. The following Item List contains those services currently offered by CCC.

Comprehensive Computer Consulting-APS Item Master List

Filter Criteria includes: Report order is by ID.

Item ID	Item Description	
Tech Sup 1	5 Hours--Monthly Technical Sup	150.00
Tech Sup 2	10 Hours--Monthly Technical Su	300.00
Tech Sup 3	15 Hours--Monthly Technical Su	450.00
Training 1	Initial Hour of On-Site Traini	95.00
Training 2	Additional Hours of On-Site Tr	80.00

In the tutorial, all transactions are described with memos. The transaction date will be the same date as the memo date unless otherwise specified within the memo. Always enter the date of the transaction as specified in the memo. Dates are very important to Peachtree and are used to age accounts receivables and accounts payables. They are also used as part of the process of paying bills and generating payroll. By default, Peachtree® Complete Accounting 2006 automatically enters the system date. In many instances, this will not be the same date as the transaction. This is particularly true when working through instructional data. Peachtree defaults its system date to your computer's system date. In order to more realistically use Peachtree, we will be changing Peachtree's system date to that of the memo date prior to entering the transactions contained in the memo. The Change System Date window is accessible by clicking on the system date on the status bar at the bottom of the screen. Start every tutorial by setting the date to the tutorial date.

Once the Change System Date window is open, you can type in the memo date or use the calendar icon to the right of the date field to select the memo date.

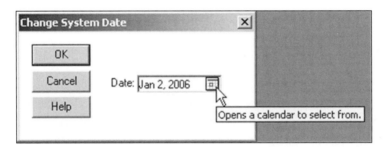

Customer names, when necessary, will be given in the transaction. All terms for customers on account are Net 30 days unless specified otherwise. The defaults for this option have already been set but confirm them nevertheless. If a memo contains more than one transaction, there will be a horizontal space separating the transactions.

MEMO

DATE: The transaction date is listed here

Transaction details are given in the body of the memo. Customer names, the type of transaction, amounts of money, and any other details needed are listed here.

Even when you are instructed how to enter a transaction step by step, you should always refer to the memo for transaction details. Once a specific type of transaction has been entered in a step-by-step manner, additional transactions will be made without having detailed instructions provided. Of course, you may always refer to instructions given for previous transactions for the steps used to enter those transactions.

ENTER SALES ON ACCOUNT

Because Peachtree® Complete Accounting 2006 operates with a business form entry screen, a sale on account is entered via an invoice accessed from the Sales/Invoicing option of the Sales Navigation button. You prepare an invoice, and Peachtree® Complete Accounting 2006 records the transaction in the Sales Journal and updates the customer's account automatically. The DO: presumes and will continue to presume that you are already in the Peachtree program and have opened the company. The following DO: steps you through changing the system date. This should be the first thing you do prior to entering transactions regardless of whether the DO: specifically provides instructions for this task.

MEMO

DATE: January 3, 2006

Bill the following: Invoice No. 101—Jose Mandano has had several questions regarding his new computer system. He spoke with Roger Alan about this and has signed up for 10 hours of technical support (Tech Sup 2) for January. Bill him for this service.

   DO: Record the sale on account shown in the memo above. This invoice is being used to bill a customer for a sale using one sales item:
Click on the date shown next to Today at the bottom of the screen
–   This is the system date button on the toolbar
Enter 1/3/06 in the **Date:** field
Click **OK**
Click on the **Sales** Navigation button

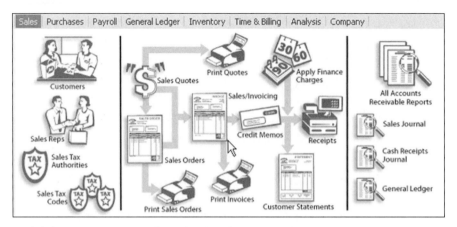

Click **Sales/Invoicing** icon in the center section of the screen.

– A blank invoice will show on the desktop

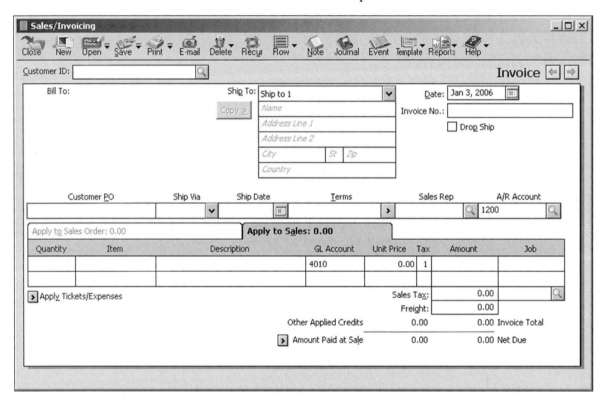

Click the magnifying glass next to **Customer ID:**
Double click Mandano, Jose, Esq.

– The customer's name is entered in the **Bill To:** field automatically

– Cursor is automatically moved to the **Ship To:** field. Since we are not shipping a product, this field is not required. Peachtree allows us to maintain up to 9 shipping addresses in addition to the billing address. These can be typed in on the invoice or selected with the pull down arrow assuming they have been entered into the customer's account previously.

Tab to **Date:** field

- Confirm that it reflects the 1/3/06 system date. Change if required.

Tab to the **Invoice No.:** field. We could insert the invoice number at this point; however, we often times do not know what the next number in the sequence should be. If left blank, Peachtree will assign the next available invoice number during the print process. This is the procedure we will follow in this book

Tab to the **Customer PO** field.

- There is no PO number to record but we could enter the customers PO number here had one been given.

Tab through the **Ship Via** and **Ship Date** fields as they are not required for this invoice.

Tabbing again brings you to the **Terms** arrow; however, the default terms of Net 30 should already be indicated.

- Using the arrow opens a window through which the terms can be viewed and/or edited.

Tab through the **Sales Rep, A/R Account** fields and the **Apply to Sales** tab until you reach the **Quantity** field.

- If our business utilized sales representatives, we could indicate which sales rep was responsible for this transaction. This information could be used to calculate total sales by sales rep.

Enter 1.00 in the **Quantity** field. Press **Enter**. (If set to manual decimal point, you do not need to enter the two zeros. Peachtree can be set to use auto decimal like a ten-key machine in the Global Options in which case the zeros are required).

- We must enter a quantity in order for Peachtree to calculate the amount of this invoice. We have sold one service contract.

Click on the magnifying glass to the right of the **Item** field, select Tech Sup 2 and click **OK** to choose this item.

You are taken to the **Description** field. Tab through this field as well as the following fields and note how Peachtree completes the remaining fields automatically.

EDIT AND CORRECT ERRORS

If an error is discovered while entering invoice information, it may be corrected by positioning the cursor in the field containing the error. You may do this by clicking in the field containing the error, tabbing to move forward through each field, or pressing Shift+Tab to move back to the field containing the error. If the error is highlighted, type the correction. If the error is not highlighted, you can correct the error by pressing the backspace or the delete key as many times as necessary to remove the error. You may then type in the correction. (Alternate method: Point to the error, highlight it by dragging the mouse through the error with the left button depressed, then type the correction.)

DO: Practice editing and making corrections to the invoice just completed:

Click the magnifying glass next to **Customer ID:**

Click **Bachoffer & Sons**, click **OK**

– Information is changed in the **Bill To:** fields.

Highlight contents of **Date:** field.

Type 1/24/06 as the date

– This removes the Jan 3, 2006 date originally entered.

Click in the **Quantity** field to highlight the 1.00.

Type 2.00. Press Enter.

To eliminate the changes made to this invoice, click the drop-down list arrow next to **Customer ID:**

Click Mandano, Jose, Esq., click **OK**

Highlight contents of **Date:** field and type 01/03/06

Click in the **Quantity** field to highlight the 2.00 and type a 1.00.

Press the **Enter** or **Tab** key

– This will complete the correction invoice.

– Compare the information you entered with the information provided in the memo and with the following completed invoice.

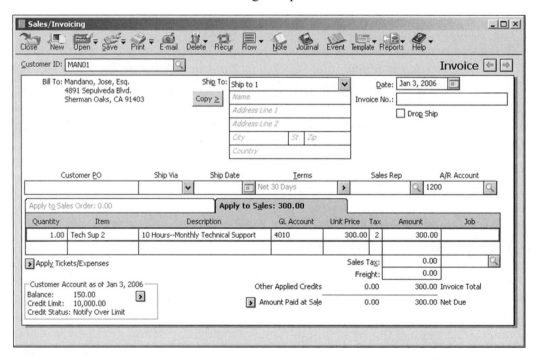

PRINT AN INVOICE

Peachtree allows us to save our invoices for batch printing at a later time, or to print them one by one as they are created. The quantity of invoices required by your company at any given point in time will generally dictate which method is used. Peachtree assigns invoice numbers during the printing process unlike other programs that assign the number during the invoice creation phase.

DO: With the invoice on the screen, print it immediately after entering the information. Click **Print** at the top of the **Sales/Invoicing** window.

This brings us to a dialog box from which we can print our invoice. Here too, we can use the Change Form option to select from numerous formats. Some are for plain paper while others require the use of preprinted forms. We will use the default selection, **Invoice**. We will also accept Peachtree's default invoice number 101. If the **First Invoice Number:** field does not have 101 in it, be sure to change it before proceeding.

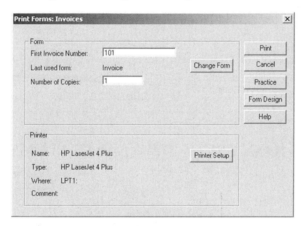

You are also presented with a **Practice** option.

– This option allows us to print a practice invoice for alignment purposes, modify the selected form or cancel print operations. You may select it to see how it works.

Click on **Practice**.

– This option would be selected at the start of a large invoice print run using preprinted forms to ensure proper alignment. After Peachtree has sent the sample invoice to the printer, you are presented with:

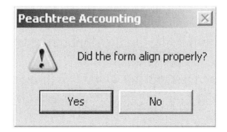

Click on **Yes**.

– This will return you to the Print Forms: Invoices options box.

Click on **Print** to complete the print process.

- If we were batch printing many invoices, Peachtree would have assigned subsequent numbers to each invoice.
- Peachtree has recorded this invoice as a result of the printing. Had we chosen to not print the invoice at this time, we would have been required to save the invoice prior to closing by clicking on the **Save** button.
- Batch printing is initiated from the Accounts Receivable Reports menu. This feature can be selected from the **Sales Navigation** button as **Print Invoices**.

Click on **Close** if you wish to exit the invoicing task

MEMO:

Date: January 3, 2006

Bill the following: Invoice No. 102—Bachoffer & Sons; Mr. Bachoffer spoke with Roger Alan regarding the need for on-site training to help him get started using the Internet. Bill him for a 5-hour on-site training session. (Remember to use Training 1 for the first hour of on-site training and Training 2 for all additional hours of training.)

ENTER TRANSACTIONS USING TWO SALES ITEMS

DO: Record a transaction on account for a sale involving two sales items:
Set the system date to 1/3/2006.
Click on **Sales/Invoicing** from the **Sales** button.
Click the drop-down list arrow next to **Customer ID:**
Double click Bachoffer & Sons.
Tab to **Date:** field.
- Confirm that it reflects the 1/3/06 system date.
Tab to the **Quantity** field.
Enter 1.00 in the **Quantity** field. Press **Enter**.
- Because the first hour is billed at a different rate than the subsequent hours, we must break this 5-hour job into two parts. This first part is only for the first hour.
Click on the magnifying glass to the right of the **Item** field, highlight Training 1 and click **OK** to choose this item.
You are taken to the **Description** field. Tab through this field as well as the following fields and note how Peachtree completes the remaining fields automatically.
When you reach the **Quantity** field again, type 4.00. Press **Enter**.
Click on the magnifying glass to the right of the **Item** field, highlight Training 2 and click **OK** to choose this item.
Tab through the remaining fields to complete the line.

Check your invoice with the data furnished in the memo and with the following example. Make corrections as needed prior to printing.

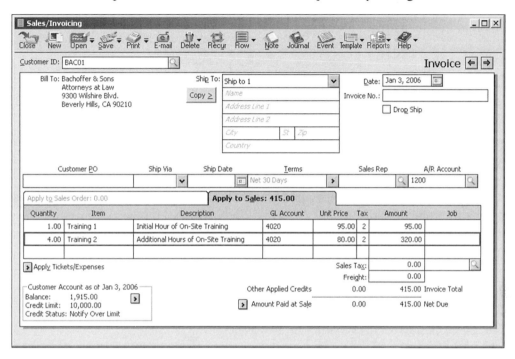

PRINTING THE INVOICE

DO: With the invoice (this will be Invoice No. 102) on the screen, print the invoice immediately after entering invoice information:

Click **Print** button at the top of the **Sales/Invoicing** window.

Peachtree will use the last form it has printed and has now selected this form for us. We can change the form by selecting Change Form and choosing from the 14 built-in options contained in the program. We could also choose to design our own form.

Accept or enter 102 as our invoice number.

– If a number other than 102 shows:

Click in the **First Invoice Number:** box

Drag to highlight the number

Type 102

Click on **Print**.

Click **Close** button at the top of the **Sales/Invoicing** window to exit this task.

ADDING A NOTE TO AN INVOICE

Peachtree allows you to add a note to any invoice created. This feature is activated by clicking on the **Note** icon in the Sales/Invoicing window.

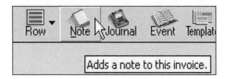

You are presented with the **Note** window. The window contains three tabs, Customer Note, Statement Note and Internal Note. The Customer Note tab is for messages that are to be printed on the invoice. You may type any message you desire into the Note field for inclusion on the invoice. The Statement Note is for messages you wish to have printed on the customer's monthly statement. The Internal Note tab attaches a note to the invoice but does not print it. The printed notes can be positioned by selecting the appropriate radio button at the bottom of the window.

To add a message thanking your customer for his/her business, you would have something like this:

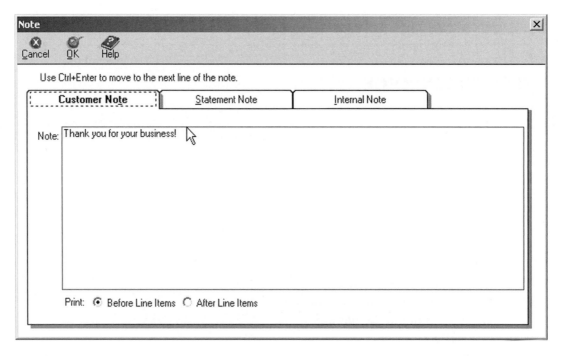

The note feature provides the user with a simple to use mechanism for communicating with the customer or keeping private notes about the customer.

PREPARE INVOICES WITHOUT STEP-BY-STEP INSTRUCTIONS

MEMO

DATE: January 5, 2006

Bill the following:

Invoice No. 103—Yu Jung needed to have telephone assistance to help him set up his Internet connection. Prepare a bill for 10 hours of technical support for January.

Invoice No. 104—Walter, Yancheski, and Yi have several new employees that need to be trained in the use of the office computer system. Bill them for 40 hours of on-site training.

Invoice No. 105—Gold, Bradley, CPA, needs to learn the basic features of Peachtree® Complete Accounting 2006, a program used by many of their customers. Bill them for 10 hours of on-site training and 15 hours of technical support for January. (Note: You will use three sales items in this transaction.)

Invoice No. 106—Kati's Illustrations has a new assistant office manager. We are providing 40 hours of on-site training for Beverly Williams. To provide additional assistance, the company has signed up for 5 hours technical support for January.

DO: Enter the four transactions in the memo above. Refer to instructions given for the two previous transactions entered.
- Remember to set the system date to 1/5/2006.
- Remember, when billing for on-site training, the first hour is billed as Training 1, and the remaining hours are billed as Training 2.
- Always use the Item list to determine the appropriate sales items for billing. Let Peachtree auto-fill the balance of the line.
- If you make an error prior to printing, correct it immediately.
- Print each invoice immediately after you enter the information for it.
- Click **Close** after Invoice No. 106 has been entered and printed.
- Your invoices prior to printing should look like the following:

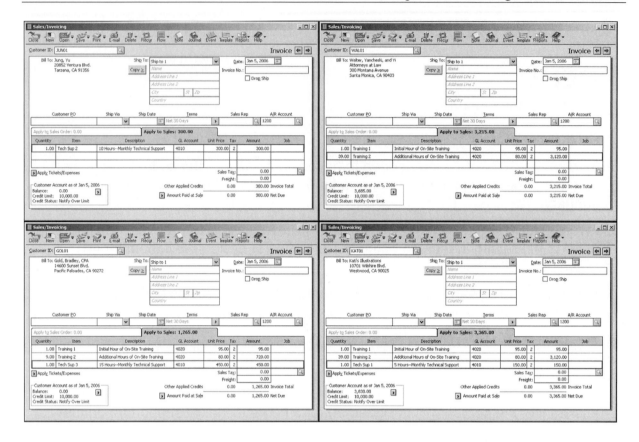

PRINT A/R REPORTS

Peachtree® Complete Accounting 2006 has several reports available that are related to accounts receivable. These reports are accessible from the **Sales** button of the Navigation Aids. Under the Reports section, we can select **All Accounts Receivables Reports**, which will bring up the following Select A Report window.

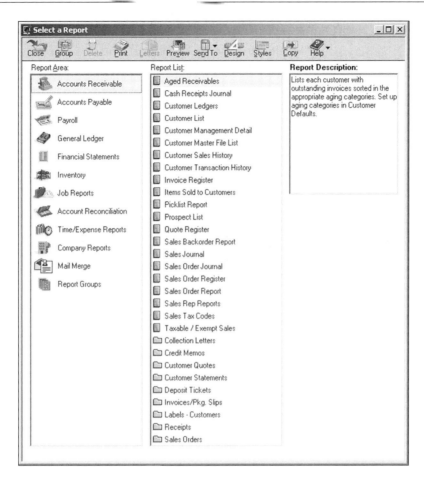

One of the most useful is the Customer Ledgers report. This report shows you the balances due from all of our credit customers. It will also summarize the current activity for each customer.

 DO: Click the **All Accounts Receivables Reports** from the **Sales** button.
Double click on **Customer Ledgers**
  – This report lists the names of all customers on account with balances. The amount column shows the total balance for each customer. This includes opening balances as well as current invoices.

Comprehensive Computer Consulting-APS						
Customer Ledgers						
For the Period From Jan 1, 2006 to Jan 31, 2006						
Filter Criteria includes: Report order is by ID. Report is printed in Detail Format.						
Customer ID Customer	**Date**	**Trans No**	**Type**	**Debit Amt**	**Credit Amt**	**Balance**
AND01 Andrews Research Corp.	1/1/06	Balance Fwd				815.00
BAC01 Bachoffer & Sons	1/1/06	Balance Fwd				1,915.00
	1/3/06	102	SJ	415.00		2,330.00

Click the **Print** button at the top of the Customer Ledgers report window.
- You may get a Windows Print dialog box. If you do click **OK**.

USE THE DRILLDOWN FEATURE

Bachoffer & Sons called Roger Alan asking about their recent invoice from 1/5/06. To obtain information regarding the invoice, we can use Peachtree's Drilldown feature from within the Customer Ledgers report. Position the cursor over the line in the report that contains invoice #102. The cursor will resemble a magnifying glass with a Z inside of it. At the same time a blue box will surround the invoice number and other transaction details allowing you to select it.

 DO: Point to the line for the **Bachoffer & Sons** invoice #102.

Comprehensive Computer Consulting-APS
Customer Ledgers
For the Period From Jan 1, 2006 to Jan 31, 2006
Filter Criteria includes: Report order is by ID. Report is printed in Detail Format.

Customer ID Customer	Date	Trans No	Type	Debit Amt	Credit Amt	Balance
AND01 Andrews Research Corp.	1/1/06	Balance Fwd				815.00
BAC01 Bachoffer & Sons	1/1/06	Balance Fwd				1,915.00
	1/3/06	102	SJ	415.00		2,330.00

Double click to select the invoice.
- Notice that you are taken back to the invoice you created earlier. Its status is reflected in the upper left corner, Unpaid. If needed, you could reprint the invoice or simply use the information presented to handle the phone call.

Click **Close** when you are finished examining the invoice.
- You are brought back to the Customer Ledgers report where you could select another invoice for examination or close the report if it is no longer needed.

CORRECT AN INVOICE AND PRINT THE CORRECTED FORM

Errors may be corrected very easily with Peachtree® Complete Accounting 2006. Because an invoice is prepared for sales on account, corrections will be made directly on the invoice. We will access the invoice via the Customer Ledgers report.

MEMO
DATE: January 7, 2006

The actual amount of time spent for on-site training increased from 10 hours to 12 hours. Change Invoice No. 105 to Gold, Bradley, CPA, to correct the actual amount of training hours to show a total of 12 hours.

DO: Modify **Invoice #105** and print a corrected invoice:

Set the system date to 1/7/2006.

Click **All Accounts Receivables Reports** in the **Sales** button.

Double click on Customer Ledgers

If necessary, scroll through the report until Invoice #105 is visible.

Position the cursor over the invoice number and double click.

– Invoice #105 appears on the screen.

Click in the **Quantity** field for the line that corresponds to the Training 2 hours.

Change the quantity from 9 hours to 11 hours.

Press **Tab** to generate a new total.

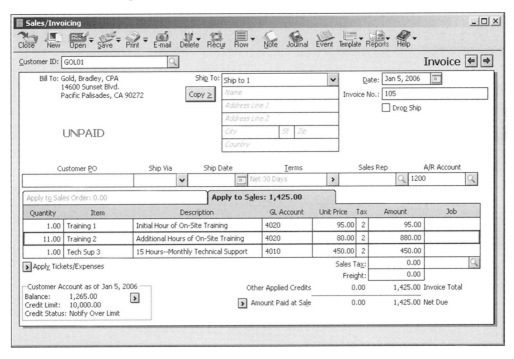

– Notice that the date remains 01/05/2006.

Click **Print** button.

Click **Close** to close the invoice form.

After editing the invoice and returning to the Customer Ledgers report, locate invoice #105 again and note that Peachtree has already updated the information in the report and shows the new balance for invoice #105 as $1,425.00.

VOID AND DELETE SALES FORMS

Deleting an invoice permanently removes it from Peachtree® Complete Accounting 2006 without leaving a trace. If you would like to maintain an audit trail for the invoice that you no longer want, it is more appropriate to void the invoice. When an invoice is voided, it remains in the Peachtree® Complete Accounting 2006 system; however, it no longer reflects a balance owed by the customer.

Void an Invoice

MEMO

DATE: January 7, 2006

We discover Yu Jung called on January 5 to cancel the 10 hours of technical support for January (This was the same day the invoice was recorded.) Because Invoice No. 103 to Yu Jung is no longer required, void the invoice.

 DO: Void the invoice above by going directly to the original invoice:
The system date should be 1/7/2006, if it is not, set it.
If necessary, click **All Accounts Reports** in the **Sales** button.
Double click on Customer Ledgers
Position the cursor over Invoice No. 103 and double click.
– Invoice No. 103 appears on the screen.
Click on the arrow next to the **Delete** icon.
– Notice that you are presented with the option to delete or void the invoice.

Click **Void**.
– You are presented with a Void Existing Invoice dialog box that is asking you for a date from which to void the invoice.

Change Date to 1/5/06.

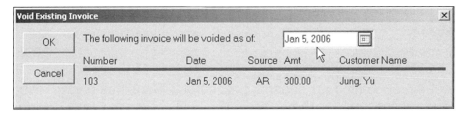

Click **OK**.

- The invoice has now been voided and you are now left with a blank Sales/Invoicing window.

Click **Close** to close the Sales/Invoicing window.

- You are now back in the Customer Ledgers report. Locate invoice #103 and note that invoice #103V has been added to this customers ledger account.

JUN01	1/5/06	103	SJ	300.00		300.00
Jung, Yu	1/5/06	103V	SJ		300.00	0.00

By creating Invoice No. 103V, Peachtree Complete has effectively reversed the transaction. This same reversal process has also occurred in the General Ledger where the controlling accounts receivable account and the related sales accounts have also been reversed.

1200	1/1/06			Beginning Balance			22,505.00
Accounts Receivable	1/3/06	101	SJ	Mandano, Jose, Esq.	300.00		
	1/3/06	102	SJ	Bachoffer & Sons	415.00		
	1/5/06	103	SJ	Jung, Yu	300.00		
	1/5/06	104	SJ	Walter, Yancheski, an	3,215.00		
	1/5/06	105	SJ	Gold, Bradley, CPA	1,425.00		
	1/5/06	106	SJ	Kati's Illustrations	3,365.00		
	1/5/06	103V	SJ	Jung, Yu		300.00	
	1/5/06	103	CRJ	Jung, Yu - Invoice: 10		300.00	
	1/5/06	103	CRJ	Jung, Yu - Invoice: 10	300.00		
				Current Period Change	9,320.00	600.00	8,720.00
	1/31/06			Ending Balance			31,225.00

4010	1/1/06			Beginning Balance			
Technical Support Income	1/3/06	101	SJ	Mandano, Jose, Esq. -		300.00	
	1/5/06	103	SJ	Jung, Yu - Item: Tech		300.00	
	1/5/06	105	SJ	Gold, Bradley, CPA - I		450.00	
	1/5/06	106	SJ	Kati's Illustrations - It		150.00	
	1/5/06	103V	SJ	Jung, Yu - Item: Tech	300.00		
				Current Period Change	300.00	1,200.00	-900.00
	1/31/06			Ending Balance			-900.00

While the effect of Invoice No. 103 has been removed from Peachtree, an audit trail remains to indicate the series of events surrounding the removal of the invoice. Because the invoice is still in Peachtree, the Note feature discussed earlier could be used to provide an explanation of the voiding.

Delete an Invoice

MEMO

DATE: January 7, 2006

Because of the upcoming tax season, Bachoffer & Sons has had to reschedule
their 5-hour training session three times. Bachoffer & Sons finally decided to
cancel the training session and reschedule it after April 15. Delete Invoice No.
102 to Mr. Bachoffer.

DO: Delete the above transaction, using Find Transactions (Ctrl+F) to locate the
invoice:
– Find Transactions is useful when you have a large number of invoices and
want to locate a specific invoice number.
– Using Find will locate the invoice without requiring you to scroll through all
the invoices in the system or even for the specific company. For example, if
customer Sanderson's transaction was on Invoice No. 3 and the invoice on the
screen was Invoice No. 1,084, you would not have to scroll through 1,081
invoices because Find would locate Invoice No. 3 instantly.
To use Find Transaction:
Click **Edit** on the menu bar.
Click **Find Transactions** (or use Ctrl+F).
Click in the **Type** column for the **Reference Number** row. Using the drop
down list, select Range.
Click in the **From** field in the same row and enter 102.
Click in the **To** field in the same row and enter 102.
Click on the **Find** icon in the middle of the dialog box.

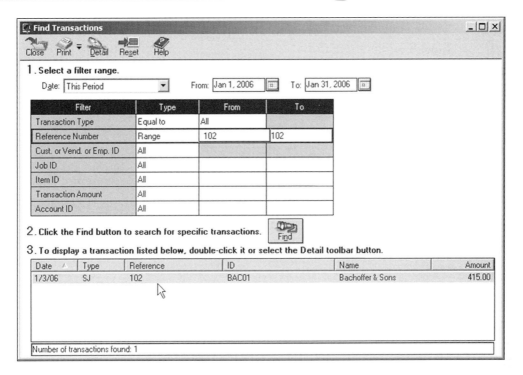

Double click on the transaction displayed in the field at the bottom of the window. This will place **Invoice No. 102** on your screen.
Click on the **Delete** icon at the top of the window.

- Notice that you are presented with the option to delete or void the invoice.
Click **Delete**.
- You are presented with a confirmation dialog box that is asking you to confirm your action to delete the invoice.

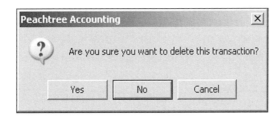

Click **Yes**.

– The invoice has now been deleted and you are now left with a blank
Sales/Invoicing window.

Click **Close** to close the Sales/Invoicing window.

The Find Transaction feature of Peachtree 2006 is a very powerful tool that allows us to retrieve data based on any number of criteria. In the first area are filters that allow us to specify the time period for the transactions we seek. Once the time period has been selected, we can activate filters to narrow down our search. The following filters are available to us:

Filter	Description
Transaction Type	Allows us to select the type of transaction, e.g. sales invoices, purchase invoices, sales orders, payroll entries, etc.
Reference Number	Allows us to specify one or a range of invoice numbers, pay check numbers, P.O. numbers, etc.
Customer, Vendor or Employee ID	Allows us to select one or a range of customer, vendor or employee numbers.
Job ID	Allows us to select one or a range of job numbers.
Item ID	Allows us to select one or a range of item numbers. These can be inventory items or service items.
Transaction Amount	Allows us to select a specific amount or a range for the transactions.
Account ID	Allows us to select one or a range of GL account numbers that were affected by the transaction.

Click the **Close** button to close the Find Transactions window. If necessary, close the Customer Ledgers report. To confirm that Invoice No. 102 is no longer in our system, we can look at a Customer Ledger report.

DO: Print a single Customer Ledger account:

Click the **All Accounts Reports** from the **Sales** button.

Single click on Customer Ledgers to highlight the report.

Click on the **Preview** icon at the top of the window.

– This will bring you to a Customers Ledger dialog box where you can use filters to customize the report.

Click in the field in the **Type** column for the **Customer ID** line

Using the drop down list arrow, change the All to Equal To.

In the same row, click in the **From** column.

Using the magnifying glass button, select Bachoffer & Sons.

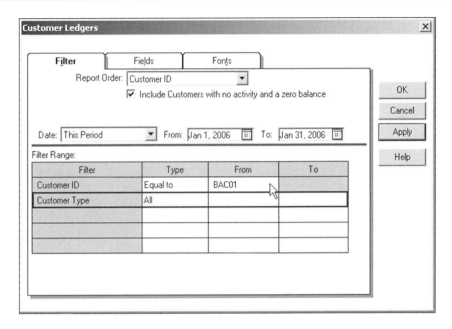

Click **OK**.

- Based on our filter selection, we are presented with a Customer Ledger report that contains only one customer, Bachoffer & Sons.
- As you can see from the report, Invoice No. 102 has been removed from the account.

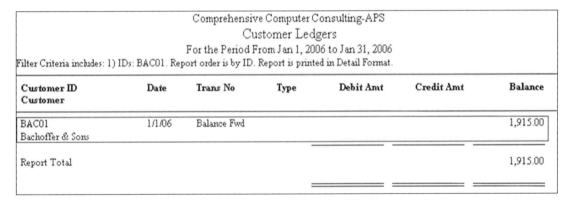

Click **Print** to print report.
Click **Close** to exit the report.
Click **Close** to exit the Select A Report window.

PREPARE CREDIT MEMOS

Credit memos are prepared to show a reduction in the amount of a transaction. If the invoice has already been sent to the customer, it is more appropriate and less confusing to make a change to an invoice by issuing a credit memo rather than voiding the invoice and issuing a new one. A credit memo notifies a customer that a change has been made.

MEMO

DATE: January 9, 2006

Prepare the following: Credit Memo No. 104-C—Walter, Yancheski, and Yi did not need 5 hours of the training billed on Invoice No. 104. Issue a Credit Memo to reduce Training 2 by 5 hours.

DO: Record a credit memo:
Set the system date to 1/9/2006.
Click on **Credit Memos** from the **Sales** button.
Click the drop-down list next to **Customer ID:**
Double click Walter, Yancheski, and Yi.
Tab to **Date:** field.
– Confirm that it reflects the 1/9/06 system date.
Tab to the **Credit No.:** field and enter 104-C
– Tying the credit memo to a specific invoice as we have done here will save you research time later on.
Click the drop-down list next to the **Apply to Invoice No.:** field
Select Invoice #104
Tab to the **Returned** column in the Training 2 row.
Enter 5.0 in the **Returned** field. Press **Enter**.
Check for accuracy and make corrections as needed prior to printing.

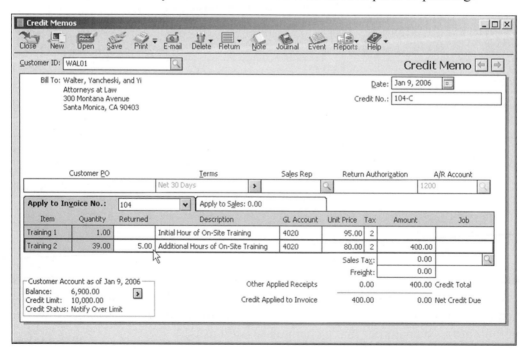

Click **Print** button at the top of the **Credit Memos** window.

Accept or enter 104-C as our invoice number. Instead of tying the credit to the invoice number, another number sequence could also be used for credits.

Click on **Print**.

Click **Close** button at the top of the window to exit this task.

VIEW CUSTOMER LEDGERS REPORT

Periodically viewing reports allows you to verify the changes that have occurred to accounts such as with the Walter, Yancheski, and Yi account. The Customer Ledgers report shows all the transactions for every customer; however, we can use the options feature to select a single customer as we did before.

DO: View a single Customer Ledger account:

Click the **All Accounts Receivable Reports** from the **Sales** button.

Single click on Customer Ledgers to highlight the report.

Click on the **Preview** icon at the top of the window.

Click in the field in the **Type** column for the **Customer ID** line

Using the drop down list arrow, change the All to Equal to.

In the same row, click in the **From** column.

Using the magnifying glass button, select Walter, Yancheski, and Yi.

Click **OK**.

- Based on our filter selection, we are presented with a Customer Ledger report that contains only one customer, Walter, Yancheski, and Yi.
- The account now reflects a $400.00 credit to the account.

Comprehensive Computer Consulting-APS
Customer Ledgers
For the Period From Jan 1, 2006 to Jan 31, 2006
Filter Criteria includes: 1) IDs: WAL01. Report order is by ID. Report is printed in Detail Format.

Customer ID Customer	Date	Trans No	Type	Debit Amt	Credit Amt	Balance
WAL01	1/1/06	Balance Fwd				3,685.00
Walter, Yancheski, and Yi	1/5/06	104	SJ	3,215.00		6,900.00
	1/9/06	104-C	SJ		400.00	6,500.00
Report Total				3,215.00	400.00	6,500.00

Click **Close** to exit the report.

Click **Close** to exit the Select A Report window.

ADD A NEW ACCOUNT TO THE CHART OF ACCOUNTS

The accounts required by a business can change from those that were set up initially. Peachtree® Complete Accounting 2006 allows you to make changes to the chart of accounts at anytime. You can add accounts, delete accounts, change account types or edit account names as needed. This can be accomplished through a maintenance procedure or can be performed "on the fly" from any number of task windows.

Roger Alan has determined that CCC has received a lot of calls from customers for assistance with hardware installation. Comprehensive Computer Consulting desires to maintain its revenue by type. It currently has income accounts for technical support and training, but does not have an account for hardware installation. Roger has made the decision that CCC will offer assistance with hardware installation on a regular basis. As a result of this decision, you will be adding another income account. This account will be used when revenue from hardware installation is earned. In addition to adding the account, you will also have to add two new services to the Item list.

 DO: Add a new account to the chart of accounts:
Click the **General Ledger** button.
Click **Chart of Accounts** in the Maintain section of the button.
Enter 4060 in the **Account ID** field.
– Peachtree will open a pull down list of the existing chart of accounts as you enter the number. This will not impact your task. Simply press the **Enter** key after entering the account number.
Enter Installation Income in the **Description** field. Press the **Enter** key.
In the **Account Type** field, use the drop down list arrow to open a list of account types.
Click **Income**.

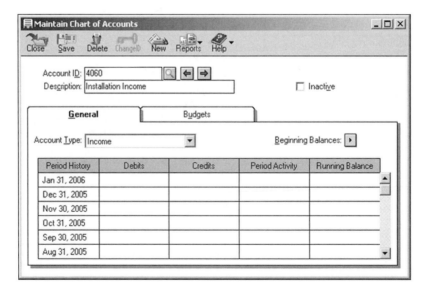

Compare your screen with the previous illustration and verify your entry.
Click **Save** at the top of the Maintain Chart of Accounts window.
Click **Close** to exit.

ADD NEW ITEMS TO LIST

Adding new accounts to the chart of accounts is not the only feature of Peachtree 2006 that will accommodate the changing needs of a business. The addition of the revenue account in the preceding activity also created the need for new service items in our inventory module. In order to use the new Installation Income account, two new items need to be added to the Item List.

 DO: Add two new service items to the Item List:
Click on the **Inventory** button.
Click the **Inventory Items** in the Maintain section of the button.
Enter Install 1 in the **Item ID:** field. Press **Enter**.
Enter Initial Hour of Installation in the **Description** field. Press **Enter**.
Click the drop down list arrow for the **Item Class** field, check Non-stock item
Tab twice to enter the **for Sales Description:** field, enter Initial hour of hardware installation.
Press **Tab** to enter the next unnamed field which is the price field. Enter 95.00.
Click on the magnifying glass next to the **GL Sales Acct:** field.
Select account 4060 Installation Income.
Click **OK**.

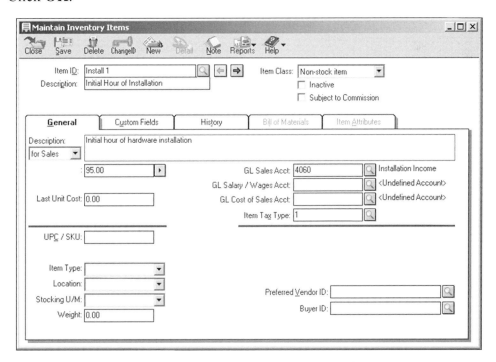

Accept all other field defaults and compare your screen with the above illustration.
   Verify that your entries match those displayed above.
Click **Save**.
Click the **New** icon to add the second service item.
Repeat the steps above to add Install 2.
The short description is Add'l Hours of Installation.
Using the pull down arrow of the **Item Class** field, select Non-stock item.
The **for Sales Description:** is Additional hours of hardware installation.
The rate is $80.00 per hour.
Select account 4060 Installation Income.
When finished adding Install 2, click **Save** to add the new item.
–   Whenever hardware installation is provided for customers, the first hour will
     be billed as Install 1, and additional hours will be billed as Install 2.
Click **Close** to exit the Maintain Inventory Items window.

VERIFY THE ADDITIONS ON THE ITEM LIST

  DO: View the Item List:
Click on the **Inventory** button.
Click the **All Inventory Reports** in the Reports section of the button.
Double click on Item List.

Comprehensive Computer Consulting-APS
Item List

Filter Criteria includes: Report order is by ID.

Item ID	Item Description	Item Class	Active?	Item Type	Qty on Hand
Install 1	Initial Hour of Installation	Non-stock item	Active		
Install 2	Add'l Hours of Installation	Non-stock item	Active		
Tech Sup 1	5 Hours--Monthly Technical Sup	Non-stock item	Active		
Tech Sup 2	10 Hours--Monthly Technical Su	Non-stock item	Active		
Tech Sup 3	15 Hours--Monthly Technical Su	Non-stock item	Active		
Training 1	Initial Hour of On-Site Traini	Non-stock item	Active		
Training 2	Additional Hours of On-Site Tr	Non-stock item	Active		

–   Our two new items have been placed at the top of the Item List since Peachtree
     alphabetizes this list by the Item ID.
Close the Item List and the Select A Report windows.

ADD A NEW CUSTOMER

Because customers are the lifeblood of a business, Peachtree® Complete Accounting 2006 allows
customers to be added "on the fly" as you create an invoice or sales receipt. You may also use
the Maintain Customer option when adding customers without the need to generate an invoice.

MEMO

DATE: January 9, 2006

Prepare the following: Invoice No. 107—A new customer, Brian McCormick, has purchased several upgrade items for his personal computer but needed assistance with the installation. CCC spent two hours installing this hardware. Invoice Mr. McCormick for 2 hours of hardware installation. His address is: 20985 Ventura Blvd., Woodland Hills, CA 91371. His telephone number is: 818-555-2058. He does not have a fax. His credit limit is $1,000; and the terms are Net 15.

DO: Record the above sale on account to a new customer:

Set the system date to 1/9/2006.

Click **Sales/Invoicing** from the **Sales** button.

In the **Customer ID:** field, use the magnifying glass to pull down our customer list. Since Mr. McCormick is not on the list, click on the **New** icon at the bottom of the window.

AND01	Andrews Research Corp.	818-555-
BAC01	Bachoffer & Sons	310-555-
BAR01	Barnes, Rachel, CPA	310-555-
CRE01	Creative Innovations	818-555-
CRE02	Creative Design Institute	310-555-
GOL01	Gold, Bradley, CPA	310-555-
HAC01	Hacene Nahid Imports	310-555-
JEN01	Jensen Ranch	310-555-
JUN01	Jung, Yu	818-555-
KAT01	Kati's Illustrations	310-555-
MAN01	Mandano, Jose, Esq.	818-555-
MAT01	Matthews, Thomas, CPA	818-555-

OK   Cancel   Find   Next   New   Sort   Help

You are taken to the Maintain Customer dialog box.

Enter MCC01 in the **Customer ID:** field.

– As you start typing, a drop down list of existing customers will appear. Ignore this list and press **Enter** after you have completed entering MCC01.

In the **Name** field, type McCormick, Brian. Press **Enter**.

In the **Contact** field, enter Brian McCormick.

Press **Enter** twice to move to the **Address** field.

Enter 20985 Ventura Blvd. in the **Address** field.

Press **Enter** twice to move to the **City, ST, Zip** field.

Enter Woodland Hills (or use pull down list to select it), press the **Tab** key, enter CA (or use pull down list to select it), press the **Tab** key, enter 91371.

Click in the field next to **Telephone 1:** and enter 818-555-2058.

Your screen should look like the illustration below. If not, make corrections before
proceeding.

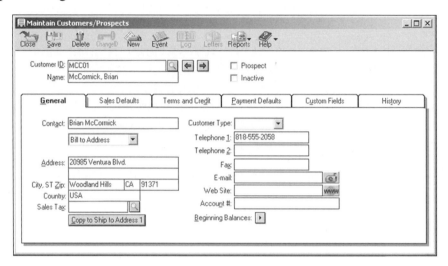

Click on the **Sales Defaults** tab.

Click on the magnifying glass next to the **GL Account** field.

Select account 4060 Installation Income and click **OK**.

Click on the **Terms and Credit tab**.

Deselect **Use Standard Terms and Credit** by clicking on the checkmark.

−   When adding a new customer, Peachtree will use defaults that have been set up
    when the company files were first created. These defaults are used every time a
    new customer is set up; however, Peachtree allows us to change these defaults
    for each customer as we are doing with Mr. McCormick.

Click in the field next to **Credit Limit**. Enter 1,000.00.

Change the field **Net Due in** to 15 days.

Compare your screen with the illustration below and verify that you have the same
information. Make corrections as necessary.

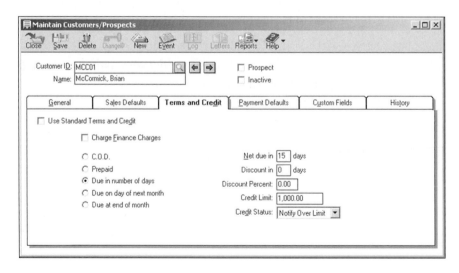

Click **Save** to save the new customer information.

Click **Close** to return to the Sales/Invoicing window.

Click the drop-down list next to **Customer ID:**

Double click McCormick, Brian.

Tab to **Date:** field.

–   Confirm that it reflects the 1/9/06 system date.

Tab to the **Quantity** field.

Enter 1.0 in the **Quantity** field. Press **Enter**.

Click the magnifying glass for **Item**, double click on Install 1.

Tab through the fields until you are returned to the **Quantity** field.

Enter 1.0 in the **Quantity** field. Press **Enter**.

Click the magnifying glass for **Item**, double click on Install 2, press **Enter**.

Before printing, verify all your entries in the invoice screen capture that follows.

Click **Print** button at the top of the **Sales/Invoicing** window.

Accept or enter 107 as our invoice number.

Click on **Print**.

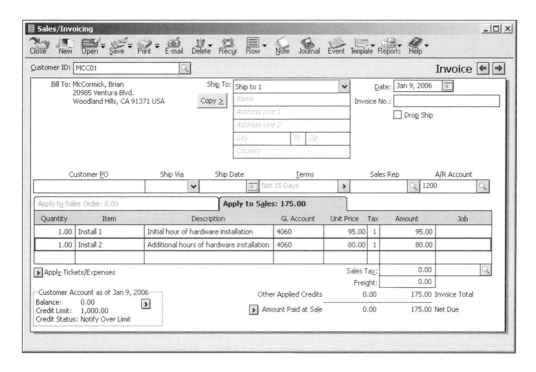

Click **Close** button at the top of the **Sales/Invoicing** window to exit this task.

MODIFY CUSTOMER RECORDS

Occasionally, information relating to a customer will change. Things such as address, telephone number, point of contact and even credit limits will change. Peachtree® Complete Accounting 2006 allows you to modify customer accounts at any time by using the Maintain Customer dialog box. This can be accessed "on the fly" as we did in the Adding a Customer activity or can be selected from the menu bar or Navigation Aid.

MEMO

DATE: January 9, 2006

Update the following account: Creative Design Institute has changed its fax number to 310-555-5959.

 DO: Edit a customer account:

Access **Customers** from the Maintain area of the **Sales** button.
Using the pull down list in the **Customer ID:** field, select Creative Design Institute.
Highlight the old number in the **Fax:** field.
Enter the new number 310-555-5959.

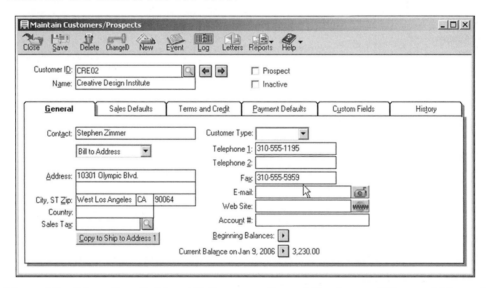

Note: All of the other fields with the exception of **Customer ID:**, could have been just as easily edited. The **Customer ID:** field can only be edited by clicking on the **ChangeID** icon at the top of the window. Attempting to change it directly in the **Customer ID:** field, will add a new account to your customer list.

Click **Save**
Close the Maintain Customers window.

RECORD CASH SALES

Not all sales in a business are on account. In many instances, payment is made at the time the service is performed. This is entered as a cash sale. When entering a cash sale, you may prepare a sales receipt through the Receipts window or prepare an invoice through the Sales/Invoicing window and apply the payment to that invoice. Peachtree® Complete Accounting 2006 records the transaction in the appropriate Journal, recording revenue and increasing cash in our default cash account unless otherwise instructed. When cash sales are recorded through the Receipts window, the transaction will appear in the Cash Receipts Journal. When the cash sale is recorded through the Sales/Invoicing window, the transaction will appear in the Sales Journal. In our textbook accounting, cash sales are recorded in the Cash Receipts Journal and so we will record our cash sales through the Receipts window. Some businesses may prefer recording cash sales through the Sales/Invoicing window so that all sales will appear in the Sales Journal. Peachtree can be set to mark the cash receipt as deposited when entered or it can create a list of checks received from which a deposit can be created. We will be using the former.

MEMO:

DATE: January 10, 2006

Prepare the following to record cash sales: Sales Receipt No. 101—Roger Alan provided 5 hours of on-site training to Barnes, Rachel, CPA, and received Rachel's Check No. 3287 for the full amount due. Prepare Sales Receipt No. 101 for this transaction.

 DO: Enter the following transaction as a cash sale:
Set the system date to 1/10/2006.
Access **Receipts** from the Tasks area of the **Sales** button.
Note: The **Deposit ticket ID:** is the first field of the window and is automatically filled in by Peachtree. The number it uses is the date it reads off the computer's internal clock. Under normal business conditions, this is ideal as deposits are typically made on a daily basis. We will manually insert our dates in this field.
Type 1/10/06 in the **Deposit ticket ID:** field.
Click the magnifying glass for the **Customer ID:** field, select Barnes, Rachel, CPA.
   –   You will automatically be moved to the **Reference:** field.
Enter the customers check number, 3287. Tab to the **Receipt Number:** field.

Note: Since most businesses do not have access to their accounting systems at the time cash sales are made, preprinted manual cash receipt forms are used. These forms are typically pre-numbered and it is this number that we would insert in the Receipt Number field. We could also enter the Receipt Number in the print dialogue box when we go to print the invoice. Once the first number has been entered here, Peachtree will sequentially number future cash receipts by adding 1 to the previous number during the current session.

Enter 101 now or wait and enter it in the print dialogue box.

Verify that the date is Jan 10, 2006. If it is not correct, enter 1/10/06.

Click in the **Quantity** field.

Enter 1.00. Press **Tab**.

Click on the magnifying glass for **Item**, double click Training 1.

Tab until you reach the **Quantity** field again.

Enter 4.00. Press **Tab**.

Click on the magnifying glass for **Item**, double click Training 2.

Tab until you reach the **Quantity** field again.

Verify your screen with the illustration below. Edit if needed.

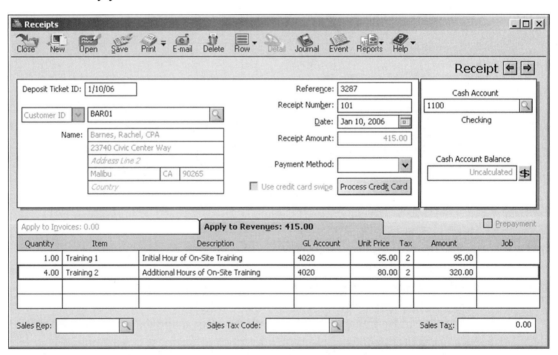

Once you have verified your data, click on the **Print** icon.

Note: You are again presented with a Print Forms dialog box; however, this time it is for Receipts. Peachtree has defaulted to a Receipt form that we can accept or change at this point in time. It has also picked up on the Receipt Number we entered on the Receipt form if you entered it earlier. If not, enter it now.

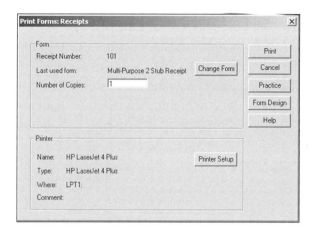

Click on **Print**.
Close the **Receipts** window.

ENTER CASH SALES TRANSACTIONS WITHOUT STEP-BY-STEP INSTRUCTIONS

> # MEMO:
> **DATE:** January 12, 2006
>
> Sales Receipt No. 102—Rachel Barnes needed additional on-site training to correct some error messages she received on her computer. Roger Alan provided 1 hour of on-site training for her and received Rachel's Check No. 3306 for the full amount due. (Even though Ms. Barnes has had on-site training previously, this is a new sales call and should have the first hour billed as Training 1.)
>
> Sales Receipt No. 103—Roger Alan provided 4 hours of on-site Internet training for Andrews Research Corp. so the company could be online. Roger received Check No. 10358 for the full amount due.

 DO: Record the two transactions listed above by repeating the procedures used to enter Sales Receipt No. 101:
- Remember, the <u>first hour for on-site training</u> is billed as <u>Training 1</u> and the <u>remaining hours</u> are billed as <u>Training 2</u>.
- Because Andrews Research Corp. already has a balance due, Peachtree will default to an invoice screen to give us the option of paying the prior balances. Because this is a cash sale, click on the **Apply to Revenue** tab in order to complete your entry.

- Always use the Item List to determine the appropriate sales items for billing.
- Print each sales receipt immediately after entering the information for it.
- If you make an error, correct it.
- Click Close after you have entered and printed Sales Receipt No. 103.
- You can add the Receipt Number as the other data is entered or let the print dialogue box add it for you by inserting a starting number there.

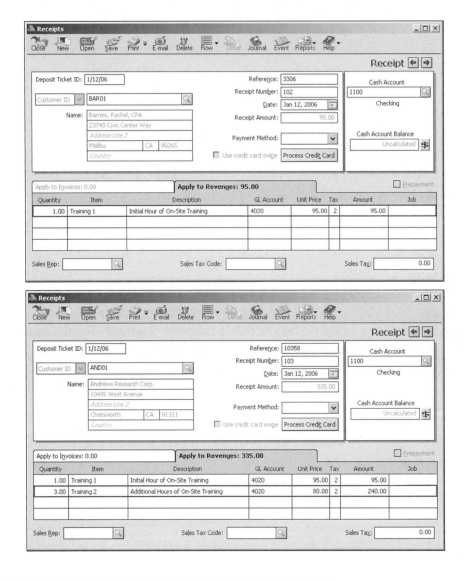

PRINT ITEMS SOLD TO CUSTOMERS REPORT

Peachtree® Complete Accounting 2006 has reports available that enable you to obtain sales information about your customers. To get information about the total amount of sales to each customer during a specific period, print an Items Sold to Customers report. The totals shown represent both cash and/or credit sales.

 DO: Click on the **All Accounts Receivable Reports** on the **Sales** button.

Double click on Items Sold to Customers.

Note: Peachtree will default its filters to all customers and for the entire current month. Should we desire one or a range of customers, or a different time period, we could click on the **Options** icon at the top of the window. We would be brought to a filters window where these parameters could be set.

Click the **Print** button on the top of the screen.

Click **OK** in the Windows Print dialog box.

Comprehensive Computer Consulting-APS
Items Sold to Customers
For the Period From Jan 1, 2006 to Jan 31, 2006
Filter Criteria includes: Report order is by Customer ID, Item ID. Report is printed in Detail Format.

Customer ID Name	Item ID	Qty	Amount	Cost of Sales	Gross Profit	Gross Margin
AND01	Training 1	1.00	95.00		95.00	100.00
Andrews Research Corp.	Training 2	3.00	240.00		240.00	100.00
		4.00	335.00		335.00	100.00
WAL01	Training 1	1.00	95.00		95.00	100.00
Walter, Yancheski, and Yi	Training 2	34.00	2,720.00		2,720.00	100.00
		35.00	2,815.00		2,815.00	100.00
Report Totals		102.00	8,925.00		8,925.00	100.00

Click **Close** to exit the Items Sold to Customers window.

Click **Close** to exit the Select A Report window.

CORRECT A SALES RECEIPT AND PRINT THE CORRECTED FORM

As it did with sales invoices and credit memos, Peachtree® Complete Accounting 2006 makes correcting errors user friendly. When an error is discovered in a transaction such as a cash sale, you can simply return to the receipt form where the transaction was recorded and correct the error.

When a correction for a cash sale is made, Peachtree® Complete Accounting 2006 not only changes the receipt, it also changes all journal and account entries for the transaction to reflect the correction. Peachtree® Complete Accounting 2006 then allows a corrected sales receipt to be printed.

In the past, we have located and selected forms for editing in one of two ways. The first method we used was to examine a related report and use Peachtree's drilldown feature to select a form.

We could use a cash receipts journal from within the accounts receivable reports to do this. The second method we used was the Find Transaction option from the Edit menu (Ctrl+F). Using this method we would set the transaction type filter to receipts. In the following activity, you will be introduced to yet a third method of finding and accessing a form. Since we are currently working with Receipts, the third method seems most appropriate but all three of these methods can be used at any time for most any form in Peachtree.

MEMO

DATE: January 13, 2006

After reviewing transaction information, you realize the date for the Sales Receipt No. 101 to Rachel Barnes, CPA, originally entered on 1/10/2006 and paid for with check number 3287, was entered incorrectly. Change the check number to 3278.

DO: Correct the error indicated in the memo above and print a corrected sales receipt:
Set the system date to 1/13/2006.
Access **Receipts** from the Tasks area of the **Sales** button.
Click **Open** at the top of the window.
Note: This will bring you to a Select Receipt window that by default, will list all cash receipts in the current period. Should we need to access a transaction for a different period, this can easily be changed by changing the period in the **Show** field in the upper right corner of the window.

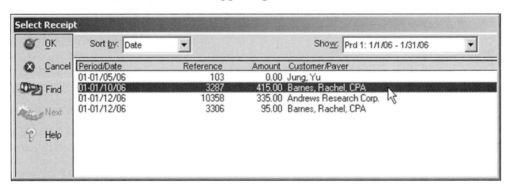

Click on the second item: Check number 3287.
Click **OK** to bring up the sales receipt.
Highlight 3287 in the **Reference:** field, type in 3278.

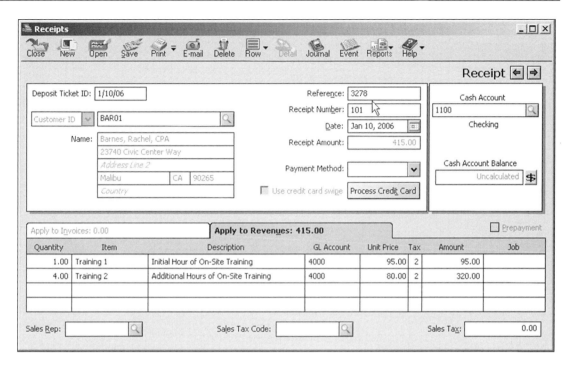

Click **Print** at the top of the window.
Close the **Receipts** window.

ANALYZE SALES

To obtain information regarding the amount of sales by income type, you can print or view a general ledger report. A general ledger report can show us all of the activity within a single account or a range of accounts. Since Comprehensive Computer Company has three major income categories, we can use a general ledger report with a filter to show only the income accounts in order to analyze how successful each category is. This provides important information for decision making and managing the business. For example, if a sales category is not generating much income, it might be wise to discontinue that income category.

DO: Print a filtered general ledger report:
Click the **General Ledger** icon in the Reports section of the **General Ledger** button.
You are taken to a General Ledger Filter window.
Click in the field in the **Type** column for the **General Ledger Account ID** line.
Click the drop down arrow list, change the All to Range.
In the same row, click in the **From** column.
Click the magnifying glass and select 4010.
In the same row, click in the **To** column.
Click the magnifying glass and select 4060.

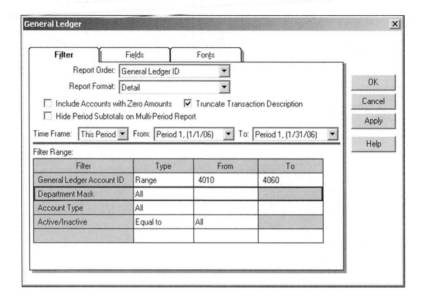

Click **OK**.

– Based on our filter selection, we are presented with a General Ledger report that contains only the income accounts.

Click **Print** to print report.

Comprehensive Computer Consulting-APS							
General Ledger							
For the Period From Jan 1, 2006 to Jan 31, 2006							
Filter Criteria includes: 1) IDs from 4010 to 4060. Report order is by ID. Report is printed with Truncated Transaction Descriptions and in Detail Format.							
Account ID **Account Description**	**Date**	**Reference**	**Jrnl**	**Trans Description**	**Debit Amt**	**Credit Amt**	**Balance**
4010	1/1/06			Beginning Balance			
Technical Support Income	1/3/06	101	SJ	Mandano, Jose, Esq. -		300.00	
	1/5/06	103	SJ	Jung, Yu - Item: Tech		300.00	
	1/5/06	105	SJ	Gold, Bradley, CPA - I		450.00	
	1/5/06	106	SJ	Kati's Illustrations - It		150.00	
	1/5/06	103V	SJ	Jung, Yu - Item: Tech	300.00		
				Current Period Change	300.00	1,200.00	-900.00
	1/31/06			Ending Balance			-900.00
4020	1/1/06			Beginning Balance			
Training Income	1/5/06	104	SJ	Walter, Yancheski, an		95.00	
	1/5/06	104	SJ	Walter, Yancheski, an		3,120.00	
	1/5/06	105	SJ	Gold, Bradley, CPA - I		95.00	
	1/5/06	105	SJ	Gold, Bradley, CPA - I		880.00	
	1/5/06	106	SJ	Kati's Illustrations - It		95.00	
	1/5/06	106	SJ	Kati's Illustrations - It		3,120.00	
	1/9/06	104-C	SJ	Walter, Yancheski, an	400.00		
	1/10/06	3278	CRJ	Barnes, Rachel, CPA -		95.00	
	1/10/06	3278	CRJ	Barnes, Rachel, CPA -		320.00	
	1/12/06	3306	CRJ	Barnes, Rachel, CPA -		95.00	
	1/12/06	10358	CRJ	Andrews Research Cor		240.00	
	1/12/06	10358	CRJ	Andrews Research Cor		95.00	
				Current Period Change	400.00	8,250.00	-7,850.00
	1/31/06			Ending Balance			-7,850.00

Click **Close** to exit the report.

RECORD CUSTOMER PAYMENTS ON ACCOUNT

When customers pay the amount they owe, Peachtree® Complete Accounting 2006 allows us to apply the payment to the invoices in the customer's account. When you start to record a payment made by a customer, you will be presented with a list of invoices that are still unpaid. You will be prompted to indicate to which invoices the payment should be applied. Some programs do not allow the user this flexibility but rather will automatically apply the payment to the oldest invoice. This will create problems in reconciling the account with your customer, whose records may show the payment applied to a different invoice.

MEMO

DATE: January 16, 2006

Record the following cash receipt: Received Check No. 0684 for $815 from Andrews Research Corp. as payment on account for his prior balance. Use 104 as the receipt number.

 DO: Record the above payment on account:

If necessary, set the system date to 1/16/06. Click **Receipts** in the **Sales** button.

The **Deposit ticket ID:** should be 1/16/06.

Note: Any time you will use the Receipts window you will need to change the date since Peachtree is reading the computer's clock rather than the system date we have set.

Click on the magnifying glass for **Customer ID:**.

Double click Andrews Research Corp.

– Notice that Peachtree will automatically open the Apply to Invoices tab since this company has unpaid invoices.

You will start in the **Reference field**. Enter the check number 0684.

Tab to the **Receipt Number** field. Since we did not issue a manual cash receipt form, we do not have a receipt number to enter here. Instead we will enter 104 which is a continuation of our numbering sequence for receipts. Note that we may have to do a little checking to see what the next number in the sequence is.

The **Date:** field should reflect the system date of 1/16/06. If you forgot to set the system date, you will need to change the date now.

In the **Apply to Invoices** tab, click in the Pay box at the end of the row that contains invoice 090.

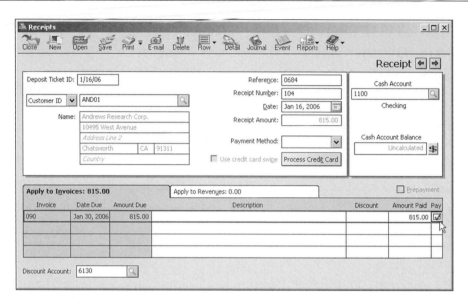

After verifying your input, click on the **Print** icon.

Click **Print**.

You may close the **Receipts** window or continue on to the next activity.

RECORD CUSTOMER PARTIAL PAYMENTS ON ACCOUNT

When customers make a partial payment, the procedures will differ slightly from those used when they made a payment in full. Rather than simply checking the Pay box, which presumes payment of the entire amount, we must enter the amount of the payment manually. For our reference we will also place a notation on the cash receipt to remind us that this was a partial payment.

MEMO

DATE: January 16, 2006

Received Check No. 8925 for $2,000 from Kati's Illustrations in partial payment of account. This receipt requires a notation of Partial Payment.

DO: Record the above partial payment on account:

If necessary, set the system date to 1/16/06. Click **Receipts** from the **Sales** button.

The **Deposit ticket ID:** should be 1/16/06.

Click on the magnifying glass for **Customer ID:**.

Double click Kati's Illustrations.

You will start in the **Reference** field. Enter the check number 8925.

Tab to the **Receipt Number** field. If you did not close the Receipts window since the last activity, this field should contain 105. If not, enter it now.

The **Date:** field should reflect the system date of 1/16/06.

In the **Apply to Invoices** tab, click in the Description field at the end of the row that contains Invoice 096. Enter Partial Payment.

Tab to the **Amount Paid** field and enter 2000.00 and press **Tab**.

Note: Peachtree will automatically checkmark the Pay box since you have indicated a payment against this line.

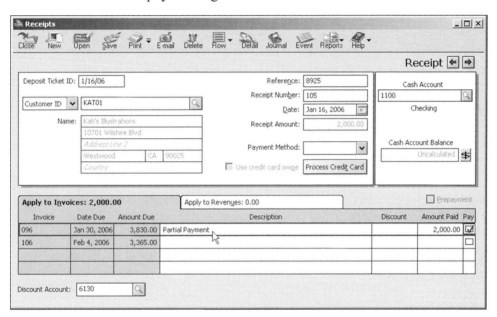

After verifying your input, click on the **Print** icon.

Click **Print**.

You may close the **Receipts** window or continue on to the next activity.

RECORD ADDITIONAL PAYMENTS ON ACCOUNT WITHOUT STEP-BY-STEP INSTRUCTIONS

> # MEMO
> **DATE:** January 16, 2006
>
> Use receipt number 106 for the first entry and allow Peachtree to assign numbers to the rest of the receipts. All receipts are being applied to the beginning balances of the customers.
>
> Received Check No. 1952 from Jensen Ranch for $3,680.
>
> Received Check No. 39251 from Thomas Matthews for $415.
>
> Received Check No. 2051 for $2,190 from Victor Productions in partial payment of account. Record a notation for this receipt: "This is a Partial Payment".
>
> Received Check No. 5632 from Jose Mandano for $150. Apply this to his invoice number 097.
>
> Received Check No. 80195 from Walter, Yancheski and Yi for $3,685. Apply this to invoice number 100.

DO: Refer to the previous steps listed to enter the above payments:
Click **Print** to go from one Receive Payments Screen to the next. Peachtree should assign the next sequential receipt number.
Click **Close** button after all payments received have been recorded.

VIEW CUSTOMER LEDGERS REPORT

In order to see the results of the transactions recorded in this chapter, you need to prepare a Customer Ledgers report. This report shows all sales, credits, and payments for each customer in Peachtree.

DO: Click the **All Accounts Receivable Reports** from the **Sales** button.
Double click on **Customer Ledgers**.
- This report lists the names of all customers on account with balances. The amount column shows the total balance for each customer. This includes opening balances as well as current invoices.

Comprehensive Computer Consulting-APS
Customer Ledgers
For the Period From Jan 1, 2006 to Jan 31, 2006
Filter Criteria includes: Report order is by ID. Report is printed in Detail Format.

Customer ID Customer	Date	Trans No	Type	Debit Amt	Credit Amt	Balance
AND01	1/1/06	Balance Fwd				815.00
Andrews Research Corp.	1/12/06	10358	CRJ	335.00	335.00	815.00
	1/16/06	0684	CRJ		815.00	0.00
BAC01	1/1/06	Balance Fwd				1,915.00
Bachoffer & Sons						
BAR01	1/10/06	3278	CRJ	415.00	415.00	0.00
Barnes, Rachel, CPA	1/12/06	3306	CRJ	95.00	95.00	0.00
CRE01	1/1/06	Balance Fwd				1,295.00
Creative Innovations						
CRE02	1/1/06	Balance Fwd				3,230.00
Creative Design Institute						
GOL01	1/5/06	105	SJ	1,425.00		1,425.00
Gold, Bradley, CPA						
HAC01	1/1/06	Balance Fwd				300.00
Hacene Nahid Imports						
JEN01	1/1/06	Balance Fwd				3,680.00
Jensen Ranch	1/16/06	1952	CRJ		3,680.00	0.00

Click the **Print** button at the top of the Customer Ledgers report window.
You may get a Windows Print dialog box. If you do, click **OK**. When printing is complete, close the report and the Select A Report window.

VIEW AND PRINT SALES JOURNAL

Peachtree® Complete Accounting 2006 creates journals for every transaction entered—for example, entering a sale on account via an invoice, it will create a Sales Journal. The Journal records each transaction and lists the accounts and the amounts for debit and credit entries. There are two ways to view journals in Peachtree. The first method is to look at Journals from the Reports feature of Peachtree Complete. Let us take a look at a Sales Journal to reflect our sales to date.

DO: Click the **Sales Journal** from the **Sales** button.
Click **OK** in the Sales Journal dialog box to accept the default settings.
Click on the **Print** icon.
- You may get a Windows Print dialog box. If you do click **OK**.

Comprehensive Computer Consulting-APS
Sales Journal
For the Period From Jan 1, 2006 to Jan 31, 2006
Filter Criteria includes: Report order is by Invoice/CM Date. Report is printed in Detail Format.

Date	Account ID	Invoice/CM #	Line Description	Debit Amnt	Credit Amnt
1/3/06	4010	101	10 Hours--Monthly Technical Support		300.00
	1200		Mandano, Jose, Esq.	300.00	
1/5/06	4010	103	10 Hours--Monthly Technical Support		300.00
	1200		Jung, Yu	300.00	
1/5/06	4020	104	Initial Hour of On-Site Training		95.00
	4020		Additional Hours of On-Site Training		3,120.00
	1200		Walter, Yancheski, and Yi	3,215.00	

The second method of viewing the journal impact is to view it from within the transaction window itself. This can be accomplished at the time the invoice is entered or we can return to the Sales/Invoicing window and view it after the fact. Let us take a look at one of our older invoices from the Sales Journal we just created.

 DO: Position the cursor over **Invoice No. 101** and double click to bring up the invoice. Click on the **Journal** icon to activate Peachtree's Behind the Scenes feature.

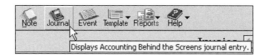

Peachtree will present you with the Behind the Scenes window that contains a Sales Journal entry for this one transaction.

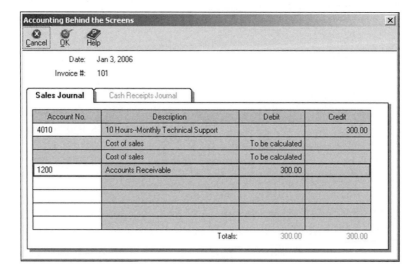

Note that account 4010 was credited and account 1200 was debited.
Close all open windows and the Sales Journal report.

PRINT THE TRIAL BALANCE

When all sales transactions have been entered, it is important to print the Trial Balance and verify that the total debits equal the total credits.

 DO: Click **General Ledger Reports** from the **General Ledger** button.
Double click on **General Ledger Trial Balance** in the **Report List** column.
Click the **Print** icon.

Comprehensive Computer Consulting-APS
General Ledger Trial Balance
As of Jan 31, 2006
Filter Criteria includes: Report order is by ID. Report is printed in Detail Format.

Account ID	Account Description	Debit Amt	Credit Amt
1100	Checking	73,305.00	
1200	Accounts Receivable	17,650.00	
1310	Office Supplies	500.00	
1500	Company Cars	49,000.00	
1510	Office Equipment	8,050.00	
2000	Accounts Payable		850.00
2210	Company Cars Loan		35,000.00
2220	Office Equipment Loan		4,000.00
3000	Roger Alan, Capital		78,075.00
3100	Retained Earnings		21,655.00
4010	Technical Support Income		900.00
4020	Training Income		7,850.00
4060	Installation Income		175.00
	Total:	148,505.00	148,505.00

Close all open windows.

As with most of Peachtree's reports, the program has selected the most logical defaults for the report. It will show only accounts with balances and will show the report as of the end of the month. Should we desire different parameters, we could click on the Options icon and select a different set of parameters. This is true of any report in this book. Unless you are told otherwise, accept the default parameters.

BACK UP AND CLOSE COMPANY

Backing up accounting work is an important part of the job. In most places of business, the rule is to back up more than less. That is to say, backing up more frequently than you need to is always better than not backing up enough. Because of the possibility of data loss on your computer, it is advised that you maintain back ups on a floppy disk. This is particularly true if you are working in a lab where the files must be shared. In this case, backing up after each session and restoring prior to starting the next session, is a must.

 DO: Click **Company** button
Click **Backup**

    Make sure there is a check in the box next to Include company name in the backup
        file name. If not, click to mark.
    Click **Back Up**
    Click the drop down list arrow for **Save in:** field
    With a formatted disk in your [A:] drive, click **3½ Floppy [A:]**
    Click **Save**
    Note: Peachtree is telling you the storage space required for the backup. Make sure
        the location to which you are backing up has sufficient capacity. If so, click
        OK. Your instructor may have you back up to another location.

After Peachtree has completed the backup, you are returned to the main screen to continue
working if you so desire. By selecting the option to include the company name, we instructed
Peachtree to use the name of our company in the file name followed by the date. Had we not
selected this option, Peachtree would have used the date only. Should you desire something other
than these options, you can change the file name to whatever is desired. As an example, you may
wish to create a backup at the end of each accounting period prior to closing and use the month
or year followed by the word end as your file name. If you back up to the same floppy every day,
Peachtree will place a new file on your disk. Obviously, you will run out of room after a few
days. You must then either delete some of the older files or use a new disk. You can prevent this
problem by backing up to the same file name each day and overwriting the previous day's file.

SUMMARY

In this chapter, cash and credit sales were entered and printed for Comprehensive Computer
Consulting using the Receipts, and the Sales/Invoicing features. Credit memos were issued.
Customer accounts were added and revised. Invoices and sales receipts were edited, deleted, and
voided. Cash payments were received and marked as deposited. All the transactions entered
reinforced the Peachtree® Complete Accounting 2006 concept of using the business form to
record transactions rather than entering information in journals. However, Peachtree® Complete
Accounting 2006 does not disregard traditional accounting methods. Instead, it performs this
function in the background.

Journals were accessed and changes were made as a result of transactions behind the scenes.
These journals were viewed and printed. The importance of reports for information and decision-
making was illustrated. Exploration of the various sales and accounts receivable reports allowed
information to be viewed from a sales standpoint and from an accounts receivable perspective.
Sales reports emphasized both cash and credit sales according to the customer or according to the
sales item generating the revenue. Accounts Receivable reports focused on amounts owed by
credit customers. The traditional trial balance emphasizing the equality of debits and credits was
also prepared.

END-OF-CHAPTER QUESTIONS

TRUE/FALSE

ENTER TRUE/FALSE IN THE SPACE PROVIDED BEFORE THE QUESTION NUMBER.

_____   1. A new customer can be added to a company's records "on the fly."

_____   2. In Peachtree® Complete Accounting 2006, error correction for a sale on account can be accomplished by editing the invoice.

_____   3. An Inventory Item List only stores information about products you purchase.

_____   4. Once transactions have been entered, modifications to a customer's account may be made only at the end of the fiscal year.

_____   5. In Peachtree® Complete Accounting 2006 all transactions must be entered with the traditional debit/credit method in the General Journal.

_____   6. Checks received for cash sales must be held in the Undeposited Funds account until the bank deposit is made.

_____   7. When a correction for a transaction is made, Peachtree® Complete Accounting 2006 not only changes the data on the form used to record the transaction, it also changes all journal account entries impacted by the transaction.

_____   8. Peachtree® Complete Accounting 2006 reports can be printed using a variety of different parameters including date ranges and account number ranges.

_____   9. Back ups should be made after every work session in Peachtree.

_____   10. A customer's payment on account is immediately recorded in the cash account.

MULTIPLE CHOICE

WRITE THE LETTER OF THE CORRECT ANSWER IN THE SPACE PROVIDED BEFORE THE QUESTION NUMBER.

_____ 1. To remove an invoice without a trace, it is ___.
A. voided
B. deleted
C. erased
D. reversed

_____ 2. To enter a cash sale, a(n) ___ is completed.
A. debit
B. invoice
C. receipt
D. both B and C are true

_____ 3.   Two primary types of lists used in this chapter are ___.
             A. receivables and payables
             B. invoices and checks
             C. registers and navigator
             D. customers and items

_____ 4.   While entering an invoice, an error may be corrected by ___.
             A. backspacing or deleting
             B. tabbing and typing
             C. dragging and typing
             D. all of the above

_____ 5.   While in the Customer Ledgers Report, it is possible to ___.
             A. change the customer's name
             B. post a payment on account
             C. access the invoice forms
             D. delete a customer

_____ 6.   Receipts represent ___.
             A. cash or checks received from customers
             B. only cash sales
             C. the balance of the accounts receivable account
             D. none of the above

_____ 7.   Peachtree® Complete Accounting 2006 uses reports to provide information about ___.
             A. the chart of accounts
             B. sales
             C. the cash account
             D. all of the above

_____ 8.   Changes to the chart of accounts may be made ___.
             A. at the beginning of a fiscal period
             B. before the end of the fiscal year
             C. at any time
             D. once established, the chart of accounts may not be modified

_____ 9.   To obtain information about sales to your customers, you can view ___.
             A. the income statement
             B. the trial balance
             C. receivables reports
             D. sales reports

_____10. When you post a customer payment on account, you ___.
A. use the Sales/Invoicing window
B. use the General Journal
C. use the Cash Deposit window
D. none of the above

FILL-IN

IN THE SPACE PROVIDED, WRITE THE ANSWER THAT MOST APPROPRIATELY
COMPLETES THE SENTENCE.

1. The report used to view all the balances on account of each customer is the _____.

2. The form prepared to show a reduction to a transaction is a(n) _____.

3. The report that proves that debits equals credits is the _____.

4. The _____ details the Accounts Receivable according to the date when they are owed.

5. To verify the company being used in Peachtree® Complete Accounting 2006, you check
the _____.

SHORT ESSAY

Discuss the differences and similarities between Peachtree Complete and a traditional textbook
approach to recording a sale on account

_____

_____

_____

_____

_____

_____

_____

_____

NAME _____

TRANSMITTAL

CHAPTER 2: COMPREHENSIVE COMPUTER CONSULTING

Attach the following documents and reports:

- ☐ Invoice No. 101: Mandano, Jose, Esq.
- ☐ Invoice No. 102: Bachoffer & Sons
- ☐ Invoice No. 103: Jung, Yu
- ☐ Invoice No. 104: Walter, Yancheski, and Yi
- ☐ Invoice No. 105: Gold, Bradley
- ☐ Invoice No. 106: Kati's Illustrations
- ☐ Customer Ledgers Report (through invoice 106)
- ☐ Corrected Invoice No. 105: Gold, Bradley
- ☐ Customer Ledgers Report (Bachoffer & Sons only)
- ☐ Credit Memo No. 104-C: Walter, Yancheski, and Yi
- ☐ Invoice No. 107: McCormick, Brian
- ☐ Receipt No. 101: Barnes, Rachel, CPA
- ☐ Receipt No. 102: Barnes, Rachel, CPA
- ☐ Receipt No. 103: Andrews Research Corp.
- ☐ Items Sold to Customers Report
- ☐ Corrected Receipt No. 101: Barnes, Rachel, CPA
- ☐ General Ledger Report (revenue accounts only)
- ☐ Receipt No. 104: Andrews Research
- ☐ Receipt No. 105: Kati's Illustrations
- ☐ Receipt No. 106: Jensen Ranch
- ☐ Receipt No. 107: Matthews, Thomas
- ☐ Receipt No. 108: Victor Productions
- ☐ Receipt No. 109: Mandano, Jose
- ☐ Receipt No. 110: Walter, Yancheski, and Yi
- ☐ Customer Ledgers Report
- ☐ Sales Journal
- ☐ General Ledger Trial Balance

END-OF-CHAPTER PROBLEM

SunCare Lawn and Pool Services

SunCare Lawn and Pool Services is owned and operated by George Gordon. George's sister and brother-in-law, also work for the company. Sylvia manages the office and keeps the books for the business. George provides lawn maintenance and supervises the lawn maintenance employees. Greg provides the pool maintenance. SunCare is located in Santa Barbara, California.

Instructions

Open SunCare Lawn and Pool Services. Add your initials to the company name. The company name will be **SunCare Lawn and Pool Services--Student's Initials**. (Type your actual initials, *not* the words *Student's Initials*.) Record the following transactions using invoices and cash receipts (Peachtree calls this just a receipt. Sales has been added for clarification). Print the invoices, receipts and reports as indicated.

The invoices and sales receipts are numbered consecutively. Invoice No. 101 is the first invoice number used in this problem. Sales Receipt No. 115 is the first cash receipt number used in this problem. In addition, payments on account will be numbered in the same sequence as cash sales. Print each document as it is completed. Always be aware of the next number in whichever document sequence you are using. Check a related report if you need to confirm the next number in the sequence.

When recording transactions, use the following Item List to determine the item(s) billed. If the transaction does not indicate the size of the pool or property, use the first category for the item—for example, LandCom 1 or LandRes 1 would be used for standard-size landscaping service for commercial and residential properties respectively. Remember that PoolCom 1 and PoolRes 1 are services for spas—not pools. The appropriate billing for a standard-size pool would be PoolCom 2 or PoolRes 2. Change your system date from the Options menu to the transaction date before entering each block of transactions.

Suncare Pool And Lawn Services
Item List

Item	Description	Amount
LandCom 1	Commercial Landscape Maintenance (Standard Size)	$150 mo.
LandCom 2	Commercial Landscape Maintenance (Med.)	250 mo.
LandCom 3	Commercial Landscape Maintenance (Lg.)	500 mo.
LandRes 1	Residential Landscape Maintenance (Standard Size)	$100 mo.
LandRes 2	Residential Landscape Maintenance (Med.)	200 mo.
LandRes 3	Residential Landscape Maintenance (Lg.)	350 mo.
PoolCom 1	Commercial Spa Service	$100 mo.
PoolCom 2	Commercial Pool Service (All pools unless specified as Lg.)	300 mo.
PoolCom 3	Commercial Pool Service (Lg.)	500 mo.
PoolRes 1	Residential Spa Service	$ 50 mo.
PoolRes 2	Residential Pool Service (All pools unless specified as Lg.)	100 mo.
PoolRes 3	Residential Pool Service (Lg.)	150 mo.
LandTrim	Trimming and Pruning	$75 hr.
LandPlant	Planting and Cultivating	50 hr.
LandWater	Sprinklers, Timers, etc.	75 hr.
LandGrow	Fertilize, Spray for Pests	75 hr.
PoolRepair	Mechanical Maintenance and Repairs	$75 hr.
PoolWash	Acid Wash, Condition	Price by the job
PoolStart	Startup for New Pools	500.00

Record Transactions

January 3, 2006

Billed Jack's Motel for monthly landscape services and monthly pool maintenance services, Invoice No. 101. (Use LandCom 1 to record the monthly landscape service fee and PoolCom 2 to record the monthly pool service fee. The quantity for each item is 1.) Terms are Net 15.

Billed RaceTeam Evans for monthly landscape and pool services at his home. Both the pool and landscaping are standard size. The terms are Net 30.

Billed Carol's Creations for 2 hours shrub trimming. Terms are Net 30.

Received Check No. 381 for $500 from Jeremy Jackson for pool startup services at his home. Since this is a cash sale, use Sales Receipt No. 115.

Received Check No. 8642 from Vivian Mantis for $150 for 3 hours of planting flowers previously billed. This is payment in full on the account.

January 14, 2006

Billed a new customer: Ronda Glades—10824 Hope Ranch St., Santa Barbara, CA 93110, 805-555-9825, terms Net 30—for monthly service on her large pool and large residential landscape maintenance. (Remember to assign the account number GLA01 and to type the last name first for the customer name.) Accept all other defaults.

Received Check No. 6758 from Jack's Motel in full payment of Invoice No. 101.

Received Check No. 987 from a new customer: Walter Paine (a neighbor of Ronda Glades) for $75 for 1 hour of pool repairs. Although this is a cash sale, we anticipate Walter becoming a regular customer. Set up his account in full. 10877 Hope Ranch St., Santa Barbara, CA 93110, 805-555-7175, fax 805-555-5717, E-mail wpaine@abc.com, terms Net 30.

Billed Pleasantville Resorts for maintenance on their large pool and large landscaping maintenance. Also bill for 5 hours planting, 3 hours trimming and 2 hours spraying on the landscaping. Terms are Net 15.

January 31, 2006

Received Check No. 1247 for $525 as payment in full from Carol's Creations.

Received Check No. 8865 from Yvette Simmons for amount due.

Billed Bloom Resorts for large pool and large landscaping maintenance (commercial). Terms are Net 15.

Billed AJ Apartments for medium-size commercial pool service and medium-size commercial landscape maintenance. Terms are Net 30.

Print Reports

Print the following reports accepting Peachtree's defaults.

Sales Journal
Cash Receipts Journal
General Ledger Trial Balance

NAME _____

TRANSMITTAL

CHAPTER 2: SUNCARE LAWN AND POOL SERVICES

Attach the following documents and reports:

- ☐ Invoice No. 101: Jack's Motel
- ☐ Invoice No. 102: Race Team Evan
- ☐ Invoice No. 103: Carol's Creations
- ☐ Sales Receipt No. 115: Jeremy Jackson
- ☐ Sales Receipt No. 116: Vivian Mantis
- ☐ Invoice No. 104: Ronda Glades
- ☐ Sales Receipt No. 117: Jack's Motel
- ☐ Sales Receipt No. 118: Walter Paine
- ☐ Invoice No. 105: Pleasantville Resorts
- ☐ Sales Receipt No. 119: Carol's Creations
- ☐ Sales Receipt No. 120: Yvette Simmons
- ☐ Invoice No. 106: Bloom Resorts
- ☐ Invoice No. 107: AJ Apartments
- ☐ Sales Journal
- ☐ Cash Receipts Journal
- ☐ General Ledger Trial Balance

Payables and Purchases: Service Business

3

LEARNING OBJECTIVES

At the completion of this chapter you will be able to:

1. Understand the concepts for computerized accounting for payables.
2. Enter, edit, correct, delete, and pay bills.
3. Add new vendors and modify vendor records.
4. View Accounts Payable transaction history.
5. View and/or print reports for vendors.
6. Record purchases in the Purchases Journal via the Purchases window.
7. Edit purchase entries.
8. Enter vendor credits.
9. Print, edit, void, and delete checks.
10. Pay for expenses using petty cash.
11. Add new General Ledger accounts.
12. Display and print the Purchases Journal, an Aged Payables Report, a Vendor Ledger Report, a Cash Disbursements Journal and a Check Register.

ACCOUNTING FOR PAYABLES AND PURCHASES

In a service business, most of the accounting for purchases and payables is simply recording and paying the bills for expenses incurred in the operation of the business. We purchase things for use in the operation of the business. Some transactions will be in the form of cash purchases, but most will be purchases on account. Bills can be paid when they are received or when they are due. For optimum cash flow management, most businesses will pay bills when they are due requiring the use of Accounts Payable. Rather than use cumbersome journals, Peachtree® Complete Accounting 2006 continues to focus on recording transactions based on the business document. You will use the Purchases/Receive Inventory and Payments features of the program to record the receipt and payment of bills. Peachtree® Complete Accounting 2006 can remind you when payments are due and can calculate and apply discounts earned for paying bills early. Payments for invoices already recorded can be made in the Select for Payment or Payments windows. If using the cash basis for accounting, Peachtree® Complete Accounting 2006 has a Write Check feature. A cash purchase can be recorded by writing a check or by using petty cash. Even though Peachtree® Complete Accounting 2006 focuses on recording transactions on the business forms used, all transactions are recorded behind the scenes in the appropriate journal. Peachtree® Complete Accounting 2006 uses a Vendor's List for all vendors with whom the company has an account. Peachtree® Complete Accounting 2006 does not refer to the Vendor List as the Accounts Payable Ledger, yet that is exactly what it is. The total of the Vendor

List/Accounts Payable Ledger will match the total of the Accounts Payable account in the Chart of Accounts/General Ledger.

As in Chapter 2, corrections can be made directly on the bill or within the appropriate journal. New accounts and vendors may be added "on the fly" as transactions are entered. Reports illustrating aged payables, cash disbursements, check register, purchases journal and vendor ledgers may be viewed and printed.

TRAINING TUTORIAL AND PROCEDURES

The following tutorial will once again work with Comprehensive Computer Consulting (CCC). As in Chapter 2, transactions will be recorded for this fictitious company. To maximize training benefits, you should:

1. Read the entire chapter *before* beginning to enter transactions for CCC.
2. Answer the end-of-chapter questions.
3. Be aware that transactions to be entered are given within a **MEMO**.
4. Complete all the steps listed for the Comprehensive Computer Consulting (CCC) tutorial in the chapter. The steps are indicated by: **DO:**
5. When you have completed a step, put an **X** on the computer next to **DO:**
6. As you complete your work, proofread carefully and check for accuracy. Double-check amounts of money.
7. If you find an error while preparing a transaction, correct it. If you find the error after the transaction has been entered, follow the steps indicated in this chapter to correct, void, or delete the transaction.
8. Print as directed in the chapter.
9. You may not finish the entire chapter in one computer session. Always back up your work at the end of your work session as described in Chapter 1.
10. When you complete your computer session, always close your company.

OPEN PEACHTREE® COMPLETE ACCOUNTING 2006 AND COMPREHENSIVE COMPUTER CONSULTING—CCC

 DO: Open Peachtree® Complete Accounting 2006 as instructed in Chapters 1 and 2
Open Comprehensive Computer Consulting (CCC):
Click **Open an existing company.**
Click the Browse button (if Comprehensive Computer Consulting is not already visible)
Click the drop down arrow for **Drives:**
Select the drive where your data files are kept

> Locate and double click on Comprehensive Computer Consulting (under the Company name text box)
>
> Check the title bar to verify that Comprehensive Computer Consulting (CCC)-Student's Initials is the open company

BEGINNING THE TUTORIAL

In this chapter, you will be entering bills incurred by the company in the operation of the business. You will also be recording the payment of bills, payments using checks, and purchases/payments using petty cash.

The Vendor List keeps information regarding the vendors with whom you do business. It is the Accounts Payable Ledger. Vendor information includes the vendor name, address, telephone number, payment terms, credit limit, and account numbers. You will be using the following list of vendors with whom CCC has an account:

Comprehensive Computer Consulting-APS Vendor List			
Filter Criteria includes: Report order is by ID.			
Vendor ID	**Vendor**	**Contact**	**Telephone 1**
COM01	ComSer Telephone Co.		818-555-4422
COM02	Computer Pro Magazine	707-555-3214	707-555-4123
JAC01	Jackson Realtors	Harvey Jackson	818-555-7412
JOH01	John's Auto Services	Joe Gonzalez	818-555-3658
MAT01	Matrix Advertising	Mel Vernon	310-555-8777
QRS01	QRS Insurance Company	Brenda Slocum	818-555-6495
SOU01	Southern CA Electric		818-555-9988
SOU02	SouthCal Gas Co.		818-555-2323
TER01	Teri's Office Supplies Wholesale	Morris Jergens	818-555-4563
WAT01	Water Works		818-555-0123
ZIP01	Zippy's Delivery Service	Joel Chang	818-555-1987

All transactions are listed on memos. The system date and transaction date will be the same date as the memo date unless otherwise specified within the transaction. Vendor names, when necessary, will be given in the transaction. Unless otherwise specified, terms are Net 30. Once a specific type of transaction has been entered in a step-by-step manner, additional transactions of the same or a similar type will be made without having instructions provided. Of course, you may always refer to instructions given for previous transactions for the steps used to enter those transactions. Verify the account Peachtree has selected for use in the transaction. In most cases, the only account that must be changed will be the expense account for each line item. If you must enter account information on a bill, clicking on the drop-down list arrow will show a copy of the Chart of Accounts.

ENTER A BILL

Peachtree® Complete Accounting 2006 provides accounts payable tracking. Entering bills as soon as they are received is an efficient and correct way to record your liabilities. Once bills have been entered, Peachtree® Complete Accounting 2006 will be able to provide up-to-date cash flow reports, and Peachtree® Complete Accounting 2006 will remind you when it's time to pay your bills. The form used to enter a bill is virtually identical to the form used to enter a sale. Significant differences include a Vendor ID in place of a Customer ID, the need for a GL expense account and the use of an Apply to Purchases tab in lieu of an Apply to Revenues tab. A major difference is that we will not be using an item list; therefore, we will not have a quantity to enter or an item to automatically fill in data for us. The business form will have these columns but they are primarily for a merchandising business and would be used to record specific inventory items. We will do this in a later chapter. We will be using the Purchase/Receive Inventory window even for services. This can be reached from the Task Menu by selecting Bills/Enter Bills in addition to the method used in the tutorial.

MEMO

DATE: January 17, 2006

Record the following bill: Matrix Advertising prepared and placed advertisements in local business publications announcing our new hardware installation service. Received a bill for $260, Matrix's Invoice No. 9875, terms Net 30.

 DO: Record the above transaction
Click **Purchase/Receive Inventory** on the **Purchases** button
Click the magnifying glass next to **Vendor ID**
Select Matrix Advertising
–   Name and address is entered as the vendor.
–   Note that our name and address are entered in the **Ship To:** field
Tab to **Date:**
–   If your system date was set correctly, the correct date should already be set. If not, you will be required to enter the correct date as follows.
–   When you type in the new date, the highlighted date will be deleted.
–   Type 01/17/06 as the date
Tab to the **Invoice No.:** field. Type the vendor's invoice number: 9875
Complete the detail section of the bill in the Apply to Purchases tab:
Click in the column for **Description**
Enter Ads for Hardware Installation Services and click **Enter**
Confirm or enter the **GL Account**. It should reflect 6100 for Advertising Expense
Tab twice to the **Amount** field. Enter 260.00

Do not click on **Save** until after the next activity

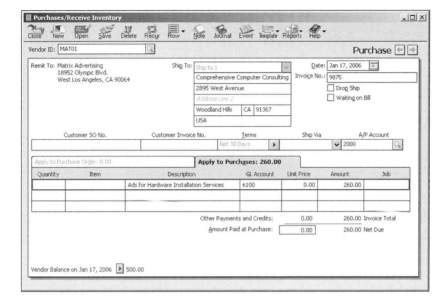

EDIT AND CORRECT ERRORS

If an error is discovered prior to clicking on the Save icon, it may be corrected by positioning the cursor in the field containing the error. You may tab forward through each field or press Shift+Tab to move back to the field containing the error. When the error is highlighted, type the correction and the previous data will be replaced. If the error is not highlighted, you can correct the error by pressing the backspace or the delete key as many times as necessary to remove the error, then type the correction. (*Alternate method:* Point to the error, highlight it by dragging the mouse through the error, then type the correction.)

 DO: Practice editing and making corrections to the bill for Matrix Advertising:
Click the magnifying glass for **Vendor ID**
Double click ComSer Telephone Co.
Tab to **Date:**
To increase the date by one day, press +
– You may use Shift+= next to the backspace key, or you may press the + key on the numerical keypad.
Press + two more times
– The date should be 01/20/06.
To decrease the date by one day, press -
– You may type a hyphen (-) next to the number 0, or you may press the hyphen (-) key on the numerical keypad.
Press - two more times
– The date should be 01/17/06.

Change the date by clicking on the calendar next to the date

Click 19 on the calendar for January 2006
Click the calendar again
Click 17 to change the date back to 01/17/2006
To change the amount, click in the **Amount** column to highlight the amount
Key in 299.00 and press the **Tab** key
Click the drop-down list arrow for **Vendor ID**
Click Matrix Advertising
Click in the **Amount** column to highlight the amount
Key in 260.00 and press the **Tab** key
Click **Save** and then **Close** buttons to record the bill and return to the main screen

PREPARE A BILL USING MORE THAN ONE EXPENSE ACCOUNT

MEMO

DATE: January 19, 2006

On the recommendation of the Roger's office manager, Carmen Mendoza, CCC is trying out several different models of fax machines on a monthly basis. Received a bill from Teri's Office Supplies Wholesale for one month's rental of a fax machine, $25, and for fax supplies, which were consumed during January, $20, Invoice No. 1035A, Terms Net 30.

DO: Record the transaction listed in the above memo. This transaction involves two expense accounts.
Click **Purchases/Receive Inventory** on the **Purchases** button
Click the magnifying glass next to **Vendor ID**
Select Teri's Office Supplies Wholesale
Tab to **Date:**

- If your system date was set correctly, the correct date should already be set. If not, you will be required to enter the correct date.

You are taken to the **Invoice No.:** field. Type the vendor's invoice number: 1035A

Complete the detail section of the bill in the Apply to Purchases tab:

Click in the column for **Description**

Enter 1 Month Fax Rental and click **Enter**

In the **GL account** column, us the look up feature, select 6170 for Equipment Rental

Tab twice to the **Amount** field. Enter 25.00

Tab to the **Description** field in the next row and enter Fax Supplies

Tab to the **GL account** column. Using the look up feature, select 6550 for Office Supplies Expense

Note: Since the supplies are being used within the month, this transaction is recorded directly as an expense rather than a prepaid expense.

Tab twice to the **Amount** field. Enter 20.00

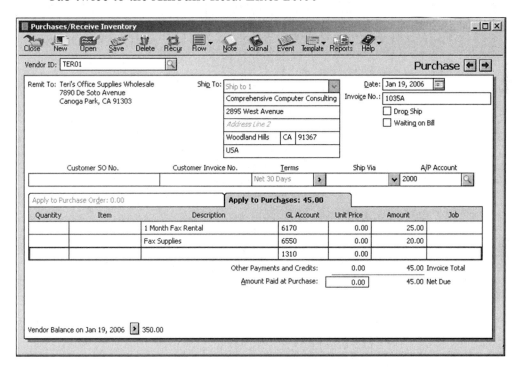

Click **Save** and then **Close** buttons to record the bill and return to the main screen

PRINT VENDOR LEDGER REPORT

To obtain information regarding individual transactions grouped by vendor, you prepare a Vendor Ledger Report. This allows you to view the vendors for whom you have recorded transactions. The vendor, the transaction date, the invoice number and the transaction amount appear in the report.

DO: Prepare a **Vendor Ledger Report**
Click **All Accounts Payable Reports** in the **Purchases** button
Double click on Vendor Ledgers
Click **Print**

Comprehensive Computer Consulting-APS
Vendor Ledgers
For the Period From Jan 1, 2006 to Jan 31, 2006

Filter Criteria includes: Report order is by ID.

Vendor ID Vendor	Date	Trans No	Type	Paid	Debit Amt	Credit Amt	Balance
COM01 ComSer Telephone Co.							0.00
COM02 Computer Pro Magazine							0.00
JAC01 Jackson Realtors							0.00
JOH01 John's Auto Services							0.00
MAT01 Matrix Advertising	1/1/06 1/17/06	Balance Fwd 9875	PJ			260.00	500.00 760.00
QRS01 QRS Insurance Company							0.00
SOU01 Southern CA Electric							0.00
SOU02 SouthCal Gas Co.							0.00
TER01 Teri's Office Supplies Wholes	1/1/06 1/19/06	Balance Fwd 1035A	PJ			45.00	350.00 395.00
WAT01 Water Works							0.00
ZIP01 Zippy's Delivery Service							0.00
Report Total						305.00	1,155.00

USE THE DRILLDOWN FEATURE

Carmen Mendoza wants more detailed information regarding the accounts used in the transaction of January 19, 2006 for Teri's Office Supplies Wholesale. In order to see these account names, Carmen will use the Drill Down feature of Peachtree® Complete Accounting 2006 while in the Vendor Ledger Report.

 DO: Point to the line for Teri's Office Supplies Wholesale invoice #1035A.
Double click to select the invoice.
– Notice that you are taken back to the invoice you created earlier. Its status is reflected in the upper left corner, Unpaid. Any information desired by Carmen can be seen on the screen.
Click **Close** when you are finished examining the invoice.

- You are brought back to the Vendor Ledgers report where you could select another invoice for examination or close the report if it is no longer needed. Close the report and the Select a Report window.

ENTER BILLS WITHOUT STEP-BY-STEP INSTRUCTIONS

MEMO

DATE: January 19, 2006

Received a bill from Computer Pro Magazine for a 6-month subscription for Roger Alan, $74, Invoice No. 1579-53, Net 30 days. (Enter as an expense.) As you save each invoice, you will be presented with a blank invoice screen.

Carmen Mendoza received office supplies from Teri's Office Supplies Wholesale, Invoice No. 8950S, $450, terms Net 30 days. These supplies will be used over a period of several months so enter as a prepaid expense.

While Carolyn Masters was on her way to a training session at Walter, Yancheski and Yi, the company car broke down. It was towed to John's Auto Services, where it was repaired. The total bill for the towing and repair is $575, Invoice No. 630, Net 30 days.

Received a bill from QRS Insurance Company for the annual auto insurance premium, $2,850, Invoice No. 3659, terms Net 30.

  DO: Enter the four transactions in the memo above.
- Refer to the instructions given for the two previous transactions entered.
- To go from one bill to the next, click the Save icon at the top of the window.
- After entering the fourth bill, click **Save** and then **Close** to record and exit the Purchases/Receive Inventory window.

Remember, when recording bills, you will need to determine/confirm the accounts used in the transaction. Although Peachtree does have defaults associated with the vendor account, they may not always be valid. The accrual method of accounting matches the expenses of a period against the revenue of the period. When you pay something in advance, it is recorded as an increase (debit) to an asset rather than an increase (debit) to an expense. At the end of the period in which the prepaid asset is used, an adjusting entry is made to the account for the amount used during the period. Unless otherwise instructed, use the accrual basis of accounting when recording the above entries. (Notice the exception in the first transaction.) To determine the appropriate accounts to use, refer to the Chart of Accounts/General Ledger drop down list as you record the above transactions. You may find it beneficial to print a chart of accounts from the General Ledger option of the Report menu and have it by your side when recording transactions.

Compare your invoices to the following prior to saving them.

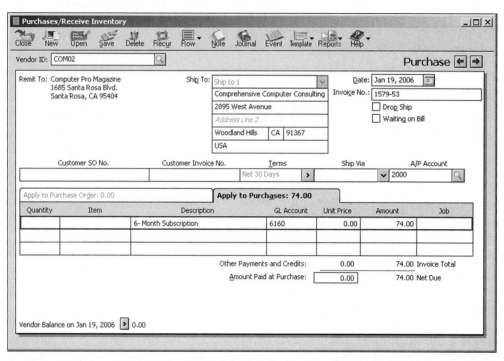

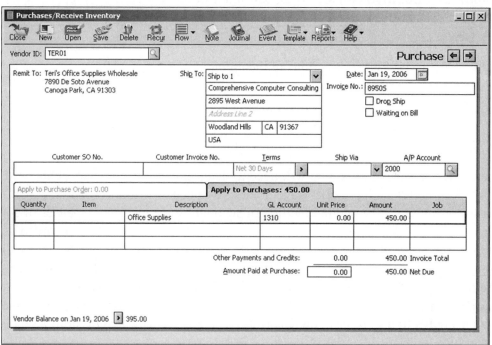

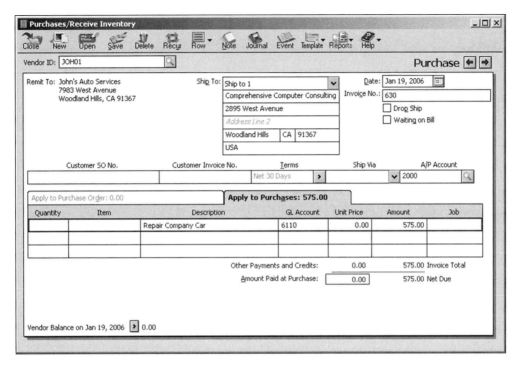

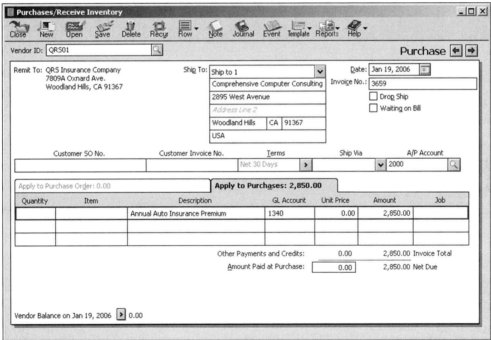

EDIT A POSTED TRANSACTION FROM THE VENDOR LEDGER REPORT

Because Peachtree® Complete Accounting 2006 makes correcting errors extremely user friendly, a transaction can be edited or changed from the Vendor Ledger Report using the drill down feature. This is a useful feature since errors are frequently identified while reviewing reports.

MEMO

DATE: January 20, 2006

Upon examination of the invoices and the bills entered, Carmen Mendoza discovers an error: The amount of the Invoice from Computer Pro Magazine was $79, not $74. Change the transaction amount for this transaction.

DO: Correct an invoice listed on a Vendor Ledger Report

Click **All Accounts Payable Reports** in the **Purchases** button

Double click on Vendor Ledgers

Point to the line for Computer Pro Magazine invoice #1579-53.

Double click to select the invoice.

Click in the Amount column to highlight the 74.00

Key in 79.00

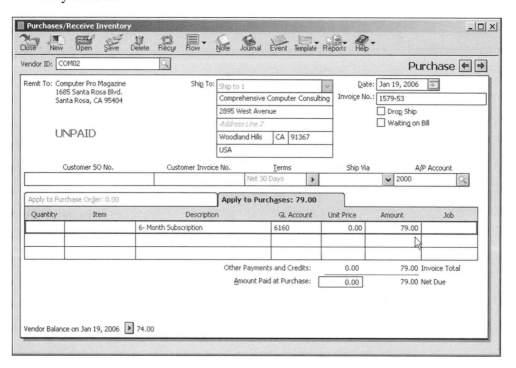

Click **Save** then **Close** when you are finished correcting the invoice.

- You are brought back to the Vendor Ledgers report where you could select another invoice for examination or correction.

Close the report and the Select a Report windows.

PREVIEW AND PRINT A PURCHASES JOURNAL

Another useful purchases related report in Peachtree® Complete Accounting 2006 is the Purchases Journal. This report lists all of our purchases just as the Vendor Ledger Report does. One primary difference is that the Purchases Journal will also show us the accounts involved in the transaction. In addition, this report will show us the transactions in chronological sequence rather than grouped by vendor. This can be useful in determining when bills should be paid.

MEMO

DATE: January 20, 2006

Several vendor invoices have been entered for Comprehensive Computer Consulting. The owner, Roger Alan, would like to view a listing of all invoices recorded so far this month.

DO: Prepare a Purchases Journal
Click the **Purchases Journal** from the **Purchases** button
Click **OK** in the Purchases Journal dialog box to accept the default settings

Comprehensive Computer Consulting-APS
Purchase Journal
For the Period From Jan 1, 2006 to Jan 31, 2006
Filter Criteria includes: Report order is by Date. Report is printed in Detail Format.

Date	Account ID Account Description	Invoice/CM #	Line Description	Debit Amount	Credit Amount
1/17/06	6100 Advertising Expense	9875	Ads for Hardware Installation Services	260.00	
	2000 Accounts Payable		Matrix Advertising		260.00
1/19/06	6170 Equipment Rental	1035A	1 Month Fax Rental	25.00	
	6550 Office Supplies Expense		Fax Supplies	20.00	
	2000 Accounts Payable		Teri's Office Supplies Wholesale		45.00
1/19/06	6160 Dues and Subscriptions	1579-53	6- Month Subscription	79.00	
	2000 Accounts Payable		Computer Pro Magazine		79.00
1/19/06	1340 Prepaid Insurance	3659	Annual Auto Insurance Premium	2,850.00	
	2000 Accounts Payable		QRS Insurance Company		2,850.00

Click on the **Print** icon
   − You may get a Windows Print dialog box. If you do click **OK**
   Note: You may use Peachtree's drill down feature in this report as well.
Close the report.

PREPARE CASH REQUIREMENTS REPORT

It is possible to get information regarding unpaid bills by simply preparing a report—no more digging through tickler files, recorded invoices, ledgers, or journals. Peachtree® Complete Accounting 2006 can prepare a Cash Requirements Report listing each unpaid bill grouped and subtotaled by vendor.

MEMO

DATE: January 23, 2006

Carmen Mendoza prints a Cash Requirements Report for Roger Alan each Monday. Because CCC is a small business, Roger likes to have a firm control over cash flow so he determines which bills will be paid during the coming week.

 DO: Prepare and print a Cash Requirements Report
Click **All Accounts Payable Reports** in the **Purchases** button
Double click on Cash Requirements
Click on **Print**

Comprehensive Computer Consulting-APS
Cash Requirements
As of Jan 31, 2006
Filter Criteria includes: Report order is by ID. Report is printed in Detail Format.

Vendor ID Vendor	Invoice/CM #	Date	Date Due	Amount Due	Disc Amt	Age
MAT01 Matrix Advertising	56789	12/27/05	1/26/06	500.00		5
MAT01 Matrix Advertising				500.00		
TER01 Teri's Office Supplies Wholesale	23498	12/23/05	1/22/06	350.00		9
TER01 Teri's Office Supplies Wholesale				350.00		
Report Total				850.00		

Notice that Peachtree has defaulted to the end of the month, January 31st as it does in many of its reports. Peachtree is showing us all bills that must be paid by January 31st. By using the Options icon, we can tell Peachtree to use a different date. Let us say, for example, that Roger wishes to know how much cash he must have to pay all bills due by the end of February. We can use the Options icon to open a dialog box into which we can enter this new date.

CHANGE REPORT OPTIONS

DO: Change the options for a Cash Requirements Report and print it
Click the **Options** icon at the top of the window
Using the pull down arrow to the right of the **Date:** field, select Exact Date
Use the calendar in the **As of:** field to select February 28
Note: Peachtree would also allow us to change the vendor ID's or vendor types to be included in the report. This would allow us to report on a single vendor, a range of vendors or even a type of vendor. We will accept the All default for these.
Click **OK**

Peachtree has again generated the report using February 28th as the due date. That is to say, all bills due on or before February 28th will now show on the report. As you can see, many more invoices have been added to the report. In fact, since none of our terms go beyond 30 days, all of the invoices in our Accounts Payable system are showing on the report. In typical usage, an accounts payable clerk would use this feature to identify the bills that must be paid on a daily and/or weekly basis. The **Option** icon performs this task within any Peachtree report that contains the icon.

Comprehensive Computer Consulting-APS
Cash Requirements
As of Feb 28, 2006
Filter Criteria includes: Report order is by ID. Report is printed in Detail Format.

Vendor ID Vendor	Invoice/CM #	Date	Date Due	Amount Due	Disc Amt	Age
COM02 Computer Pro Magazine	1579-53	1/19/06	2/18/06	79.00		10
COM02 Computer Pro Magazine				79.00		
JOH01 John's Auto Services	630	1/19/06	2/18/06	575.00		10
JOH01 John's Auto Services				575.00		
MAT01 Matrix Advertising	56789 9875	12/27/05 1/17/06	1/26/06 2/16/06	500.00 260.00		33 12
MAT01 Matrix Advertising				760.00		
QRS01 QRS Insurance Company	3659	1/19/06	2/18/06	2,850.00		10
QRS01 QRS Insurance Company				2,850.00		
TER01 Teri's Office Supplies Wholesale	23498 1035A 8950S	12/23/05 1/19/06 1/19/06	1/22/06 2/18/06 2/18/06	350.00 45.00 450.00		37 10 10
TER01 Teri's Office Supplies Wholesale				845.00		
Report Total				5,109.00		

Click on **Print**

Close the report and the Select a Report windows.

DELETE A BILL

Peachtree® Complete Accounting 2006 makes it possible to delete any bill that has been recorded. No adjusting entries are required in order to do this. Simply access the original form used to enter the bill and delete it. The form may be accessed from either the Purchases Journal or the Vendor Ledgers report. It may also be accessed through the Find Transaction feature (Ctrl+F) discussed in Chapter 2.

MEMO

DATE: January 26, 2006

After reviewing the Cash Requirement Report, Carmen Mendoza realizes that the bill recorded for *Computer Pro Magazine*, invoice #1579-53, should have been recorded for *Computer Tech Magazine*, a new vendor.

DO: Delete the bill recorded for *Computer Professionals Magazine*

From the **Edit** menu, click on **Find Transactions** (or use Ctrl+F)

In the **Reference Number** row, use the pull down arrow in the **Type** column to select Range

In the **From** column, type in the invoice number, 1579-53 and repeat this in the **To** column

Click on the **Find** button

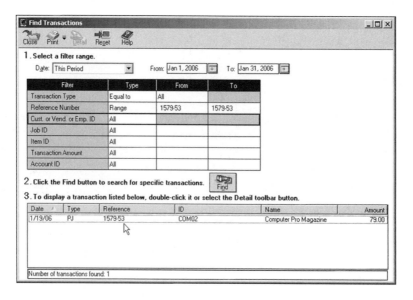

Double click on the transaction displayed in the bottom of the window
– The transaction will be displayed on the screen.
Click on the **Delete** icon
You are presented with a deletion confirmation dialog box, click **Yes**
Click **Close** to exit the Purchase/Receive Inventory and the Find Transactions
windows.

ADD A NEW VENDOR WHILE RECORDING A BILL

When entering bills, vendors are selected using Peachtree's lookup feature. If the vendor is not in the Vendor List, Peachtree® Complete Accounting 2006 allows you to add a new vendor "on the fly" while entering a bill. To add a new vendor, you click on the **New** icon contained in the **Vendor ID:** list window to open a Maintain Vendor dialog box.

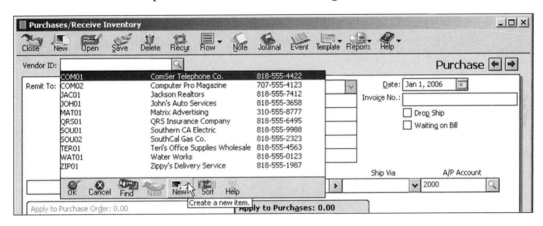

Once open, the Maintain Vendor dialog box can be used to add the new vendor. When the new vendor information is complete, you may select the new vendor and finish entering the rest of the transaction.

MEMO

DATE: January 26, 2006

Record the bill for a 6-month subscription to *Computer Tech Magazine*. The transaction date is 01/19/06, Invoice No. 1579-53, Terms Net 15, amount $79. This is recorded as an expense. The address and telephone for *Computer Tech Magazine* is 12405 Menlo Park Drive, Menlo Park, CA 94025 (510) 555-3829. The vendor has assigned us its account number 8347A. They have extended a credit limit of $1,000.00 to us.

DO: Record the above bill to a new customer:

  Click **Purchases/Receive Inventory** from the **Purchases** button.

   In the **Vendor ID:** field, use the magnifying glass to pull down the vendor list.

  Since Computer Tech Magazine is not on the list, click on the **New** icon at the bottom of the window.

 – You are taken to the Maintain Vendor dialog box.

 – Enter COM03 in the **Vendor ID:** field.

 – As you start typing, a drop down list of existing vendors will appear. Ignore this list and press **Enter** after you have completed entering COM03. We have elected to use the first three letters of a vendors name followed by a number sequence if the letter combination is already in use. Since COM is already in use by two other vendors, we must use COM03. You may use any structure for assigning vendor account numbers in a real working situation.

  In the **Name:** field, type Computer Tech Magazine. Press **Enter**.

  Click in the **Account #:** field and enter 8347A

  Click in the **Address:** field.

  Enter 12405 Menlo Park Drive.

  Press **Enter** twice to move to the **City, ST, Zip:** field.

  Enter Menlo Park, press the **Tab** key, enter CA, press the **Tab** key, enter 94025, press the **Tab** key. Tab between each component of this line.

  Click in the field next to **Telephone 1:** and enter 510-555-3829.

  Your screen should look like the illustration below. If not, make corrections before proceeding.

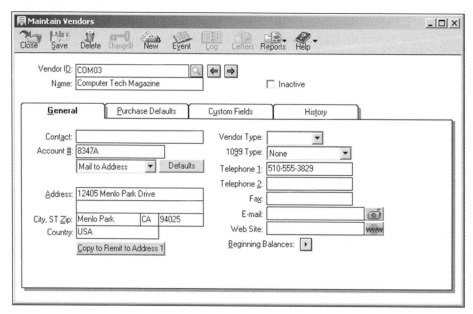

  Click on the **Purchase Defaults** tab.

Click on the magnifying glass next to the **Expense Acct:** field.

– The account we select here is the default account Peachtree will use each time we enter an invoice from this vendor. For vendors who supply us with a single item such as Computer Tech, this is particularly useful.

Select account 6160 Dues and Subscriptions and click **OK**.

Click on arrow to the right of **Terms:**.

Deselect **Use Standard Terms** by clicking on the checkmark next to it.

– When adding a new vendor, Peachtree will use certain defaults that have been set up when the company files were first created. These defaults are used every time a new vendor is set up; however, Peachtree allows us to change these defaults for each vendor as we have done with Computer Tech Magazine.

Click in the field next to **Net Due in**. Enter 15.

Click in the field next to **Credit Limit**. Enter 1,000.00.

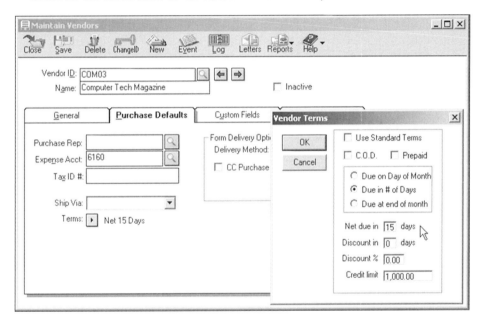

Compare your screen with the illustration above and verify that you have the same information. Make corrections as necessary.

Click **OK** to exit the Vendor Terms dialog box.

Click **Save** to save the new vendor information.

Click **Close** to return to the Purchases/Receive Inventory window.

Click the drop-down list next to **Vendor ID:**

Double click Computer Tech Magazine

In the **Invoice #:** enter 1579-53

Tab to **Date:** field.

– The date should be 1/19/06, enter that date.

Complete the detail section of the bill in the Apply to Purchases tab:

Click in the column for **Description**

Enter 6 Month Subscription

Tab to the **GL account** column. Confirm that it reflects GL account 6160 for Dues
    and Subscriptions
Tab twice to the **Amount** field. Enter 79.00
Click on **Save** and then **Close**

Instead of deleting and re-entering the invoice, we could have merely edited the existing invoice
changing the vendor to the new vendor. In either case, we will end up with the following:

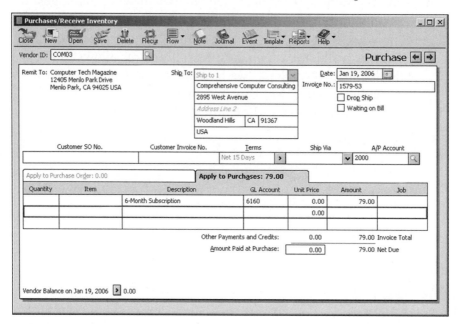

MODIFY VENDOR RECORDS

Occasionally, information regarding a vendor will change. Peachtree® Complete Accounting
2006 allows vendor accounts to be modified at any time by editing the Vendor List.

MEMO

DATE: January 26, 2006

Because Brenda Slocum received a promotion, the contact person for QRS
Insurance Company has been changed to Guadalupe Hernandez.

DO: Modify the vendor records as indicated
         Click **Vendors** from the **Purchases** button.
         Click the magnifying glass for **Vendor ID:**
         Double click QRS Insurance Company

In the General tab, highlight the name in the **Contact:** field
Type Guadalupe Hernandez
Click **Save** to record the change
Click **Close** in the Maintain Vendors window

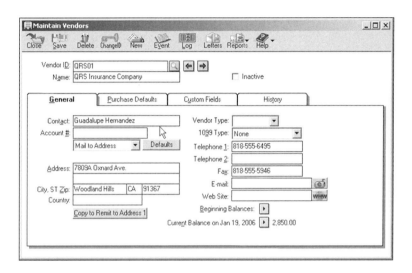

ENTER A CREDIT FROM A VENDOR

Credit memos are prepared to record a reduction to a transaction. With Peachtree® Complete Accounting 2006, you use the Credit Memo window to record credit memos received from vendors acknowledging a return of or an allowance for a previously recorded bill and/or payment. The amount of a credit memo is deducted from the amount owed on the invoice to which it is linked.

MEMO

DATE: January 26, 2006

Received Credit Memo No. CM789 for $5 from Teri's Office Supplies Wholesale for a return of damaged fax paper.

DO: Access the Credit Memo window and record the credit memo shown above
Click **Credit Memo** in the **Purchases** button.
Click the magnifying glass for **Vendor ID:**.
Double click Teri's Office Supplies Wholesale.
Tab to or click the **Date:**.
Confirm or type 01/26/06.
Enter CM789 in the **Credit #:** field.

Select Invoice #1035A in the **Apply to Invoice No.:** field.
Look for Fax Supplies in the **Description** column.
Click in the **Amount** column of the row containing Fax Supplies.
Type 5.00

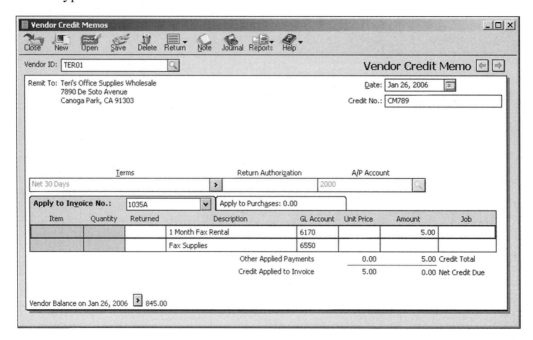

Click **Save** and then **Close** to record the credit and exit

VIEW CREDIT IN THE VENDOR LEDGERS REPORT

When recording the credit in the last transaction, Peachtree® Complete Accounting 2006 has listed the transaction in the Purchases Journal just as it would any other invoice. The primary difference is that it is debiting accounts payable and crediting the expense (asset) account used in the original transaction. The impact of this invoice can be seen grouped with the other vendor invoices in a Vendor Ledgers report. It would also be viewable in the Purchases Journal in chronological sequence. Let us take a look at our credit in the Vendor Ledgers Report.

    DO: View credit in the Vendor Ledgers Report
                Click **All Accounts Payable Reports** in the **Purchases** button
                Double click on Vendor Ledgers Report
                Click the **Options** icon at the top of the window
                Click the drop down list arrow, click in the **Type** column for the **Vendor ID:** field,
                      select **Equal To**
                Click in the **From** field and use the lookup feature (click the magnifying glass) to
                      select Teri's Office Supplies Wholesale

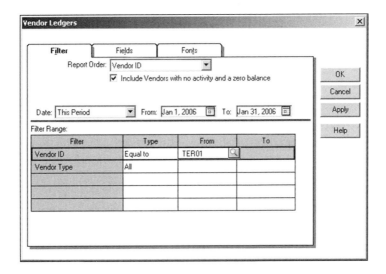

Click **OK**

You are presented with a Vendor Ledger Report for just Teri's Office Supplies
Wholesale:

Comprehensive Computer Consulting-APS
Vendor Ledgers
For the Period From Jan 1, 2006 to Jan 31, 2006

Filter Criteria includes: 1) IDs: TER01. Report order is by ID.

Vendor ID Vendor	Date	Trans No	Type	Paid	Debit Amt	Credit Amt	Balance
TER01	1/1/06	Balance Fwd					350.00
Teri's Office Supplies Wholes	1/19/06	1035A	PJ			45.00	395.00
	1/19/06	8950S	PJ			450.00	845.00
	1/26/06	CM789	PJ	*	5.00		840.00
Report Total					5.00	495.00	840.00

As you can see, Peachtree has applied the $5.00 credit memo to our account with Teri's Office
Supplies Wholesale, leaving a balance due of $840.00. Later in the chapter, when we pay our
bills, we will see that Peachtree has applied this credit to invoice 1035A and reduced the amount
we must pay.

Close the Vendor Ledgers report and the Select a Report window.

PAYING BILLS WITH SELECT FOR PAYMENT

When using Peachtree® Complete Accounting 2006, you may choose one of three ways to pay
your bills. The methods range from telling Peachtree to pay all bills that are due before a certain
date to writing a check for a specific expense. Although we can manually write a check and
simply tell Peachtree the check number we used, it is best to let Peachtree write the checks for
us. Let us look at each of these three ways to generate a check from within Peachtree and see
when each should be used.

Payment Method	Description
Select for Payment	Use this feature to pay all invoices due on or before a specific date. You may use both the net due date and the discount date in your filter. Peachtree will combine invoices to the same vendor and will allow for batch check processing. This is the most efficient use of Peachtree's payment feature. Peachtree also now has an electronics payment option but this feature is disabled in the educational version of the program.
Payments	Feature allows you to select and pay individual invoices from a specific vendor. This is a more selective process and gives you more control over which invoices are to be paid. This window will also allow you to record cash payments for inventory as well as pay existing invoices. This window can also be reached from the Tasks menu by selecting Bills/Pay Bills.
Write Checks	A simplified version of the Payments window, this option allows the user to quickly generate a check for a specific expense or asset item. It cannot be used to pay existing invoices or to record the purchase of inventory although the payment can be split into multiple accounts.

MEMO

DATE: January 27, 2006

Whenever possible, Carmen Mendoza pays the bills on a weekly basis. She will be paying bills today and must pay all bills due between today and next Friday when she pays bills again. This means she must pay bills due before 2/3/06. If she does not pay all bills due by this date, they will become past due by the time she again pays bills. Pay all bills due before 2/3/06.

DO: Pay bills due on or before 2/3/06
Click on **Select for Payment** from the **Purchases** button
Confirm the check date as 1/27/06, which should be your system date
In the field labeled **Invoices Due Before:**, enter the date 2/3/06
In the field labeled **or Discounts Lost By:**, enter the date 2/3/06
– Although none of our vendors have furnished us invoices with discount dates, we should still use the **Discounts Lost By** field since this would typically be used in a real world situation. By changing the dates in both of these fields, we will be paying all invoices with net dates before 2/3/06 as well as all invoices with discount dates before 2/3/06.
Confirm that the radio buttons for **All Invoices** and **All Vendors** are selected

– Using these filters, we could limit which invoices and/or which vendors to include in our criteria for payment.

When filled out correctly, your **Select for Payment - Filter Selection** window should look like this:

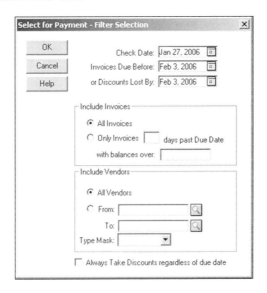

Click **OK**

Note: You are taken to a Select for Payment window that will list all invoices that meet the criteria established in the filter selection. Note that this window is very similar to the Apply to Invoices tab of the Receipts feature. Peachtree uses windows in the Purchases area that are very similar to the windows in the Sales related functions.

The red checkmarks in the Pay column indicate these two bills have been selected for payment.

Inv. Date	Due Date	Vendor Name	Invoice#	Balance	Discount Amt	Pay Amount	Pay
Dec 23, 2005	Jan 22, 2006	Teri's Office Supplies W	23498	350.00		350.00	☑
Dec 27, 2005	Jan 26, 2006	Matrix Advertising	56789	500.00		500.00	☑

Leave the Select for Payment screen open and continue to the next section.

PRINTING CHECKS FOR BILLS

After the invoices have been marked for payment, you must print them. The normal procedure would be to allow Peachtree to print the checks for you. A company would purchase one of numerous check formats available for the program and print directly on these forms. If for whatever reason, checks were handwritten, you would still need to go through the print process and print the checks on blank paper. This process assigns the check numbers to the payments. If there is more than one amount due for a vendor, Peachtree® Complete Accounting 2006 totals the amounts due to the vendor and prints one check to the vendor. It will include a remittance advice telling the vendor which invoices are being paid with the check. If discounts are available, Peachtree will deduct these amounts when calculating the amount to be paid. It will also show that it has taken these discounts on the remittance advice.

 DO: Print the checks for the bills paid
          Click the **Print** icon to be taken to the Print Forms: Disbursement Checks dialog
             box

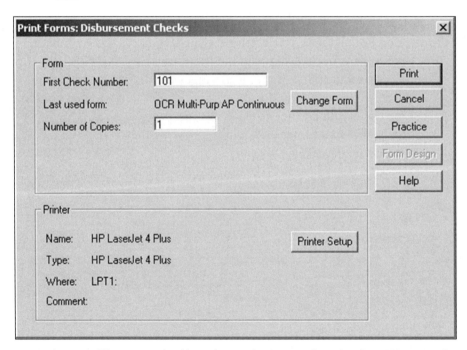

Peachtree will automatically select a form to print checks. We can change this by
    clicking on the **Change Form** button. Since we are printing on plain paper,
    the choice does not matter much.

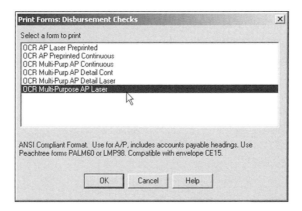

Select **OCR Multi-Purpose AP Laser** and Click **OK** to accept.

You are taken back to the Print Forms: Disbursement Checks dialog box where you can enter the starting check number. In future check runs, Peachtree will enter the next available number for you. The number should be that which is preprinted on your check forms. We will start with the number 101. Enter 101.

Click **Print**

Because Peachtree would expect you to insert the check forms in your printer, it may pause at this point waiting for you to insert the check forms and tell it to continue. Although we will not be inserting blank checks, we must still tell the printer to continue. See your instructor for these instructions.

After printing the checks, Peachtree will ask you to confirm that they printed properly. If for some reason the check printing process were interrupted and it became necessary to reprint, the starting check number would change and different check numbers would be used. Click **Yes**

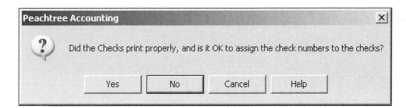

REVIEW BILLS THAT HAVE BEEN PAID

In order to avoid any confusion about payment of a bill, Peachtree® Complete Accounting 2006 marks the bill paid (except Balance Fwd amounts) through the use of an asterisk. Scrolling through the recorded bills in a Vendor Ledgers report, you will see the invoices that were just paid marked with an asterisk.

DO: Prepare a Vendor Ledgers report
Click **All Accounts Payable Reports** in the **Purchases** button

Double click on Vendor Ledgers

Note that the bills we just paid have been posted to the customer accounts using a CDJ (Cash Disbursements Journal) posting reference.

Comprehensive Computer Consulting-APS
Vendor Ledgers
For the Period From Jan 1, 2006 to Jan 31, 2006

Filter Criteria includes: Report order is by ID.

Vendor ID Vendor	Date	Trans No	Type	Paid	Debit Amt	Credit Amt	Balance
COM01 ComSer Telephone Co.							0.00
COM02 Computer Pro Magazine							0.00
COM03 Computer Tech Magazine	1/19/06	1579-53	PJ			79.00	79.00
JAC01 Jackson Realtors							0.00
JOH01 John's Auto Services	1/19/06	630	PJ			575.00	575.00
MAT01 Matrix Advertising	1/1/06	Balance Fwd					500.00
	1/17/06	9875	PJ			260.00	760.00
	1/27/06	101	CDJ		500.00		260.00
QRS01 QRS Insurance Company	1/19/06	3659	PJ			2,850.00	2,850.00
SOU01 Southern CA Electric							0.00
SOU02 SouthCal Gas Co.							0.00
TER01 Teri's Office Supplies Wholes	1/1/06	Balance Fwd					350.00
	1/19/06	1035A	PJ			45.00	395.00
	1/19/06	8950S	PJ			450.00	845.00
	1/26/06	CM789	PJ	*	5.00		840.00
	1/27/06	102	CDJ		350.00		490.00
WAT01 Water Works							0.00

Print and close the report and the Select a Report window.

PETTY CASH

Frequently, a business will need to pay for small expenses with cash. These might include expenses such as postage, office supplies, and miscellaneous expenses. For example, rather than write a check for postage due of 75 cents, you would use money from petty cash. Peachtree® Complete Accounting 2006 allows you to establish a petty cash account to pay for these small expenditures. Normally, a Petty Cash Voucher is prepared manually; and, if available, the receipt for the transaction is stapled to it. It is important in a business to keep accurate records of the petty cash expenditures. Procedures for control of the Petty Cash fund need to be established to prohibit access to and unauthorized use of the cash. Periodically, the petty cash expenditures are recorded in Peachtree so that the records of the company accurately reflect all expenses incurred in the operation of the business and the petty cash fund can be replenished.

ADD PETTY CASH ACCOUNT TO THE CHART OF ACCOUNTS

Peachtree® Complete Accounting 2006 allows accounts to be added to the Chart of Accounts list at any time. Petty Cash is identified as a "Cash" account type so it will be placed at the top of the Chart of Accounts along with checking and savings accounts.

DO: Add Petty Cash to the Chart of Accounts
Click **Chart of Accounts** from the **General Ledger** button
Type 1150 in the **Account ID:** field
Click **OK** or press the **Enter** key
Type Petty Cash in the **Description:** field
Confirm that the **Account Type:** is Cash
Click **Save** and then **Close**

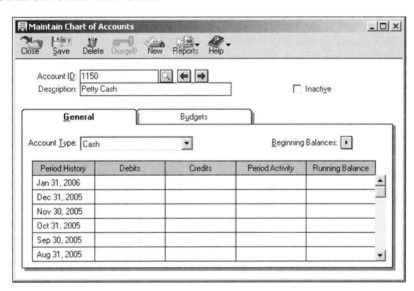

ESTABLISH PETTY CASH FUND BY USING WRITE CHECKS

Once the account has been created, the petty cash fund custodian must have money in order to pay for small expenses. A check must be written and cashed to obtain petty cash funds. This may be accomplished with Peachtree's Write Checks feature. The Write Checks window allows us to generate a check to an individual or company from our Vendor List or to type in a payee who is not on our list. Carmen Mendoza will be our petty cash custodian and so we will write a check for $100 to her. She is not currently on our Vendor List and so we will manually type in her name on the check to explore that feature. Alternatively, we could have added Carmen to our

Vendor list in order to simplify writing future checks since as petty cash custodian, she will in all probability be receiving a check every month.

MEMO

DATE: January 28, 2006

Roger instructs Carmen Mendoza to issue a check for $100 to the Petty Cash Fund that she will maintain.

DO: Record the payment of $100 from checking to establish petty cash:

Click **Write Checks** from the **Purchases** button

Confirm that the **Cash Account:** shown on the right side of the Write Checks window is 1100. If not, enter the account number.

Tab to the **Pay to the Order of:** field, type Carmen Mendoza

Tab to **Check Number:** field. Since Peachtree will assign the check number when it prints the check, tab to the **Date:** field.

Confirm the check date as 1/28/06

Tab to the **$** field, enter 100.00

Tab to the **Memo:** field. Enter Establish Petty Cash Fund

Click on the magnifying glass to the right of the **Expense Account:** field. Select account number **1150 Petty Cash**

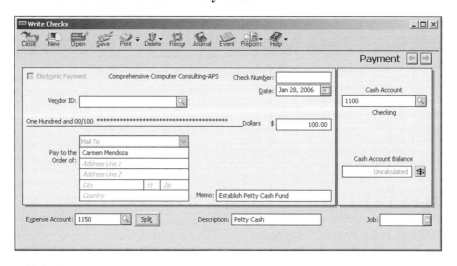

Click the **Print** icon

Enter or confirm that Peachtree will be using check number 103

Click **Print**

Close the Write Checks window or leave open for the next activity.

RECORD REPLENISHMENT OF PETTY CASH

As petty cash is used to pay for small expenses in the business, these payments are recorded in a manual register. Once a month the fund must be replenished in order to correctly record the expenditures in our books. At the same time, the fund is brought back up to its previous balance for next month's expenditures. It might be necessary to replenish the fund at mid-month. This is not a problem and would be recorded in the same manner as the end-of-month replenishment.

MEMO

DATE: January 31, 2006

Carmen Mendoza needs to record the petty cash expenditures made during the month: postage due, 34 cents; purchased staples and paper clips, $3.57; reimbursed Carolyn Masters for gasoline purchased for company car, $13.88.

DO: Record the replenishment of the petty cash fund:

If necessary, click **Write Checks** from the **Purchases** button

Confirm that the cash account used for the check is 1100

Tab to the **Pay to the Order of:** field, type **Carmen Mendoza**

Tab to **Check Number**: field. Since Peachtree will assign the check number when it prints the check, tab to the date field.

Confirm the check date as 1/31/06

Tab to the **$** field, enter 17.79

Tab to the **Memo:** field. Enter Petty Cash Replenishment

Because our transaction involves more than one account, click on the **Split** button to the right of **Expense Account:** field

On the first line of the Split Transaction window, enter Account No. 6250 and the amount 0.34

On the second line, enter Account No. 1310 and the amount 3.57

On the third line, enter Account No. 6110 and accept the amount 13.88

Account No.	Description	Amount	Job
6250	Postage and Delivery Expense	0.34	
1310	Office Supplies	3.57	
6110	Automobile Expense	13.88	

Amount Distributed:	17.79
Amount Remaining:	0.00
Transaction Total:	17.79

Compare your screen with the above making any corrections needed
Click **OK**
Print check as stated previously using check number 104
Close the Write Checks window

PAY BILLS BY USING THE PAYMENTS WINDOW

Although it is more efficient to record all bills in the Purchases/Receive Inventory window and pay them through the Select for Payment window, Peachtree® Complete Accounting 2006 also allows bills to be paid by creating a check without going through Accounts Payable. We can accomplish this through either the Write Checks window used previously or the Payments window. If we choose to use the Payments window, the transaction for the check is created but the check itself will not be created until it is printed. Let us use the Payments window to become familiar with it. Peachtree has stored various bits of information about the vendors and the services we buy from them. As such, many fields will be completed automatically. Always confirm that names, addresses, dates and general ledger accounts selected by Peachtree are what we require. The memo field will print the vendor account number field.

MEMO

DATE: January 31, 2006

Create checks to pay the following bills:

Jackson Realtors—rent for the month, $1,500
ComSer Telephone Co.—telephone bill for the month, $350
Southern CA Electric—electric bill for the month, $250
Water Works—water bill for the month, $35
SouthCal Gas Co.—heating bill for the month, $175

DO: Create checks to pay the bills listed above:
Click **Payments** from the **Purchases** button
Using the lookup feature, select Jackson Realtors
Most of the fields in the upper portion of the check will fill in automatically.
    Confirm the date as 1/31/06
Click in the **Description** column in the lower portion of the check
Enter Rent for January
Confirm the **GL Account** as 6290 Rent Expense
Tab to the **Amount** field, enter 1500.00

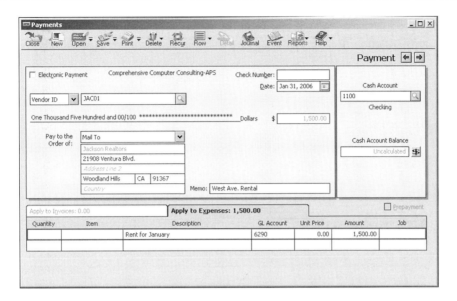

Compare your entry with the above and correct as needed.

Click **Save**

Do not print any of the checks being entered at this time

Repeat the steps indicated above to record payment of the telephone, electric, water, and gas bills

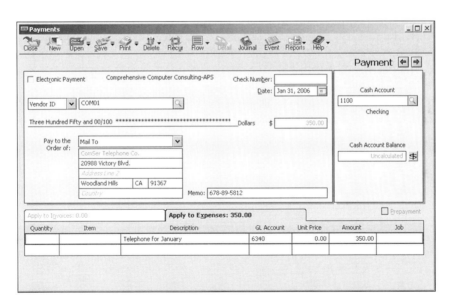

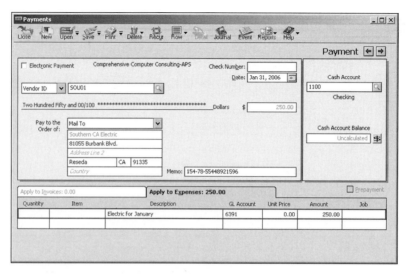

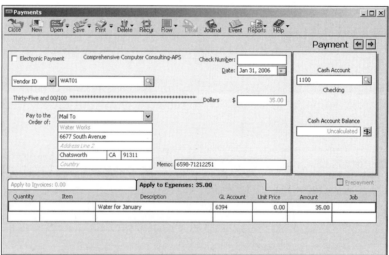

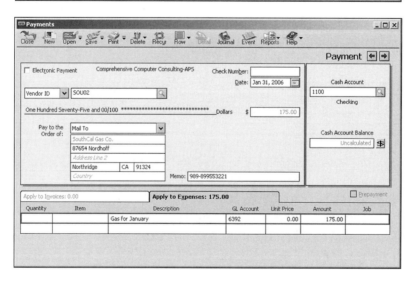

ENTER THE CHECK FOR THE ELECTRIC BILL A SECOND TIME

Enter it the second time exactly like the first. Click **Save** when finished.

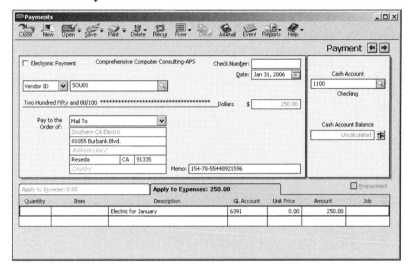

Duplicate Check

EDIT PAYMENT TRANSACTION

Mistakes can occur in business—even when creating a payment transaction. Peachtree®
Complete Accounting 2006 allows for these to be edited at anytime prior to printing. The
transaction must be edited in the Payments window since this is where it was created. To bring
up a transaction already created, you may use either the Payments window itself or use the drill
down feature in any report showing the transaction such as a Check Register or a Cash
Disbursements Journal. Since we have not introduced either of these reports yet, we will use the
Payments window to retrieve the transaction for editing.

> # MEMO
>
> **DATE:** January 31, 2006
>
> Once the transaction for the rent had been entered, Carmen realized that it
> should have been for $1,600. Edit the check created for Jackson Realtors.

DO: Revise the check created to pay the rent
Click **Payments** from the **Purchases** button
Click on the **Open** icon at the top of the window
Select the $1,500.00 payment to Jackson Realtors

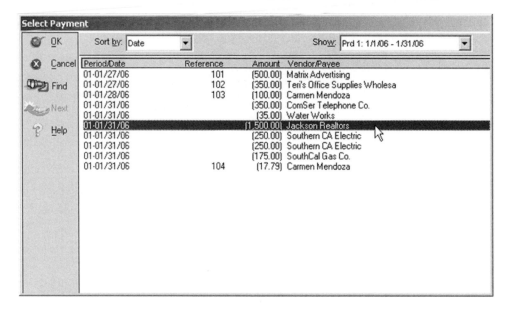

Click **OK**

Highlight the 1500.00 in the **Amount** field and enter 1600.00

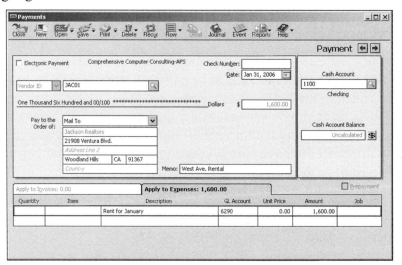

Click **Save** and **Close**

PREPARE A CHECK REGISTER REPORT

Prior to printing checks, it is important to review the information about the checks. The Check Register provides detailed information regarding each check. Information indicates the date, the payee, the cash account used, and the paid amount of the check. If printed after the checks have been generated, it will also indicate the check number.

MEMO

DATE: January 31, 2006

Prior to printing checks, Carmen prints a Check Register to confirm all the transactions she has entered for payment.

 DO: Print a Check Register Report:

Click **All Accounts Payable Reports** from the **Purchases** button
Double click Check Register from the reports listed
Note: The register shows checks 101 through 104 that have been printed in prior activities. The unprinted checks are those with no check number assigned. Unless changes are made prior to printing, Peachtree will create a check for each of these transactions in the amounts shown.

Click **Print**

Comprehensive Computer Consulting-APS
Check Register
For the Period From Jan 1, 2006 to Jan 31, 2006
Filter Criteria includes: Report order is by Date.

Check #	Date	Payee	Cash Account	Amount
101	1/27/06	Matrix Advertising	1100	500.00
102	1/27/06	Teri's Office Supplies Wh	1100	350.00
103	1/28/06	Carmen Mendoza	1100	100.00
104	1/31/06	Carmen Mendoza	1100	17.79
	1/31/06	Jackson Realtors	1100	1,600.00
	1/31/06	ComSer Telephone Co.	1100	350.00
	1/31/06	Southern CA Electric	1100	250.00
	1/31/06	Water Works	1100	35.00
	1/31/06	SouthCal Gas Co.	1100	175.00
	1/31/06	Southern CA Electric	1100	250.00
Total				3,627.79

Leave your report on screen for the next activity.

DELETE PAYMENT TRANSACTION

Deleting a payment transaction completely removes the transaction and any information associated with it from Peachtree® Complete Accounting 2006. Make sure you definitely want to remove the transaction before deleting it; because once it is deleted, it cannot be recovered for printing. It is preferable to delete a transaction prior to printing the check. Once a check has been printed it is better to void the check rather than to delete it because a voided check is maintained in the company records, whereas no record is kept of a deleted check.

MEMO

DATE: January 31, 2006

In reviewing the register for the checking account, Carmen Mendoza discovered that two checks were written to pay the electric bill. Delete the second check.

DO: Delete the second entry for the electric bill
    –   Notice that there are two transactions showing for Southern CA Electric.
Double click anywhere in the row for the second entry for Southern CA Electric
Click the **Delete** icon at the top of the window
Choose **Delete** from the choices offered
When asked to confirm the deletion, click **Yes**
Close the Payments window. Note that the second check has been removed
Close the Check Register report
Do not close the Select A Report window until after the next activity

PRINT CHECKS

Checks may be printed as they are entered, or as we have elected to do, they may be printed at a later time. When checks are to be printed, Peachtree® Complete Accounting 2006 enters them in the journal without a check number. In this way, you can identify unprinted checks in the Check Register. The appropriate check number is assigned to the check during printing as well as to the Check Register. Peachtree® Complete Accounting 2006 has safeguards built in to assist a company in cash controls. For example, if the check for rent of $1,500 had been printed, Peachtree® Complete Accounting 2006 would not allow a second check for $1,600 to be printed unless a new check number is assigned. This is because we are printing on pre-numbered forms and once a check has been written, it cannot be rewritten. As a matter of practice in a small business, the owner or a person different than the one writing checks should sign the checks. In order to avoid any impropriety, more than one person can be designated to review checks.

MEMO

DATE: January 31, 2006

Carmen needs to print checks and obtain Roger Alan's signature so the checks can be mailed.

DO: Print the checks for rent and utility bills

From the Select A Report menu under Accounts Payable, double click on Disbursement Checks

You are presented with the same check formats that are offered when printing checks through Select for Payment and Write Checks windows

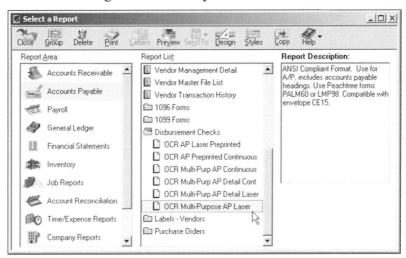

Double click on OCR Multi-Purpose AP Laser

You are taken to an Options window where you can filter which checks are to be printed. To print all of the pending checks, accept the defaults in this window

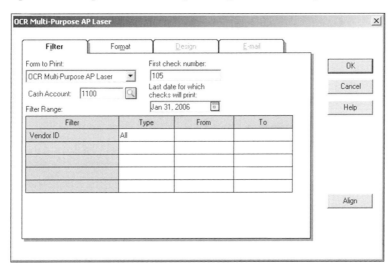

Click **OK**

If brought to a Windows Print dialog box, click **OK**

A dialog box appears asking for confirmation of proper printing, select **Yes**

Close the Select A Report window

VOID CHECKS

Peachtree® Complete Accounting 2006 allows checks to be voided rather than deleted. Voiding a check changes the amount of the check to zero but keeps a record of the transaction.

MEMO

DATE: January 31, 2006

The telephone bill should not have been paid until the first week of February. Void the check written for the telephone expense.

DO: Void the check written for the telephone expense:
Use the steps given previously to access the Check Register
Double click anywhere in the row for ComSer Telephone Co.
Click on the **Delete** icon at the top of the window
Choose **Void** from the options offered
You are presented with a Void Existing Checks dialog box

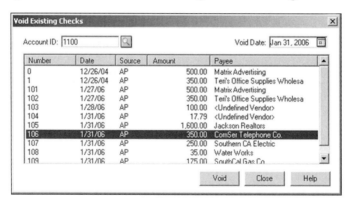

With check number 106 highlighted, click on the **Void** button at the bottom of the window
You are asked to confirm the void. Click **Yes**
Close the Void Existing Checks window
Close the Payments window
Close all report windows

PRINT POST PRINTING CHECK REGISTER

Peachtree® Complete Accounting 2006 creates the Check Register in order by check number. A separate register can be created for each cash account used by a business. If there are any gaps between numbers or duplicate check numbers, this information is provided on the report. It will also reflect any voided checks.

MEMO

DATE: January 31, 2006

To see a listing of all checks printed, print a Check Register.

   DO: View a Check Register
Click **All Accounts Payable Reports** from the **Purchases** button
Double click Check Register from the reports listed

Comprehensive Computer Consulting-APS
Check Register
For the Period From Jan 1, 2006 to Jan 31, 2006
Filter Criteria includes: Report order is by Date.

Check #	Date	Payee	Cash Account	Amount
101	1/27/06	Matrix Advertising	1100	500.00
102	1/27/06	Teri's Office Supplies Wh	1100	350.00
103	1/28/06	Carmen Mendoza	1100	100.00
104	1/31/06	Carmen Mendoza	1100	17.79
105	1/31/06	Jackson Realtors	1100	1,600.00
106	1/31/06	ComSer Telephone Co.	1100	350.00
107	1/31/06	Southern CA Electric	1100	250.00
108	1/31/06	Water Works	1100	35.00
109	1/31/06	SouthCal Gas Co.	1100	175.00
106V	1/31/06	ComSer Telephone Co.	1100	-350.00
Total				3,027.79

Notice that Peachtree has assigned check numbers to all of the transactions. It has also added check number 106V at the bottom of the register which neutralizes Check Number 106 written to ComSer Telephone Co. It is in this manner that Peachtree keeps track of all checks written.
Click **Print**
Close the **Check Register** but leave the **Select A Report** window open for the next activity

PRINT AGED PAYABLES REPORT

It is important in a business to maintain a good credit rating by insuring that payments are made on time. In order to avoid overlooking a payment, the Aged Payables report lists the vendors to whom the company owes money and shows how long the money has been owed.

MEMO

DATE: January 31, 2006

Prepare the Aged Payables report for Roger Alan.

DO: Prepare an Aged Payables report
Double click Aged Payables from the reports listed

Comprehensive Computer Consulting-APS
Aged Payables
As of Jan 31, 2006
Filter Criteria includes: Report order is by ID. Report is printed in Detail Format.

Vendor ID Vendor Contact Telephone 1	Invoice/CM #	0 - 30	31 - 60	61 - 90	Over 90 days	Amount Due
COM03 Computer Tech Magazine 510-555-3829	1579-53	79.00				79.00
COM03 Computer Tech Magazine		79.00				79.00
JOH01 John's Auto Services Joe Gonzalez 818-555-3658	630	575.00				575.00
JOH01 John's Auto Services		575.00				575.00
MAT01 Matrix Advertising Mel Vernon 310-555-8777	9875	260.00				260.00
MAT01 Matrix Advertising		260.00				260.00

Notice that the bills we paid earlier do not appear on this report. It will show only those invoices that are still outstanding. If they are past due, they will appear in a column other than 0-30.

Click **Print**

Close the Aged Payables report

PRINT VENDOR LEDGER REPORT

The Vendor Ledger Report will show us all of the activity in each vendor's account during the month. This will include purchases, credits and cash payments made. It will also show us the current balance owed to the vendor. It is a useful report to generate when there is a difference between the balance we show and the statement received from the vendor at the end of the month.

MEMO

DATE: January 31, 2006

Prepare a Vendor Ledger Report to give to Roger Alan.

DO: Prepare and print a Vendor Ledgers report

Click **All Accounts Payable Reports** in the **Purchases** button

Double click on Vendor Ledgers

Click **Print**

Comprehensive Computer Consulting-APS
Vendor Ledgers
For the Period From Jan 1, 2006 to Jan 31, 2006
Filter Criteria includes: Report order is by ID.

Vendor ID Vendor	Date	Trans No	Type	Paid	Debit Amt	Credit Amt	Balance
COM01	1/31/06	106	CDJ		350.00	350.00	0.00
ComSer Telephone Co.	1/31/06	106V	CDJ		350.00	350.00	0.00
COM02 Computer Pro Magazine							0.00
COM03 Computer Tech Magazine	1/19/06	1579-53	PJ			79.00	79.00
JAC01 Jackson Realtors	1/31/06	105	CDJ		1,600.00	1,600.00	0.00
JOH01 John's Auto Services	1/19/06	630	PJ			575.00	575.00
MAT01 Matrix Advertising	1/1/06	Balance Fwd					500.00
	1/17/06	9875	PJ			260.00	760.00
	1/27/06	101	CDJ		500.00		260.00

Do not close the report until after the next activity

VIEW A SINGLE VENDOR LEDGER

To view a single vendor's report, we would use the Options icon to change the filter for this report and have it display only one vendor.

DO: View a single Vendor Ledger
Click on the **Options** icon
In the **Type** column, change All to Equal To
In the **Vendor ID** row, click in the **From** field
Using the look up feature, select Teri's Office Supplies Wholesale
Click **OK**

Comprehensive Computer Consulting-APS
Vendor Ledgers
For the Period From Jan 1, 2006 to Jan 31, 2006
Filter Criteria includes: 1) IDs: TER01. Report order is by ID.

Vendor ID Vendor	Date	Trans No	Type	Paid	Debit Amt	Credit Amt	Balance
TER01	1/1/06	Balance Fwd					350.00
Teri's Office Supplies Wholes	1/19/06	1035A	PJ			45.00	395.00
	1/19/06	8950S	PJ			450.00	845.00
	1/26/06	CM789	PJ	*	5.00		840.00
	1/27/06	102	CDJ		350.00		490.00
Report Total					355.00	495.00	490.00

Click **Close** to exit the Vendor Ledgers report
Do not close the Select A Report window until after the next activity

VIEW AND PRINT A CASH DISBURSEMENTS JOURNAL

The Cash Disbursements Journal is another way to look at cash that has been disbursed. It differs from the Check Register in that it shows more detail. Not only does it show the check number and to whom the check was written but it also shows us the debit side of the transaction. That is, on what the money was spent. This is a good report for use by management or the owner of the business to insure that his cash disbursements are legitimate.

DO: Prepare and print a Cash Disbursements Journal
Double click on Cash Disbursements Journal
Click **Print**

Comprehensive Computer Consulting-APS
Cash Disbursements Journal
For the Period From Jan 1, 2006 to Jan 31, 2006
Filter Criteria includes: Report order is by Date. Report is printed in Detail Format.

Date	Check #	Account ID	Line Description	Debit Amount	Credit Amount
1/27/06	101	2000	Invoice: 56789	500.00	
		1100	Matrix Advertising		500.00
1/27/06	102	2000	Invoice: 23498	350.00	
		1100	Teri's Office Supplies Wholesale		350.00
1/28/06	103	1150	Petty Cash	100.00	
		1100	Carmen Mendoza		100.00
1/31/06	104	6250	Postage and Delivery Expense	0.34	
		1310	Office Supplies	3.57	
		6110	Automobile Expense	13.88	
		1100	Carmen Mendoza		17.79
1/31/06	105	6290	Rent for January	1,600.00	
		1100	Jackson Realtors		1,600.00
1/31/06	106	6340	Telephone for January	350.00	
		1100	ComSer Telephone Co.		350.00
1/31/06	106V	6340	Telephone for January		350.00
		1100	ComSer Telephone Co.	350.00	
1/31/06	107	6391	Electric for January	250.00	
		1100	Southern CA Electric		250.00
1/31/06	108	6394	Water for January	35.00	
		1100	Water Works		35.00
1/31/06	109	6392	Gas for January	175.00	
		1100	SouthCal Gas Co.		175.00
	Total			3,727.79	3,727.79

Close the Cash Disbursement Journal and the Select A Report window

BACK UP CCC DATA AND CLOSE COMPANY

Whenever an important work session is complete, you should always back up your data. If your data disk is damaged or an error is discovered at a later time, the backup disk may be restored and the information used for recording transactions. As in previous chapters, you should close the company at the end of each work session.

 DO: Follow the instructions given in Chapters 1 and 2 to back up data for Comprehensive Computer Consultants and to close the company. Refer to Appendix A for instructions on making a duplicate disk

SUMMARY

In this chapter, bills were recorded and paid, checks were written, and reports were prepared. The petty cash fund was established and used for payments of small expense items. Check transactions were voided, deleted, and corrected. Accounts were added and modified. The Aged Payables report provided information regarding bills that had not been paid. The Vendor Ledgers report showed us the impact of our purchasing and payment activities. The Check Register and Cash Disbursements Journal gave us different views of our expenditures.

END-OF-CHAPTER QUESTIONS

TRUE/FALSE

ANSWER THE FOLLOWING QUESTIONS IN THE SPACE PROVIDED BEFORE THE QUESTION NUMBER.

_____ 1. Credit Memos are prepared to record a reduction to a transaction.

_____ 2. When you use Peachtree® Complete Accounting 2006, only checks printed by Peachtree will be recorded.

_____ 3. Drill down is a Peachtree® Complete Accounting 2006 feature that allows detailed information to be displayed.

_____ 4. A cash purchase can be made by writing a check or by using petty cash.

_____ 5. Peachtree® Complete Accounting 2006 selects commonly used defaults when reports are created.

_____ 6. A Check Register will show only those checks that have been printed.

_____ 7. The accrual method of accounting matches the income of the period with the cash received for sales.

_____ 8. A Check Register will show us any duplicate check numbers or gaps between check numbers.

_____ 9. The Vendor Ledgers keep track of all checks written in the business.

_____ 10. If a check has been edited, it cannot be printed.

MULTIPLE CHOICE

WRITE THE LETTER OF THE CORRECT ANSWER IN THE SPACE PROVIDED BEFORE THE QUESTION NUMBER.

_____ 1. When using Peachtree® Complete Accounting 2006, bills can be entered _____.
   A. when they are paid
   B. when they are received
   C. neither A nor B
   D. both A and B

_____ 2. A check may be entered in ___.
   A.   the Write Checks window
   B.   the Payments window
   C.   both A and B
   D.   neither A nor B

_____ 3. When you enter a bill, typing the first letter(s) of a vendor's code on the Vendor ID line, Peachtree _____.
   A.   enters the vendor's name on the line if the name is in the Vendor List
   B.   displays a look up list of vendor names
   C.   displays the Address Info tab for the vendor
   D.   indicates that you want to type the vendor name completely

_____ 4. To erase an incorrect amount in a bill, you may ___, then key the correction.
   A.   drag through the amount to highlight
   B.   position the cursor in front of the amount and press the delete key until the amount has been erased
   C.   position the cursor after the amount and press the backspace key until the amount has been erased
   D.   all of the above

_____ 5. When a bill is entered, the date on the business form will default to ____ .
   A.   today's date
   B.   the system date
   C.   Peachtree does not enter a date
   D.   the invoice date

_____ 6. A correction to a bill that has been recorded can be made ____.
   A.   on the bill
   B.   directly in the Vendor Ledger
   C.   in the Purchases Journal
   D.   none of the above

_____ 7. When a bill is deleted, ___.
   A.   the amount is changed to 0.00
   B.   the word _deleted_ appears as the Memo
   C.   it is removed without a trace
   D.   a bill cannot be deleted

_____ 8. To increase the date on a bill by one day, ___.
   A. press the + key
   B. press the - key
   C. tab
   D. press the # key

_____ 9. If a bill is recorded in the Purchases/Receive Inventory window, it is best to pay the bill by ___.
   A. writing a manual check
   B. using the Write Checks window
   C. using petty cash
   D. using the Select for Payment window

_____ 10. When entering several bills at once on the Purchases/Receive Inventory window, it is most efficient to ___to go to the next blank screen.
   A. click Previous
   B. click Save
   C. click OK
   D. click Preview

FILL-IN

IN THE SPACE PROVIDED, WRITE THE ANSWER THAT MOST APPROPRIATELY COMPLETES THE SENTENCE.

1. The _____ section of the Purchases/Receive Inventory business form is used to record the information detailing what is being purchased.

2. Two reports in Peachtree® Complete Accounting 2006 that can be viewed or printed that show the checks we have recorded are: _____ and _____ .

3. Three different reports in Peachtree® Complete Accounting 2006 that can be viewed or printed that show Accounts Payable are: _____, _____and _____.

4. The icon used to add a vendor "on the fly" is called _____.

5. Petty Cash is identified as a _____ account type so it will be placed at the top of the Chart of Accounts along with checking and savings accounts.

SHORT ESSAY

When writing a check using the Write Check window, you will see a button called **Split** displayed. Explain what the term **Split** means when used in this application. How would it apply if we were writing a check for office supplies and office furniture?

_____

_____

_____

_____

_____

_____

_____

_____

_____

_____

NAME   _____

TRANSMITTAL

CHAPTER 3: COMPREHENSIVE COMPUTER CONSULTING

Attach the following documents and reports:

- ☐   Vendor Ledger Report
- ☐   Purchases Journal
- ☐   Cash Requirements Report (as of January 31, 2006)
- ☐   Cash Requirements Report (as of February 28, 2006)
- ☐   Check No. 101: Matrix Advertising
- ☐   Check No. 102: Teri's Office Supplies Wholesale
- ☐   Check No. 103: Carmen Mendoza
- ☐   Check No. 104: Carmen Mendoza
- ☐   Check Register (Prior to final check printing)
- ☐   Check No. 105: Jackson Realtors
- ☐   Check No. 106: ComSer Telephone Co.
- ☐   Check No. 107: Southern CA Electric
- ☐   Check No. 108: Water Works
- ☐   Check No. 109: SouthCal Gas Co.
- ☐   Check Register (After final check printing)
- ☐   Aged Payable Report
- ☐   Vendor Ledgers Report
- ☐   Cash Disbursements Journal

END-OF-CHAPTER PROBLEM

SUNCARE LAWN AND POOL SERVICES

Chapter 3 continues with the transactions for bills, bill payments, and purchases for SunCare Lawn and Pool Services. Even though it is a family-owned business, cash control measures have been implemented. Sylvia prints the checks and any related reports; Greg initials his approval of the checks; and George, the owner, signs the checks.

INSTRUCTIONS

Continue to use the data file for SunCare. Open the company. Record the bills, bill payments, and cash purchases using procedures contained within the chapter. Always read the transactions carefully and review the Chart of Accounts when selecting or confirming transaction accounts. Print reports as indicated. All checks should be generated by Peachtree® Complete Accounting 2006—not by writing the check yourself. Start with Check No. 101 and continue the sequence unbroken throughout the activity. Checks should be drawn on the Cash in Bank account 1100. Use the MultiP AP Chks 1 Stub form for checks. Refer back to the chapter when in doubt as to how to enter a transaction.

RECORD TRANSACTIONS

January 2

Use the Purchases/Receive Inventory window to record the following bills:

Received a bill from Western Communications for cellular phone service for January, $485, Invoice No. 1109, Net 10.

Received a bill from the Office Solutions for supplies purchased, $275, Invoice No. 58-9826, Net 30. (This is a prepaid expense.)

Add Petty Cash to the Chart of Accounts. (Use 1150 as the account number)

Use the Write Checks window to issue a $50 check made out to Petty Cash, to establish a Petty Cash Fund. (Use Check No. 101 and the Cash in Bank account for your cash account). Be sure to change your expense account. Use OCR Multi-Purpose AP Laser for the check form.

Received a bill from Lionel's Motors for truck service and repairs, $519, Invoice No. 1-62, Net 10, (There is only one expense account that can be used for this bill. We will be changing the name to something more appropriate in Chapter 4.)

Received a bill from Fuel Line Company for anticipated gasoline usage for the month of January, $375, Invoice No. 853, Net 10.

Received a bill from Power Corp. for a repair of the office air conditioner, $150, Invoice No. 87626, Net 30.(The air conditioner is part of the building.)

January 9

Use the Purchases/Receive Inventory window to record the following bills:

Received a bill from TJ Disposal for disposing of lawn, tree, and shrub trimmings, $180, Invoice No. 667, Net 30.

Received a bill from CA Water Company for January, $25, Invoice No. 098-1, Net 10.

Print a Cash Requirements Report as of January 16 (the day up to which we will be paying bills).

SunCare is doing a check run today to pay bills. It does not plan on doing another check run until January 16 and so it needs to pay all bills due or discounts lost before January 16. (Use Select for Payment to pay bills and confirm that Peachtree will start the check run with Check No. 102.) Print all checks.

Record the receipt of a bill from Quality Maintenance. Add this new vendor as you record the transaction (Vendor ID should be QUA01). Our account number will be 56709-2. Additional information needed to do a complete set up is: 1234 State Street, Santa Barbara, CA 93110, 805-555-0770, the default expense account will be 6330 Equipment Repairs. Terms will be Net 10. The bill was for the repair of the lawn mower, $75, Invoice No. 5-1256, Net 10, accept all other defaults.

Change the telephone number for TJ Disposal. The new number is 805-555-3798.

Prepare and print the Vendor Ledgers Report.

January 16

Enter the transactions:

Received a $10 credit from Quality Maintenance. It was noted that not all maintenance requested was performed. Associate it with the original invoice. The credit memo was numbered 1015-CM.

Record the replenishment of Petty Cash to pay for postage, $24.64, and office supplies, $21.59 (this is an expense rather than an asset).

Write a check to Quality Maintenance to buy a lawn fertilizer spreader as a cash purchase of equipment, $349. Print the check.

Print a Cash Requirements Report as of January 21.

SunCare is doing a check run today to pay bills. It does not plan on doing another check run until January 21. Pay all bills due on or before January 21; print the checks.

Prepare and print a Purchases Journal.

Prepare and print a Cash Disbursements Journal.

Prepare and print a Check Register.

Prepare and print an Aged Payables Report

Back up your data and close the company.

NAME _____

TRANSMITTAL

CHAPTER 3: SUNCARE LAWN & POOL SERVICES

Attach the following documents and reports:

☐ Check No. 101: Petty Cash

☐ Cash Requirements Report for January 16, 2006

☐ Check No. 102: Fuel Line Company

☐ Check No. 103: Lionel's Motors

☐ Check No. 104: Western Communications

☐ Vendor Ledgers Report

☐ Check No. 105: Petty Cash Replenishment

☐ Check No. 106: Quality Maintenance – Cash Purchase

☐ Cash Requirements Report for January 23, 2006

☐ Check No. 107: CA Water Company

☐ Check No. 108: Quality Maintenance

☐ Purchases Journal

☐ Cash Disbursements Journal

☐ Check Register

☐ Aged Payables Report

General Accounting and End-Of-Period Procedures: Service Business

LEARNING OBJECTIVES

At the completion of this chapter, you will be able to:

1. Complete the end-of-period procedures.
2. Change account names, delete accounts, and make accounts inactive.
3. Record depreciation and enter the adjusting entries required for accrual-basis accounting.
4. Record owner's equity transactions for a sole proprietor including capital investment and owner withdrawals.
5. Reconcile the bank statement, record bank service charges, and other reconciliation adjustments.
6. Print General Ledger Trial Balance, Income Statement, and Balance Sheet.
7. Export reports to Microsoft® Excel
8. Perform end-of-period backup and advance the period.

GENERAL ACCOUNTING AND END-OF-PERIOD PROCEDURES

As previously stated, the Peachtree® Complete Accounting 2006 user interface operates from the standpoint of the business document rather than an accounting form, journal, or ledger. While Peachtree® Complete Accounting 2006 does incorporate all of these items into the program, in many instances they operate behind the scenes. Peachtree® Complete Accounting 2006 contains a simple end-of-period closing for both its monthly financial statements and the annual financial statements. At the end of the fiscal year, Peachtree® Complete Accounting 2006 transfers the net income into the Retained Earnings account and automatically prepares the books for the next accounting cycle. Closing the fiscal year will remove transaction details from the system. Since some businesses must still deal with transaction detail well into the next fiscal year, Peachtree® Complete Accounting 2006 does not require you to close the year at the end of the year. Since the program allows you to keep two fiscal years open at the same time, it is generally recommended that you do not officially close the year until near the end of the next fiscal year. In the meantime, all of the transaction detail is maintained and is viewable. Should there be a requirement to view older detail, backup can be restored and detailed information viewed.

A period is ended when we advance Peachtree to the next period. Even though a formal "closing" does not have to be performed within Peachtree® Complete Accounting 2006, when you use accrual-basis accounting, several transactions must be recorded to reflect all expenses and income for the period. For example, bank statements must be reconciled and any charges or bank collections need to be recorded. During the business period, the CPA for the company will review things such as account names, adjusting entries, depreciation schedules, owner's equity adjustments, and so on. Sometimes, changes and adjustments will be suggested by your accountant. These changes and adjustments would be entered into the system prior to closing the period.

Once necessary adjustments have been made, reports reflecting the end-of-period results of operations should be prepared. For archive purposes at the end of the fiscal year an additional backup disk is prepared and stored. Ideally, backups will be made and kept at the end of each month as well.

TRAINING TUTORIAL AND PROCEDURES

For the following tutorial, we will once again work with Comprehensive Computer Consulting (CCC). As in Chapters 2 and 3, transactions will be recorded for this fictitious company. To maximize training benefits, you should:

1. Read the entire chapter *before* beginning to enter transactions for CCC.
2. Answer the end-of-chapter questions.
3. Be aware that transactions to be entered are given within a **MEMO**.
4. Complete all the steps listed for the Comprehensive Computer Consulting (CCC) tutorial in the chapter. The steps are indicated by: **DO:**
5. When you have completed a step, put an **X** on the button next to **DO:**
6. As you complete your work, proofread carefully and check for accuracy. Double-check amounts of money.
7. If you find an error while preparing a transaction, correct it. If you find the error after the transaction has been entered, follow the steps indicated in this chapter to correct, void, or delete the transaction.
8. Print as directed in the chapter.
9. You may not finish the entire chapter in one computer session. Always back up your work at the end of your work session as described in Chapter 1.
10. When you complete your computer session, always close your company.

OPEN PEACHTREE® COMPLETE ACCOUNTING 2006 AND COMPREHENSIVE COMPUTER CONSULTING

DO: Open Peachtree® Complete Accounting 2006 as instructed in prior Chapters
Open Comprehensive Computer Consulting (CCC):
Click **Open an existing company.**
Click the **Browse** button (if Comprehensive Computer Consulting is not already visible)
Click the drop down arrow for **Drives:**
Select the drive where your data files are kept

Locate and double click on **Comprehensive Computer Consulting** (under the
Company name text box)
Check the title bar to verify that Comprehensive Computer Consulting -Student's
Initials is the open company

BEGINNING THE TUTORIAL

In this chapter, you will be recording end-of-period adjustments, reconciling bank statements,
changing account names, and preparing traditional end-of-period reports. Because Peachtree®
Complete Accounting 2006 does not perform a traditional "closing" of the books, you will learn
how to advance the period to prepare the books for the next month.

All transactions are listed on memos. The transaction date will be the same as the memo date
unless otherwise specified within the transaction. Once a specific type of transaction has been
entered in a step-by-step manner, additional transactions of the same or a similar type will be
made without instructions being provided. Of course, you may always refer to instructions given
for previous transactions for ideas or for steps used to enter those transactions. To determine the
account used in the transaction, refer to the Chart of Accounts, which is also the General Ledger.

CHANGE THE NAME OF EXISTING ACCOUNTS IN THE CHART OF ACCOUNTS

Even though transactions have been recorded during the month of January, Peachtree® Complete
Accounting 2006 makes it a simple matter to change the name of an existing account. Once the
name of an account has been changed, all transactions using the "old" name are updated and
show the "new" account name.

MEMO

DATE: January 31, 2006

Upon the recommendation from the company's CPA, Roger Alan decided to
change the account named Company Cars to Business Vehicles.

 DO: Change the account name of Company Cars
Click on **Chart of Accounts** from the **General Ledger** button
Using the lookup feature, select account number 1500 Company Cars
Peachtree should automatically move to the **Description** field and highlight the
     current description. Enter Business Vehicles
Click **Save** and then **Close**
To confirm the change, we will examine a Chart of Accounts report.

Click on **All General Ledger Reports** from the **General Ledger** button
Double click on Chart of Accounts
- Notice that the name of the account appears as Business Vehicles in the Chart of Accounts.

Comprehensive Computer Consulting-APS
Chart of Accounts
As of Jan 31, 2006

Filter Criteria includes: Report order is by ID. Report is printed with Accounts having Zero Amounts and in Detail Format.

Account ID	Account Description	Active?	Account Type
1100	Checking	Yes	Cash
1150	Petty Cash	Yes	Cash
1200	Accounts Receivable	Yes	Accounts Receivable
1310	Office Supplies	Yes	Other Current Assets
1340	Prepaid Insurance	Yes	Other Current Assets
1400	Employee Advances	Yes	Other Current Assets
1500	Business Vehicles	Yes	Fixed Assets
1505	Depreciation, Company Cars	Yes	Fixed Assets
1510	Office Equipment	Yes	Fixed Assets

Follow the steps above to change the names of:
 2210 - Company Cars Loan to Business Vehicles Loan
 6110 - Automobile Expense to Business Vehicles Expense
 6181 - Auto Insurance Expense to Business Vehicles Insurance
 6220 - Loan Interest Expense to Interest on Loans
 1505 - Depreciation, Company Cars to Accum Depr Business Vehicles
 1515 - Depreciation, Office Equipment to Accum Depr Office Equipment

Verify changes were made with a Chart of Accounts report

MAKE AN ACCOUNT INACTIVE

If you are not using an account and do not have plans to use it in the near future, the account may be made inactive. The account remains visible; however, it may not be used in transactions. After two years of inactivity, the account may be deleted.

MEMO

DATE: January 31, 2006

At present, CCC does not plan to purchase its own building. The accounts, Mortgage Expense and Property Tax Expense should be made inactive.

DO: Make the accounts listed above inactive
Click **Chart of Accounts** from the **General Ledger** button
Using the lookup feature, select account number 6225 Mortgage Expense
Click in the box next to **Inactive**

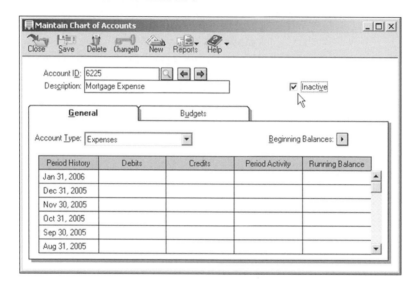

Click **Save**
Follow the steps above to make 6850 Property Tax Expense inactive
Click **Save** and then **Close**

DELETE AN EXISTING ACCOUNT FROM THE CHART OF ACCOUNTS

If your Chart of Accounts contains an account that you have not used and do not plan to use, making it inactive is not sufficient. Instead, Peachtree® Complete Accounting 2006 allows the account to be deleted. However, as a safeguard, Peachtree® Complete Accounting 2006 does prevent the deletion of an account once it has been used even if it simply contains an opening or an existing balance or if it is used in any other area of the program. As mentioned before, an account that has been used must be made inactive for a period of two years before it can be deleted. An account that has never been used can be deleted at anytime.

MEMO

DATE: January 31, 2006

In addition to previous changes to account names, Roger Alan finds that he does not use nor will he use the expense account: Contributions. Delete this account from the Chart of Accounts. In addition, Roger wants you to delete the Dues and Subscriptions account.

DO: Delete the Contributions expense account
Scroll through accounts until you see Contributions, click 6140 Contributions
Click the **Delete** icon at the top of the window
You will be presented with a Delete Confirmation box

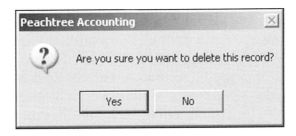

Click **Yes**
- The account has now been deleted.
Repeat the above steps for the deletion of 6160 Dues and Subscriptions
- As soon as you try to delete Dues and Subscriptions, a Warning appears stating, "Cannot Delete Account (6160) because there is a non-zero balance in some period(s)." Since the account is being used by Peachtree, it cannot be deleted.

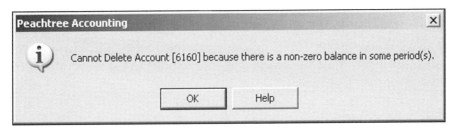

Click **OK**
- The account remains in the Chart of Accounts.
Close the Maintain Chart of Accounts window

ADJUSTMENTS FOR ACCRUAL-BASIS ACCOUNTING

As previously stated, the accrual basis of accounting matches expenses to the income they helped earn. This is accomplished in order to arrive at an accurate figure for net income. Thus, the revenue is earned at the time the service is performed or the sale is made no matter when the actual cash is received. The cash basis of accounting records income or revenue at the time cash is received no matter when the sale was made or the service performed. The same holds true when a business buys things or pays bills. In accrual-basis accounting, the expense is recorded at the time the bill is received or the purchase is made regardless of the actual payment date. In cash-basis accounting, the expense is not recorded until it is paid. While Peachtree is capable of performing accounting functions under a cash-basis system, you would have been required to tell

Peachtree this when the company was first created. Once accrual or cash-basis accounting is selected, Peachtree® Complete Accounting 2006 will not permit switching the basis of your accounting.

There are several internal transactions that must be recorded when you are using the accrual basis of accounting in order to close the period. These entries are called adjusting entries. For example, equipment does wear out and will eventually need to be replaced. Rather than wait until replacement to record the use of the equipment, one makes an adjusting entry to allocate the use of equipment as an expense for each period of its useful life. This is called depreciation. In addition, a business can pay for expenses in advance. These are recorded as assets and as they are used, they become expenses of the business. For example, insurance for the entire year would be used up month by month and should, therefore, be a monthly expense. Commonly, the insurance is prepaid for the entire year. Until the insurance is used, it is an asset. Each month, the portion of the insurance used becomes an expense for the month.

ADJUSTING ENTRIES—PREPAID EXPENSES

During the operation of a business, companies purchase supplies to have on hand for use in the operation of the business. In accrual-basis accounting, the supplies are considered to be prepaid expenses and are recorded as assets (something the business owns) until they are used in the operation of the business. As the supplies are used, the amount used becomes an expense for the period. The same system applies to other things paid for in advance, such as insurance. At the end of the period, an adjusting entry must be made to allocate the amount of assets used to expenses. These adjustments must be recorded as transactions in the General Journal.

MEMO

DATE: January 31, 2006

NOTE from Roger—
Carmen, remember to record the monthly adjustment for Prepaid Vehicle Insurance. $2,850 is the amount we paid for the year. Also, we used $325 worth of supplies this month. Please adjust accordingly.

DO: Record the adjusting entries for office supplies expense and business vehicle insurance expense in the General Journal.
Access the General Journal:
Click **General Journal Entry** from the **General Ledger** button
Confirm or type Jan 31, 2006 in the **Date** field
In the **Reference field**, enter ADJ01. This is for our reference only and is not required

Tab to or click the **GL Account** column

Click the drop-down list arrow for **GL Account**, double click 6181 Business
        Vehicles Insurance

In the **Description** field, enter Adjusting Entry, Insurance

Tab to or click in **Debit** column

- The $2,850 given in the memo is the amount for the year; calculate the amount
  of the adjustment for the month:

Click **Calculator** on the custom toolbar

Enter 2850 by clicking the numbers or using the key pad

- Be sure Num Lock is on. There should be a light by Num Lock on/or above the
  10-key pad. If not, press Num Lock to activate.

Press / for division

Key 12

Press = or **Enter** to see the answer 237.50

Click the **Close** button to close the Calculator

- For additional calculator instructions refer to Chapter 1.

Enter the amount of the adjustment 237.50 in the **Debit** column

Tab to or click **GL Account**

Click the drop-down list arrow for **GL Account**

Double click 1340 Prepaid Insurance

- The description will be entered automatically.

Tab to or click the **Credit** column

Type 237.50

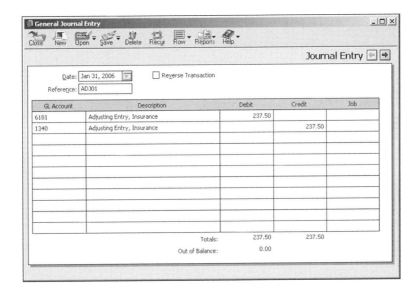

Click **Save**

- Notice that Peachtree brings you to a blank General Journal window and
  automatically changes the Reference to the next number, ADJ02. It will
  continue to do this between entries until the window is closed.

Repeat the above procedures to record the adjustment for the office supplies used
– The amount given in the memo is the actual amount of the supplies used in January.

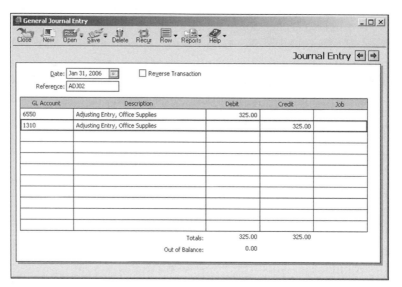

Click **Save**

ADJUSTING ENTRIES—DEPRECIATION

Using the accrual basis of accounting requires companies to record an expense for equipment used in the operation of the business. Unlike supplies—where you can actually see, for example, the paper supply diminishing—it is very difficult to see how much of a computer has been "used up" during the month. To account for the fact that machines do wear out and do need to be replaced, an adjustment is made for depreciation. This adjustment correctly matches the expenses of the period against the revenue of the period. The adjusting entry for depreciation is made in the General Journal.

MEMO

DATE: January 31, 2006

Having received the necessary depreciation schedules, Carmen records the adjusting entry for depreciation: Business Vehicles, $583 per month; Equipment, $142 per month.

DO: Record a compound adjusting entry for depreciation of the equipment and the business vehicles in the General Journal:

Confirm or enter 01/31/06 as the **Date**

In the **Reference field**, confirm or enter ADJ03

Tab to or click the **GL Account** column

Click the drop-down list arrow for **GL Account**, double click 6150 Depreciation Expense

In the **Description** field, enter Record Depreciation for the Month

Tab to or click **Debit,** enter 725.00

Tab to or click **GL Account**

Click the drop-down list arrow for **GL Account**

Double click 1505 Accum. Depr. Business Vehicles

Tab to or click the **Credit** column

Type 583.00

Tab to or click **GL Account**

Click the drop-down list arrow for **GL Account**

Double click 1515 Accum. Depr. Office Equipment

Tab to or click the **Credit** column

Type 142.00

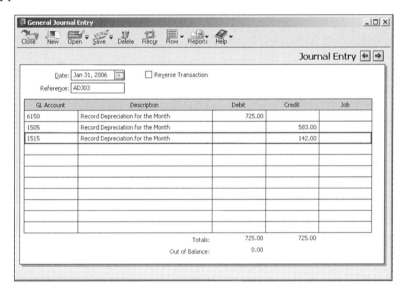

Click **Save** and then **Close** to record the adjustment and close the **General Journal Entry** window

VIEW GENERAL JOURNAL

Once transactions have been entered in the General Journal, it is important to view them. Peachtree® Complete Accounting 2006 maintains a General Journal and allows it to be viewed or printed at any time.

DO: View the Journal for January
Click **General Journal** in the Reports area of the **General Ledger** button
– Accept the defaults and Click **OK**

			Comprehensive Computer Consulting-APS		
			General Journal		
			For the Period From Jan 1, 2006 to Jan 31, 2006		

Filter Criteria includes: Report order is by Date. Report is printed with Accounts having Zero Amounts and with Truncated Transaction Descriptions and in Detail Format.

Date	Account ID	Reference	Trans Description	Debit Amt	Credit Amt
1/31/06	6181	ADJ01	Adjusting Entry, Insurance	237.50	
	1340		Adjusting Entry, Insurance		237.50
1/31/06	6550	ADJ02	Adjusting Entry, Office Supplies	325.00	
	1310		Adjusting Entry, Office Supplies		325.00
1/31/06	6150	ADJ03	Record Depreciation for the Month	725.00	
	1505		Record Depreciation for the Month		583.00
	1515		Record Depreciation for the Month		142.00
		Total		1,287.50	1,287.50

Print or close the report without printing

OWNER WITHDRAWALS

In a sole proprietorship an owner cannot receive a paycheck because he or she owns the business. An owner withdrawing money from a business—even to pay personal expenses—is similar to withdrawing money from a savings account. A withdrawal simply decreases the owner's capital. Peachtree® Complete Accounting 2006 allows you to establish a separate account for owner withdrawals. If a separate account is not established, owner withdrawals may be subtracted directly from the owner's capital account.

MEMO

DATE: January 31, 2006

Roger Alan requests his monthly withdrawal. Prepare the check for his monthly withdrawal, $2,500.

DO: Write Check No. 110 to Roger Alan for $2,500 withdrawal
Click on **Write Checks** from the **Purchases** button
Enter Roger Alan in the **Pay to the Order of:** field
Confirm or type Jan 31, 2006 in the **Date:** field

Verify that the cash account used is 1100.
Enter 2,500.00 in the **Dollar** field
Enter Monthly Draw in the **Memo:** field
Using the look up feature, select 3020 - Roger Alan, Drawing in the **Expense Account:** field

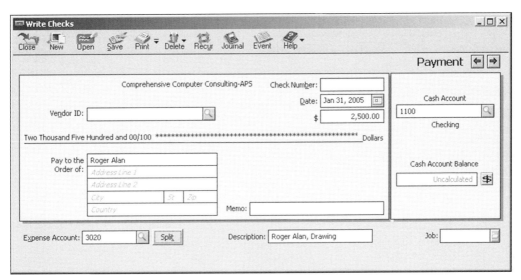

Click **Print** following instructions in previous chapters
Click **Close**

ADDITIONAL CASH INVESTMENT BY OWNER

An owner may decide to invest more of his or her personal cash in the business at any time. The new investment is entered into the owner's investment account and into cash. The investment will be recorded in the General Journal although Receipts could also be used.

MEMO
DATE: January 31, 2006

Roger Alan received money from a certificate of deposit. Rather than reinvest in another certificate of deposit, he decided to invest an additional $5,000 in CCC.

DO: Record the additional cash investment by Roger Alan in the General Journal
Access the Journal as previously instructed
The **Date** should be 01/31/06
Enter MEMO01 in the **Reference** field

The description for both entries should be Additional Investment
Debit account 1100 - Checking, $5,000
Credit account 3000 - Roger Alan, Capital, $5,000

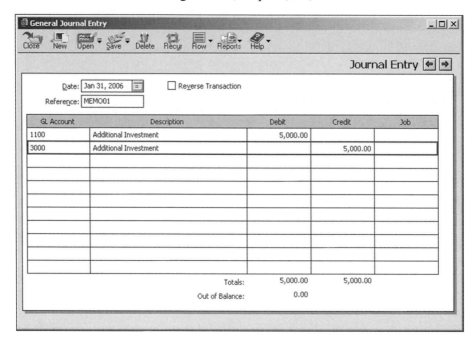

Click **Save** but do not close the General Journal Entry window

NONCASH INVESTMENT BY OWNER

Investments in a business may be made at any time by an owner. The investment may be cash; but it may also be something such as reference books, equipment, tools, buildings, and so on. Additional investments by an owner or owners is added to owner's equity. In the case of a sole proprietor or partnership, the investment is added to the donator's Capital account.

MEMO

DATE: January 31, 2006

Originally, Roger Alan planned to have an office in his home as well as in the company and purchased new office furniture for his home. He decided the business environment would appear more professional if the new furniture were in the office rather than his home. Roger gave the new office furniture to CCC as an additional owner investment. The value of the investment is $3,000.

DO: Record the additional investment by Roger Alan in the General Journal
The **Date** should be 01/31/06
Enter MEMO02 in the **Reference** field
Debit 1510 Office Equipment, $3,000
Credit 3000 Roger Alan, Capital, $3,000
The description for both entries should be Additional Investment, Furniture

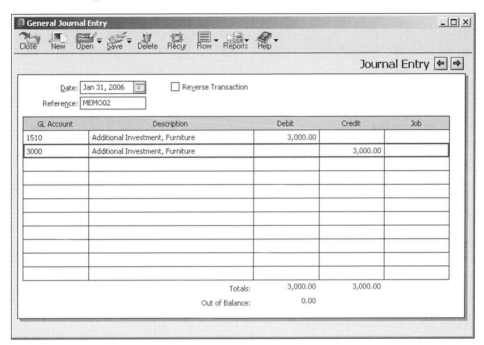

Click **Save** and then **Close**

VIEW BALANCE SHEET

Although a Balance Sheet would not be prepared in a manual accounting system until the end of the accounting period after expenses and revenues have been closed, Peachtree has the capability of generating a Balance Sheet at any time. Since revenues and expenses are not balance sheet accounts, and would keep the Balance Sheet from balancing, Peachtree will add Net Income into the Equity section of the Balance Sheet. Additionally, the Drawing account will be included in the Equity section since it also would normally close to Capital. By including these items on the Balance Sheet, Peachtree is in essence showing you a Statement of Owner's Equity as well as a Balance Sheet.

DO: View a Standard Balance Sheet:
Click **All Financial Statements** from the **General Ledger** button
Double click on <Standard> Balance Sheet

- As with all other reports, Peachtree will allow the user to create custom formats. The built in Balance Sheet will always be the one labeled Standard

You will be presented with a Balance Sheet dialog box. Accept all defaults and click **OK**

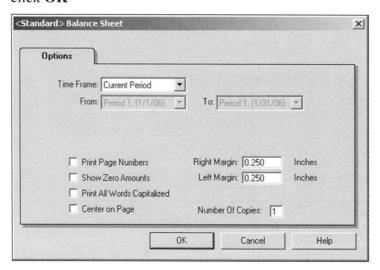

Scroll through the report
- Notice the Equity section, especially Net Income.

LIABILITIES AND CAPITAL

Current Liabilities		
Accounts Payable	$ 4,254.00	
Total Current Liabilities		4,254.00
Long-Term Liabilities		
Business Vehicles Loan	35,000.00	
Office Equipment Loan	4,000.00	
Total Long-Term Liabilities		39,000.00
Total Liabilities		43,254.00
Capital		
Roger Alan, Capital	86,075.00	
Roger Alan, Drawing	(2,500.00)	
Retained Earnings	21,655.00	
Net Income	4,609.28	
Total Capital		109,839.28
Total Liabilities & Capital	$	153,093.28

Close the report and associated windows when you are finished.

BANK RECONCILIATION

Each month, the checking account should be reconciled with the bank statement to make sure that the balances agree. The bank statement will rarely have an ending balance that matches the balance of the checking account. This is due to several factors: outstanding checks (written by the business but not paid by the bank), deposits in transit (deposits that were made too late to be included on the bank statement), bank service charges, interest earned on checking accounts, collections made by the bank, and errors made by the company and/or by the bank.

In order to have an accurate balance in the checking account, it is important that the differences between the bank statement and the checking account be reconciled. If something such as a service charge or a collection made by the bank appears on the bank statement, it needs to be recorded in the checking account.

Reconciling a bank statement is an appropriate time to find any errors that may have been recorded in the checking account. The reconciliation may be out of balance because a transposition was made (recording $94 rather than $49), a transaction was recorded backwards, a transaction was recorded twice, or a transaction was not recorded at all. If a transposition was made, the error may be found by dividing the difference by 9. For example, if $94 was recorded when the actual transaction amount was $49, you would be out of balance by the difference or $45. The number 45 can be evenly divided by 9. This indicates that your error probably was a transposition. If the error can be evenly divided by 2, the transaction may have been entered backwards. For example, if you were out of balance $200, look to see if you had any $100 transactions. Perhaps you recorded a $100 debit, and it should have been a credit (or vice versa).

OPEN ACCOUNT RECONCILIATION

To begin the reconciliation, you need to open the Account Reconciliation window from the General Ledger button. Peachtree allows for reconciliation of any cash account in the General Ledger. We have only one external cash account, 1100 Checking. The reconciliation process will involve comparing the transactions listed on the bank statement with the transactions recorded into or out of this account.

MEMO

DATE: January 31, 2006

Received the bank statement from Southern California Bank. The bank statement is dated January 31, 2006. Carmen Mendoza needs to reconcile the bank statement and print a Reconciliation Report for Roger Alan.

DO: Reconcile the bank statement for January

Select **Account Reconciliation** from the **General Ledger** button

You are presented with the Account Reconciliation window

Using the lookup feature, select 1100 Checking as the **Account to Reconcile:**

Note: The Checks and other Credits are listed in the bottom of the window

and the Deposits and other Debits are listed at the top of the window

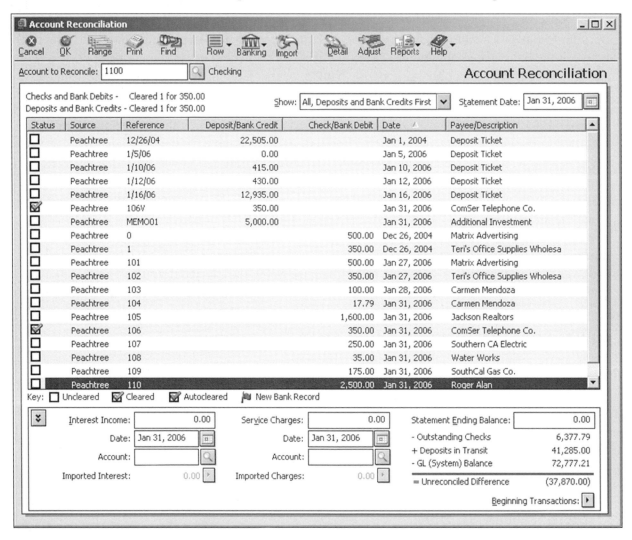

Peachtree has created a single list that contains all of the transactions that have decreased or increased the account. A scroll bar will appear to access any un-displayed items should the list be longer. The first column of the list contains a box that can be clicked with the mouse to indicate the item's presence on the bank statement. There is also a **Statement Ending Balance** field into which we will enter the ending balance from the bank statement as well as fields for interest earned and bank service charges.

ENTER BANK STATEMENT INFORMATION

Information appearing on the bank statement is entered into the Account Reconciliation window as the next step. This information includes bank service charges and interest earned as well as the ending statement balance. Remember, the dates shown for the checks on the bank statement are the dates the checks were processed by the bank, not the dates the checks were written. Deposits will generally appear with the same dates, as they are hand-carried to the bank on the day they are recorded.

SOUTHERN CALIFORNIA BANK
12345 West Colorado Avenue
Woodland Hills, CA 91377
(818) 555-3880

BANK STATEMENT FOR:

Comprehensive Computer Consulting
2895 West Avenue
Woodland Hills, CA 91367

Acct. # 123-456-7890			January 2006
Beginning Balance 1/1/06			$37,870.00
1/10/06 Deposit	415		38,285.00
1/12/06 Deposit	430		38,715.00
1/15/05 Deposit	3,835.00		42,550.00
1/16/06 Deposit	9,100.00		51,650.00
1/26/06 Check 101		500	51,150.00
1/26/06 Check 102		350	50,800.00
1/26/06 Check 103		100	50,700.00
1/31/06 Vehicle Loan Pmt.: $467.19 Principal, $255.22 Interest		722.41	49,977.59
1/31/06 Office Equip. Loan Pmt.: $53.39 Principal, $29.17 Interest		82.56	49,895.03
1/31/06 Service Chg.		8	49,887.03
1/31/06 Interest Earned	66.43		49,953.46
Ending Balance 1/31/06			**49,953.46**

DO: Continue to reconcile the bank statement above with the checking account
Note: The date next to the check on the bank statement is the date the check cleared the bank, not the date the check was written. If you are unable to complete the reconciliation in one session, you may leave the reconciliation and return to it later. If you do not return to complete the reconciliation you will not be reconciled

In the **Statement Ending Balance** field, enter, 49,953.46

Compare the bank statement with the Account Reconciliation window

Click in the Clear boxes of the items that appear on both statements using the scroll bars to display additional items

–   Check 106 and 106V will be marked automatically even though the two transactions do not appear on the bank statement since they represent a voided check. Leave them marked as cleared.

Look at the right side of the Account Reconciliation window

There is an **Unreconciled Difference** of (746.54)

–   This is caused by the items on the bank statement that did not appear in the Account Reconciliation window

ADJUSTING AND CORRECTING ENTRIES—BANK RECONCILIATION

As you complete the reconciliation, you may find errors that need to be corrected or transactions that need to be recorded. In our reconciliation, we note that the bank statement contains two electronic loan payments, a bank service charge and interest earned which do not appear in our Account Reconciliation window. Peachtree has included an Adjust icon at the top of the Account Reconciliation window that can be used to record additional transactions as needed. Errors that are noted should be corrected directly on the business form in which they occurred. That is to say, if a manually written check was entered into Peachtree incorrectly, we should bring up the receipt through the Receipts window and make the change directly on the business form. When we enter adjustments using the Adjust feature or make corrections on any business form that affects the cash account, these changes will appear in the Account Reconciliation window.

DO: Enter the electronic loan payments, the bank service charge and the interest earned shown on the bank statement.

Click on the **Adjust** icon at the top of the window

A blank General Journal is brought up.

Confirm the date 1/31/06

Enter RECON01 in the **Reference:** field

In the **GL Account** column, enter account 2210

In the **Description** field, enter Electronic Loan Payment for Vehicle

In the **Debit column**, enter 467.19

In the **GL Account** column, enter account 6220

In the **Debit column**, enter 255.22

In the **GL Account** column, enter account 1100

In the **Credit column**, enter 722.41

In the **GL Account** column, enter account 2220

In the **Description** field, enter Electronic Loan Payment for Equipment

In the **Debit column**, enter 53.39

In the **GL Account** column, enter account 6220

In the **Debit column**, enter 29.17

In the **GL Account** column, enter account 1100

In the **Credit column**, enter 82.56

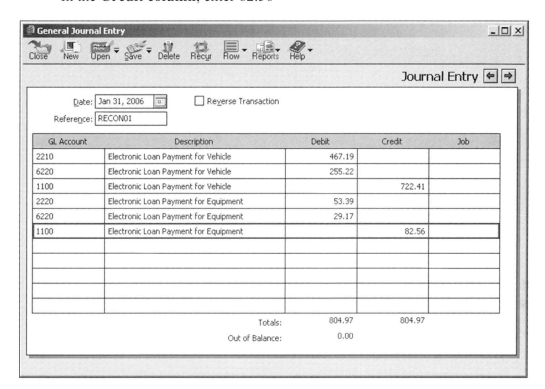

Click **Save** and then **Close**

In the field marked **Service Charges:**, enter 8.00 and press **Tab**

Enter or confirm **1/31/06** in the **Date** field. Press **Tab**

In the **Account** field, enter 6120

Click in the **Interest Income:** field and enter 66.43. Press **Tab**

Enter or confirm **1/31/06** in the **Date** field. Press **Tab**

In the **Account** field, enter 7010

Press **Enter**

Peachtree has added the General Journal items to the reconciliation item lists.

Using the Clear column, click on the items just added marked as RECON01. The interest and service charge are automatically cleared by Peachtree.

If all has been entered correctly, the **Unreconciled Difference** should be 0.00. If a balance remains, go back and check to make sure all of the cleared items have a checkmark in front of them. If they do and you are still out of balance, check each item carefully to make sure the amounts are identical. When you are finished, your Account Reconciliation window should look like the following:

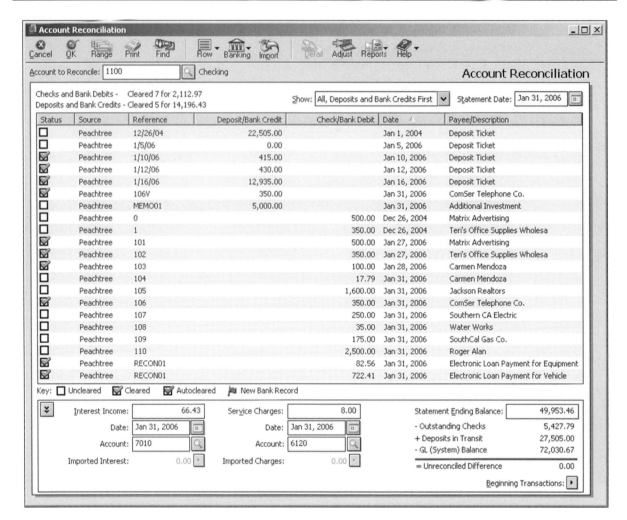

Note: The Account Reconciliation window contained several other features that we
did not use. Two of these are Range and Row. They are both designed for use
in high volume situations. Row allows us to clear all items or to unclear all
items. In some cases, where hundreds of transactions have cleared but only a
few items remain uncleared, it is best to clear all rows and then individually
unclear the items that have not cleared. Range enables us to clear a series of
consecutive checks. It will prompt us for a beginning and an ending check
number for the range to clear. Both Banking and Import allow for a variety of
Internet options to import statement and transaction detail electronically but
this is not available in the Educational Version. Print provides you with a
current in progress reconciliation report while the Report option provides a
quick link to all reports associated with this window.

Click **OK** to complete the reconciliation process

PRINT AN ACCOUNT RECONCILIATION REPORT

One of Peachtree's many reports is an Account Reconciliation Report. This report summarizes all of the activity from the account reconciliation process. It is a good idea to print this report and maintain a file copy of it every time you reconcile an account. One of the useful features of the report is to provide a list of uncleared items that will carry over into the next month.

DO: Print an Account Reconciliation Report
Click on the **All Accounts Reconciliation Reports** in the **General Ledger** button
Double click **Account Reconciliation** from the Select a Report window
Click on the **Print** icon at the top of the window

Comprehensive Computer Consulting-APS
Account Reconciliation
As of Jan 31, 2006
1100 - Checking
Bank Statement Date: January 31, 2006
Filter Criteria includes: Report is printed in Detail Format.

Beginning GL Balance				59,525.00
Add: Cash Receipts				13,780.00
Less: Cash Disbursements				(5,527.79)
Add (Less) Other				4,253.46
Ending GL Balance				72,030.67
Ending Bank Balance				49,953.46
Add back deposits in transit				
	Jan 5, 2006	1/5/06		
	Jan 1, 2004	12/26/04	22,505.00	
Total deposits in transit				22,505.00
(Less) outstanding checks				
	Dec 26, 2004	0	(500.00)	
	Dec 26, 2004	1	(350.00)	
	Jan 31, 2006	104	(17.79)	
	Jan 31, 2006	105	(1,600.00)	
	Jan 31, 2006	107	(250.00)	
	Jan 31, 2006	108	(35.00)	
	Jan 31, 2006	109	(175.00)	
	Jan 31, 2006	110	(2,500.00)	
Total outstanding checks				(5,427.79)
Add (Less) Other				
	Jan 31, 2006	MEMO01	5,000.00	
Total other				5,000.00
Unreconciled difference				
Ending GL Balance				72,030.67

Note: In the event the company has more than one account that has been reconciled, additional reports for these accounts can be obtained by clicking on the Options icon at the top of the window and using the drop down arrow to select a different account. Should you desire to see this feature, you can

open Bellwether Garden Supply and view this report from within the sample
company.
Click **Close**
Close the Select a Report window

VIEW THE ACCOUNT REGISTER FOR CHECKING

Once the bank reconciliation has been completed, it is wise to scroll through the checking
account register to view the effect of the reconciliation on the account. You will notice that the
adjusting items we entered as RECON1 have been added to the account as well as the service
charge and interest earned. All are listed as Other under Type. This report provides a
comprehensive summary of all activity into and out of the checking account. The report is
virtually identical to a General Ledger report except the Account Register maintains a running
balance after each transaction.

DO: View the Account Register for the Checking account
Click on the **All Accounts Reconciliation Reports** in the **General Ledger** button
Double click on Account Register

Comprehensive Computer Consulting-APS
Account Register
For the Period From Jan 1, 2006 to Jan 31, 2006
1100 - Checking

Filter Criteria includes: Report order is by Date.

Date	Trans No	Type	Trans Desc	Deposit Amt	Withdrawal Amt	Balance
			Beginning Balance			59,525.00
1/10/06	1/10/06	Deposit	Barnes, Rachel, CPA	415.00		59,940.00
1/12/06	1/12/06	Deposit	Barnes, Rachel, CPA	95.00		60,035.00
		Deposit	Andrews Research Corp.	335.00		60,370.00
1/16/06	1/16/05	Deposit	Mandano, Jose, Esq.	150.00		60,520.00
		Deposit	Walter, Yancheski, and Yi	3,685.00		64,205.00
1/16/06	1/16/06	Deposit	Andrews Research Corp.	815.00		65,020.00
		Deposit	Kati's Illustrations	2,000.00		67,020.00
		Deposit	Jensen Ranch	3,680.00		70,700.00
		Deposit	Matthews, Thomas, CPA	415.00		71,115.00
		Deposit	Victor Productions	2,190.00		73,305.00
1/27/06	101	Withdrawal	Matrix Advertising		500.00	72,805.00
1/27/06	102	Withdrawal	Teri's Office Supplies Wholes		350.00	72,455.00
1/28/06	103	Withdrawal	Carmen Mendoza		100.00	72,355.00
1/31/06	01/31/06	Other	Interest Income	66.43		72,421.43
1/31/06	01/31/06	Other	Service Charge		8.00	72,413.43
1/31/06	104	Withdrawal	Carmen Mendoza		17.79	72,395.64
1/31/06	105	Withdrawal	Jackson Realtors		1,600.00	70,795.64
1/31/06	106	Withdrawal	ComSer Telephone Co.		350.00	70,445.64
1/31/06	106V	Withdrawal	ComSer Telephone Co.		-350.00	70,795.64
1/31/06	107	Withdrawal	Southern CA Electric		250.00	70,545.64
1/31/06	108	Withdrawal	Water Works		35.00	70,510.64
1/31/06	109	Withdrawal	SouthCal Gas Co.		175.00	70,335.64
1/31/06	110	Withdrawal	Roger Alan		2,500.00	67,835.64
1/31/06	MEMO01	Other	Additional Investment	5,000.00		72,835.64
1/31/06	RECON01	Other	Electronic Loan Payment fo		722.41	72,113.23
1/31/06	RECON01	Other	Electronic Loan Payment fo		82.56	72,030.67
			Total	18,846.43	6,340.76	

Print and then click **Close**

Close the Select a Report window

VIEW THE GENERAL JOURNAL

After entering several transactions, it is helpful to view the General Journal. In the journal, all transactions entered through the General Journal Entry window or during the reconciliation process will appear in traditional debit/credit format.

DO: View the **General Journal** for January

Click **General Journal** from the Reports area of the **General Ledger** button

You are taken to a General Journal dialog box, accept the default setting, click **OK**

Note: You can easily identify the various types of entries by looking in the Reference column. If you recall, we used ADJ for our adjusting entries and RECON for our reconciliation entries. See how easily you can find these.

Comprehensive Computer Consulting-APS
General Journal
For the Period From Jan 1, 2006 to Jan 31, 2006

Filter Criteria includes: Report order is by Date. Report is printed with Accounts having Zero Amounts and with Truncated Transaction Descriptions and in Detail Format.

Date	Account ID	Reference	Trans Description	Debit Amt	Credit Amt
1/31/06	1100	01/31/06	Interest Income	66.43	
	7010		Interest Income		66.43
	1100		Service Charge		8.00
	6120		Service Charge	8.00	
1/31/06	6181	ADJ01	Adjusting Entry, Insurance	237.50	
	1340		Adjusting Entry, Insurance		237.50
1/31/06	6550	ADJ02	Adjusting Entry, Office Supplies	325.00	
	1310		Adjusting Entry, Office Supplies		325.00
1/31/06	6150	ADJ03	Record Depreciation for the Month	725.00	
	1505		Record Depreciation for the Month		583.00
	1515		Record Depreciation for the Month		142.00
1/31/06	1100	MEMO01	Additional Investment	5,000.00	
	3000		Additional Investment		5,000.00
1/31/06	1510	MEMO02	Additional Investment, Furniture	3,000.00	
	3000		Additional Investment, Furniture		3,000.00
1/31/06	2210	RECON01	Electronic Loan Payment for Vehicle	467.19	
	6220		Electronic Loan Payment for Vehicle	255.22	
	1100		Electronic Loan Payment for Vehicle		722.41
	2220		Electronic Loan Payment for Equipment	53.39	
	6220		Electronic Loan Payment for Equipment	29.17	
	1100		Electronic Loan Payment for Equipment		82.56
		Total		10,166.90	10,166.90

Print then click **Close**

THE WORKING TRIAL BALANCE

The account adjustments that were required for Comprehensive Computer Consulting were minor and were obvious. For a larger company or one whose books are more complicated, the adjustment process requires more analysis. To assist the accountant in performing this analysis, Peachtree® Complete Accounting 2006 can generate a Working Trial Balance. This Trial Balance is similar to a regular Trial Balance except space is provided to enter the adjustments that will be required.

MEMO

DATE: January 31, 2006

Because it is the end of the month, prepare a Working Trial Balance.

DO: Prepare a Working Trial Balance
Click **All General Ledger Reports** from the Reports area of the **General Ledger** button
Double click on Working Trial Balance

	Comprehensive Computer Consulting-APS						
	Working Trial Balance						
	As of Jan 31, 2006						
Filter Criteria includes: Report order is by ID. Report is printed with Accounts having Zero Amounts and in Detail Format.							
Account ID **Account Description**	**Last FYE Bal**	**Current Bal**	**Debit Adj**	**Credit Adj**	**End Bal**	**Reference**	
1100 Checking	59,525.00	72,030.67	_____	_____	_____	_____	
1150 Petty Cash	0.00	100.00	_____	_____	_____	_____	
1200 Accounts Receivable	22,505.00	17,650.00	_____	_____	_____	_____	
1310 Office Supplies	500.00	628.57	_____	_____	_____	_____	
1340 Prepaid Insurance	0.00	2,612.50	_____	_____	_____	_____	
1400 Employee Advances	0.00	0.00	_____	_____	_____	_____	
1500 Business Vehicles	49,000.00	49,000.00	_____	_____	_____	_____	
1505 Accum Depr Business Vehicles	0.00	-583.00	_____	_____	_____	_____	

Note: The accountant would use the Working Trial Balance to reflect the current balance in each account in the General Ledger. Space is provided to show debit and/or credit adjustments as well as an ending balance. When the adjusting process is completed, the Working Trial Balance with its written adjustments, can be entered into Peachtree® Complete Accounting 2006 to complete the adjusting process.
Click **Print** and then **Close**
Close the Select a Report window

PRINT THE GENERAL LEDGER TRIAL BALANCE

The Trial Balance, which looks most like that prepared in a manual accounting system, is the General Ledger Trial Balance. It would be prepared after the adjusting entries have been made. It can be used as a final check to insure that all the accounts reflect the desired balances prior to printing the financial statements. If it is determined that an account requires additional adjusting, entries can be made and another Trial Balance can be quickly and easily printed.

 DO: Print the General Ledger Trial Balance
Click **All General Ledger Reports** in the **General Ledger** button
Double click on General Ledger Trial Balance

	Comprehensive Computer Consulting-APS		
	General Ledger Trial Balance		
	As of Jan 31, 2006		
Filter Criteria includes: Report order is by ID. Report is printed in Detail Format.			
Account ID	**Account Description**	**Debit Amt**	**Credit Amt**
1100	Checking	72,030.67	
1150	Petty Cash	100.00	
1200	Accounts Receivable	17,650.00	
1310	Office Supplies	628.57	
1340	Prepaid Insurance	2,612.50	
1500	Business Vehicles	49,000.00	
1505	Accum Depr Business Vehicles		583.00
1510	Office Equipment	11,050.00	
1515	Accum Depr Office Equipment		142.00
2000	Accounts Payable		4,254.00
2210	Business Vehicles Loan		34,532.81
2220	Office Equipment Loan		3,946.61
3000	Roger Alan, Capital		86,075.00
3020	Roger Alan, Drawing	2,500.00	
3100	Retained Earnings		21,655.00
4010	Technical Support Income		900.00
4020	Training Income		7,850.00
4060	Installation Income		175.00
6100	Advertising Expense	260.00	
6110	Business Vehicles Expense	588.88	
6120	Bank Service Charges	8.00	
6150	Depreciation Expense	725.00	
6160	Dues and Subscriptions	79.00	
6170	Equipment Rental	20.00	
6181	Business Vehicles Insurance	237.50	
6220	Interest on Loans	284.39	
6250	Postage and Delivery Expense	0.34	
6290	Rent Expense	1,600.00	
6391	Electricity Expense	250.00	
6392	Heating Expense--Gas	175.00	
6394	Water Expense	35.00	
6550	Office Supplies Expense	345.00	
7010	Interest Income		66.43
	Total:	160,179.85	160,179.85

Click **Print**
Close the report and the Select a Report window

PREPARE AND PRINT CASH FLOW FORECAST

In planning for the cash needs of a business, Peachtree® Complete Accounting 2006 can prepare a Cash Flow Forecast. This report is useful when projecting cash requirements. It is important to know if your company will have enough cash on hand to meet its obligations. A company with too little cash on hand may have to borrow money to pay its bills, while a company with excess cash may miss out on investment opportunities or the opportunity to distribute profits to the owner(s). Peachtree® Complete Accounting 2006 Cash Flow Forecast does not analyze investments or loans. It simply projects the amount you will be receiving if all those who owe you money pay on time and the amounts you will be spending to pay your accounts payable on time.

MEMO

DATE: January 31, 2006

Prepare Cash Flow Forecast for February 2006.

 DO: Prepare Cash Flow Forecast for February 2006
Click **Cash Manager** from the **Analysis** button
You are presented with a numeric forecast.

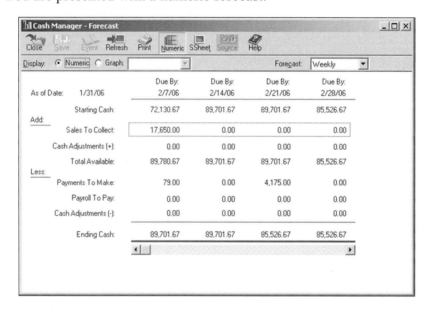

Note: The drop down arrow in the upper right corner of the window allows us to select the frequency for forecast of the report. We can forecast cash on a weekly, biweekly or monthly basis. Your selection should reflect weekly.

Notice how Peachtree shows us both the projected cash receipts and projected cash payments on a week-by-week basis. Peachtree® Complete Accounting 2006 allows us to forecast as far as a year into the future. Realistically, only the next few weeks will contain accurate information. This is sufficient for a manager to determine whether the company will encounter a deficit in the cash balance.

Click on Graph radio button to obtain a graphical representation

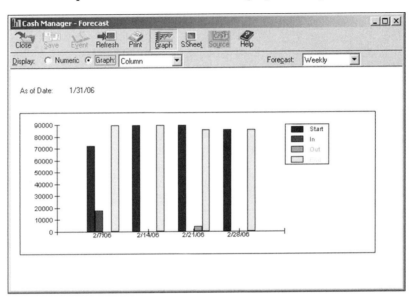

Click on **Numeric** to return to original report
Click **Print**
Click **Close**

STATEMENT OF CASH FLOW

Another report that details the amount of cash flow in a business is the Statement of Cash Flows. Peachtree calls this a Standard Cash Flow. This report organizes information regarding cash in three areas of activities: Operating Activities, Investing Activities, and Financing Activities. The report also explains the changes in the cash balance during the period.

MEMO
DATE: January 31, 2006

Prepare End of Month Financial Statements for January, 2006.

 DO: Prepare Standard Cash Flow for January

Click **All Financial Statements** from the Reports area of the **General Ledger**
    button
Double click on <Standard> Cash Flow
You are presented with a Cash Flow Options dialog box

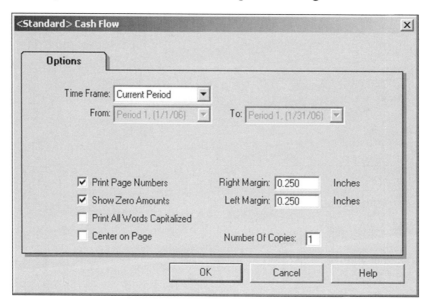

Accept the defaults and click **OK**
Click **Print**
Click **Close**

PRINT STANDARD INCOME STATEMENT

Because all revenues and expenses have been recorded, and adjustments have been made for the
period, an Income Statement can be prepared. This statement is also known as a Profit and Loss
Statement. Peachtree® Complete Accounting 2006 can generate a current period income
statement or show a 2-year comparison for analysis purposes. We will print the former.

 DO: Print a **Standard Income Statement**
        All Financial Statements from the Reports area of the **General Ledger** button
        Double click on <Standard> Income Statement
        You are presented with a <Standard> Income Statement dialog box

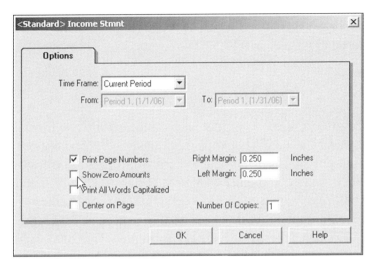

Deselect **Show Zero Amounts** and click **OK**
Click **Print** and **Close**

PRINT STANDARD BALANCE SHEET

The Balance Sheet proves the fundamental accounting equation: Assets = Liabilities + Owner's Equity. When all transactions and adjustments for the period have been recorded, a balance sheet should be prepared.

DO: Print a <Standard> Balance Sheet
If necessary, click **All Financial Statements** from the Reports area of the **General Ledger** button
Double click on <Standard> Balance Sheet
You are presented with a <Standard> Balance Sheet Options dialog box
Accept the defaults and click **OK**

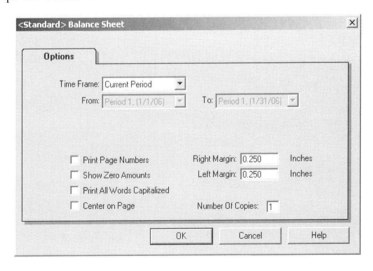

Click **Print**
Close the report and the Select a Report window

EXPORTING REPORTS TO EXCEL

Many of the reports prepared in Peachtree® Complete Accounting 2006 can be exported to Microsoft® Excel. This allows you to take advantage of extensive filtering options available in Excel, hide detail for some but not all groups of data, combine information from two different reports, change titles of columns, add comments, change the order of columns, and to experiment with "what if" scenarios. Additionally, you can use Excel's charting capabilities to create custom charts and graphs of your accounting data. In order to use this feature of Peachtree® Complete Accounting 2006 you must also have Microsoft Excel 97 or higher. The 2006 version has also added a utility to convert to PDF (Portable Document Format). It is the icon next to the Excel icon and requires only a filename. Since a reader is required to use this feature, it is not included in the tutorial.

DO: Optional Exercise: Export a report from Peachtree® Complete Accounting 2006 to Excel

Click **General Ledger Reports** from the **General Ledger** button
Double click General Ledger Trial Balance
Click on the **Excel** icon at the top of the screen
You are presented with a Copy Report to Excel dialog box
Peachtree will default to creating a new workbook but we could just as easily add this as a new sheet in an existing workbook by selecting the Add a new worksheet to an existing Microsoft Excel workbook option.

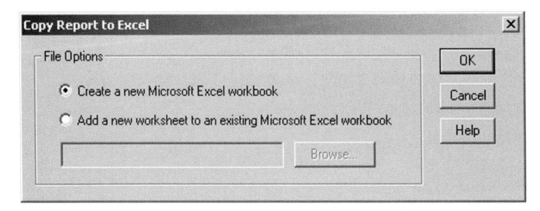

Click **OK** to accept defaults

	A	B	C	D
1	Account ID	Account Description	Debit Amt	Credit Amt
2	1100	Checking	72,030.67	
3	1150	Petty Cash	100.00	
4	1200	Accounts Receivable	17,650.00	
5	1310	Office Supplies	628.57	
6	1340	Prepaid Insurance	2,612.50	
7	1500	Business Vehicles	49,000.00	
8	1505	Accum Depr Business Vehicles		583.00
9	1510	Office Equipment	11,050.00	
10	1515	Accum Depr Office Equipment		142.00
11	2000	Accounts Payable		4,254.00
12	2210	Business Vehicles Loan		34,532.81
13	2220	Office Equipment Loan		3,946.61
14	3000	Roger Alan, Capital		86,075.00
15	3020	Roger Alan, Drawing	2,500.00	
16	3100	Retained Earnings		21,655.00
17	4010	Technical Support Income		900.00
18	4020	Training Income		7,850.00
19	4060	Installation Income		175.00
20	6100	Advertising Expense	260.00	
21	6110	Business Vehicles Expense	588.88	
22	6120	Bank Service Charges	8.00	
23	6150	Depreciation Expense	725.00	
24	6160	Dues and Subscriptions	79.00	
25	6170	Equipment Rental	20.00	
26	6181	Business Vehicles Insurance	237.50	
27	6220	Interest on Loans	284.39	
28	6250	Postage and Delivery Expense	0.34	
29	6290	Rent Expense	1,600.00	
30	6391	Electricity Expense	250.00	
31	6392	Heating Expense--Gas	175.00	
32	6394	Water Expense	35.00	
33	6550	Office Supplies Expense	345.00	
34	7010	Interest Income		66.43
35				
36		Total:	160,179.85	160,179.85

Click **Print**

Comprehensive Computer Consulting-APS
General Ledger Trial Balance
As of Jan 31, 2006

Account ID	Account Description	Debit Amt	Credit Amt
1100	Checking	72,030.67	
1150	Petty Cash	100.00	
1200	Accounts Receivable	17,650.00	
1310	Office Supplies	628.57	
1340	Prepaid Insurance	2,612.50	
1500	Business Vehicles	49,000.00	
1505	Accum Depr Business Vehicles		583.00
1510	Office Equipment	11,050.00	
1515	Accum Depr Office Equipment		142.00
2000	Accounts Payable		4,254.00
2210	Business Vehicles Loan		34,532.81
2220	Office Equipment Loan		3,946.61
3000	Roger Alan, Capital		86,075.00
3020	Roger Alan, Drawing	2,500.00	
3100	Retained Earnings		21,655.00
4010	Technical Support Income		900.00
4020	Training Income		7,850.00
4060	Installation Income		175.00
6100	Advertising Expense	260.00	
6110	Business Vehicles Expense	588.88	
6120	Bank Service Charges	8.00	
6150	Depreciation Expense	725.00	
6160	Dues and Subscriptions	79.00	
6170	Equipment Rental	20.00	
6181	Business Vehicles Insurance	237.50	
6220	Interest on Loans	284.39	
6250	Postage and Delivery Expense	0.34	
6290	Rent Expense	1,600.00	
6391	Electricity Expense	250.00	
6392	Heating Expense--Gas	175.00	
6394	Water Expense	35.00	
6550	Office Supplies Expense	345.00	
7010	Interest Income		66.43
	Total:	160,179.85	160,179.85

Note: Peachtree® Complete Accounting 2006 created a formal header as well as the print setting needed to print this report. Any changes that may be needed can be made directly in the spreadsheet or in the header for the spreadsheet prior to printing. In the illustration above, a default landscape orientation was changed to portrait.

Click **Close** button in the top right corner of the Excel title bar to close Excel

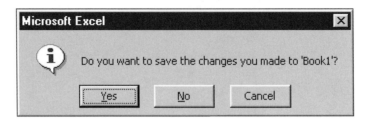

Click **No** to close the workbook without saving
Close the report and the Select a Report window

END-OF-PERIOD BACKUP

Once all end-of-period procedures have been completed, a regular backup and a second backup of the company data should be made and filed as an archive copy. Preferably this copy will be located someplace other than on the business premises. The archive or file copy is set aside in case of emergency or in case damage occurs to the original and current backup copies of the company data. There are a number of Internet companies that will provide Internet site-based storage for data backups as well.

DO: Back up company data and prepare an archive copy of the company data
Insert your backup disk in the **A:** drive
Click **File** on the menu bar, click **Back Up**
In the Back Up Company dialog box, select **Include company name in the
backup file name** by clicking in the blank field to the left of it
Using the **Save in:** drop down arrow, select **A:** and Click **Save**
Click **OK**
Label this disk **Archive, 1-31-2006**

PASSWORDS

Not every employee of a business should have access to all the financial records for the company. In some companies, only the owner will have complete access. In others, one or two key employees will have full access while other employees are provided limited access based on the jobs they perform. Passwords are secret words used to control access to data. Peachtree® Complete Accounting 2006 has several options available when assigning passwords.

In order to assign any passwords at all, you must have an administrator. The administrator has unrestricted access to all Peachtree® Complete Accounting 2006 functions and sets up users and user passwords, and assigns areas of transaction access for each user. Areas of access can be limited to transaction entry for certain types of transactions or a user may have unrestricted access into all areas of Peachtree® Complete Accounting 2006 and company data.

A password should be kept secret at all times. It should be something that is easy for the individual to remember, yet difficult for someone else to guess. Birthdays, names, initials, and similar devices are not good passwords because the information is too readily available. Never write down your password where it can be easily found or seen by someone else.

ADVANCE TO THE NEXT PERIOD

In order for Peachtree® Complete Accounting 2006 to produce interim (monthly) financial statements, it is necessary to inform Peachtree that we are finished with a given period (month) and are ready to begin recording data for the next period. We accomplish this by advancing to the next accounting period.

As part of this process, we will be asked to generate a number of end-of-period reports, primarily the journals that recorded the transactions that occurred during the month. It is always wise to have a printed or "hard copy" of the data. This copy should be kept on file as an additional backup to the data stored on your disk. If your disk becomes damaged, you will still have the paper copy of your transactions available for re-entry into the system and/or research.

MEMO

DATE: January 31, 2006

Now that the closing transactions have been performed, advance the system to period - 02 Feb 1, 2006 - Feb 28, 2006 and print the end-of-period reports.

  DO: Advance the period and print end-of-period reports
Click on **Change Accounting Period** from the **General Ledger** button
Click on **02 Feb 1, 2006 - Feb 28, 2006**

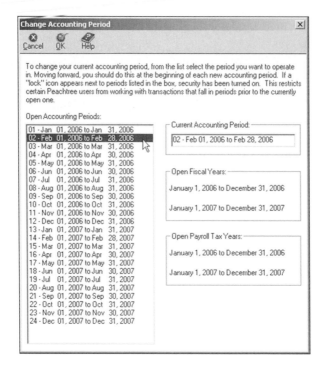

Click **OK**

You are presented with a dialog box asking whether you desire to print end-of-
period reports. If these reports had already been printed as part of your end-
of-period routine, you would answer no. Since we have not printed these
reports, we will do so at this time.

Click **Yes**

You are presented with a Print Reports dialog box. This window lists the reports
that will be printed by default. If any of these reports have already been
printed, they can be deselected at this time to prevent reprinting them.
Circumstances can cause the list to vary.

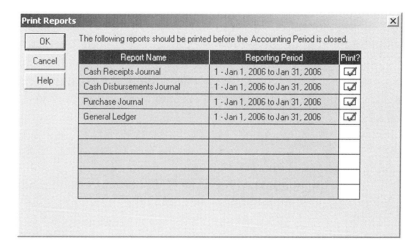

Click **OK**

Note: Peachtree® Complete Accounting 2006 will now print the reports that were selected in the Print Report dialog box. When finished, you are presented with the option to run an internal audit:

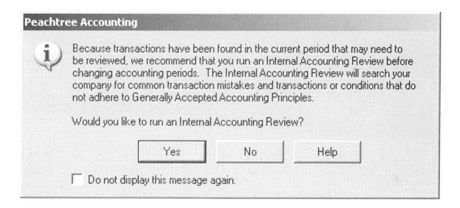

We will answer no since this is an advanced topic.

Note in the lower left-hand corner of your screen, that the system has been moved to Period 2.

You are now ready to begin recording transactions for the month of February.

ACCESS TRANSACTION FOR PREVIOUS PERIOD

Even though the month of January has been "closed," transactions still appear in the account ledgers, the journals, and so on. There will be times when we will need to access an invoice or a cash receipt or some other transaction from a prior accounting period. Peachtree® Complete

Accounting 2006 stores this data and keeps it available as we move from period to period. Once a transaction has been completed, the detail will no longer show up in our current reports; however, we can use the Options feature to change the date(s) of the report so that they will reflect the older transactions as well. What this means is that if we wish to see a cash receipt from last month, say the cash receipt from Rachel Barnes, we are still able to even though January has been closed.

 DO: Access cash receipt from prior period
Click **Cash Receipts Journal** from the Reports section of the **Sales** button
You are presented with an Options window, click **OK**
Note: The report you are presented is for the current period, 1 Feb - 29 Feb. Since you have collected no cash in February, the report will show no data.

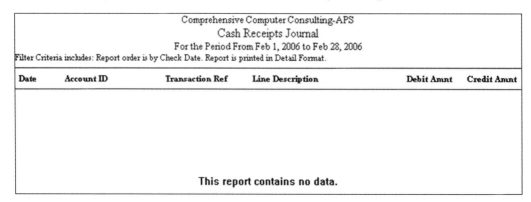

Comprehensive Computer Consulting-APS
Cash Receipts Journal
For the Period From Feb 1, 2006 to Feb 28, 2006
Filter Criteria includes: Report order is by Check Date. Report is printed in Detail Format.

Date	Account ID	Transaction Ref	Line Description	Debit Amnt	Credit Amnt

This report contains no data.

Click on the **Options** icon at the top of the window
In order to view the Cash Receipts from January, we will need to change the date so that our report will include the cash receipts from last month. There are a number of options to do this. For example, using the drop down arrow from the **Date:** field, click **This Year**

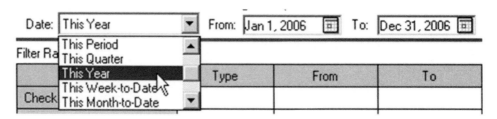

Click **OK**
Position the cursor over one of the lines for Rachel Barnes cash receipt for 1/10/06. It will turn into a magnifying glass.

Comprehensive Computer Consulting-APS
Cash Receipts Journal
For the Period From Jan 1, 2006 to Dec 31, 2006
Filter Criteria includes: Report order is by Check Date. Report is printed in Detail Format.

Date	Account ID	Transaction Ref	Line Description	Debit Amnt	Credit Amnt
1/5/06	1200	103	Invoice: 103		300.00
	1200		Invoice: 103V	300.00	
	1100		Jung, Yu		
1/10/06	4020	3278 (Z)	Initial Hour of On-Site Training		95.00
	4020		Additional Hours of On-Site Training		320.00
	1100		Barnes, Rachel, CPA	415.00	

Double click to view the original cash receipt.

The original cash receipt is brought up on screen for viewing. All of the details can be examined including the deposit ticket ID, the check number and which General Ledger accounts were used in the transaction in the prior period.

Close the Receipts window

Close the Cash Receipts Journal

EDIT TRANSACTION FROM PREVIOUS PERIOD

If it is determined that an error was made in a previous period, Peachtree® Complete Accounting 2006 does allow a correction to be made. Be aware though, that it is not advisable to change transactions from prior accounting periods. Doing so will alter the financial statements, journals, ledger reports and other reports printed at the end of the accounting period. In most businesses, the accounting manager will decide when an error is significant enough to warrant making the change in the accounting period in which the error took place. It is also important to note that, while Peachtree® Complete Accounting 2006 allows these changes to be made easily, many larger programs do not allow such changes without significant system administrator involvement. Before it will record any changes for previous periods, Peachtree® Complete Accounting 2006 requires that you confirm the change in a dialog box warning you that the change involves a transaction date that is outside the current period for the company. As an alternative to changing a specific transaction, an error can also be corrected by changing the account that contains the error and using a capital account like Retained Earnings as the offsetting account. Since any change to the income or loss would have been closed to Capital anyway, this allows a change to be made without affecting the Income Statement.

MEMO

DATE: February 1, 2006

After reviewing the journal and reports printed at the end of January, Roger Alan finds that the amount of supplies used was $350, not $325. Make the correction to the adjusting entry of January 31.

DO: Change the Office Supplies adjusting entry to $350 from $325
          Click **General Journal** from the Reports area of the **General Ledger** button
          Change the **Date:** to **This Year**
          Click **OK**
          Find the entry for adjusting Office Supplies (ADJ02 in the Reference column)
          Double click on any line in this entry
          You are returned to the original General Journal entry
          Highlight the Amount 325.00 and change to 350.00 in both the **Debit** and **Credit**
              columns
          Click **Save**
          You are presented with a confirmation window

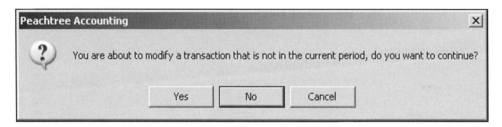

          Click **Yes**
          Close the General Journal Entry window
          Close the General Journal report window

As a result of the change we just made, we have altered all of our financial statements and most other reports. To illustrate this, let us take a look at an Income Statement created after the change.

DO: Print the Income Statement
          Click **Print Financial Statements** from the Reports area of the **General Ledger**
              button
          Double click <Standard> Income Stmnt
          Deselect **Show Zero Amounts**
          Change the **Time Frame** to Current 3 Periods
          Click **OK**

```
                    Comprehensive Computer Consulting-APS
                              Income Statement
                    For the Two Months Ending February 28, 2006

                              Current Month                Year to Date

Revenues
Technical Support Income      $      900.00    10.01   $       900.00    10.01
Training Income                    7,850.00    87.31        7,850.00    87.31
Installation Income                  175.00     1.95          175.00     1.95
Interest Income                       66.43     0.74           66.43     0.74

Total Revenues                     8,991.43   100.00        8,991.43   100.00


Cost of Sales

Total Cost of Sales                    0.00     0.00            0.00     0.00

Gross Profit                       8,991.43   100.00        8,991.43   100.00

Expenses
Advertising Expense                  260.00     2.89          260.00     2.89
Business Vehicles Expense            588.88     6.55          588.88     6.55
Bank Service Charges                   8.00     0.09            8.00     0.09
Depreciation Expense                 725.00     8.06          725.00     8.06
Dues and Subscriptions                79.00     0.88           79.00     0.88
Equipment Rental                      20.00     0.22           20.00     0.22
Business Vehicles Insurance          237.50     2.64          237.50     2.64
Interest on Loans                    284.39     3.16          284.39     3.16
Postage and Delivery Expense           0.34     0.00            0.34     0.00
Rent Expense                       1,600.00    17.79        1,600.00    17.79
Electricity Expense                  250.00     2.78          250.00     2.78
Heating Expense--Gas                 175.00     1.95          175.00     1.95
Water Expense                         35.00     0.39           35.00     0.39
Office Supplies Expense              370.00     4.12          370.00     4.12

Total Expenses                     4,633.11    51.53        4,633.11    51.53

Net Income                    $    4,358.32    48.47   $     4,358.32    48.47
```

Note: If you compare this Income Statement with the one printed at the end of the period, you will note that the Net Income has changed from $4,383.32 to $4,358.32, a difference of $25.00. If we were to look at the Balance Sheet, it would also show that assets and equity had changed by $25.00. In a real working situation, you would have been required to reprint all of the end-of-period reports.

Click **Print**

Close the Income Statement

Close the Select a Report window

POST-CLOSING TRIAL BALANCE

In a manual accounting system a Post-Closing Trial Balance is created to verify the closing process and to prove the equality of debits and credits. Since Peachtree® Complete Accounting 2006 does not close the expense and revenue accounts after completing an end-of-month closing, and will not allow the books to become out of balance, there is no need for a Post-Closing Trial Balance. Remember though, that you can generate a Trial Balance at any time you desire one.

END-OF-CHAPTER BACKUP AND CLOSE COMPANY

As in previous chapters, you should back up your company and close the company.

 DO: Follow instructions previously provided to back up company files, close CCC

SUMMARY

In this chapter, end-of-period adjustments were made, the bank reconciliation was performed, backup and archive disks were prepared, and the period was advanced. Account name changes were made, accounts were deleted and others were made inactive. Even though Peachtree® Complete Accounting 2006 focuses on entering transactions on business forms, this chapter presented transaction entry directly into the General Journal. Owner withdrawals and additional owner investments were made. Many of the different report options available in Peachtree® Complete Accounting 2006 were examined, and the exporting of reports to Excel was explored. A variety of reports were printed. Correction of errors was explored, and changes to transactions in "closed" periods were made. The process and impact of advancing the period was examined.

END-OF-CHAPTER QUESTIONS

TRUE/FALSE

ANSWER THE FOLLOWING QUESTIONS IN THE SPACE PROVIDED BEFORE THE QUESTION NUMBER.

_____ 1. Accrual-basis accounting matches the income from the period and the expenses for the period in order to determine the net income or net loss for the period.

_____ 2. In Peachtree® Complete Accounting 2006, the General Journal is a book of entry.

_____ 3. An account may be deleted at any time.

_____ 4. In a sole proprietorship, an owner's name must be added to the Vendor List for recording withdrawals.

_____ 5. Additional investments made by an owner may be cash or non-cash items.

_____ 6. Peachtree® Complete Accounting 2006 keeps every transaction recorded in a journal.

_____ 7. Peachtree® Complete Accounting 2006 keeps the Bank Reconciliation report in memory.

_____ 8. Once an account has been used in a transaction, no changes may be made to the account name.

_____ 9. Anything identified as a service charge or as interest earned during the bank reconciliation process must be entered manually in the General Journal when the reconciliation is complete.

_____ 10. A Balance Sheet is prepared to prove the equality of debits and credits.

MULTIPLE CHOICE

WRITE THE LETTER OF THE CORRECT ANSWER IN THE SPACE PROVIDED BEFORE THE QUESTION NUMBER.

_____ 1. To close a period, you must have a(n) ___.
A. transaction password
B. administrator
C. entry password
D. none of the above

_____ 2. When an account name such as "cars" is changed to "automobiles," all related accounts such as car "depreciation" ___.
A. should to be changed to "automobile depreciation"
B. are automatically changed to "automobile depreciation"
C. cannot be changed
D. must be deleted and re-entered

_____ 3. The report that proves Assets = Liabilities + Owner's Equity is the ___.
A. Trial Balance
B. Income Statement
C. Profit and Loss Statement
D. Balance Sheet

_____ 4. When the period is advanced, the expense and revenue accounts are closed and their balances are transferred to ____.
A. Retained Earnings
B. Net Income
C. both Net Income and Retained Earnings
D. none of the above because they are not closed

_____ 5. An Income Statement can be shown for ___ .
A. the current month
B. the current quarter
C. year-to-date
D. all of the above

_____ 6. A bank statement may ___.
A. show service charges or interest not yet recorded
B. be missing deposits in transit or outstanding checks
C. both of the above
D. none of the above

_____ 7. The General Journal report shows ___.
  A. all transactions no matter where they were recorded
  B. only those transactions recorded in the General Journal
  C. only transactions recorded in the Receipts window
  D. only those transactions that have been edited

_____ 8. A backup disk ___.
  A. is a duplicate of the company data
  B. is prepared in case of emergencies or errors on current disks
  C. must be restored before information can be used
  D. all of the above

_____ 9. An error known as a transposition can be found by ___ during reconciliation.
  A. dividing the amount out of balance by 9
  B. dividing the amount out of balance by 2
  C. multiplying the difference by 9, then dividing by 2
  D. dividing the amount out of balance by 5

_____ 10. The Balance Sheet report shows _____.
  A. the revenues and expenses for the company
  B. adherence to the accounting equation
  C. the equality of the debits and credits
  D. all of the above

FILL-IN

IN THE SPACE PROVIDED, WRITE THE ANSWER THAT MOST APPROPRIATELY COMPLETES THE SENTENCE.

1. Bank reconciliations should be performed on a(n) _____ basis.

2. Export of report data between Peachtree® Complete Accounting 2006 and _____ can be made in order to perform "what if" scenarios and create presentation graphics.

3. An owner's paycheck is considered a(n) _____.

4. The two methods of accounting are _____ basis and _____ basis.

5. The _____ shows both the cash we expect to receive and the cash we must pay out in future periods.

SHORT ESSAY

Describe the Bank Reconciliation process as performed in Peachtree® Complete Accounting 2006.

_____

_____

_____

_____

_____

_____

_____

_____

_____

_____

_____

_____

_____

_____

_____

_____

NAME _____

TRANSMITTAL

CHAPTER 4: COMPREHENSIVE COMPUTER CONSULTING

Attach the following documents and reports:

- ☐   Check No. 110: Roger Alan
- ☐   Account Reconciliation as of January 31, 2006
- ☐   Account Register from January 1- January 31, 2006
- ☐   General Journal from January 1- January 31, 2006
- ☐   Working Trial Balance as of January 31, 2006
- ☐   General Ledger Trial Balance as of January 31, 2006
- ☐   Weekly Cash Flow Forecast as of 1/31/06
- ☐   Standard Cash Flow, January 2006
- ☐   Standard Income Statement, January 2006
- ☐   Standard Balance Sheet, January 31, 2006
- ☐   General Ledger Trial Balance from Excel (optional)
- ☐   Cash Receipts Journal, January 1 - January 31, 2006
- ☐   Cash Disbursements Journal, January 1 - January 31, 2006
- ☐   Purchases Journal from January 1- January 31, 2006
- ☐   General Ledger, January 1 - January 31, 2006
- ☐   Standard Income Statement, Two Months Ending February 28, 2006

END-OF-CHAPTER PROBLEM

SunCare Lawn and Pool Services

Chapter 4 continues with the end-of-period adjustments, bank reconciliation, archive disks, and advancing the period for SunCare Lawn and Pool Services. The company does use a certified public accountant for guidance and assistance with appropriate accounting procedures. The CPA has provided information for Sylvia to use for her adjusting entries.

Instructions

Continue to use the data file for SunCare. Open the company. Record the adjustments and other transactions using the procedures you were taught in the chapter. Review bank reconciliation procedures carefully prior to completing the reconciliation at month's end. Always read the transaction carefully and confirm the accounts selected by Peachtree when recording transactions. Print the reports and journals as indicated.

Record Transactions

January 31—Enter the following:

Change the names of the following accounts:
Automobile Expense to Business Trucks Expense
Auto Insurance Expense to Business Trucks Insurance

Make the following accounts inactive:
Recruiting Expense
Travel & Entertainment Expense

Delete the following accounts:
Amortization Expenses
Contributions
Mortgage Interest Expense
Property Tax Expense

Print the Chart of Accounts by clicking **All General Ledger Reports** from the **General Ledger** button and double clicking on Chart of Accounts

January 31—Enter the following using ADJ 01 for the Reference:

Enter adjusting entries in the General Journal for:
    Office Supplies Used, $185. Description: Office Supplies Used for January
    Depreciation for the month:
        Business Trucks, $950
        Equipment, $206.25

Description for all accounts used: Depreciation Expense for January

Record the business trucks insurance expense for the month, $250. Description: Insurance Expense for January. Insurance was prepaid.

Enter transactions for Owner's Equity using Peachtree's Write Checks feature:

The owner, George Gordon withdraws $1,000. Description: Withdrawal for January (Print the check, Check No. 109)

Additional non-cash investment by owner consisting of $1,500 worth of lawn equipment is made. Description: Additional Investment: Equipment. Use MEMO 01 for the Reference.

Prepare Bank Reconciliation and Enter Adjustments for the Reconciliation using RECON 01 for the Reference:

– Be sure to enter adjustments as in the chapter.

SANTA BARBARA COASTAL BANK
1234 Coast Highway
Santa Barbara, CA 93100
(805) 555-9310
BANK STATEMENT FOR:

SunCare Lawn and Pool Services
18527 State Street
Santa Barbara, CA 93103

Acct. # 987-352-9152			January 2006
Beginning Balance 1/1/06			$23,850.00
1/1/05 Deposit	1,450.00		25,300.00
1/3/06 Deposit	650.00		25,950.00
1/14/06 Deposit	525.00		26,475.00
1/18/06 Check 101		50.00	26,425.00
1/18/06 Check 102		375.00	26,050.00
1/18/06 Check 103		669.00	25,381.00
1/18/06 Check 104		485.00	24,896.00
1/31/06 Service Chg.		10.00	24,886.00
1/31/06 Business Trucks Loan Pmt: 160.64 Interest, 795.54 Principal		956.18	23,929.82
1/31/06 Interest Earned	59.63		23,989.45
Ending Balance 1/31/06			23,989.45

Print: Account Reconciliation Report
         General Ledger Trial Balance
         Standard Income Statement
         Standard Cash Flows
         Standard Balance Sheet

Advance the period:
         Advance to Period 02 - Feb 01, 2006 - Feb 28, 2006 printing the General Journal, Cash
         Receipts Journal, Cash Disbursements Journal, and General Ledger reports. Do not run
         the internal audit.

Edit a Transaction from a closed period:
         Discovered an error in the amount of office supplies used. The amount used should be
         $175, not $185.

February 1, 2006—Print the following reports:

         General Journal changing the Date field to This Year
         General Ledger Trial Balance changing the As of Date to Period 1
         Cash Manager Forecast
         Standard Cash Flows changing the Time Frame to Current 3 Periods
         Corrected Standard Income Statement changing the Time Frame to Current 3 Periods
         Corrected Standard Balance Sheet changing the Time Frame to Current 3 Periods

NAME _____

TRANSMITTAL

CHAPTER 4: SUNCARE LAWN AND POOL SERVICES

Attach the following documents and reports:

☐ Chart of Accounts, January 31, 2006
☐ Check No. 109: George Gordon
☐ Account Reconciliation Report as of January 31, 2006
☐ General Ledger Trial Balance as of January 31, 2006
☐ Standard Income Statement for month ended January 31, 2006
☐ Standard Cash Flow for month ended January 31, 2006
☐ Standard Balance Sheet, January 31, 2006
☐ General Journal, January 1 - January 31, 2006
☐ Cash Receipts Journal, January 1 - January 31, 2006
☐ Cash Disbursements Journal, January 1 - January 31, 2006
☐ General Ledger, January 1 - January 31, 2006
☐ General Journal from January 1, 2006 to December 31, 2006
☐ General Ledger Trial Balance as of January 31, 2006
☐ Cash Manager Forecast, 2/1/06
☐ Standard Cash Flow, for two months ended February 28, 2006
☐ Income Statement for two months ended February 28, 2006
☐ Balance Sheet as of February 28, 2006

END OF SECTION 1— Handy Helpers Practice Set: Service Business

The following is a comprehensive practice set combining all the elements of Peachtree® Complete Accounting 2006 studied in the first section of the text. In this practice set, you will keep the books for a company for one month. Entries will be made to record invoices, receipt of payments on invoices, cash sales, receipt and payment of bills, and credit memos for invoices and bills. Account names will be added, changed, deleted, and made inactive. Customer and vendor names will be added to the appropriate lists. Formal reports including the General Ledger Trial Balance, Income Statement, and Balance Sheet will be prepared. Adjusting entries for depreciation, supplies used, and insurance expense will be recorded. A bank reconciliation will be prepared. The period will be advanced.

HANDY HELPERS

Located in Beverly Hills, California, Handy Helpers is a service business providing assistance with errands, shopping, home repairs, simple household chores, and transportation for children and others who do not drive. Rates are on a per-hour basis and differ according to the service performed. The business operates 7 days a week in order to accommodate it's customers.

Handy Helpers is a sole proprietorship owned and operated by Harriet Cervantes. Harriet has one assistant, Carol Hasting, helping her with errands, scheduling of duties, and doing the bookkeeping for Handy Helpers. In addition, a part-time employee, Jean Hastie, works weekends for Handy Helpers.

INSTRUCTIONS

Open Handy Helpers. Add your initials to the company name. The company name will be **Handy Helpers-Student's Initials**. (Type your actual initials, *not* the words *Student's Initials*.) The following lists are used for all sales items, customers, and vendors. You will be adding additional customers and vendors throughout the practice set. When entering transactions, you are responsible for any descriptions and references you wish to include in transactions. Unless otherwise specified, the terms for each sale or bill will be the terms specified on the Customer or Vendor List.

Customers:

Handy Helpers Customer List			
Filter Criteria includes: 1) Customers only. Report order is by ID.			
Customer ID	**Customer**	**Contact**	**Telephone 1**
ALB01	Albert, Mark	Mark Albert	310-555-5779
ANT01	Anton, George	George Anton	310-555-1332
BAR01	Barker, Carla	Carla Barker	310-555-7762
CLA01	Clark, Bernice	Bernice Clark	310-555-5577
COL01	Collins, Rodney	Rodney Collins	310-555-4563
CON01	Conner, Christy	Christy Conner	310-555-9871
DEL01	DeLuna, Stephen	Stephen DeLuna	310-555-9637
EDW01	Edwards, Paula	Paula Edwards	310-555-9182
JAC01	Jacobs, Marylou	Marylou Jacobs	310-555-5321
KAB01	Kabir, Abdul	Abdul Kabir	310-555-5925
STE01	Steller, Raymond	Raymond Steller	310-555-6648

Vendors:

Handy Helpers Vendor List			
Filter Criteria includes: Report order is by ID.			
Vendor ID	**Vendor**	**Contact**	**Telephone 1**
AVE01	Avenue Florist	Avenue Florist	310-555-8523
FIR01	First Auto Repairs	First Auto Repairs	310-555-4489
ONE01	One Stop Gas	Saleem Kennedy	310-555-9267
STA01	Stacy's Stationers	Stacy Shaylin	310-555-1148

Sales Items:

Handy Helpers Item List			
Filter Criteria includes: Report order is by ID.			
Item ID	**Item Description**	**Item Class**	**Active?**
Errands	Household Errands	Non-stock item	Active
Household	Household Chores	Non-stock item	Active
Party	Party Planning and Supervision	Non-stock item	Active
Pets	Pet Sitting	Non-stock item	Active
Repairs	Repair Service	Non-stock item	Active
Shopping	Client Shopping	Non-stock item	Active
Transport	Transportation	Non-stock item	Active

Each Item is priced per hour. Unless otherwise specified within the transactions, a minimum of one hour is charged for any service provided. As you can see, there is no difference in amount between the first hour of a service and subsequent hours of service.

RECORD TRANSACTIONS

Enter the transactions for Handy Helpers and print as indicated. Always print invoices, sales receipts, checks, and so on as they are entered even though receipts are not on the transmittal. Accept all defaults unless otherwise instructed. Apply all cash receipts to the oldest invoices unless otherwise instructed.

Daily Transactions for January 2006:

Find all accounts with the name Automobile as part of the account name. Change every occurrence of Automobile to Business Vehicle. (There should be 5 changes)

Find all accounts with the name Office Equipment as part of the account name. Change every occurrence of Office Equipment to Office Furniture/Equipment. Abbreviate if necessary. (There should be 3 changes)

Change the account type for accounts 1420 and 1520 from Fixed Asset to Accumulated Depreciation.

Make the following inactive: Mortgage Expense, Property Tax Expense, Travel Expense

Delete the following accounts: Sales, Recruiting Expense, Contributions, Amortization Expense

Add 1150 - Petty Cash to the Chart of Accounts.

Print a Chart of Accounts. Use this report to identify accounts needed in the transactions.

1/1/06

Write a check to Harriet Cervantes for $100 to establish a Petty Cash fund. Use Check No. 100. Use OCR Multi-Purpose AP Laser for the form.

Christy Conner is having a party in two weeks. Bill Christy Conner for 3 hours of party planning. Refer to the Item List for the appropriate sales item. Invoice No. 35, terms, Net 30. Print the invoice using the Invoice form and invoice number 35.

Dr. Steller has arranged for you to feed and walk his dogs every day. Bill Dr. Steller for pet sitting, 1 hour per day for 7 days (put this all on one bill). Terms, Net 15.

We were out of paper, ink cartridges for the laser printer, computer disks, and various other office supplies that we need to have on hand. Received a bill—Invoice No. 1806-1—from Stacy's Stationers for $350 for the office supplies we received today.

Every week we put fresh flowers in the office in order to provide a welcoming environment for any customers who happen to come to the office. Received a bill—Invoice No. 887—from Avenue Florist for $25 for office flowers for the week. (Flower Expense)

1/2/06

Dr. Anton almost forgot his wife's birthday. He called Handy Helpers with an emergency request for help. The store will bill the doctor for the actual gift purchased. Bill Dr. George Anton, 3 hours of shopping for his wife's birthday gift.

Carla Barker needed to have her shelves relined. You did part of the house this week and will return next week to continue the work. Bill her for 5 hours of household chores.

1/3/06

Stephen's mother has several doctor appointments. Mr. DeLuna has asked Handy Helpers to take her to these appointments. Bill Stephen DeLuna for 3 hours of transportation.

1/4/06

Received a bill—Invoice No. 81056—from One Stop Gas, $125 for the weekly gasoline charge.

Received checks from the following customers on account: Dr. George Anton, Check No. 713 for $275, use Receipt # 501 as your starting receipt number; Rodney Collins, Check No. 3381 for $250; Stephen DeLuna, Check No. 6179 for $450; Abdul Kabir, Check No. 38142 for $1,000.

1/5/06

Leona Jacobs has a birthday party to attend. Her mother, Marylou, has hired Handy Helpers to take her to the party and stay with her while she is there. Bill Marylou Jacobs, 3 hours of transportation for the birthday party. (This transportation charge also includes the time at the party.)

1/6/06

Prepare Sales Receipt No. 505 to record a cash sale. Received Check No. 2894 for 1 hour of errands for a new customer: Clarence Riker, 18062A Camden Drive, Beverly Hills, CA 90410, 310-555-7206, terms Net 10 days, credit limit $1,000.00. Print the sales receipt.

Prepare Cash Requirements report using an exact date of 1/13/06. Print the report.

Since Harriet will not be paying bills again until January 13, pay all bills due prior to January 13. Print the checks—be sure that the check run starts with Check No. 101.

1/7/06

Christy Conner is having a party January 19th. Bill Christy Conner for 4 hours of party planning.

Stephen's mother has several additional doctor appointments. Mr. DeLuna has asked Handy Helpers to take her to these appointments. Bill Stephen DeLuna for 4 hours of transportation.

Dr. Steller was pleased with Handy Helpers' service and has arranged to have Handy Helpers feed and walk his dogs every day on a permanent basis. Bill Dr. Steller for pet sitting, 1 hour per day for 7 days.

1/8/06

Bernice Clark really likes the floral arrangements in the office of Handy Helpers. She has asked that flowers be brought to her home and arranged throughout the house. When Harriet completes the placement of the flowers in the house, Bernice gives her Check No. 387 for 1 hour of errands and 1 hour of household chores, $40.

1/9/06

Received checks from the following customers: Dr. Steller, No. 7891, $500; Ms. Jacobs, No. 97452, $200; Ms. Clark, No. 395, $600; Ms. Edwards, No. 178, $50; Mr. Albert, No. 3916, $750.

Received a bill—Invoice No. 943—from Avenue Florist for $25 for office flowers for the week.

Received a bill—Invoice No. 81085—from One Stop Gas, $100 for the weekly gasoline charge.

1/10/06

Abdul Kabir has arranged for Handy Helpers to supervise and coordinate the installation of new tile in his master bathroom. Bill Mr. Kabir for 4 hours of repair service for hiring the subcontractor, scheduling the installation for 1/15 and 1/16, and contract preparation.

1/11/06

Carla Barker needed to have her shelves relined. Harriet did part of the house last week and completed the work today. Bill Ms. Barker for 5 hours of household chores.

Returned faulty printer cartridge. Received Credit Memo No. CM5 from Stacy's Stationers, $75. Associate it with the original invoice #1806-1.

1/13/06

Pay all bills for the amounts due on or before January 20. (Hint: There should be one check again.) Print the check.

Correct the invoice issued to Carla Barker on 1/11/06. The number of hours billed should be 7 instead of 5. Print the corrected invoice.

Print Aged Receivables report as of 1/13/06.

1/14/06

Christy Conner is having a party on the 19th. Bill Christy Conner for 2 hours of party planning.

1/15/06

Bernice Clark was really pleased with the floral arrangements Harriet did last week. She has asked that flowers be brought to her home and arranged throughout the house on a weekly basis. This week when Harriet completes the placement of the flowers in the house, Bernadette gives her Check No. 421 for 1 hour of errands and 1 hour of household chores.

1/17/06

Received a bill—Invoice No. 81109—from One Stop Gas, $150 for the weekly gasoline charge.

Received a bill—Invoice No. 979—from Avenue Florist for $25 for office flowers for the week.

The bathroom tile was installed on 1/15 and 1/16. The installation was completed to Mr. Kabir's satisfaction. Bill him for 16 hours of repair service.

1/18/06

Bernice Clark's neighbor, Dr. Josef Paloff, really liked the flowers in Bernice's house and asked Harriet to bring flowers to his home and office. This week he gave her a $40.00 Check No. 90-163 for 1 hour of errands and 1 hour of household chores. Add him to the customer list: Dr. Josef Paloff, 236 West Canon Drive, Beverly Hills, CA 90210, 310-555-0918, Net 10, credit limit $1,000.00.

1/19/06

Tonight is Christy's big party. She has arranged for both Harriet and Jean to supervise the party from 3 p.m. until 1 a.m. Bill Christy for 20 hours of party planning and supervision.

1/20/06

Record the checks received from customers for the week, (Receipt Number should start with 514): Mr. DeLuna, No. 9165, $175; Ms. Barker, No. 7-303, $150; Dr. Steller, No. 89162, $175; Ms. Jacobs, No. 5291, $75.

Pay all bills for the amounts due on or before January 27. (Hint: There should be two checks.) Print the checks.

1/22/06

Bernice Clark gave Harriet Check No. 439 for 1 hour of errands and 1 hour of household chores in payment for the flowers that were brought to her home and arranged throughout the house this week.

1/23/06

The party went so smoothly Saturday that Harriet went home at 11 p.m. rather than 1 a.m. Issue a Credit Memo to Christy Conner for 2 hours of party planning and supervision. Use CM48 and associate the credit with invoice #48.

Paula Edwards arranged to have her pets cared for by Handy Helpers during the past 7 days. Bill her for 1 hour of pet sitting for each day.

1/24/06

Harriet arranged for theater tickets and dinner reservations for Dr. Anton. Bill him for 1 hour of errands.

Received a bill—Invoice No. 81116—from One Stop Gas, $110 for the weekly gasoline charge.

Received a bill—Invoice No. 1002—from Avenue Flowers for $25 for office flowers for the week.

1/25/06

Write a check to Stacy's Stationers for the purchase of a new printer for the office, $500.

1/27/06

Dr. Steller had arranged for Handy Helpers to feed and walk his dogs every day. Bill Dr. Steller for pet sitting, 1 hour per day for the past two weeks.

Write checks to pay bills for rent and utilities. The utility companies and the rental agent will need to be added to the Vendor List to record future invoices. Select a logical default expense account for each vendor. Vendor information is provided in each transaction:

> Monthly telephone bill: $192, CaliTone Telephone, 2015 Wilshire Boulevard, Beverly Hills, CA 90210, 310-555-8888, Net 20 days. Acct # 45678L43

> January rent for office space: $1,500, Franklin Rentals, 3016 Franklin Boulevard, Beverly Hills, CA 90210, 310-555-1636, Net 10 days.

> Monthly water bill: $153, Beverly Hills Water, 9916 Sunset Boulevard, Beverly Hills, CA 90210, 310-555-1961, Net 30 days. Acct # 897543CA-23BH-5

Monthly gas and electric bill: $296, California Power, 10196 Olympic Boulevard, West Los Angeles, CA 90016, 310-555-9012, Net 30 days.

Pay bills for all amounts due before February 3.

1/31/06

Replenish the Petty Cash Fund. The Petty Cash record indicates that $6.92 was spend on postage to mail invoices to customers, $23.16 was used to purchase office supplies (these are both expenses).

Write a check for $2,400.00 to We Kover U Insurance Brokers, 1026 Sunset Blvd, Beverly Hills, CA 90210, 310-565-1953. The check prepays our vehicle insurance policy for January 1, 2006 through December 31, 2006.

Prepare a Check Register for January. Confirm that your check numbering is unbroken.

Record payments received from customers: Ms. Conner, No. 4692, $150; Dr. Steller, No. 7942, $175; Ms. Edwards, No. 235, $175; Dr. Anton, No. 601, $75; Ms. Barker, No. 923-10, $75.

Print Customer Ledgers report.

Record adjusting entries for:
> Business Vehicle Insurance, $200 expired
> Office Supplies Used, $150
> Depreciation: Business Vehicles, $500
> > Office Furniture and Equipment, $92

Write a check for a withdrawal by Harriet Cervantes, $1,000.

Because a fax machine is a business necessity, Harriet decided to give her new fax machine to Handy Helpers. Record this additional $350 investment of equipment by Harriet Cervantes.

Franklin Rentals decreased the amount of rent to $1,000 per month. Correct and reprint the check for rent. (Ignore that a blank check with the same number may not be available)

End of the Month: January 31, 2006

Prepare the bank reconciliation using the bank statement on the following page. Record any adjustments necessary as a result of the bank statement. Print an Account Reconciliation report.

Print the following reports as of 1/31/06:
> General Ledger Trial Balance
> Cash Flow Forecast for February 2006
> Statement of Cash Flows
> Standard Income Statement
> Standard Balance Sheet

Advance the period to 02 - February 01, 2006 to February 28, 2006 and print all reports selected by Peachtree in the Print Reports dialog box. No need to run an internal audit.

BEVERLY HILLS BANK
1234 Rodeo Drive
Beverly Hills, CA 90210
(419) 585-0310

BANK STATEMENT FOR:

Handy Helpers
27800 Beverly Boulevard
Beverly Hills, CA 90210

Acct. # 887-902-7521			January 2006
Beginning Balance 1/1/06			$21,550.00
1/3/06 Check 100		100.00	$21,450.00
1/4/06 Deposit	1975.00		$23,425.00
1/6/06 Deposit	25.00		$23,450.00
1/7/06 Check 101		50.00	$23,400.00
1/8/06 Deposit	40.00		$23,440.00
1/9/06 Deposit	2100.00		$25,540.00
1/14/06 Check 102		25.00	$25,515.00
1/15/06 Deposit	40.00		$25,555.00
1/18/06 Deposit	40.00		$25,595.00
1/20/06 Deposit	575.00		$26,170.00
1/26/06 Check 103		500.00	$25,670.00
1/28/06 Check 106		192.00	$25,478.00
1/28/06 Check 107		1000.00	$24,478.00
1/29/06 Check 108		153.00	$24,325.00
1/31/06 Check 112		30.08	$24,294.92
1/31/06 Payment: Business Vehicle Loan: Interest $86.06; Principal $445.15		531.21	$23,763.71
1/31/06 Payment: Office Equipment Loan: Interest $10.33; Principal $53.42		63.75	$23,699.96
1/31/06 Service Charge		15.00	$23,684.96
1/31/06 Interest	42.50		$23,727.46
Ending Balance 1/31/06			$23,727.46

NAME _____

TRANSMITTAL

END OF SECTION 1—
Handy Helpers Practice Set: Service Business

Attach the following documents and reports (note that receipts are not included):

- ☐ Chart of Accounts
- ☐ Check No. 100: Petty Cash
- ☐ Invoice No. 35: Christy Conner
- ☐ Invoice No. 36: Raymond Steller
- ☐ Invoice No. 37: George Anton
- ☐ Invoice No. 38: Carla Barker
- ☐ Invoice No. 39: Stephen DeLuna
- ☐ Invoice No. 40: Marylou Jacobs
- ☐ Cash Requirements report as of January 13, 2006
- ☐ Check No. 101: Avenue Florist
- ☐ Invoice No. 41: Christy Conner
- ☐ Invoice No. 42: Stephen DeLuna
- ☐ Invoice No. 43: Raymond Steller
- ☐ Invoice No. 44: Abdul Kabir
- ☐ Invoice No. 45: Carla Barker
- ☐ Check No. 102: Avenue Florist
- ☐ Invoice No. 45 (Corrected): Carla Barker
- ☐ Aged Receivables as of January 13, 2006
- ☐ Invoice No. 46: Christy Conner
- ☐ Invoice No. 47: Abdul Kabir
- ☐ Invoice No. 48: Christy Conner
- ☐ Check No. 103: First Auto Repairs
- ☐ Check No. 104: One Stop Gas
- ☐ Credit Memo CM48: Christy Conner
- ☐ Invoice No. 49: Paula Edwards
- ☐ Invoice No. 50: George Anton
- ☐ Check No. 105: Stacy's Stationers
- ☐ Invoice No. 51: Raymond Steller
- ☐ Check No. 106: CaliTone Telephone

- ☐ Check No. 107: Franklin Rentals
- ☐ Check No. 108: Beverly Hills Water
- ☐ Check No. 109: California Power
- ☐ Check No. 110: Avenue Florist
- ☐ Check No. 111: Stacy's Stationers
- ☐ Check No. 112: Harriet Cervantes (Petty Cash)
- ☐ Check No. 113: We Kover U Insurance Brokers
- ☐ Check Register
- ☐ Customers Ledger report
- ☐ Check No. 114: Harriet Cervantes
- ☐ Check No. 107 (Corrected): Franklin Rentals
- ☐ Account Reconciliation report
- ☐ General Ledger Trial Balance
- ☐ Cash Flows - Forecast
- ☐ Statement of Cash Flows
- ☐ Standard Income Statement
- ☐ Standard Balance Sheet
- ☐ General Journal
- ☐ Cash Receipts Journal
- ☐ Cash Disbursements Journal
- ☐ Sales Journal
- ☐ Purchases Journal
- ☐ General Ledger

Sales and Receivables: Merchandising Business

5

LEARNING OBJECTIVES

At the completion of this chapter, you will be able to:

1. Enter sales transactions for a retail business.
2. Prepare invoices that use sales tax, exceed a customer's credit limit and use discount pricing levels.
3. Prepare transactions for cash sales with sales tax.
4. Add new accounts to the Chart of Accounts.
5. Add additional price levels to merchandise inventory items.
6. Add new customers and modify existing customer records.
7. Delete and void invoices.
8. Prepare credit memos with and without refunds.
9. Record customer payments on account with and without discounts.
10. Prepare and print Sales related reports to include Customer Ledgers report, Aged Receivables, Sales Journal, Cash Receipts Journal and Invoice Register.
11. Prepare and print Inventory related reports to include an Item List, Item Price List and an Items Sold to Customers report.

ACCOUNTING FOR SALES AND RECEIVABLES IN A MERCHANDISING BUSINESS

Peachtree® Complete Accounting 2006 uses an invoice created in the Sales/Invoicing module to record credit sales transactions rather than a traditional Sales Journal with debits and credits and special columns. All entries will, nevertheless, be automatically recorded in a Sales Journal by Peachtree to be subsequently posted to the General Ledger. Peachtree will frequently create journals in the background. Entries made through this module will also be entered into the Subsidiary Accounts Receivable ledger. A new customer can be added "on the fly" as transactions are entered should the need arise.

Cash sales do not involve accounts receivable and will be recorded in the Receipts module of Peachtree® Complete Accounting 2006. The program allows us to apply cash receipts either to sales or to existing invoices. By choosing to apply cash to sales, we are recording a cash sale. By choosing to apply cash receipts to existing invoices, we are recording a payment on account. Cash could also be applied to an invoice created in the Sales/Invoicing feature as a second method of recording cash sales. The first method puts the cash in a Cash Receipts Journal while the second places it in the Sales Journal. We will use the first method.

For a retail business, Peachtree® Complete Accounting 2006 tracks inventory, maintains information on reorder points and quantities, tracks the quantity of merchandise on hand, maintains information on the value of the inventory, and can inform you of the percentage of sales for each inventory item. Discounts to certain types of customers can be given as well as prompt-payment discounts.

Unlike many computerized accounting programs, Peachtree® Complete Accounting 2006 makes error correction easy. A sales form may be edited, voided, or deleted in the same window where it was created or via an account register. If a sales form has been printed prior to correction, it may be reprinted after the correction has been made.

A multitude of reports are available when using Peachtree® Complete Accounting 2006. Accounts receivable related reports include Customer Ledgers and Aged Receivables, Cash Receipts Journal, Sales Journal and Invoice Register reports. Inventory related reports include Item List, Item Price List and Inventory profitability reports. In addition, the traditional accounting reports such as General Ledger Trial Balance, Income Statement, and Balance Sheet are available.

TRAINING TUTORIAL

The following tutorial is a step-by-step guide to recording sales (both cash and credit) for a fictitious company with fictitious employees. This company is called High Ridge Ski Shoppe. In addition to recording transactions, you will prepare several reports for High Ridge Ski Shoppe using Peachtree® Complete Accounting 2006. The tutorial for High Ridge Ski Shoppe will continue in Chapters 6 and 7, when accounting for payables, bank reconciliation, financial statement preparation, and advancing an accounting period for a merchandising business will be completed.

COMPANY PROFILE: HIGH RIDGE SKI SHOPPE

High Ridge Ski Shoppe is a sporting goods store located in Mammoth Lakes, California. High Ridge Ski Shoppe specializes in equipment, clothing, and accessories for skiing and snowboarding and is open only in the winter. The company is a partnership between Eric Boyd and Matt Wayne. Each partner has a 50 percent share of the business, and both devote all of their efforts to High Ridge Ski Shoppe. There is a full-time bookkeeper and manager, Renee Squires, who oversees purchases, maintains the inventory, and keeps the books for the company.

OPEN A COMPANY—HIGH RIDGE SKI SHOPPE

Access Peachtree® Complete Accounting 2006, and open the company.

 DO: Open Peachtree® Complete Accounting 2006 as instructed in Chapters 1 and 2

Open High Ridge Ski Shoppe:
Click **Open an existing company.**
Click the **Browse** button (if High Ridge Ski Shoppe is not already visible)
Click the drop down arrow for **Drives:**
Select the drive where your data files are kept
Locate and double click on High Ridge Ski Shoppe (under the **Company name** text box)
Check the title bar to verify that High Ridge Ski Shoppe is the open company

VERIFYING AN OPEN COMPANY

 DO: Verify the title bar heading:

> **Peachtree Accounting: High Ridge Ski Shoppe**
> File   Edit   Maintain   Tasks   Analysis   Options   Reports

ADD YOUR NAME TO THE COMPANY NAME

Because each student in the course will be working for the same companies and printing the same documents, personalizing the company name to include your name will help identify many of the documents you print during your training.

 DO: Add your name to the company name
Click on the **Maintain** menu option at the top of your screen
Click **Company Information**
Click to the right of **High Ridge Ski Shoppe**
Add a dash and your three letter initials. For example, Alex P. Smith would type -APS
Click **OK**
The change will not show until the company has been opened again.
Click on the **File** menu option
Click on **Open Company**
When prompted for confirmation that you wish to close the current company, answer yes.
Double click on **High Ridge Ski Shoppe**.
–   The title bar now shows High Ridge Ski Shoppe–(Your Initials)

BEGINNING THE TUTORIAL

In this chapter you will be entering both accounts receivable transactions and cash sales transactions for a retail company that charges its customers sales tax. Much of the organization of Peachtree® Complete Accounting 2006 is dependent on lists. The three primary types of lists you will use in the tutorial for receivables are a Customers/Prospects List, Chart of Accounts and Inventory Item list.

The names, addresses, telephone numbers, credit terms, credit limits, and balances for all established credit customers are contained in the Customers/Prospects List. The Customers/Prospects List can also be referred to as the Accounts Receivable Ledger. Peachtree® Complete Accounting 2006 does not use this term; however, this list contains the detailed information one would find in an Accounts Receivable Ledger.

You will be using the following Customer List for established credit customers. You will be adding customers to this list as you progress through the tutorial.

High Ridge Ski Shoppe
Customer List

Filter Criteria includes: 1) Customers only. Report order is by ID.

Customer ID	Customer	Contact	Telephone 1
CHA01	Chang, Melissa	Melissa Chang	619-555-8441
CLA01	Clarence, Caroline	Caroline Clarence	619-555-4697
DAV01	Davidson, Fred	Fred Davidson	619-555-9431
EDD01	Eddy, David	David Eddy	619-555-5113
FIN01	Finnigan, Sean	Sean Finnigan	619-555-9770
HIG011	High Ridge School	Sheryl Roy	619-555-1234
MON01	Montello, Jacob	Jacob Montello	619-555-8624
PLA01	Platter, Susan	Susan Platter	619-555-7563
ROD01	Rodriguez, Jose	Jose Rodriguez	619-555-2585
TAN01	Tanner, Kathy	Kathy Tanner	619-555-2258
TAN02	Tanamura, Hideto	Hideto Tanamura	619-555-1257
VAL01	Vallejo, Martin	Martin Vallejo	619-555-9152
WAL01	Walsh, Victor	Victor Walsh	619-555-8733

Sales are often made up of various types on income. In High Ridge Ski Shoppe there are a number of income accounts. Our two primary accounts are 4011 - Clothing & Accessories Sales and 4012 - Equipment Sales. We will use the same item list feature used in Chapter 2. The difference is that High Ridge Ski Shoppe is a merchandising company and will use the item list for its inventory rather than services.

The Inventory Module will track various details about the items included on the list. It can track the vendor, the last price paid, ten levels of pricing as well as reorder points and reorder quantities. The following item list shows the various items of merchandise being sold by High Ridge Ski Shoppe.

High Ridge Ski Shoppe
Item List

Filter Criteria includes: Report order is by ID.

Item ID	Item Description	Item Class	Active?	Item Type	Qty on Hand
BIN10	Ski Bindings, Deluxe	Stock item	Active		20.00
BIN15	Ski Bindings, Standard	Stock item	Active		18.00
BIN20	Ski Bindings, ProBind	Stock item	Active		7.00
BOT10	Boot Case, Canvas	Stock item	Active		12.00
GLO10	Gloves, Insulated	Stock item	Active		15.00
GLO15	Gloves, Deluxe	Stock item	Active		42.00
HAT10	Hats, Polartec	Stock item	Active		30.00
LIP10	Lip Balm	Stock item	Active		122.00
PAN10	Ski Pants, Microfiber	Stock item	Active		75.00
PAN15	Snowboard Pants, Microfiber	Stock item	Active		25.00
PAR10	Parkas, Down filled	Stock item	Active		75.00
POL10	Ski Poles, Economy	Stock item	Active		18.00
SB10	Ski Boots, Polartec II	Stock item	Active		15.00
SB15	Ski Boots, Ultra Pro	Stock item	Active		20.00
SB20	Ski Boots, High Performance	Stock item	Active		10.00
SK10	Snow Skis, Model XB04	Stock item	Active		16.00
SK15	Snow Skis, Downhill	Stock item	Active		12.00
SK20	Snow Skis, Model X348	Stock item	Active		8.00
SK25	Skis, Pro Snow Deluxe	Stock item	Active		5.00
SNB20	Snowboard, Deluxe	Stock item	Active		25.00
SNO10	Snowboard, Standard	Stock item	Active		32.00
SNO15	Snowboard Bindings, Standard	Stock item	Active		16.00
SNO20	Snowboard Boots, Deluxe	Stock item	Active		12.00
SOC10	Ski Socks, Thermal	Stock item	Active		75.00
SUN10	Sunglasses, Polarized Lens	Stock item	Active		50.00
SWE10	Sweaters, Cashmere	Stock item	Active		44.00
SWE15	Sweater, Ski	Stock item	Active		18.00
UND10	Long Underwear, Thermal	Stock item	Active		33.00
WAX10	Ski Wax, Beeswax	Stock item	Active		312.00

As in previous chapters, all transactions are described with memos. The transaction date will be the same date as the memo date unless otherwise specified within the memo. Always enter the date of the transaction as specified in the memo. Dates are very important to Peachtree and are used to age accounts receivables and accounts payables. They are also used as part of the process of paying bills and generating payroll. By default, Peachtree® Complete Accounting 2006 automatically enters the system date. In many instances, this will not be the same date as the transaction. This is particularly true when working through instructional data. Peachtree defaults its system date to your computer's system date. In order to more realistically use Peachtree, we will be changing Peachtree's system date to that of the memo date prior to entering the transactions contained in the memo. Review the process for changing the system date in Chapter 1 if necessary.

Customer names, when necessary, will be given in the transaction. All terms for customers on account are Net 30 days unless specified otherwise. The defaults for this option have already been set but confirm them nevertheless. If a memo contains more than one transaction, there will be a horizontal space separating the transactions.

Even when you are instructed how to enter a transaction step by step, you should always refer to the memo for transaction details. Once a specific type of transaction has been entered in a step-by-step manner, additional transactions will be made without having detailed instructions provided. Of course, you may always refer to instructions given for previous transactions for the steps used to enter those transactions.

ENTER SALES ON ACCOUNT

Because Peachtree® Complete Accounting 2006 operates with a business form entry screen, a sale on account is entered via an invoice accessed from the Sales/Invoicing option of the Sales Navigation button. You prepare an invoice including sales tax and payment terms information, and Peachtree® Complete Accounting 2006 records the transaction in the Sales Journal and updates the customer's account automatically.

MEMO

DATE: January 3, 2006

Bill the following: Invoice No. 101—An established customer, Victor Walsh, purchased a pair of Ultra Pro ski boots for $75.00 on account. Terms are Net 15.

DO: Record the sale on account shown in the invoice above. This invoice is used to bill a customer for a sale using one sales item:

Click on the date shown next to Today at the bottom of the screen
  – This is the system button on status bar
Enter 1/3/06 in the **Date:** field
Click **OK**
Click on the **Sales** Navigation button
Click **Sales/Invoicing** icon in the Tasks section of the button.
  – A blank invoice will show on the screen

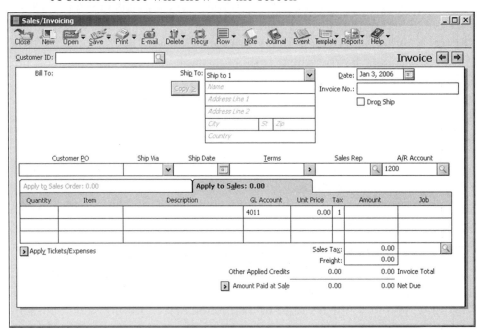

Click the magnifying glass next to Customer ID:

Double click Walsh, Victor

- Information in the **Bill To:** field is completed automatically
- Cursor is automatically moved to the **Ship To:** field. Since we are not shipping the boots, we will leave this blank.

Click in the **Date:** field

- Confirm that it reflects the 1/3/06 system date
- We could insert the invoice number at this point; however, we often times do not know what the next number in the sequence should be. If left blank, Peachtree will assign the next available invoice number during the print process. This is the procedure we will follow in this book

Tab to the **Terms** arrow and confirm terms of Net 15.

Tab to the **Quantity** field.

Click on and enter 1.00 in the **Quantity** field. Press **Enter**. We must enter a quantity in order for Peachtree to calculate the amount of this invoice. We have sold one pair of ski boots.

Click on the magnifying glass to the right of the **Item** field, select Ski Boots, Ultra Pro (Item SB15) and click **OK** to choose this item.

- You are taken to the **Description** field. Tab through this field as well as the following fields and note how Peachtree completes the remaining fields automatically. In addition, the sales tax is calculated and added at the bottom of the invoice.

EDIT AND CORRECT ERRORS

If an error is discovered while entering invoice information, it may be corrected by positioning the cursor in the field containing the error. You may do this by clicking in the field containing the error, tabbing to move forward through each field, or pressing Shift+Tab to move back to the field containing the error. If the error is highlighted, type the correction. If the error is not highlighted, you can correct the error by pressing the backspace or the delete key as many times as necessary to remove the error. You may then type in the correction. (Alternate method: Point to the error, highlight it by dragging the mouse through the error with the left button depressed, then type the correction.)

 DO: Practice editing and making corrections to the invoice just completed:

Click the magnifying glass next to **Customer ID:**

Select Chang, Melissa, click **OK**

- Information is changed in the **Bill To:** field.

Highlight contents of **Date:** field.

Type 1/19/06 as the date

- This removes the Jan 3, 2006 date originally entered.

Click in the **Quantity** field to highlight the 1.00.

Type 2.00. Press **Enter**.

To eliminate the changes made to Invoice No. 101, click the drop-down list arrow next to **Customer ID:**

Select Walsh, Victor, click **OK**

Highlight contents of **Date:** field.

Type 01/03/06

Click in the **Quantity** field to highlight the 2.00.

Type a 1.00.

Press the Enter or Tab key

–   This will complete the invoice.

–   The invoice has been returned to the correct customer, date, and quantity. Compare the information you entered with the information provided in the memo and with the following completed invoice.

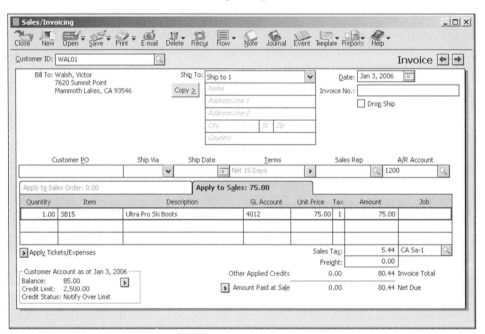

PRINT AN INVOICE

DO: With the invoice on the screen, print it immediately after entering the information.

Note: This will be Invoice No. 101

Click **Print** at the top of the Sales/Invoicing window.

Accept or enter 101 as our invoice number.

Click on **Print**.

The invoice is printed and you are presented with a blank invoice.

ENTER TRANSACTIONS USING MORE THAN ONE SALES ITEM AND SALES TAX

Frequently, sales to customers will be for more than one item. For example, new bindings are usually purchased along with a new pair of skis. Invoices can be prepared to bill a customer for several items at once.

MEMO

DATE: January 3, 2006

Bill the following: Invoice No. 102—Every year Dr. Jacob Montello gets new ski equipment. Bill him for his equipment purchase for this year: skis, Model XB04 $425; Deluxe ski bindings, $175; High Performance ski boots, $250; and Economy ski poles, $75.

DO: Record a transaction on account for a sale involving multiple sales items:

Set the system date to 1/3/2006.

Click the **Sales/Invoicing** from the **Sales** button.

Click the drop-down list arrow next to **Customer ID:**

Double click Montello, Jacob.

Tab to **Date:** field.

– Confirm that it reflects the 1/3/06 system date.

Tab to the **Quantity** field.

Enter 1.00 in the **Quantity** field. Press **Enter**.

Click on the magnifying glass to the right of the **Item** field, highlight Snow Skis, Model XB04 (Item SK10) and click **OK** to choose this item.

You are taken to the **Description** field. Tab through this field as well as the following fields and note how Peachtree completes the remaining fields automatically.

When you reach the **Quantity** field again, type 1.00. Press **Enter**.

Click on the magnifying glass to the right of the **Item** field, highlight Ski Bindings, Deluxe (Item BIN10) and click **OK** to choose this item.

Tab through the remaining fields to complete the line.

Repeat the above steps to enter the information for the ski boots and the ski poles. Peachtree will add new rows to the invoice as needed. Rows not displayed can be accessed with the added scroll bar.

Check your invoice with the data furnished in the memo and with the following example. Make corrections as needed prior to printing.

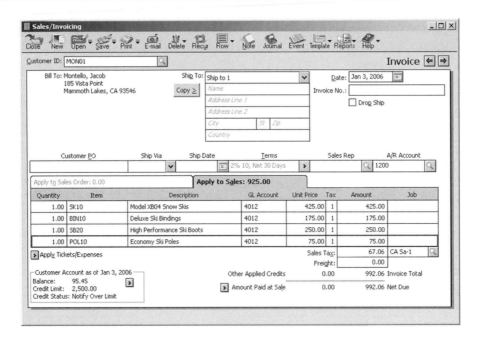

Print the invoice by following the instructions provided for Invoice No.101

PREPARE INVOICES WITHOUT STEP-BY-STEP INSTRUCTIONS

MEMO

DATE: January 3, 2006

Bill the following: Invoice No. 103—High Ridge School purchases equipment and clothing for the ski team. This year the school purchases 5 pairs of Model XB04 skis, $425 each; 5 pairs of Standard bindings, $159.99 each; and 5 sets of Economy ski poles, $75 each. Terms 2/10 Net 30.

Invoice No. 104—Susan Platter purchased a new ski outfit: 1 parka, $249; a hat, $25; a cashmere sweater, $150; 1 pair of ski pants, $129; long underwear, $68; insulated ski gloves, $79; ski socks, $15.95; sunglasses, $39.95; and a matching ski boot case, $49.95. Terms Net 15.

Invoice No. 105—Hideto Tanamura broke his snowboard when he was going down his favorite run, "Dragon's Back." He purchased our Deluxe model without bindings for $499.95, Terms 1/10 Net 30.

Invoice No. 106—Victor Walsh decided to buy some new powder skis and bindings. Bill him for Pro Snow Deluxe snow skis, $599, and ProBind ski bindings, $179. Terms Net 15.

DO: Enter the four transactions in the memo above. Refer to instructions given for the two previous transactions entered.

- Remember to set the system date to 1/3/2006.
- Always use the Item list to determine the appropriate sales items for billing. Let Peachtree auto-fill the balance of the line.
- If you make an error prior to printing, correct it immediately.
- Print each invoice immediately after you enter the information for it.
- Click **Close** after Invoice No. 106 has been entered and printed.

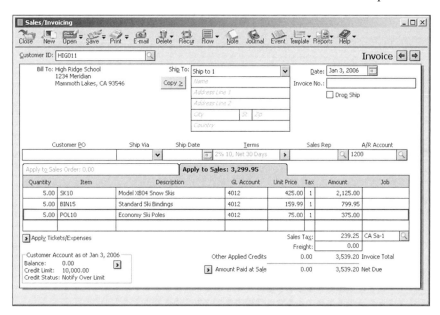

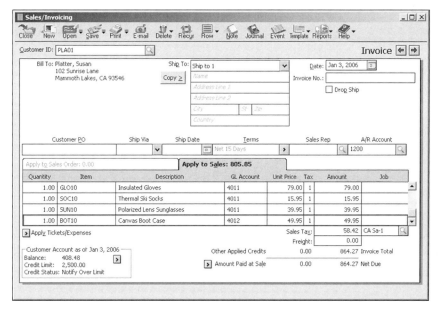

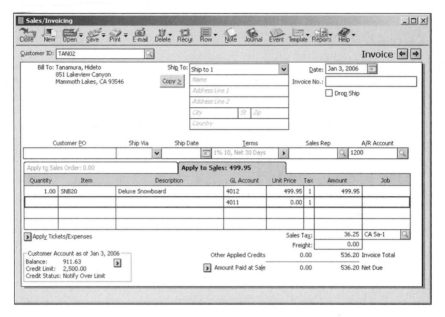

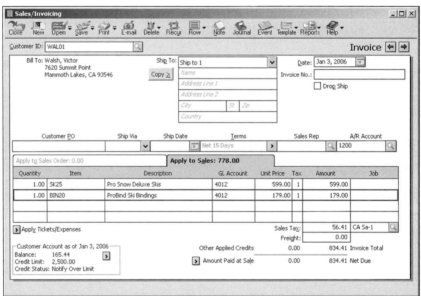

ENTER A TRANSACTION EXCEEDING A CUSTOMER'S CREDIT LIMIT

As you may recall from Chapter 2, when a customer is added through the Maintain Customer feature, a credit limit is established for that customer. This credit limit is used to provide a warning whenever a customer's purchases exceed the established amount. Peachtree® Complete Accounting 2006 does allow a transaction for a customer to exceed the established credit limit, but a warning box appears with information regarding the transaction amount and the credit limit for a customer.

MEMO

DATE: January 5, 2006

Bill the following: Invoice No. 107—Melissa Chang decided to get a new Deluxe snowboard, $499.95; Standard snowboard bindings, $189.99; snowboard boots, $249; and a canvas case to carry her boots, $49.95. Terms are Net 30.

DO: Prepare and print Invoice No. 107 as instructed previously
  - Always use the Item List to determine the appropriate sales items for billing.
  - If you make an error, correct it.
  - Print the invoice immediately after you enter the information for it.

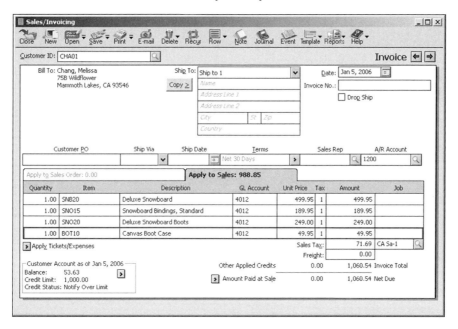

Click **Print** after Invoice No. 107 has been entered. You are presented with the following warning message

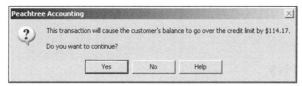

  - If you click **No**, you are returned to the invoice in order to make changes
  - If you click **Yes**, the system returns to the print dialog box for printing

Click **Yes** to print and record the transaction
Click **Close**

PREPARE CUSTOMER LEDGERS REPORT

In order to see the results of all the transactions for our customers, you need to prepare a
Customer Ledgers report. This report shows all sales, credits, and payments for each customer in
Peachtree.

MEMO

DATE: January 5, 2006

Prepare and print a Customer Ledgers report so that the owners can see exactly
how much each customer owes to High Ridge Ski Shoppe.

DO: Prepare a Customer Ledgers report for all customers for all transactions:
Click the Sales/Receivables Reports from the Sales button.
Double click on **Customer Ledgers**.
- This report lists the names of all customers on account with balances. This
  includes opening balances as well as current invoices.

High Ridge Ski Shoppe
Customer Ledgers
For the Period From Jan 1, 2006 to Jan 31, 2006
Filter Criteria includes: Report order is by ID. Report is printed in Detail Format.

Customer ID Customer	Date	Trans No	Type	Debit Amt	Credit Amt	Balance
CHA01	1/1/06	Balance Fwd				53.63
Chang, Melissa	1/5/06	107	SJ	1,060.54		1,114.17
CLA01	1/1/06	Balance Fwd				455.00
Clanence, Caroline						
DAV01	1/1/06	Balance Fwd				650.00
Davidson, Fred						
EDD01	1/1/06	Balance Fwd				1,136.00
Eddy, David						
FIN01	1/1/06	Balance Fwd				417.00
Finnigan, Sean						
HIG011	1/3/06	103	SJ	3,539.20		3,539.20
High Ridge School						
MON01	1/1/06	Balance Fwd				95.45
Montello, Jacob	1/3/06	102	SJ	992.06		1,087.51
PLA01	1/1/06	Balance Fwd				408.48
Platter, Susan	1/3/06	104	SJ	864.27		1,272.75

Click the **Print** button at the top of the Customer Ledgers report window.
You may get a Windows Print dialog box. If you do click **OK**.

USE THE DRILLDOWN FEATURE

Drilldown is a feature of Peachtree® Complete Accounting 2006 that allows you to view
additional information within a report. For example, an invoice may be viewed when the
Customer Ledgers report is on the screen simply by using the Drilldown feature.

MEMO

DATE: January 5, 2006

The bookkeeper, Renee Squires, could not remember if Invoice No. 107 was for
ski equipment or snowboard equipment. With the Customer Ledgers report on
the screen, use Drilldown to view Invoice No. 107.

   DO: Use Drilldown to view Invoice No. 107
Position the cursor over any part of the report showing information about Invoice
No. 107
– The cursor will turn into a magnifying glass with a letter **Z** inside.
Double click
– Invoice No. 107 appears on the screen.
– Check to make sure the four items on the invoice are: Deluxe snowboard,
Standard Snowboard Bindings, Deluxe Snowboard Boots, and Canvas Boot
Case.
With Invoice No. 107 on the screen, proceed to the next section.

CORRECT AN INVOICE AND PRINT THE CORRECTED FORM

Peachtree® Complete Accounting 2006 allows corrections and revisions to an invoice even if the
invoice has been printed. The invoice may be corrected by going directly to the original invoice
or by accessing the original invoice via the Accounts Receivable Register. An invoice can be on
view in Drilldown and still be corrected. The ability to allow such changes can be controlled by
the program's administrator assignment of rights to users. It is in this manner that internal
control can be established. Peachtree can also be set to maintain an audit trail to track all such
changes by the individual making them allowing auditors to spot suspicious changes.

MEMO
DATE: January 5, 2006

While viewing Invoice No. 107 for Melissa Chang, the bookkeeper, Renee Squires, realizes that Melissa had requested that her equipment be delivered to her home. This service is provided to established customers for a nominal fee of $25.00. The delivery fee is not taxable. Make the correction and reprint the invoice.

DO: Correct Invoice No. 107 while showing on the screen in Drilldown
Click on the arrow to the right of the **Ship To:** box
Use the pull down arrow to open up the ship address options
Note: When entering customers using the Maintain Customer feature, Peachtree allows the insertion of up to 9 shipping addresses in addition to the billing address. They would be selectable from this drop down menu.
Using the scroll bar, select the first item on the list, Bill to Address

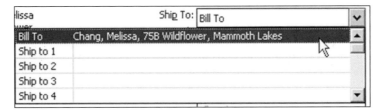

Alternatively, one could also use the Copy button next to the Ship To window when the Ship To address is the same as the Bill To address.

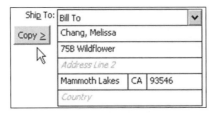

Access a new entry line at the bottom of the invoice
–   Position the cursor in the **Job** column of the last row and hit **Tab**
Click in the **Description** field and enter Delivery Charge
Tab to the **GL Account** field and select 4020 Freight Income
Tab to the **Tax** field and select 2 Exempt
Tab to the **Amount** field enter 25.00
Click the **Print** icon at the top of the screen
Click **Yes** to authorize Melissa exceeding her credit limit

Click **Print** to print the corrected invoice
Close the Sales/Invoicing window
– Note that the report reflects the new invoice amount
Close the Customers Ledgers report and the Select a Report windows

ADDING NEW ACCOUNTS TO THE CHART OF ACCOUNTS

Because account needs can change as a business is in operation, Peachtree® Complete Accounting 2006 allows you to make changes to the Chart of Accounts at any time. An account may be added by accessing the Maintain Chart of Accounts feature. It is also possible to add an account to the Chart of Accounts "on the fly" while adding an item to another list.

MEMO

DATE: January 5, 2006

Although returns are rare, it has been decided that when they do occur they should be recorded into a separate Sales Returns account. To accommodate sales returns, add a new income account, 4016 Sales Returns and Allowances to the Chart of Accounts.

 DO: Click **Chart of Accounts** in the first section of the **General Ledger** button.
Enter 4016 in the **Account ID** field.
Enter Sales Returns and Allowances in the **Description** field. Press the **Enter** key.
In the **Account Type** field, use the drop down list arrow to open a list of account types.
Select Income.
Click **Save** at the top of the Maintain Chart of Accounts window.
Click **Close** to exit.

ADD NEW ITEMS TO LIST

In order to accommodate the changing needs of a business, all Peachtree® Complete Accounting 2006 lists allow you to make changes at any time. As an example, if a new sales item is required we can use the Maintain Inventory Item feature to add it. The Item List stores information about the items High Ridge Ski Shoppe sells. In the previous activity, we had a need for an item to record the delivery charges that were added to the invoice. Although we were able to type in all the information we required, having delivery services as an item would make adding delivery charges an easier process. Both stocked and non-stocked items can be added to our inventory to make them available in our item list when creating invoices.

MEMO

DATE: January 5, 2006

Add a new item to our inventory list for Delivery Services. Use account 4020 Freight Income for the Delivery Services item GL account. It is a non-stock item and has a flat rate price of $25.00.

 DO: Add a new inventory item:
Click **Inventory Items** from the **Inventory** button
Enter DELIVERY in the **Item ID** field
Enter Delivery Service Fee in both **Description** fields
Select Non-stock item in the **Item Class** field
Enter 25.00 in the **Price Level 1:** field
Using the magnifying glass next to the **GL Sales Acct:** field, select 4020 Freight Income
Using the magnifying glass next to the **Item Tax Type:** field, select 2 Exempt
Click **Save** and then **Close**

CORRECT AN INVOICE TO INCLUDE DISCOUNT PRICING

MEMO

DATE: January 6, 2006

Received a call from High Ridge School. While processing their invoice they noted they were billed at full price for the equipment recently purchased. Due to the volume they purchase, they are supposed to receive special level 2 prices. Correct the invoice to High Ridge School to reflect level 2 pricing.

 DO: Correct invoice to High Ridge School:
Click **Sales/Invoicing** from the **Sales** button.
Click on the **Open** icon at the top of the window
Double click on Invoice Number 103 for High Ridge School
In the first row for snow skis, click in the **Unit Price** column
Using the drop down arrow, select Price Level 2

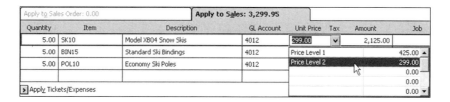

Repeat for the ski bindings and ski poles
Click on the **Print** icon
Click **Print** to print the corrected invoice
Close the **Sales/Invoicing** window

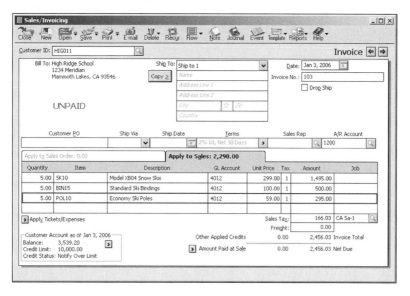

VIEW A CUSTOMER LEDGERS REPORT

After editing the invoice, you may get a detailed report regarding the customer's transactions by creating a Customer Ledgers report for High Ridge School.

DO: View a single customer ledger account:
Click the **All Accounts Receivables Reports** from the **Sales** button.
Single click on Customer Ledgers to highlight the report.
Click on the **Preview** icon at the top of the window.
– This will bring you to a Customer Ledgers dialog box where you can use filters to customize the report.
Click in the field in the **Type** column for the **Customer ID** line
Using the drop down list arrow, change the All to Equal To.
In the same row, click in the **From** column.
Using the magnifying glass button, select High Ridge School.
Click **OK**.

– Based on our filter selection, we are presented with a Customer Ledger report that contains only one customer, High Ridge School.

\multicolumn{7}{c}{High Ridge Ski Shoppe}
\multicolumn{7}{c}{Customer Ledgers}
\multicolumn{7}{c}{For the Period From Jan 1, 2006 to Jan 31, 2006}
\multicolumn{7}{l}{Filter Criteria includes: 1) IDs: HIG011. Report order is by ID. Report is printed in Detail Format.}
Customer ID Customer	**Date**	**Trans No**	**Type**	**Debit Amt**	**Credit Amt**	**Balance**
HIG011 High Ridge School	1/3/06	103	SJ	2,456.03		2,456.03
Report Total				2,456.03		2,456.03

High Ridge School's new balance reflects the lower price levels.
Click **Close** to exit the report.

ADD A NEW CUSTOMER

Peachtree® Complete Accounting 2006 allows customers to be added "on the fly" as you create an invoice or sales receipt. You may also use the Maintain Customer option when adding customers without the need to generate an invoice.

MEMO

DATE: January 8, 2006

Add the following new customer: High Ridge Recreation Center, 985 Old Mammoth Road, Mammoth Lakes, CA 93546, Contact: Melaine Clark, Phone: 619-555-2951, Fax: 619-555-1592, E-mail: highrec@abc.com Terms: 1%10 Net 30, Credit Limit: 5,000, Taxable, Tax Item: CA Sales Tax, as of 1/8/2006 there is a 0.00 opening balance for the customer. Use ID HIG012. We are using a three-digit suffix since High Ridge is used by many businesses in the area.

 DO: Add a new customer using the Maintain Customer dialog box.
Click on **Customers** from the **Sales** button.
Enter HIG012 in the **Customer ID:** field.
In the **Name** field, type High Ridge Recreation Center. Press **Enter**.
In the **Contact** field, enter Melaine Clark.
Press **Enter** twice to move to the **Address** field.
Enter 985 Old Mammoth Road in the Address field.
Press **Enter** twice to move to the **City, ST, Zip** field.
Enter Mammoth Lakes, press the **Tab** key, enter CA, press the **Tab** key, enter
93546. Use the pull down arrows to select items where applicable.
Click the magnifying glass for **Sales Tax** and double click CA Sa-1

Click in the field next to **Telephone 1**: and enter 619-555-2951.

Click in the **Fax:** field and enter 619-555-1592

Click in the **E-mail:** and enter highrec@abc.com

Your screen should look like the following illustration. If not, make corrections
before proceeding.

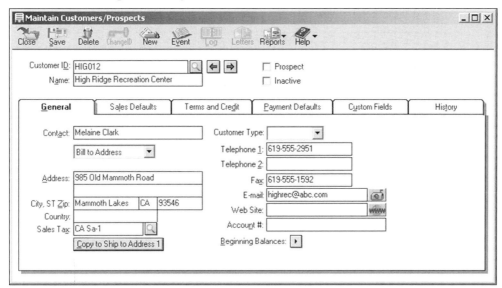

Click on the **Sales Defaults** tab.

Click on the magnifying glass next to the GL Sales Account field.

Select account **4012 Equipment Sales** and click **OK**.

Click on **Terms and Credit** tab.

Deselect **Use Standard Terms and Credit** by clicking the checkmark next to it.

Click in the field next to **Credit Limit**. Enter **5,000.00**.

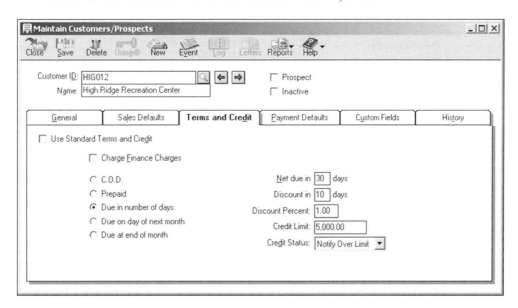

Compare your screen with the illustration above and verify that you have the same information. Make corrections as necessary.

Click **Save** to save the new customer information.

Click **Close**.

Verify the addition of High Ridge Recreation Center by viewing a Customer List report.

High Ridge Ski Shoppe
Customer List

Filter Criteria includes: 1) Customers only. Report order is by ID.

Customer ID	Customer	Contact	Telephone 1
CHA01	Chang, Melissa	Melissa Chang	619-555-8441
CLA01	Clarence, Caroline	Caroline Clarence	619-555-4697
DAV01	Davidson, Fred	Fred Davidson	619-555-8431
EDD01	Eddy, David	David Eddy	619-555-5113
FIN01	Finnigan, Sean	Sean Finnigan	619-555-9770
HIG011	High Ridge School	Sheryl Roy	619-555-1234
HIG012	High Ridge Recreation Center	Melaine Clark	619-555-2951
MON01	Montello, Jacob	Jacob Montello	619-555-8624
PLA01	Platter, Susan	Susan Platter	619-555-7563
ROD01	Rodriguez, Jose	Jose Rodriguez	619-555-2585
TAN01	Tanner, Kathy	Kathy Tanner	619-555-2258
TAN02	Tanamura, Hideto	Hideto Tanamura	619-555-1257
VAL01	Vallejo, Martin	Martin Vallejo	619-555-9152
WAL01	Walsh, Victor	Victor Walsh	619-555-8733

RECORD A SALE TO A NEW CUSTOMER

Once a new customer has been added, sales may be recorded for that customer.

MEMO

DATE: January 8, 2006

Record a sale of 5 standard snowboards and 5 Model XB04 snow skis to High Ridge Recreation Center. Because the sale is to a nonprofit organization, use Level 2 prices.

DO: Record the above sale on account to a new customer:

Click the **Sales/Invoicing** from the **Sales** button.

Click the drop-down list arrow next to **Customer ID:**

Double click High Ridge Recreation Center.

Tab to **Date:** field.

– Confirm that it reflects the 1/8/06 system date.

Tab to the **Quantity** field.

Enter 5.00 in the **Quantity** field. Press **Enter**.

Click on the magnifying glass to the right of the **Item** field, highlight Snowboard, Standard (Item SNO10) and click **OK** to choose this item.

Tab to the **Unit Price** field.

Using the drop down arrow, select Price Level 2

Repeat for the five skis

Check your invoice with the data furnished in the memo and with the following example. Make corrections as needed prior to printing.

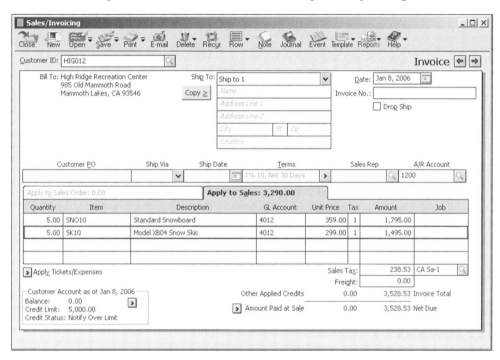

Print the invoice by following the instructions provided for Invoice No. 101

MODIFY CUSTOMER RECORDS

Occasionally information regarding a customer will change. Peachtree® Complete Accounting 2006 allows customer accounts to be modified at any time through the Maintain Customers feature.

MEMO

DATE: January 8, 2006

In order to update Melissa Chang's account, change her credit limit to $2,500.00. It is decided High Ridge Recreation Center will always get Level 2 pricing so set this as their default.

DO: Edit a customer account:

Access **Customers** from the Maintain area of the **Sales** button.
Using the pull down list in the **Customer ID:** field, select Chang, Melissa.
Click on the **Terms and Credit** tab
Highlight the old number in the **Credit Limit** field.
Enter the new amount 2,500.00.
Click **Save**
Using the pull down list in the **Customer ID:** field, select High Ridge Recreation
Click on the **Sales Defaults** tab
Using the pull down list in the **Pricing Level:** field, select Price Level 2
Click **Save** and then **Close**.

VOID AND DELETE SALES FORMS

Deleting an invoice or sales receipt permanently removes it from Peachtree® Complete Accounting 2006 without leaving a trace. If you want to correct financial records for the invoice that you no longer want, it is more appropriate to void the invoice. When an invoice is voided, it remains in the Peachtree® Complete Accounting 2006 system, but Peachtree® Complete Accounting 2006 doesn't count it. Voiding an invoice should be used only if there have been no payments made on the invoice. If any payment has been received, a Credit Memo would be appropriate for recording a return.

Void an Invoice

MEMO

DATE: January 8, 2006

Victor Walsh returned the ski boots he purchased for $80.44 including tax on January 2. He had not made any payments on this purchase. Void Invoice No. 101.

DO: Void the above transaction using Find Transactions to locate the invoice:

–   Find Transactions is useful when you have a large number of invoices and want to locate an invoice for a particular customer.

–   Using Find Transactions will locate the invoice without requiring you to scroll through all the invoices for the company. For example, if customer Sanderson's transaction was on Invoice No. 7 and the invoice on the screen was 784, you would not have to scroll through 777 invoices Using the Open command because Find would locate Invoice No. 7 instantly.

To use Find Transactions:

Click **Edit** on the menu bar.

Click **Find Transactions**.

Click in the blank field of the **Type** column for **Reference Number**. Using the
    drop down list, select Range.

Click in the **From** field in the same row and enter 101.

Click in the **To** field in the same row and enter 101.

Click on the **Find** icon in the middle of the dialog box.

Double click on the transaction displayed in the field at the bottom of the window.
    This will place Invoice No. 101 on your screen.

Click on the **Delete** icon at the top of the window.

– Notice that you are presented with the option to delete or void the invoice.

Click **Void**.

– You are presented with a Void Existing Invoice dialog box that is asking you
    for a date from which to void the invoice.

Change **Date** to 1/3/06.

Click **OK**.

– The invoice has now been voided and you are now left with a blank
    Sales/Invoicing window.

Click **Close** to close the Sales/Invoicing window.

Delete an Invoice

MEMO

DATE: January 8, 2006

Hideto Tanamura lost his part-time job. He decided to repair his old snowboard
and return the new one he purchased from High Ridge Ski Shoppe. Delete
Invoice No. 105.

    DO: Delete Invoice No. 105 by going directly to the original invoice

If the **Find** Transactions window is not on the screen, click **Edit** on the menu bar.

Click **Find Transactions**.

Click in the blank field of the **Type** column for **Reference Number**. Using the
    drop down list, select Range.

Click in the **From** field in the same row and enter 105.

Click in the **To** field in the same row and enter 105.

Click on the **Find** icon in the middle of the dialog box.

Double click on the transaction displayed in the field at the bottom of the window.
    This will place Invoice No. 105 on your screen.

Click on the **Delete** icon at the top of the window.
- Notice that you are presented with the option to delete or void the invoice. Click **Delete**.
- You are presented with a confirmation dialog box that is asking you to confirm your action to delete the invoice.

Click **Yes**.
- The invoice has now been deleted and you are now left with a blank Sales/Invoicing window.

Click **Close** to close the Sales/Invoicing window; and if necessary, close the Find Transactions window.

Verify both changes viewing an Invoice Register report.

Click the **All Accounts Receivables Reports** from the **Sales** button.

Double click on Invoice Register.

Notice that the deleted invoice #105 no longer appears.

Notice than Invoice No. 101V has been created to cancel Invoice No. 101.

High Ridge Ski Shoppe
Invoice Register
For the Period From Jan 1, 2006 to Jan 31, 2006
Filter Criteria includes: Report order is by Invoice/CM Number.

Invoice/CM #	Date	Quote No	Name	Amount
101	1/3/06		Walsh, Victor	80.44
101V	1/3/06		Walsh, Victor	-80.44
102	1/3/06		Montello, Jacob	992.06
103	1/3/06		High Ridge School	2,456.03
104	1/3/06		Platter, Susan	864.27
106	1/3/06		Walsh, Victor	834.41
107	1/5/06		Chang, Melissa	1,087.35
108	1/8/06		High Ridge Recreation Center	3,528.53
Total				9,762.65

PREPARE CREDIT MEMOS

Credit memos are prepared to show a reduction to a transaction. If the invoice has already been sent to the customer, it is more appropriate and less confusing to make a change to a transaction by issuing a credit memo rather than voiding the invoice and issuing a new invoice. A credit memo notifies a customer that a change has been made to a transaction.

MEMO
DATE: January 10, 2006

Prepare Credit Memo No. CM107 for Melissa Chang to show a reduction to her account for the return of the boot carrying case purchased for $49.95 on Invoice No. 107.

DO: Record a credit memo:

Set the system date to 1/10/2006.

Click the **Credit Memos** from the **Sales** button.

Click the drop-down list next to **Customer ID:**

Double click **Chang, Melissa**.

Tab to **Date:** field.

–   Confirm that it reflects the 1/10/06 system date.

Click on the arrow next to the **Apply to Invoice No.:** field

Select 107

Click in the **Returned** field of the row containing the Canvas Boot Case.

–   You will have to use the scroll bar at right to get to it.

Enter **1.00** in the **Returned** field. Press **Enter**.

–   Note how Peachtree completes the remaining fields automatically. Check your invoice with the data furnished in the memo and with the following example. Make corrections as needed prior to printing.

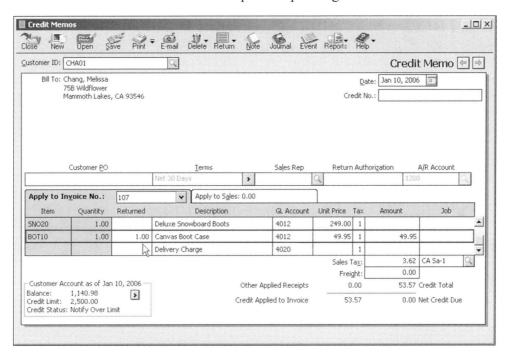

Click **Print** button at the top of the Sales/Invoicing window.

Enter CM107 in the **First CM Number:** field

> *Note:* Using CM followed by the invoice number of the invoice with the return makes it easier to associate the two documents. Peachtree does not need the number association and so any numbering sequence can be used.

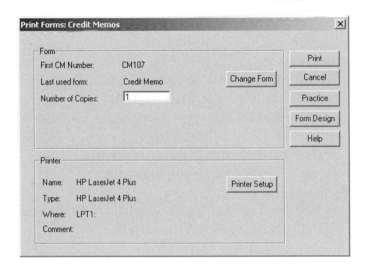

Click on **Print** then **Close**

VIEW AND PRINT AN AGED RECEIVABLES REPORT

To determine which invoices are still open—ones that have not been paid—Peachtree® Complete Accounting 2006 allows you to print a report titled Aged Receivables. This report shows information regarding the type of transaction (Invoice or Credit Memo), the transaction date, the Invoice or Credit Memo number, customer ID, customer, contact, telephone number and the total amount due. In addition, the invoices will be categorized by age in order to identify past due invoices.

MEMO

DATE: January 10, 2006

Renee needs to prepare and print an Aged Receivables report to give to the owners, Eric and Matt, so they can see which invoices are open.

 DO: Prepare and print an Aged Receivables report
Click **All Accounts Receivables Reports** from the **Sales** button
Double click on Aged Receivables
Click on the **Print** icon at the top of the window
Click **Close**

High Ridge Ski Shoppe
Aged Receivables
As of Jan 31, 2006
Filter Criteria includes: Report order is by ID. Report is printed in Detail Format.

Customer ID Customer Contact Telephone 1	Invoice/CM #	0 - 30	31 - 60	61 - 90	Over 90 days	Amount Due
CHA01	89	53.63				53.63
Chang, Melissa Melissa Chang 619-555-8441	107	1,033.78				1,033.78
CHA01 Chang, Melissa		1,087.41				1,087.41
CLA01 Clarence, Caroline Caroline Clarence 619-555-4697	90	455.00				455.00
CLA01 Clarence, Caroline		455.00				455.00

RECORD CASH SALES WITH SALES TAX

Not all sales in a business are on account. In many instances, payment is made at the time the service is performed. This is entered as a cash sale. When entering a cash sale, you may prepare a sales receipt through the Receipts window or prepare an invoice through the Sales/Invoicing window and apply the payment to that invoice. Peachtree® Complete Accounting 2006 records the transaction in the appropriate Journal, recording revenue and increasing cash in our default cash account unless otherwise instructed. When cash sales are recorded through the Receipts window, the transaction will appear in the Cash Receipts Journal. When the cash sale is recorded through the Sales/Invoicing window, the transaction will appear in the Sales Journal. In textbook accounting, cash sales are generally recorded in the Cash Receipts Journal and so we will record our cash sales through the Receipts window. Some businesses may prefer recording cash sales through the Sales/Invoicing window so that all sales will appear in the Sales Journal. Peachtree can be set to mark the cash receipt as deposited when entered or it can create a list of checks received from which a deposit can be created. We will be using the former.

Cash Receipts require the use of a unique Reference number. When payments are made with checks, the check serves as this unique number. When payment is made with currency or credit cards, this creates a problem. Most businesses would record cash receipts only once at the end of the day comprising the total of the cash receipts for the day. The date itself could be used as the reference. Since we will be recording cash more than once in our tutorial, we will use a numbering system consisting of the customer's initials followed by the date for all transactions involving credit cards or currency. In addition, we will create a customer called CASH for use in all such transactions. Receipt numbers are optional but we will use them.

MEMO:

DATE: January 11, 2006

Record the following cash sale from Morrie Tavish: Received cash from a customer who purchased a pair of sunglasses, $39.95; a boot case, $49.95; and some lip balm, $1.19. Use MT011106 in the Reference field.

 DO: Enter the above transaction as a cash sale to a cash customer

Click **Receipts** from the tasks area of the **Sales** button.

Note: The Deposit ticket ID is the first field of the window and is automatically filled in by Peachtree. The number it uses is the date it reads off the computer's internal clock. Under normal business conditions, this is ideal as deposits are typically made on a daily basis. We will manually insert our dates in this field.

Type 1/11/06 in the **Deposit ticket ID** field.

Click the magnifying glass for the **Customer ID:** field

Click on the **New** icon

Enter CASH in the **Customer ID:** field

Enter Cash Customer in the **Name:** field

Using the magnifying glass next to **Sales Tax** field, select CA Sa-1

Click **Save** and **Close** on the Maintain Customers/Prospects screen

Click the magnifying glass for the **Customer ID:** field

Select CASH

– You will automatically be moved to the **Reference** field.

Enter **MT011106**. Tab to the **Receipt Number** field.

Note: Since most businesses do not have access to their accounting systems at the time cash sales are made, preprinted manual cash receipt forms are used. These forms are typically pre-numbered and it is this number that we would insert in the Receipt Number field. Once the first number has been entered, Peachtree will sequentially number future cash receipts by adding 1 to the previous number during the current session.

Enter 1000.

Verify that the date is Jan 11, 2006. If it is not correct, enter 1/11/06.

Click in the **Quantity** field.

Enter 1.00. Press **Tab**.

Click on the magnifying glass for **Item**, double click Sunglasses, Polarized Lens.

Tab until you reach the **Quantity** field again.

Enter 1.00. Press **Tab**.

Click on the magnifying glass for **Item**, double click Boot Case, Canvas.

Tab until you reach the **Quantity** field again.

Enter 1.0, press **Tab**
Click on the magnifying glass for **Item**, double click Lip Balm.
Verify your screen with the illustration below. Edit if needed.

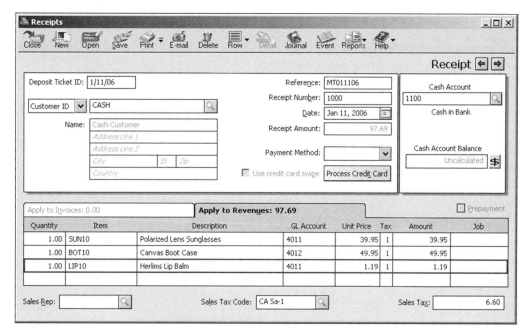

Once you have verified your data, click on the **Print** icon.
Click on **Print**.
Close the Receipts window.

ACCEPTING CREDIT CARDS

From an accounting perspective, a credit card sale is treated exactly like a cash sale. Peachtree®
Complete Accounting 2006 has the capability to accept and authorize a number of different types
of credit cards. In order to accomplish this, a Payments Methods list must be created and the user
must subscribe to an on-line credit card service. The educational version of Peachtree® Complete
Accounting 2006 does not have the on-line credit card service enabled but we can create a
Payments list and simulate the process. Once the Payments Methods list has been entered, you
can select the appropriate credit card when preparing a Cash Receipt.

The credit cards Peachtree is capable of accepting include American Express, Discover,
MasterCard, and Visa. Except for American Express, the credit card deposits are made into the
checking or bank account, and bank fees for the charge cards are deducted directly from the bank
account. Because American Express is not a "bank" charge card, charge receipts are sent to
American Express, and American Express sends a check to the company for the amount of the
charge, less American Express fees. In other words, they are recorded as a receivable.

MEMO

DATE: January 11, 2006

In order to prepare High Ridge Ski Shoppe to accept credit cards, enter the following payment methods through the Customer Defaults window: Cash/Check, Visa, MasterCard, Discover.

 DO: Create a Payment Methods list:
Click **Maintain** from the menu bar
Click **Default Information**
Click **Customers**

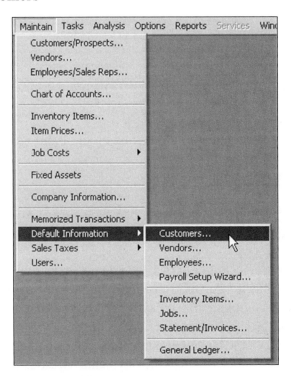

Click on the **Pay Methods** tab
In **Field 1**, enter Cash/Check as the Payment Method
In **Field 2**, enter Visa as the Payment Method
In **Field 3**, enter MasterCard as the Payment Method
In **Field 4**, enter Discover as the Payment Method

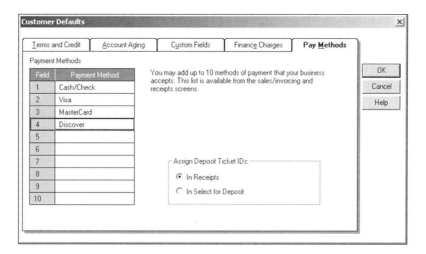

Note: We have elected to not include American Express since many businesses do not accept it as a payment method.

Click **OK** to accept the list.

ENTERING A CREDIT CARD SALE

MEMO

DATE: January 11, 2006

A customer purchases a pair of ski pants, $129.00 and pays using a Visa card. Credit card information is as follows: card holder: Harriet Brown, card number: 4605-8383-9019-8105, expires: 02/07. Use HB011106 in the Reference field.

DO: Record the credit card sale

Click **Receipts** from the tasks area of the **Sales** button.

Type 1/11/06 in the **Deposit ticket ID** field.

Click the magnifying glass for the **Customer ID:** field

Select Cash Customer

You will automatically be moved to the **Reference** field.

Enter HB011106. Tab to the **Receipt Number** field.

Enter 1001.

Verify that the date is Jan 11, 2006. If it is not correct, enter 1/11/06.

Click in the **Quantity** field.

Enter 1.00. Press **Tab**.

Click on the magnifying glass for **Item**, double click Ski Pants, Microfiber.

Click on the drop down arrow to the right of the **Payment Method** field

Select **Visa**

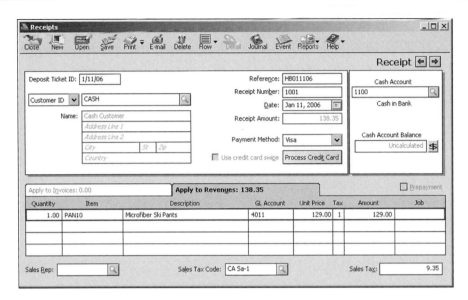

Click on the **Process Credit Card** button under the **Payment Method:** field
You are brought to a Credit Card Information window
Enter Harriet Brown in the **Cardholder's Name** field
Click in the **Credit Card Number** field, enter 4605-8383-9019-8105
Click in the **Expiration Date** field for month, enter 02 for year, 07

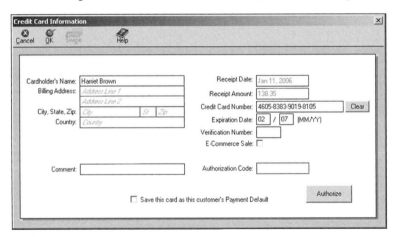

Note: If we were a subscriber to the service, we could authorize the payment by
    clicking on the Authorize button.
Click **OK**
Click **Print** twice
Leave the **Receipts** window open for the next activity

RECORD SALES PAID BY CHECK

A sale paid for with a check is considered a cash sale. A sales receipt is prepared to record the
sale.

MEMO

DATE: January 11, 2006

We do take checks for sales even if a customer is from out of town. Record the sale of 2 packs of ski socks at $15.95 each to a cash customer using Check No. 5589.

 DO: With the blank Receipt window on the screen, enter the above transaction
Click the magnifying glass for the **Customer ID:** field
Select Cash Customer
Type 5589 in the **Reference** field.
Tab to the **Receipt Number** field and enter or verify 1002.
Verify that the date is Jan 11, 2006. If it is not correct, enter 1/11/06.
The **Payments Method** field should reflect Cash/Check. Change it as needed.
Click in the **Quantity** field and enter 2.00. Press **Tab**.
Click on the magnifying glass for **Item**, double click Ski Socks, Thermal.
Click **Print** twice to print the receipt

ENTER CASH SALES TRANSACTIONS WITHOUT STEP-BY-STEP INSTRUCTIONS

MEMO

DATE: January 12, 2006

After a record snowfall, the store is really busy. Use Cash Customer as the customer name for the transactions. Record the following cash, check, and credit card sales:

Cash Receipt No. 1003—A cash customer used Check No. 196 to purchase a ski parka, $249.00; ski pants, $129.00; and a ski sweater, $89.95.

Cash Receipt No. 1004—A cash customer used a MasterCard to purchase a standard snow-board, $389.95; deluxe snowboard boots, $249.00; and standard snowboard bindings, $189.95. Credit card information is as follows: cardholder's name, George Smit, credit card number, 8765-9843-8321-3846, expires 11/08.

Cash Receipt No. 1005—A cash customer, Eunice Portage, purchased deluxe gloves for $89.95 using cash.

DO: Repeat the procedures used to enter prior Cash Receipts to record the additional transactions listed above:
- Always use the Item List to determine the appropriate sales items for billing.
- Use 1/12/06 for the Deposit ID:
- Print each Cash Receipt immediately after entering the information for it.
- Check your data with the following screen captures.
- If you make an error, correct it.
- Click **Close** after you have entered and printed Cash Receipt No. 1005.

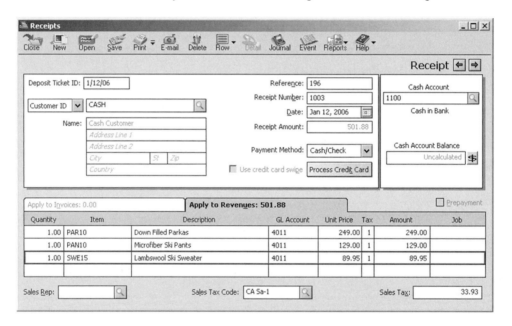

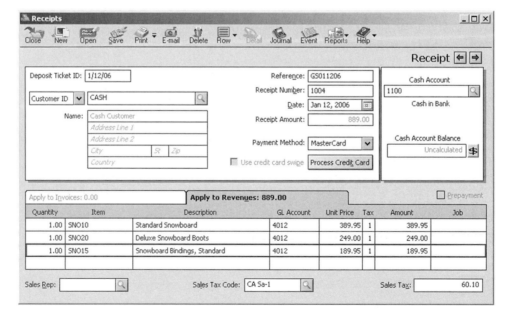

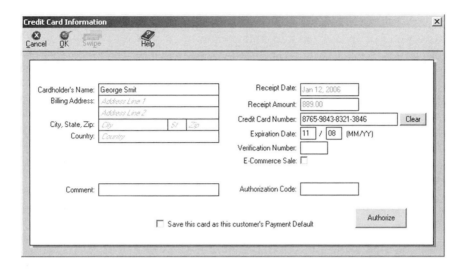

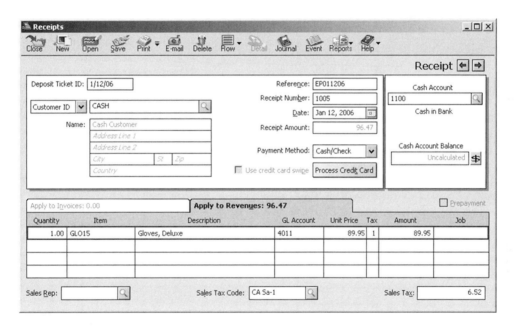

PRINT ITEMS SOLD TO CUSTOMERS REPORT

Peachtree® Complete Accounting 2006 has reports available that enable you to obtain sales information about your customers. To get information about the total amount of sales to each customer during a specific period, print an Items Sold to Customers report. The totals shown represent both cash and/or credit sales. The Items Sold to Customers report analyzes the quantity of merchandise sold to each customer by item, gives the sales value of the merchandise, gives the cost of each item, and calculates the cost of goods sold for each item, and the percentage of gross margin for each item. Information regarding the total inventory sold is also provided. This includes the cost of goods sold for the inventory, and the gross margin for the inventory of merchandise sold. As with most Peachtree reports, we can make modifications to suit our needs.

MEMO

DATE: January 13, 2006

Near the middle of the month, Renee prepares an Items Sold to Customers report to obtain information about sales and merchandise costs. Modify this report to include the Item Description and move it to the right of the Item ID column. Reduce the width of the Customer and Item ID columns.

DO: Prepare the above report

Click on the **All Accounts Receivable Reports** on the **Sales** button.

Double click on Items Sold to Customers.

Note: Peachtree does not include the Item Description by default. Since this is a useful item, we will add it to the report.

Click the **Options** icon on the top of the screen.

Click on the **Fields** tab of the Items Sold to Customers window

Scroll down using the scroll bar until you locate **Item Description**

Place a red checkmark in the **Show** column by clicking the box

Note: This process will also select the Item Description row. This is apparent due to the black box that now surrounds the row. Any row can be selected by clicking anywhere in the row. Be sure that the Item Description row is surrounded with a black box.

Click on the **Move Up** button

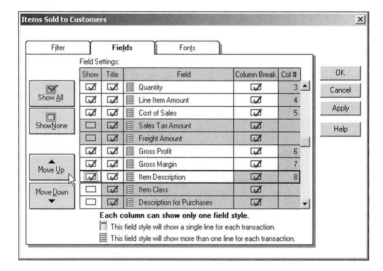

Note: Peachtree has moved this field up one position in the listing of fields.

Continue clicking on Move Up until Item Description is just above the

Contact field. If you move too far up, use the Move Down button to place the Item Description field just below the Item ID field.

Click **OK** to display the report.

Click the **Design** icon at the top of the window

Position the cursor over the blue line separating the **Customer ID** from the **Name** columns at the top of the report. Your cursor should turn into a double headed arrow.

· · 1 · · ·	· · 2 · · ·	· · 3 · · ·	· · 4 · · ·	· · 5 · · ·	· · 6 · · ·	· · 7 · · ·	· · 8 · · ·	· · 9 · · ·

High Ridge Ski Shoppe
Items Sold to Customers
For the Period From Jan 1, 2006 to Jan 31, 2006
Filter Criteria includes: Report order is by Customer ID, Item ID. Report is printed in Detail Format.

Customer ID	Name	Item ID	Item Description	Qty	Amount
CASH	Cash Customer	BOT10	Boot Case, Canvas	1.00	49.95
		GLO15	Gloves, Deluxe	1.00	89.95

Left mouse click and drag to the left stopping before you hit **Customer ID**.

Repeat for the Item ID field.

Click **Print**.

Click **OK** in the Windows Print dialog box.

Close the report without saving the modifications when you are finished.

High Ridge Ski Shoppe
Items Sold to Customers
For the Period From Jan 1, 2006 to Jan 31, 2006
Filter Criteria includes: Report order is by Customer ID, Item ID. Report is printed in Detail Format.

Customer ID	Name	Item ID	Item Description	Qty	Amount	Cost of Sales	Gross Profit	Gross Margin
CASH	Cash Customer	BOT10	Boot Case, Canvas	1.00	49.95	19.66	30.29	60.64
		GLO15	Gloves, Deluxe	1.00	89.95	42.32	47.63	52.95
		LIP10	Lip Balm	1.00	1.19	0.69	0.50	42.02
		PAN10	Ski Pants, Microfiber	2.00	258.00	1.38	256.62	99.47
		PAR10	Parkas, Down filled	1.00	249.00	123.00	126.00	50.60
		SNO10	Snowboard, Standard	1.00	389.95	198.00	191.95	49.22
		SNO15	Snowboard Bindings, Stan	1.00	189.95	89.32	100.63	52.98
		SNO20	Snowboard Boots, Deluxe	1.00	249.00	99.00	150.00	60.24
		SOC10	Ski Socks, Thermal	2.00	31.90	13.94	17.96	56.30
		SUN10	Sunglasses, Polarized Len	1.00	39.95	13.66	26.29	65.81
		SWE15	Sweater, Ski	1.00	89.95	49.00	40.95	45.53
				13.00	1,638.79	649.97	988.82	60.34
CHA01	Chang, Melissa		Delivery Charge		25.00		25.00	100.00
		BOT10	Boot Case, Canvas					60.64
		SNB20	Snowboard, Deluxe	1.00	499.95	205.00	294.95	59.00
		SNO15	Snowboard Bindings, Stan	1.00	189.95	89.32	100.63	52.98
		SNO20	Snowboard Boots, Deluxe	1.00	249.00	99.00	150.00	60.24
				3.00	963.90	393.32	570.58	59.19

CORRECT A CASH RECEIPT AND PRINT THE CORRECTED FORM

As it did with sales invoices and credit memos, Peachtree® Complete Accounting 2006 makes correcting errors user friendly. When an error is discovered in a transaction such as a cash sale, you can simply return to the receipt form where the transaction was recorded and correct the error.

When a correction for a cash sale is made, Peachtree® Complete Accounting 2006 not only changes the receipt, it also changes all journal and account entries for the transaction to reflect the correction. Peachtree® Complete Accounting 2006 then allows a corrected sales receipt to be printed.

MEMO

DATE: January 13, 2006

After reviewing transaction information, you realize that the check number for Cash Receipt No. 1002 was entered as 5589 incorrectly. Change the check number to 5598.

DO: Correct the error indicated in the memo above, and print a corrected Cash Receipt
Click **Receipts** from the Tasks area of the **Sales** button.
Click on the **Open** icon at the top of the window
Locate the incorrect check number (Reference Number) **5589** and double click
Click in the **Reference** field, enter 5598
Click **Print** twice

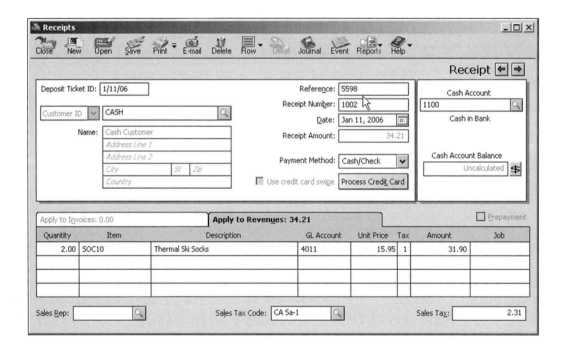

VIEW AND PRINT TAXABLE/EXEMPT SALES REPORT

The Taxable/Exempt Sales report shows a summary breakout of all taxable and exempt sales along with the related sales tax. The report provides a breakdown by taxing authority. Some businesses conduct business in more than one tax area. This might mean more than one state, or it might mean different tax rates within the same state, such as by county. The data can be used to prepare various state tax reports.

MEMO
DATE: January 13, 2006

Prepare and print a Taxable/Exempt Sales report.

DO: View and print the Taxable/Exempt Sales report
Click on the **All Accounts Receivable Reports** on the **Sales** button.
Using the scroll bar, locate the Taxable/Exempt Sales report and double click
Click **Print**
Close the report and the Select a Report windows

High Ridge Ski Shoppe
Taxable / Exempt Sales
For the Period From Jan 1, 2006 to Jan 31, 2006
Filter Criteria includes: Report is printed in Summary Format.

Authority ID	Authority Description	Tax Rate	Taxable Sale	Tax Amount	Exempt Sales	Total Sales
CA Sa-1	CA Sales Tax	7.25000	10,666.54	773.33		10,666.54
CA Sa-1	CA Sales Tax				25.00	25.00
CA Sa-1	Total CA Sales Tax		10,666.54	773.33	25.00	10,691.54

RECORD CUSTOMER PAYMENTS ON ACCOUNT

When customers pay the amount they owe, Peachtree® Complete Accounting 2006 allows us to apply the payment to the invoices in the customer's account. When you start to record a payment made by a customer, you will be presented with a list of invoices that are still unpaid. You will be prompted to indicate to which invoices the payment should be applied. Some programs do not allow the user this flexibility but rather will automatically apply the payment to the oldest invoice. This can create problems in reconciling the account with your customer, whose records may show the payment applied to a different invoice.

MEMO

DATE: January 13, 2006

Record the receipt of Check No. 765 for $975 from Martin Vallejo as payment in full on his account.

DO: Record the above payment on account:

Click **Receipts** in the **Sales** button.

The **Deposit ticket ID:** should be 1/13/06.

Click on the magnifying glass for **Customer ID:**.

Double click Vallejo, Martin

- Notice that Peachtree will automatically open the Apply to Invoices tab since this customer has an unpaid invoice.

You will start in the **Reference** field. Enter the check number 765.

Tab to the **Receipt Number** field, leave this field empty. We will enter the receipt number when we print.

The **Date:** field should reflect the system date of 1/13/06. If you forgot to set the system date, you will need to change the date now.

In the Apply to Invoices tab, click in the **Pay** box at the end of the row that contains the invoice.

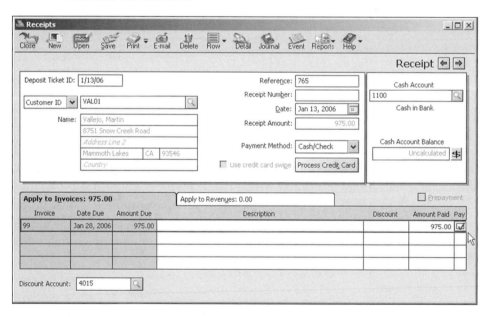

After verifying your input, click on the **Print** icon.

Enter 1006 in the **Receipt Number** field.

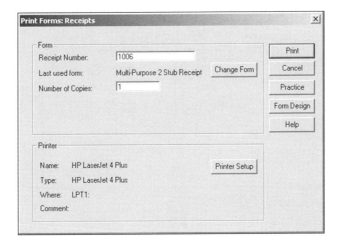

Click **Print**
Close **Receipts** window

RECORD CUSTOMER PAYMENT ON ACCOUNT WITH CREDIT

If you recall, Melissa Chang returned a boot case on 1/9/2006. At that time, we applied the credit #CM107 to the invoice on which the case was originally billed (Invoice #107). Peachtree has automatically applied this credit to that invoice. When we apply a payment to that invoice, it will reflect the new balance after deducting the credit.

MEMO
DATE: January 13, 2006

Melissa Chang sent Check No. 1026 for $1,085.60 to pay her account in full.

 DO: Record the payment by Melissa Chang to her outstanding invoices
Click **Receipts** in the **Sales** button.
The **Deposit ticket ID:** should be 1/13/06
Click on the magnifying glass for **Customer ID:**
Double click Chang, Melissa
You will start in the **Reference** field. Enter the check number 1026
Tab to the **Date:** field. It should reflect the system date of 1/13/06. If you forgot to set the system date, you will need to change the date now
In the **Apply to Invoices** tab, click in the **Pay** box at the end of the row that contains the Invoice NO. 1500
Click in the **Pay** box for Invoice Number 107

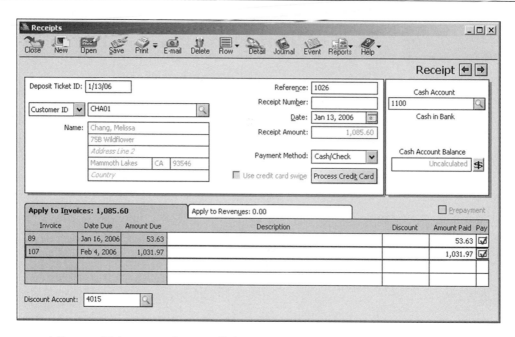

After verifying your input, click on the **Print** icon
Enter or verify 1007 in the **Receipt Number** field and click **Print**
Close the Receipts window

RECORD PAYMENT ON ACCOUNT FROM A CUSTOMER QUALIFYING FOR AN EARLY-PAYMENT DISCOUNT

Each customer may be assigned terms as part of the customer information. When terms such as 1% 10, Net 30 or 2% 10, Net 30 are given, customers whose payments are received within ten days of the invoice date are eligible to deduct 1% or 2% from the amount owed when making their payments. Peachtree will deduct these automatically if they have been earned. Peachtree will only know if the discounts have been earned if proper dates are used for both invoicing and cash receipts. In any event, one can override Peachtree by clicking in the Discount column and inserting the discount amount manually. This is particularly useful if payment was delayed for reasons not the fault of the payer and discounts are still offered.

MEMO
DATE: January 13, 2006

Received payment from High Ridge Recreation Center for Invoice No.108. Check No. 981-13 was for $3493.24 as full payment. Record the payment and the 1% discount for early payment under the invoice terms of 1% 10, Net 30.

DO: Record the receipt of the check and apply the discount to the above transaction
Click **Receipts** in the **Sales** button.
The **Deposit ticket ID:** should be 01/13/06.
Click on the magnifying glass for **Customer ID:**.
Double click High Ridge Recreation Center
You will start in the **Reference** field. Enter the check number 981-13.
Tab to the **Date:** field. It should reflect the system date of 1/13/06. If you forgot to
     set the system date, you will need to change the date now.
In the **Apply to Invoices** tab, click in the **Pay** box at the end of the row that
     contains Invoice Number 108

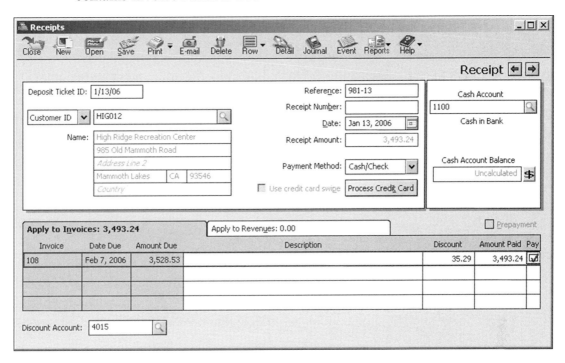

After verifying your input, click on the **Print** icon
Enter or verify Receipt number 1008
Click **Print** twice
Leave the Receipts window open for the next activity

RECORD ADDITIONAL PAYMENTS ON ACCOUNT WITHOUT STEP-BY-STEP INSTRUCTIONS

MEMO

DATE: January 14, 2006

Received Check No. 152 from Victor Walsh for $919.41

Received Check No. 8252 dated January 11 and postmarked 1/12 for $2,406.91 from High Ridge School. Even though the date we are recording the payment is after the discount date, the check was postmarked within the discount period. Use 01/12/06 as the date for this cash receipt.

Received Check No. 1051 from David Eddy for $500 in partial payment of his account. Be sure to record the payment in the Amount Paid column and add "Partial Payment" in the Description column.

Received Check No. 563 from Susan Platter for $408.48 in payment of her oldest invoice.

Received Check No. 819 from Hideto Tanamura for $100 in partial payment of his account.

DO: Refer to the previous steps listed to enter the above payments:
Click **Print** to go from one Receive Payments Screen to the next. Peachtree should assign the next sequential receipt number.
Click **Close** button after all payments received have been recorded.

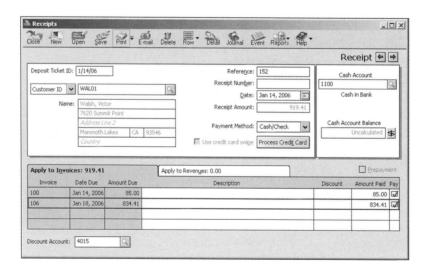

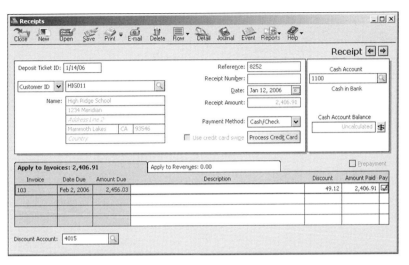

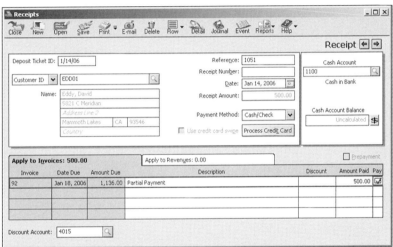

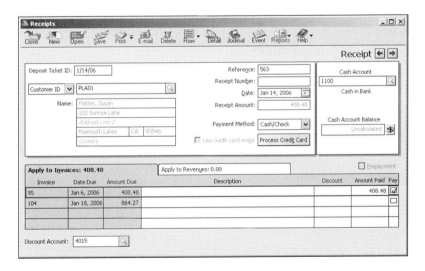

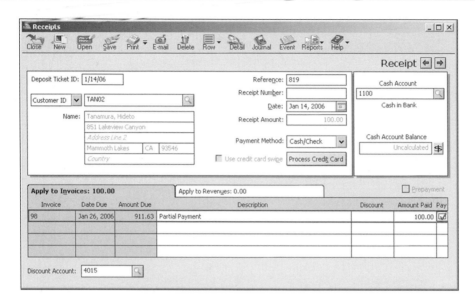

RECORD PAYMENT ON ACCOUNT FROM A CUSTOMER LOSING AN EARLY-PAYMENT DISCOUNT

Not all customers will submit payments in time to earn the discounts offered. Peachtree will automatically remove the discount in the Apply to Invoice window when payments are received after the discount date. Although this can be manually overridden, a company will typically not allow discounts past the discount date.

MEMO

DATE: January 15, 2006

Received Check No. 3951 from Dr. Jacob Montello for $1,087.51. Note that this is past the discount date (no discount earned).

DO: Refer to the previous steps listed to enter the above payment:
Note: The Discount column contains no discount for this invoice since the payment date recorded for the receipt is past the 10 days allowed.

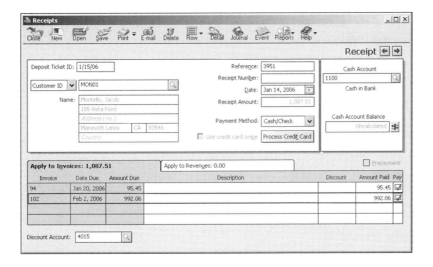

VIEW AND PRINT CUSTOMERS LEDGERS REPORT

In order to see the transactions for customers, you need to prepare a report called Customer Ledgers report. This report shows all sales, credits, and payments for each customer on account and for the customer named Cash Customer. The report also shows the balance remaining on account for the individual customers. It is a far more detailed report than a schedule of accounts receivable in that it shows all activity in the account during the reporting period rather than just a balance owed.

 DO: Prepare a Customer Ledgers report for all customers for all transactions:
Click the **All Accounts Receivables Reports** from the **Sales** button.
Double click on Customer Ledgers.
- This report lists the names of all customers and their activity for this period. The balance column shows the total balance for each customer. This includes opening balances as well as ending balances.

High Ridge Ski Shoppe
Customer Ledgers
For the Period From Jan 1, 2006 to Jan 31, 2006
Filter Criteria includes: Report order is by ID. Report is printed in Detail Format.

Customer ID Customer	Date	Trans No	Type	Debit Amt	Credit Amt	Balance
CASH	1/11/06	MT011106	CRJ	97.69	97.69	0.00
Cash Customer	1/11/06	HB011106	CRJ	138.35	138.35	0.00
	1/11/06	S598	CRJ	34.21	34.21	0.00
	1/12/06	196	CRJ	501.88	501.88	0.00
	1/12/06	GS011206	CRJ	889.00	889.00	0.00
	1/12/06	EP011206	CRJ	96.47	96.47	0.00
CHA01	1/1/06	Balance Fwd				53.63
Chang, Melissa	1/5/06	107	SJ	1,085.54		1,139.17
	1/10/06	CM107	SJ		53.57	1,085.60
	1/13/06	1026	CRJ		1,085.60	0.00

Click the **Print** button at the top of the Customer Ledgers report window.
Close the report
Leave the Select a Report window open for the next activity.

PRINT AGED RECEIVABLES REPORT

A report that will show you the balance owed by each customer is the Aged Receivables report. The report presents the total balance owed by each customer as of a certain date.

MEMO
DATE: January 15, 2006

The owners, Eric and Matt, want to see how much each customer owes to High Ridge Ski Shoppe. Print an Aged Receivables report.

DO: Print an Aged Receivables report
With the Select a Report window still on the screen, double click Aged Receivables
Using the **Options** button, set the date to 01/15/06 and click **OK**
Click **Print**

High Ridge Ski Shoppe
Aged Receivables
As of Jan 15, 2006
Filter Criteria includes: Report order is by ID. Report is printed in Detail Format.

Customer ID Customer Contact Telephone 1	Invoice/CM #	0 - 30	31 - 60	61 - 90	Over 90 days	Amount Due
CLA01 Clanence, Caroline Caroline Clarence 619-555-4697	90	455.00				455.00
CLA01 Clanence, Caroline		455.00				455.00
DAV01 Davidson, Fred Fred Davidson 619-555-8431	91	650.00				650.00
DAV01 Davidson, Fred		650.00				650.00

Close the report and the Select a Report windows

PREPARE AND PRINT A DEPOSITS IN TRANSIT REPORT

When cash sales are made and payments on accounts are received, Peachtree® Complete Accounting 2006 is currently set to record the receipts as being deposited on the day of the receipt. On days when more than one cash payment is received, Peachtree® Complete Accounting 2006 will combine these into a single deposit using the **Deposit Ticket ID**. Should the need arise to look at the deposits that have been made during the month, the Deposit in Transit report provides all the information needed to analyze our cash receipts.

MEMO

DATE: January 15, 2006

Prepare and print a Deposits in Transit report to show the cash deposits that have been made thus far this month.

DO: Prepare and print the Deposits in Transit report
Click **All Account Reconciliation Reports** from the **General Ledger** button
Double click Deposits In Transit report
Click **Print**
Close the report and the Select a Report windows

High Ridge Ski Shoppe
Deposits in Transit
As of Jan 31, 2006
1100 - Cash in Bank
Filter Criteria includes: 1) Uncleared Transactions; 2) Deposits. Report order is by Number.

Trans No	Date	Reference	Trans Desc	Trans Amt	Deposit Amt
1/11/06	1/11/06	MT011106	Cash Customer	270.25	97.69
		HB011106	Cash Customer		138.35
		5598	Cash Customer		34.21
1/12/06	1/12/06	196	Cash Customer	1,487.35	501.88
		GS011206	Cash Customer		889.00
		EP011206	Cash Customer		96.47
1/13/06	1/13/06	765	Vallejo, Martin	5,553.84	975.00
		1026	Chang, Melissa		1,085.60
		981-13	High Ridge Recreation Center		3,493.24
1/14/06	1/14/06	152	Walsh, Victor	4,334.80	919.41
		8252	High Ridge School		2,406.91
		1051	Eddy, David		500.00
		563	Platter, Susan		408.48
		819	Tanamura, Hideto		100.00
1/15/06	1/14/06	3951	Montello, Jacob	1,087.51	1,087.51
			Total	12,733.75	12,733.75

RECORD THE RETURN OF A CHECK BECAUSE OF NONSUFFICIENT FUNDS

If a customer pays you with a check that does not clear because there are insufficient funds, it will be returned to you unpaid. Since the funds were not deposited to your account, they must be taken out as well as the associated bank charges. In addition, the Accounts Receivable account must be updated to show the amount the customer owes you for the check that bounced. Remember that the customer not only owes you the previous balance, but now also owes you for the fees associated with the bounced check. By deleting the cash receipt associated with the bounced check, we remove the deposit from our cash account and reinstate the customer's accounts receivable. We must now account for both the fee charged by the bank to us and the fee we will charge our customer for the inconvenience. To do this we will add the fee onto the customer's invoice. Since the fee will consist of the amount we pay the bank as well as our charge to the customer, we must both reduce our cash account and show a returned check service charge revenue. The problem is that when we add the fee to the customer's invoice, we are allowed only one credit. This means that both the amount we pay to the bank and the extra amount we charge the customer for the bounced check will be credited to the same account, cash. To correct this, we must create a General Journal entry to split the credit portion of the entry.

As an example, let us assume that the bank charges us a $10.00 returned check fee. This means, that they have deducted $10.00 from our bank account. Let us also assume that we charge our customer $15.00 for a returned check. If we invoice the customer for the $15.00, the debit is to Accounts Receivable but we are allowed only one credit on the invoice for this amount. The reality is we should be crediting Cash for $10.00 and a Returned Check Revenue account for the other $5.00. Since we can only have one credit we will place the $15.00 in the Revenue account and use a General Journal entry to debit $10.00 out of the account and credit it into the Cash account.

MEMO

DATE: January 15, 2006

While attempting to clear Jacob Montello's Check No. 3951 for $1087.51 electronically, our bank was informed there were insufficient funds in his account. They notified us immediately. The bank imposed a $10 service charge for the NSF check. High Ridge Ski Shoppe charges a $15 fee for NSF checks. Delete the cash receipt associated with this check and add the service charge to his invoice. Add the Return Check Charges item to the Item List and create an appropriate GL account to associate with this item. Prepare the required General Journal entry to adjust the Return Check Revenue account.

DO: Delete Jacob Montello's Cash Receipt and add the returned check charge to his Invoice Number 102. Add Return Check Service Charge to the Item List and Return Check Revenue to the Chart of Accounts. Prepare the required General Journal entry.

Click **Receipts** in the **Sales** button.

Click the **Open** icon at the top of the window

Double click on the item from Jacob Montello, (Reference 3951)

Click **Delete**

Click **Yes** to confirm the deletion

Click **Close** to exit the Receipts window

Click the **All Accounts Receivables Reports** from the **Sales** button.

Double click on **Customer Ledgers**.

Locate Invoice Number 102 for Jacob Montello (MON01) and double click anywhere in the line

– This will bring up Sales Invoice Number 102

Click at the end of the line for ski poles and press tab until you have a blank line at the bottom of the invoice (or make the window longer)

Enter 1 in the **Quantity** field

Tab to the **Item** field. Using the magnifying glass, open the Item List

Since no item exists for a bank service charge, click on the **New** icon

Enter BAD CHECK in the **Item ID** field

Enter Returned Check Service Charge in the **Description** field

Select Non-stock item in the **Item Class** field

Enter 15.00 in the **Price Level 1:** field

Using the magnifying glass next to the **GL Sales Acct:** field, open the Chart of Accounts

Since no account exists for a bank service charge, click on the **New** icon

Type 4040 in the **Account ID** field

Enter Returned Check Revenue in the **Description** field

Select Income in the **Account Type** field

Click **Save** and then **Close** on the Maintain Chart of Accounts

Select account 4040 as the **GL Sales Acct**

Using the magnifying glass next to the **Item Tax Type:** field, select 2 Exempt

Click **Save** and then **Close**

Select BAD CHECK from the Item List

Click **Print**

Click **Close**

Close the report and the Select a Report windows

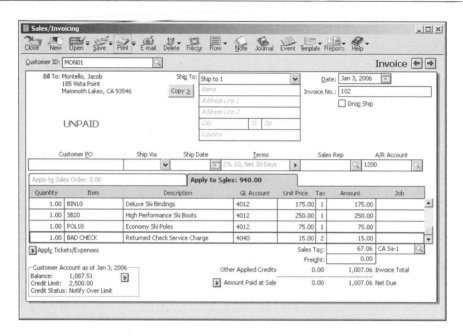

Click **General Journal Entry** from the **General Ledger** button
Confirm that the date is 01/15/06. If not, enter 01/15/06
Enter NSFADJ in the **Reference** field
Tab to the **Account No.** field, select 4040 Return Check Revenue
Type Adjust Returned Check Revenue in the **Description** field
Tab to the **Debit** field, enter 10.00
Tab to the **Account No.** field, select 1100 Cash in Bank
Tab to the **Credit** field, enter 10.00
Click **Save** and then **Close**

Peachtree® Complete Accounting 2006 can handle an NSF check in a number of ways. The above method, while not providing the best audit trail, is an easier method. The above procedures will remove the cash receipt completely from our system. It will still show on our bank statement first as a deposit and then as a deduction. Since the deposit and the deduction cancel each other, it does not matter whether it appears in our records. The only evidence of this transaction that will appear in our records is the reduction of our account by $10 for the service charge. This will also appear on the bank statement.

ISSUE A CREDIT MEMO AND A REFUND CHECK

If merchandise is returned and the invoice has been paid in full or the sale was for cash, a refund check must be issued at the same time that the credit memo is prepared. This is a three-step process that involves creating a credit memo, issuing a check and then applying the check to the credit memo.

MEMO

DATE: January 15, 2006

One of the members of the High Ridge School team has his own high performance ski poles and so the school returned one set of ski poles purchased for $59 January 3 on Invoice No. 103. They have already paid their bill in full. Record the return and issue a check refunding the $59 plus tax.

  DO: Prepare a Credit Memo to record the return of the ski poles and issue a refund check

Click the **Credit Memos** from the **Sales** button.
Click the drop-down list next to **Customer ID:**
Double click **High Ridge School**
Tab to **Date:** field.
–   Confirm that it reflects the 01/15/06 system date.
Tab to the **Credit No.** field.
Enter CM103
Tab to the **Quantity** field.
Enter 1.0 in the **Quantity** field. Press **Enter**.
Click on the magnifying glass to the right of the **Item** field, highlight Ski Poles, Economy (Item POL10) and click **OK** to choose this item.
      Note: Be sure to change the unit price to Price Level 2
Click **OK**
Click **Print**

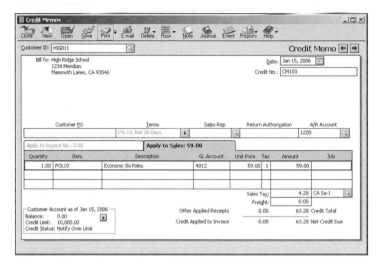

Close the Credit Memos window

Click **Payments** from the **Purchases** button

Note: If prompted, make sure Cash in Bank is the default cash account

Using the drop down arrow, change **Vendor ID** to **Customer ID**

Click on the magnifying glass and select High Ridge School

Click in the **Description** field, enter Refund Check for Ski Poles

Tab to the **Amount** field, enter 62.01

Note: This amount will be explained later

Print the check using **First Check Number** 1005

Close the Payments window

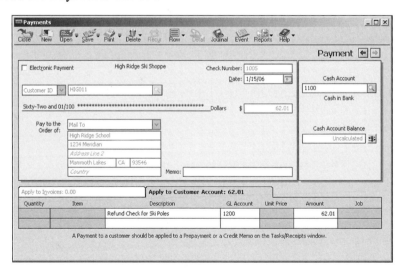

Click **Receipts** in the **Sales** button.
Enter 1/15/06 in the **Deposit ticket ID:** field
Using the magnifying glass, select High Ridge School
Enter REFUND011506 in the Reference field
Confirm the date, 01/15/06
Check the **Pay** boxes at the end of Invoice items CM103 and 1006
Print the receipt using number 1015 and close the Receipts window

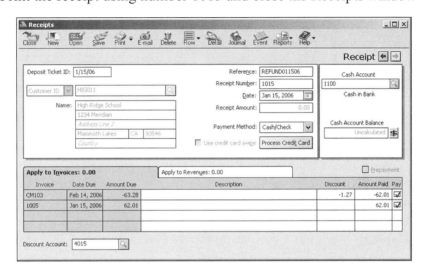

Since the customer took a 2% discount when paying us for the original order, we had to apply the discount to the refund as well. This is why we only paid High Ridge $62.01. It might be easier to first look in the Receipts window for any customer due a refund to see what the actual amount owed really comes to prior to creating the refund check.

PRINT JOURNALS

Even though Peachtree® Complete Accounting 2006 displays registers and reports in a manner that focuses on the transaction—that is, entering a sale on account via an invoice rather than a Sales Journal or a General Journal—it still keeps the transaction in a journal. Sales on account are kept in a Sales Journal while cash sales and payments on account are kept in a Cash Receipts Journal. We can view or print these journals through Peachtree's reports feature.

DO: Print the Sales Journal and Cash Receipts Journal
Click on **Sales Journal** from the **Sales** button
Click **OK** to accept the defaults
Click the **Print** icon and close the report with the **Close** icon
Select Cash Receipts Journal from the list presented
Click **OK** to accept the defaults
Click the **Print** icon and close the report

High Ridge Ski Shoppe
Sales Journal
For the Period From Jan 1, 2006 to Jan 31, 2006
Filter Criteria includes: Report order is by Invoice/CM Date. Report is printed in Detail Format.

Date	Account ID	Invoice/CM #	Line Description	Debit Amnt	Credit Amnt
1/3/06	2200	101	CA Sa-1: CA Sales Tax		5.44
	4012		Ultra Pro Ski Boots		75.00
	5000		Cost of sales	30.00	
	1120		Cost of sales		30.00
	1200		Walsh, Victor	80.44	
1/3/06	2200	102	CA Sa-1: CA Sales Tax		67.06
	4012		Model XB04 Snow Skis		425.00
	5000		Cost of sales	201.00	
	1120		Cost of sales		201.00
	4012		Deluxe Ski Bindings		175.00
	5000		Cost of sales	75.00	
	1120		Cost of sales		75.00
	4012		High Performance Ski Boots		250.00
	5000		Cost of sales	105.00	
	1120		Cost of sales		105.00
	4012		Economy Ski Poles		75.00
	5000		Cost of sales	30.00	
	1120		Cost of sales		30.00
	4040		Returned Check Service Charge		15.00
	1200		Montello, Jacob	1,007.06	
1/3/06	2200	103	CA Sa-1: CA Sales Tax		166.03
	4012		Model XB04 Snow Skis		1,495.00
	5000		Cost of sales	1,005.00	
	1120		Cost of sales		1,005.00
	4012		Standard Ski Bindings		500.00
	5000		Cost of sales	295.00	
	1120		Cost of sales		295.00
	4012		Economy Ski Poles		295.00
	5000		Cost of sales	150.00	
	1120		Cost of sales		150.00
	1200		High Ridge School	2,456.03	

High Ridge Ski Shoppe
Cash Receipts Journal
For the Period From Jan 1, 2006 to Jan 31, 2006
Filter Criteria includes: Report order is by Check Date. Report is printed in Detail Format.

Date	Account ID	Transaction Ref	Line Description	Debit Amnt	Credit Amnt
1/3/06	1200	101	Invoice: 101		80.44
	1200		Invoice: 101V	80.44	
			Walsh, Victor		
1/11/06	2200	MT011106	CA Sa-1: CA Sales Tax		6.60
	4011		Polarized Lens Sunglasses		39.95
	5000		Cost of sales	13.66	
	1120		Cost of sales		13.66
	4012		Canvas Boot Case		49.95
	5000		Cost of sales	19.66	
	1120		Cost of sales		19.66
	4011		Herlims Lip Balm		1.19
	5000		Cost of sales	0.69	
	1120		Cost of sales		0.69
	1100		Cash Customer	97.69	

PRINT THE GENERAL LEDGER TRIAL BALANCE

When all sales transactions have been entered, it is important to print the trial balance and verify that the total debits equal the total credits.

DO: Print the General Ledger Trial Balance
Click on **All General Ledger Reports** from the **General Ledger** button

Double click on General Ledger Trial Balance
Click the **Print** icon
Close the report and the Select a Report windows

High Ridge Ski Shoppe
General Ledger Trial Balance
As of Jan 31, 2006
Filter Criteria includes: Report order is by ID. Report is printed in Detail Format.

Account ID	Account Description	Debit Amt	Credit Amt
1100	Cash in Bank	34,402.22	
1120	Merchandise Inventory	52,504.05	
1200	Accounts Receivable		250.78
1311	Office Supplies	1,600.00	
1312	Sales Supplies	575.00	
1340	Prepaid Insurance	250.00	
1511	Office Equipment	5,000.00	
1521	Store Fixtures	4,500.00	
2100	Visa Payable		150.00
2200	Sales Tax Payable		1,238.36
2510	Office Equipment Loan Payable		3,000.00
2520	Store Fixtures Loan Payable		2,500.00
3010	Capital, Eric Boyd		20,000.00
3012	Capital, Matthew Wayne		20,000.00
3050	Retained Earnings		46,683.95
4011	Clothing & Accessory Sales		1,515.84
4012	Equipment Sales		9,091.70
4015	Sales Discounts	83.14	
4020	Freight Income		25.00
4040	Returned Check Revenue		5.00
5000	Cost of Goods Sold	5,546.22	
	Total:	104,460.63	104,460.63

CUSTOMER EVENT LOG

The Customer Event Log can be accessed to obtain information regarding individual customers. This log is accessed in the Maintain Customer window. Once a customer has been selected, the Log button at the top of the window is clicked.

The Log contains a listing of events relevant to our activities with that customer. This would include sales invoices, receipts and other accounting activities that we are engaged in with this customer.

DO: View the Customer Event Log
Click **Customers** from the **Sales** button
Using the magnifying glass for **Customer ID**, select High Ridge School
Click on the **Log** button

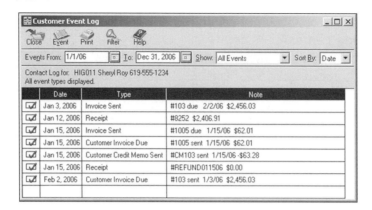

Close the Customer Event Log and the Maintain Customer windows

CUSTOMER ANALYSIS

A business may wish to know how profitable each of its customers is. While all of the reports we have examined thus far in the book related to sales have given us some information about the customer, none of them have expressed how profitable each customer is. Peachtree® Complete Accounting 2006 is capable of generating a report that gives us this information. It is called the Customer Sales History report. This report will show us by customer the amount of the sales, the cost of goods sold, the gross profit and the gross margin percent. This allows us to quickly and easily see how profitable each customer is.

DO: Print the Customer Sales History report
Click on **All Accounts Receivable Reports** from the **Sales** button
Double click on Customer Sales History
Click the **Print** icon
Close the report and the Select a Report windows

High Ridge Ski Shoppe
Customer Sales History
For the Period From Jan 1, 2006 to Jan 31, 2006
Filter Criteria includes: Report order is by Customer ID. Report is printed in Summary Format.

Customer ID	Name	Amount	Cost of Sales	Gross Profit	Gross Margin
CASH	Cash Customer	1,638.79	649.97	988.82	60.34
CHA01	Chang, Melissa	963.90	393.32	570.58	59.19
EDD01	Eddy, David				
HIG011	High Ridge School	2,231.00	1,420.00	811.00	36.35
HIG012	High Ridge Recreation Center	3,290.00	1,995.00	1,295.00	39.36
MON01	Montello, Jacob	940.00	411.00	529.00	56.28
PLA01	Platter, Susan	805.85	316.93	488.92	60.67
TAN02	Tanamura, Hideto				
VAL01	Vallejo, Martin				
WAL01	Walsh, Victor	778.00	360.00	418.00	53.73
Report Totals		10,647.54	5,546.22	5,101.32	47.91

BACK UP HIGH RIDGE SKI SHOPPE DATA

Whenever an important work session is complete, you should always back up your data. If your data disk is damaged or an error is discovered at a later time, the backup disk may be restored and the information used for recording transactions. No matter what type of business, the backup procedure remains the same. In addition, it is always wise to make a duplicate of your data disk just in case the disk is damaged in some way.

 DO: Follow the instructions given in earlier Chapters to back up data for High Ridge Ski Shoppe.

SUMMARY

In this chapter, cash, bank charge card, and credit sales were prepared for High Ridge Ski Shoppe, a retail business, using receipts and invoices. Credit memos and refund checks were issued, and customer accounts were added and revised. Invoices and cash receipts were edited, deleted, and voided. Cash payments were received and deposited. The Chart of Accounts was modified, and new items were added to the Item List "on the fly". All the transactions entered reinforced the Peachtree® Complete Accounting 2006 concept of using the business form to record transactions rather than entering information in journals. However, Peachtree® Complete Accounting 2006 performs this function in the background. Journals were accessed and printed. The importance of reports for information and making decision was illustrated. Sales reports analyzed sales both according to the customer and according to the sales item generating the revenue. Aged receivable reports focused on amounts owed by credit customers. The traditional trial balance emphasizing the equality of debits and credits was prepared.

END-OF-CHAPTER QUESTIONS

TRUE/FALSE

ANSWER THE FOLLOWING QUESTIONS IN THE SPACE PROVIDED BEFORE THE QUESTION NUMBER.

_____ 1. If an invoice has been paid in full, a refund check should be issued along with a credit memo.

_____ 2. Peachtree® Complete Accounting 2006 automatically applies a payment received to the most current invoice.

_____ 3. Sales tax will be calculated automatically on an invoice if a customer is marked taxable.

_____ 4. A new sales item may be added only at the beginning of a period.

_____ 5. A new customer may be added "on the fly."

_____ 6. Report formats can be customized.

_____ 7. One must click on the Apply Discounts button in order for discounts to be applied to invoices being paid.

_____ 8. Cash sales can be recorded through the Receipts window or through the Sales/Invoicing window on invoices and a payment applied.

_____ 9. If a customer issues a check that is returned marked NSF, you may charge the customer the amount of the bank charges and any penalty charges you impose.

_____ 10. Sales tax must be calculated manually and added to sales invoices.

MULTIPLE CHOICE

WRITE THE LETTER OF THE CORRECT ANSWER IN THE SPACE PROVIDED BEFORE THE QUESTION NUMBER.

_____ 1. Information regarding details of a customer's balance may be obtained by viewing _____.
   A. the General Ledger Trial Balance
   B. the Customer Sales History Report
   C. the Customer Ledgers Report
   D. an invoice for the customer

_____ 2. Even though transactions are entered via business documents such as invoices and receipts, Peachtree® Complete Accounting 2006 keeps track of all transactions ___.
   A. in a chart
   B. in a register
   C. on a graph
   D. in a journal

_____ 3. If a transaction is ___, it will not show up in the Customer Ledgers Report.
   A. voided
   B. deleted
   C. corrected
   D. canceled

_____ 4. A bank credit card sale is accounted for exactly like a ___.
   A. cash sale
   B. sale on account until reimbursement is received from a bank
   C. sale on account
   D. bank deposit

_____ 5. If a compound entry is created, this means that the debit and/or credit side of the transaction is split between two or more ___.
   A. accounts
   B. customers
   C. journals
   D. reports

_____ 6. When adding a customer "on the fly," you are required to ___.
   A. exit the task you are in without saving
   B. complete the task you are in before adding the customer
   C. open a window in which the new customer can be added
   D. none of the above—a customer cannot be added "on the fly"

_____ 7. The Item List stores information about ___.
    A. each item that is out of stock
    B. each item in stock
    C. each customer with an account
    D. each item a company sells

_____ 8. A report prepared to obtain information about the sales and associated merchandise
    costs by item is a ___.
    A. Stock Report
    B. Income Statement
    C. Items Sold to Customers Report
    D. Customer Sales History

_____ 9. If a customer has a balance for an amount owed and a return is made, a credit memo
    is prepared and ___.
    A. a refund check may be issued
    B. the amount of the return may be applied to the balance owed at the time the
       balance due is paid
    C. the customer determines whether to apply the amount to the balance owed or to
       get a refund check
    D. all of the above

_____ 10. Sales information regarding an item sold by the company is generally entered ___.
    A. in the Invoice Register
    B. when adding an inventory item
    C. only when creating the company
    D. only when the last item in stock is sold

FILL-IN

IN THE SPACE PROVIDED, WRITE THE ANSWER THAT MOST APPROPRIATELY
COMPLETES THE SENTENCE.

1. A report showing all sales, credits, and payments for each customer on account as well as the
   remaining balance on the account is the _____ report.

2. When you make the daily bank deposit, the report that shows the detail of the deposit is
   called a _____ report.

3. The only fields that must be filled in for Peachtree to calculate and enter all the correct
   information to complete the sales invoice are the _____ and _____ .

4. Peachtree® Complete Accounting 2006 allows you to view detailed information within most
   reports by using the _____ feature.

5. When you receive payments from customers, Peachtree® Complete Accounting 2006 places the amount received in the account called _____.

SHORT ESSAY

Describe the use of Find Transactions. Based on chapter information, what filters are used to instruct Find Transactions to limit its search?

_____

_____

_____

_____

_____

_____

_____

_____

_____

_____

_____

_____

_____

_____

_____

_____

_____

NAME _____

TRANSMITTAL

CHAPTER 5: HIGH RIDGE SKI SHOPPE

Attach the following documents and reports:

- ☐ Invoice No. 101: Victor Walsh
- ☐ Invoice No. 102: Jacob Montello
- ☐ Invoice No. 103: High Ridge School
- ☐ Invoice No. 104: Susan Platter
- ☐ Invoice No. 105: Hideto Tanamura
- ☐ Invoice No. 106: Victor Walsh
- ☐ Invoice No. 107: Melissa Chang
- ☐ Customer Ledgers Report
- ☐ Invoice No. 107 (Corrected): Melissa Chang
- ☐ Invoice No. 103 (Corrected): High Ridge School
- ☐ Invoice No. 108: High Ridge Recreation Center
- ☐ Credit Memo No. CM107: Melissa Chang
- ☐ Aged Receivables Report
- ☐ Cash Receipt No. 1000: Cash Customer
- ☐ Cash Receipt No. 1001: Cash Customer
- ☐ Cash Receipt No. 1002: Cash Customer
- ☐ Cash Receipt No. 1003: Cash Customer
- ☐ Cash Receipt No. 1004: Cash Customer
- ☐ Cash Receipt No. 1005: Cash Customer
- ☐ Items Sold to Customers Report
- ☐ Sales Receipt No. 1002 (Revised): Cash Customer
- ☐ Taxable/Exempt Sales Report
- ☐ Cash Receipt No. 1006: Martin Vallejo
- ☐ Cash Receipt No. 1007: Melissa Chang
- ☐ Cash Receipt No. 1008: High Ridge Recreation Center
- ☐ Cash Receipt No. 1009: Victor Walsh
- ☐ Cash Receipt No. 1010: High Ridge School
- ☐ Cash Receipt No. 1011: David Eddy
- ☐ Cash Receipt No. 1012: Susan Platter
- ☐ Cash Receipt No. 1013: Hideto Tanamura
- ☐ Cash Receipt No. 1014: Jacob Montello

☐   Customers Ledgers Report

☐   Aged Receivables Report

☐   Deposits In Transit Report

☐   Invoice No. 102 (Revised)

☐   Credit Memo No. CM103: High Ridge School

☐   Check No. 1005: High Ridge School

☐   Cash Receipt No. 1015: High Ridge School

☐   Sales Journal

☐   Cash Receipts Journal

☐   General Ledger Trial Balance

☐   Customer Sales History Report

END-OF-CHAPTER PROBLEM

ALOHA SUN CLOTHING CO.

Aloha Sun Clothing Co. is a men's and women's clothing store located in San Luis Obispo, California, specializing in resort wear. The store is owned and operated by Nalani Kalaniki and Maile Kahala. Maile keeps the books and runs the office for the store, and Nalani is responsible for buying merchandise and managing the store. Both partners sell merchandise in the store, and they have some college students working part time during the evenings and on the weekends.

INSTRUCTIONS

Open Aloha Sun Clothing Co. Add your initials to the company name. The company name will be **Aloha Sun Clothing Co.--Student's Initials**. (Type your actual initials, *not* the words *Student's Initials*.) Record the following transactions using invoices and cash receipts (Peachtree calls this just a receipt. Sales has been added for clarification). Print the invoices, receipts and reports as indicated.

When recording transactions, use the Item List to determine the item(s) sold. All transactions are taxable unless otherwise indicated. You may be required to select the Sales Tax Code in order for Peachtree to calculate sales tax in certain transactions. Terms for sales on account are the standard terms assigned to each customer individually. If a customer exceeds his or her credit limit, accept the transaction. If the customer makes a return and does not have a balance on account, prepare a refund check for the customer. Invoices begin with number 15, are numbered consecutively. Cash Receipts begin with number 25, are also numbered consecutively. Checks should begin with number 201 and are numbered consecutively. Credit Memos should be linked to the original transaction. If a transaction can be printed, print the transaction when it is entered.

LISTS

Aloha Sun Clothing Co.
Customer List

Filter Criteria includes: 1) Customers only. Report order is by ID.

Customer ID	Customer	Contact	Telephone 1
ALF01	Alfie, Mary	Mary Alfie	805-555-6489
CHA01	Chan, Carrie	Carrie Chan	805-555-7561
ELK01	Elkhorn, Eleanor	Eleanor Elkhorn	805-555-1267
KET01	Ketterling, Ray	Ray Ketterling	805-555-9514
LAN01	Lanka, Laura	Laura Lanka	805-555-9744
LAR01	Larkin, Rod	Rod Larkin	805-555-2486
LOM01	Lomark, Terry	Terry Lomark	805-555-3323
LOR01	Lorenzo, Ami	Ami Lorenzo	805-555-3310
MAR01	Marquez, Ellie	Ellie Marquez	805-555-4782
PET01	Petre, Gary	Gary Petre	805-555-5348
REI01	Reid, Tabitha	Tabitha Reid	805-555-7566
SAN01	Sanders, Jimmy	Jimmy Sanders	805-555-1332
TAN01	Tanaka, Ryoichi	Ryoichi Tanaka	805-555-1488
WAL01	Wall, Alec	Alec Wall	805-555-9547
WAT01	Watkins, Manny	Manny Watkins	805-555-8764

```
                           Aloha Sun Clothing Co.
                                Item List

Filter Criteria includes: Report order is by ID.

Item ID        Item Description           Item Class     Active?    Item Type    Qty on Hand
        BEL01  Belt, Canvas, Men's        Stock item     Active                       40.00
        BEL02  Belt, Leather, Men's       Stock item     Active                       30.00
        BEL03  Belt, Fashion, Women's     Stock item     Active                       18.00
        BLO01  Blouse, Women's            Stock item     Active                      100.00
        DRE01  Dress, Women's Sundress    Stock item     Active                       25.00
        DRE02  Dress, Two-Piece           Stock item     Active                       10.00
        PAN01  Pants, Men's               Stock item     Active                      100.00
        PAN02  Pants, Women's             Stock item     Active                       30.00
        SAN02  Sandals, Women's           Stock item     Active                      100.00
        SCA01  Scarf, Chiffon             Stock item     Active                       36.00
        SHI01  Shirt, Men's Hawaiian      Stock item     Active                      100.00
        SHI02  Shirt, Men's, Pierre Clariean  Stock item Active                       25.00
        SHO01  Men's Shoes                Stock item     Active                      100.00
        SHO02  Shoes, Women's             Stock item     Active                       24.00
        SHR01  Shorts, Men's              Stock item     Active                       20.00
        SHR02  Shorts, Women's            Stock item     Active                       20.00
        SUN01  Sunglasses Deluxe Aviator  Stock item     Active                       50.00
        SUN02  Sunglasses, Women's Designer  Stock item  Active                       38.00
        TIE01  Tie, Striped               Stock item     Active                      100.00
```

RECORD TRANSACTIONS

January 3, 2006:

Add your initials to the company name. The company name will be **Aloha Sun Clothing Co.-- Student's Initials**. (Type your actual initials, *not* the words "Student's Initials")

Prepare Invoice No. 15 to record the sale on account for 1 canvas belt for $29.95, 1 pair of men's shorts for $39.95, and a men's Hawaiian shirt for $39.95 to Terry Lomark. Print the invoice.

Received Check No. 3305 from Carrie Chan for $325 in payment of her account balance. Be sure to use Receipt No. 25.

Record the sale on account of 1 pair of deluxe aviator sunglasses for $89.95 to Ryoichi Tanaka.

Record the sale of a sundress on account to Gary Petre, for his wife, for $79.95.

Add a new customer: San Luis Recreation Center, use (SAN02 for Customer ID) 451 Marsh Street, San Luis Obispo, CA 93407, Contact person is Katie Gregg, 805-555-2241, Credit Terms are 2% 10 Net 30, Credit Limit $5,000. Because San Luis Recreation Center is a nonprofit organization, use Price Level 2. They are taxable for CA Sales Tax. Use 4011 as the GL Sales Acct.

Sold 5 Men's Hawaiian shirts on account to San Luis Recreation Center for $29.95 each, 5 pair of men's shorts for $29.95 each. Confirm that Peachtree used Level 2 pricing.

Sold 1 woman's blouse for $59.95 to Jerri Garth. Received Check No. 378 for the full amount including tax. Record sale as a cash customer. (If necessary, refer to steps provided within the chapter for instructions on creating a cash customer. Cash sales are taxable. Use Acct 4011 as the GL Sales Acct.) Issued Cash Receipt No. 26. Print the Cash Receipt.

Sold a Dress, 2-piece to Thersa Adesso for $99.95. The customer paid with her Visa, number 4536-9382-0292-3857, expiration date 04/08. Record the sale.

Sold a scarf to Patty Harrison for $19.95 plus tax for cash. Record the sale.

January 5:

Received payments from the following customers. Be sure to confirm the payment method.

> Elenore Elkhorn, $598.00, Check No. 145
>
> Manny Watkins, $375, Check No. 4015
>
> Ami Lorenzo, $750, Check No. 8915-02
>
> Alec Wall, $834.99, Check No. 6726

January 14:

Ami Lorenzo returned a Pierre Clariean shirt she had purchased for her husband. She purchased it for $54.99 plus tax. Record the return. Check the balance of her account. If there is no balance, issue a refund check. Use CM001 for the Credit Memo number since there is no invoice to which it can be linked.

Sold 3 men's Hawaiian shirts to Richard Ralph, a cash customer, for $39.95 each plus tax. Richard used his MasterCard for payment, card number 8787-9843-1212-0008, expiration date 09/07.

Sold on account 1 Dress, 2 piece for $99.95, 1 pair of sandals for $79.95, and a belt for $39.95 to Ray Ketterling for his daughter.

Sold 1 pair of women's shorts for $34.95 to a cash customer. Accepted Check No. 8160 for payment.

Received a partial payment on account from Laura Lanka, $250, Check No. 2395.

Received payment in full from Jimmy Sanders, Check No. 9802.

Sold 3 pairs of men's pants for $75.00 each, 3 men's Pierre Clairean shirts for $54.99 each, 3 canvas belts for $29.95 each, 2 pairs of men's shoes for $90.00 each, 2 ties for $55.00 each, and 1 pair of women's designer sunglasses for $95.00 to Tabitha Reid on account. Her Christmas shopping for next year is now complete.

Sold 1 pair of women's designer sunglasses for $95.00, 2 two-piece dresses for $99.95 each, and 2 pairs of women's shoes for $65.00 on account to Manny Watkins as a gift for his wife.

January 16, 2006

Received $1,338.03 from Gary Petre as payment in full on account, Check No. 2311. The payment was postmarked 1/12/2006. Be sure to use this date as the receipt date in order to give him the discount on invoice 17.

Received the belt purchased by Ray Ketterling. The original price of the belt was $39.95. Prepare a Credit Memo applying the return to the invoice on which it was purchased.

January 19, 2006

Received an NSF notice from the bank for the check for $1338.03 from Gary Petre. Enter the necessary transaction for this non-sufficient funds check. Use Gary's Invoice No. 17 to record the bank charge. The bank charges Aloha $10, and Aloha Sun charges its customers $15 for all NSF checks. (If necessary, refer to steps provided within the chapter for instructions on adding accounts or items necessary to record this transaction.)

Print the following reports:

Customer Ledgers
Items Sold to Customers report
Deposit in Transit report
General Ledger Trial Balance

NAME _____

TRANSMITTAL

CHAPTER 5: ALOHA SUN CLOTHING CO.

Attach the following documents and reports:

- ☐   Invoice No. 15: Terry Lomark
- ☐   Cash Receipt No. 25: Carrie Chan
- ☐   Invoice No. 16: Ryoichi Tanaka
- ☐   Invoice No. 17: Gary Petre
- ☐   Invoice No. 18: San Luis Recreation Center
- ☐   Cash Receipt 26: Cash Customer
- ☐   Cash Receipt No. 27: Cash Customer
- ☐   Cash Receipt No. 28: Cash Customer
- ☐   Cash Receipt No. 29: Eleanor Elkhorn
- ☐   Cash Receipt No. 30: Manny Watkins
- ☐   Cash Receipt No. 31: Ami Lorenzo
- ☐   Cash Receipt No. 32: Alex Wall
- ☐   Credit Memo CM001: Ami Lorenzo
- ☐   Check No. 201: Ami Lorenzo
- ☐   Cash Receipt No. 33: Ami Lorenzo
- ☐   Cash Receipt No. 34: Cash Customer
- ☐   Invoice No. 19: Ray Ketterling
- ☐   Cash Receipt No. 35 Cash Customer
- ☐   Cash Receipt No. 36 Laura Lanka
- ☐   Cash Receipt No. 37: Jimmy Sanders
- ☐   Invoice No. 20: Tabitha Reid
- ☐   Invoice No. 21: Manny Watkins
- ☐   Cash Receipt No. 38: Gary Petre
- ☐   Credit Memo CM17: Ray Ketterling
- ☐   Invoice No. 17 Duplicate: Gary Petre
- ☐   Customers Ledgers Report
- ☐   Items Sold to Customers Report
- ☐   Deposit in Transit Report
- ☐   General Ledgers Trial Balance

Payables and Purchases: Merchandising Business

LEARNING OBJECTIVES

At the completion of this chapter you will be able to:

1. Understand the concepts for computerized accounting for payables in a merchandising business.
2. Prepare, view, and print purchase orders and checks.
3. Add, modify and print reports for merchandise inventory.
4. Enter items received against purchase orders
5. View and print a Cash Requirements report.
6. Enter purchase invoices, enter vendor credits, and pay invoices.
7. Edit and correct errors in invoices and purchase orders.
8. Add new vendors and modify vendor records.
9. View accounts payable transaction history from the Purchase Journal.
10. View and/or print reports for vendors, inventory and purchase transactions.
11. Edit, void, and delete invoices, purchase orders, and checks.
12. Display and print a Taxable/Exempt Sales report, an Aged Payables report and a Vendor Ledgers report.

ACCOUNTING FOR PAYABLES AND PURCHASES

In a merchandising business, much of the accounting for purchases and payables consists of ordering merchandise for resale and paying invoices for that merchandise inventory as well as expenses incurred in the operation of the business. Purchases are for things used in the operation of the business. Some transactions will be in the form of cash purchases; others will be purchases on account. Invoices will be paid when they are due. Merchandise received must be checked against purchase orders, and completed purchase orders must be closed. Rather than use cumbersome journals, Peachtree® Complete Accounting 2006 continues to focus on recording transactions based on the business document; therefore, you use the Purchases/Receive Inventory and payment features of the program to record the receipt and payment of invoices. While Peachtree® Complete Accounting 2006 does not refer to it as such, the Vendor List is the same as the Accounts Payable Subsidiary Ledger.

Peachtree® Complete Accounting 2006 can remind you when inventory needs to be ordered and when payments are due. Purchase orders can be prepared when ordering merchandise. The program automatically tracks inventory and uses the cost method selected by the user to value the inventory. Peachtree® Complete Accounting 2006 can calculate and apply discounts earned when paying invoices early. Payments can be made by recording payments in the

Purchases/Receive Inventory or the Payments windows. A cash purchase can be recorded by writing a check, by using a credit card, or by using petty cash. Even though Peachtree® Complete Accounting 2006 focuses on recording transactions on the business forms used, all transactions are recorded behind the scenes in the appropriate journal.

As in previous chapters, corrections can be made directly on the invoice. New accounts and vendors may be added "on the fly" as transactions are entered. Purchase orders, invoices, or checks may be voided or deleted. Reports illustrating vendor balances, aged payables, sales tax liability, transaction history, and other accounts payable related reports may be viewed and printed.

TRAINING TUTORIAL AND PROCEDURES

The following tutorial will once again work with High Ridge Ski Shoppe. As in Chapter 5, transactions will be recorded for this fictitious company. Refer to procedures given in Chapter 5 to maximize training benefits.

OPEN PEACHTREE® COMPLETE ACCOUNTING 2006 AND HIGH RIDGE SKI SHOPPE

DO: Open Peachtree® Complete Accounting 2006 as previously instructed
Open High Ridge Ski Shoppe:
Click **Open an existing company.**
Click the **Browse** button (if High Ridge Ski Shoppe is not already visible)
Click the drop down arrow for **Drives:**
Select the drive where your data files are kept
Locate and double click on High Ridge Ski Shoppe (under the **Company name** text box)
Check the title bar to verify that High Ridge Ski Shoppe-Student Initials is the open company as instructed in previous chapters

BEGINNING THE TUTORIAL

In this chapter you will be entering purchases of merchandise for resale in the business and entering invoices received by the company in the operation of the business. You will also be recording the payment of invoices and purchases using checks and credit cards.

The Vendor List keeps information regarding the vendors with which you do business. This information includes the vendor names, addresses, telephone number, fax number, e-mail address, payment terms, credit limits, and account numbers. You will be using the following list for vendors with which High Ridge Ski Shoppe has an account:

High Ridge Ski Shoppe-APS
Vendor List

Filter Criteria includes: Report order is by ID.

Vendor ID	Vendor	Contact	Telephone 1
ABB01	Abbey's Bindings	Abbey Shalte	303-555-1269
ADV01	Adventurer Boots	Miles Armen	719-555-1235
CLI01	Cline Ski Supply	Pete Cline	303-555-8732
ETC01	ETC Accessories	Hamid Asati	310-555-4565
HIG01	High Ridge Power Co.		619-555-3214
HIG02	High Ridge Telephone Co.		619-555-8800
HIG03	High Ridge Water Co.		619-555-6464
JAC01	Jaclin's Shoes	Jaclin Todd	310-555-9988
JAY01	Jay's Office Supply	Jay Morganstein	619-555-9321
LAN01	Lang Property Mgmt.	Cheryl Lang	619-555-8254
SLO01	Slope Gear, Inc.	Marti Duncan	719-555-8214
STA01	State Board of Equalization		

All transactions are listed on memos. The transaction date will be the same date as the memo date unless otherwise specified within the transaction. Be sure to change your system date to reflect the date of the transaction. Vendor names, when necessary, will be given in the transaction. Unless otherwise specified, terms are 2% 10, Net 30. Once a specific type of transaction has been entered in a step-by-step manner, additional transactions of the same or a similar type will be made without having instructions provided. Of course, you may always refer to instructions given for previous transactions for ideas or for steps used to enter those transactions. To determine the account used in the transaction, refer to the Chart of Accounts. When entering account information on an invoice, clicking on the drop-down list arrow will show a copy of the Chart of Accounts. The Item List can be used in a similar manner when entering merchandise ordered.

VIEW AND PRINT THE INVENTORY REORDER WORKSHEET

Peachtree® Complete Accounting 2006 has an Inventory Reorder Worksheet that can be used to show you a listing of the inventory items that need to be reordered. This list uses a minimum order quantity that was entered into the system when the item was originally set up in the Maintain Inventory Item window. It also provides a space to manually enter a reorder quantity based on both a reorder quantity and any special needs that management may have.

MEMO
DATE: January 17, 2006

View and print the Inventory Reorder Worksheet to determine which items need to be ordered.

 DO: Display the Inventory Reorder Worksheet
Click **All Inventory Reports** from the **Inventory** button
Double click Inventory Reorder Worksheet
Print the report (Make sure it is as of January 17, 2006)

High Ridge Ski Shoppe
Inventory Reorder Worksheet
As of Jan 17, 2006
Filter Criteria includes: 1) Stock/Assembly; 2) Below Minimum. Report order is by Item ID. Report is printed with Truncated Long Descriptions.

Item ID Desc for Sales Desc for Purch	Pref Vendor ID Pref Vendor Na	Qty on Hand	Qty on Order	Sales BOs	Min Stock	Reorder Qty	Qty to Orde
BIN20 ProBind Ski Bindings	ABB01 Abbey's Bindings	6.00	0.00	0.00	7.00	9.00	_____
BOT10 Canvas Boot Case	ETC01 ETC Accessories	10.00	0.00	0.00	12.00	15.00	_____
GLO10 Insulated Gloves Gloves	SLO01 Slope Gear, Inc.	14.00	0.00	0.00	15.00	18.00	_____
POL10 Economy Ski Poles Ski Poles	CLI01 Cline Ski Supply	13.00	0.00	0.00	15.00	20.00	_____
SK10 Model XB04 Snow Skis Snow Skis	CLI01 Cline Ski Supply	5.00	0.00	0.00	8.00	10.00	_____
SK20 Model X348 Snow Skis	CLI01 Cline Ski Supply	8.00	0.00	0.00	10.00	12.00	_____

Close the report and the **Select a Report** windows
Keep this report available for a later activity

PURCHASE ORDERS

Using the Peachtree® Complete Accounting 2006 Purchase Order feature helps you order and track your inventory. Information regarding the items on order or the items received may be obtained at any time. Once all the merchandise has been received, Peachtree® Complete Accounting 2006 marks the purchase order completed. In the event items must be cancelled, the purchase order can be manually closed. As with other business forms, Peachtree® Complete Accounting 2006 will allow you to customize your purchase orders to fit the needs of your individual company or to use the purchase order format that comes with the program.

PREPARE PURCHASE ORDERS TO ORDER MERCHANDISE

Primarily, purchase orders are prepared to order merchandise; but they may also be used to order non-inventory items like supplies or services. Purchase orders are used as part of the company's internal control system to ensure that only properly authorized goods and services are ordered. The completed purchase order is mailed to the Vendor to place the order.

MEMO
DATE: January 17, 2006

With only 10 pairs of snowboard boots in stock in the middle of January, Eric and Matt decide to order an additional 15 pairs of boots in assorted sizes from Adventurer Boots for $99 per pair. Prepare Purchase Order No. 101.

DO: Prepare Purchase Order No. 101 for 15 pairs of snowboard boots
Click **Purchase Orders** from the **Purchases** button
In the **Vendor ID** field, use the magnifying glass to select Adventurer Boots
Click in the **Quantity** field, enter 15
Tab to the **Item** field and use the magnifying glass to select SNO20 Snowboard
Boots, Deluxe.

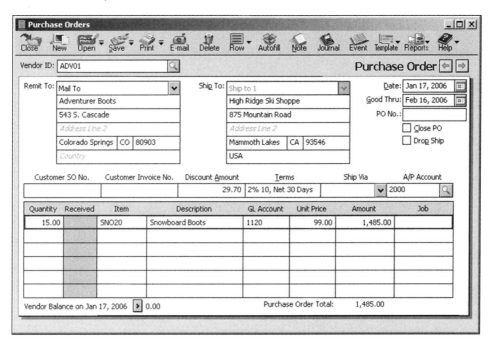

Click **Print**

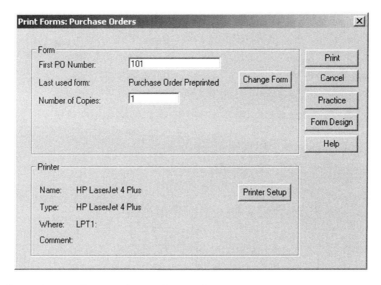

Confirm 101 as the starting PO number
Click **Print**

PREPARE A PURCHASE ORDER FOR NEW ITEMS

As a store expands into new product lines, it will be required to add new items and new vendors to the existing lists. These can be added prior to generating a purchase order or can be added "on the fly" while the purchase order is being created.

MEMO

DATE: January 17, 2006

Prepare a purchase order for 3 SLE10 Deluxe Sleds @ $50 each (minimum stock 3, reorder quantity 4), and 2 TOB10 Speeder Toboggans @ $110 each (minimum stock 2, reorder quantity 3) that will sell for $99.95 and $199.95 respectively. Both of these items will use 4012 Equipment Sales as the GL account for sales. They will be purchased from a new vendor: Flying Frost, Inc., (use FLY01 as the Vendor ID) 7105 Camino del Rio, Durango, CO 81302, Contact: Lyle Jenkins, Phone: 303-555-7765, Fax: 303-555-5677, E-mail: flyingfrost@ski.com, Terms: 2% 10 Net 30, Credit Limit: $2000.

DO: Prepare a purchase order and add a new vendor and new items
Click **Purchase Orders** from the **Purchases** button
Click on the magnifying glass to the right of the **Vendor ID** field
Click on the **New** button
Enter FLY01 in the **Vendor ID** field
Tab to the **Name** field, enter Flying Frost, Inc.
Tab to the **Contact** field, enter Lyle Jenkins
Tab to the **Address** field, enter 7105 Camino del Rio
Tab to the **City** field, enter Durango, press **Tab** and enter CO press **Tab** and enter 81302
Click in the **Telephone 1:** field, enter 303-555-7765
Tab to the **Fax:** field, enter 303-555-5677
Tab to the **E-mail:** field, enter flyingfrost@ski.com

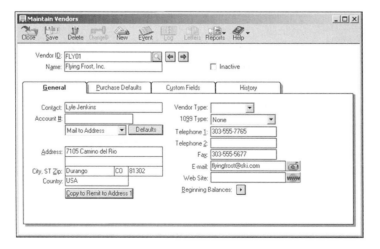

Click on the **Purchase Defaults** tab
Click on the arrow to the right of **Terms**
Deselect **Use Standard Terms**
Enter 10 in the **Discount in** field
Enter 2.00 in the **Discount %** field
Enter 2000.00 in the **Credit Limit** field

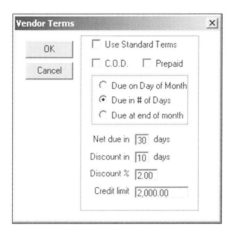

Click **OK**
Click **Save** and then **Close** to return to the Purchase Order window
Click on the magnifying glass to the right of the **Vendor ID** field, select Flying
    Frost, Inc.
Click in the **Quantity** field, enter 3.00
Tab to the **Item** field and use the magnifying glass to open the **Item** list
Click on **New**
Enter SLE10 in the **Item ID** field
Tab to the **Description** field, enter Sled, Deluxe
Click in the **Price Level 1:** field, enter 99.95
Tab to the **Stocking U/M:** field, enter EACH
Click in the **GL Sales Acct:** field, enter 4012
Click in the **Minimum Stock:** field, enter 3.00
Click in the **Reorder Quantity:** field, enter 4.00
Click on the magnifying glass to the right of the **Preferred Vendor ID** field and
    select Flying Frost, Inc.
      Note: There are numerous additional fields in the Maintain Inventory Items
              window, however; we will accept the default on any field not
              specifically mentioned in the tutorial due to space constraints. Feel
              free to examine the other fields and relate them to your manual
              accounting experience.

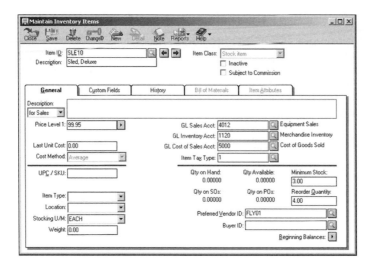

Click on **Save** and then **Close**

Click on the magnifying glass for the **Item** field, select SLE10 Sled, Deluxe

Tab to the **Unit Price** field, enter 50.00

Note: Since this is the first time we are purchasing this item, we must manually enter the price. The next time this item is ordered, the last price will fill in automatically. This will not necessarily reflect the current price and may require changing if the item is offered for a different price.

Click in the **Quantity** field, enter 2.00

Tab to the **Item** field and use the magnifying glass to open the Item list

Click on **New**

Enter the information for the toboggan in the same manner as for the sled

Click on **Save** and then **Close** to return to the Purchase Order

Click on the magnifying glass to the right of the Item field, select TOB10 Toboggan, Speeder

Tab to the **Unit Price** field, enter 110.00

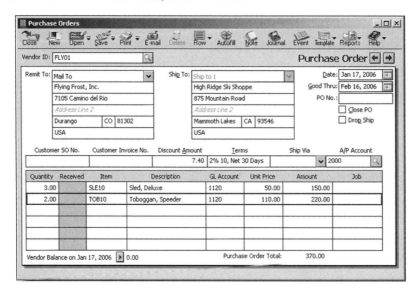

Click **Print**

Verify PO number as 102 and click **Print**

ENTER PURCHASE ORDERS WITHOUT STEP-BY-STEP INSTRUCTIONS

MEMO
DATE: January 17, 2006

Prepare and print purchase orders for the following:

25 pairs of Insulated Gloves @ $36.50 each from Slope Gear, Inc.

12 pairs of Economy Ski Poles @ $30.00 each from Cline Ski Supply

DO: Prepare and print the purchase orders indicated above.
Compare your completed purchase orders with the ones below:

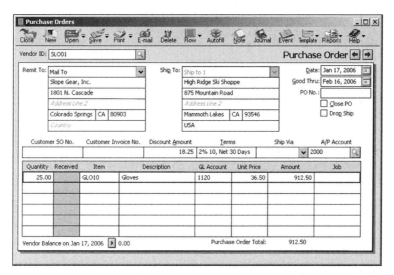

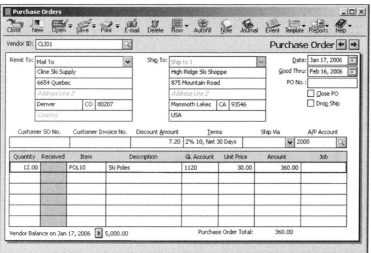

VIEW AND PRINT PURCHASE ORDER REGISTER

A number of reports related to purchase orders exists within Peachtree. Different reports will show varying degrees of detail. The simplest of these reports is the Purchase Order Register that will show us what purchase orders have been issued, when, to whom and the amount. This report will reflect all purchase orders issued during the accounting period regardless of whether they have been closed or not.

MEMO

DATE: January 17, 2006

Eric and Matt need to see which purchase orders have been created. View the Purchase Orders Register.

DO: Prepare and print the purchase orders indicated above.
Click **All Accounts Payable Reports** from the **Purchases** button
Double click Purchase Order Register
Print the report
Close the report and the Select a Report windows

High Ridge Ski Shoppe
Purchase Order Register
For the Period From Jan 1, 2006 to Jan 31, 2006
Filter Criteria includes: Report order is by Date.

PO No	Date	Good Thru	Vendor ID	Amount
101	1/17/06	2/16/06	ADV01	1,485.00
102	1/17/06	2/16/06	FLY01	370.00
103	1/17/06	2/16/06	SLO01	912.50
104	1/17/06	2/16/06	CLI01	360.00
				3,127.50

CHANGE MINIMUM STOCK LEVEL AND REORDER QUANTITY FOR AN ITEM

Any time that you determine that your reorder point and/or reorder quantity for a specific item in your inventory is too low or too high, you can change it by editing the inventory item using Maintain Inventory Item.

MEMO

DATE: January 17, 2006

Review the Inventory Reorder Worksheet created earlier in the chapter. Note that the Insulated Gloves have a Minimum Stock level of 15 and a Reorder Quantity of 18. Eric and Matt determine that they should have a minimum of 20 pairs of Insulated Gloves on hand at all times. Further, they would like to increase the Reorder Quantity to 25 on this very popular item.

DO: Change the Minimum Stock level and Reorder Quantity as indicated above
Click **Inventory Items** from the Maintain section of the **Inventory** button
Using the magnifying glass to the right of the **Item ID** field, select Gloves, Insulated
Click in the **Minimum Stock** field, enter 20
Tab to the **Reorder Quantity** field, enter 25

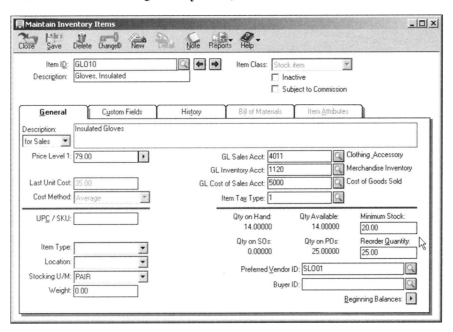

Click **Save** and then **Close**

VIEW AND PRINT THE PURCHASE ORDER REPORT

Another purchase related report that provides us with the details of which items have been ordered is the Purchase Order Report. This report provides information regarding what has been ordered, the quantity ordered, and the quantity received. This information is provided only for open purchase orders.

MEMO

DATE: January 17, 2006

More detailed information regarding the stock on hand, stock ordered, and stock needed to be ordered needs to be provided. View and print the Purchase Order Report.

DO: View and print the Purchase Order Report
Click **All Accounts Payable Reports** from the **Purchases** button
Double click Purchase Order Report
Print the report

High Ridge Ski Shoppe
Purchase Order Report
For the Period From Jan 1, 2006 to Dec 31, 2007
Filter Criteria includes: Report order is by Purchase Order Number. Report is printed with Truncated Descriptions.

PO No	PO Date	Vendor ID Vendor Name	PO State	Item ID Line Description	Qty Ordered	Qty Received	Qty Remaining
101	1/17/06	ADV01 Adventurer Boots	Open	SNO20 Snowboard Boots	15.00	0.00	15.00
102	1/17/06	FLY01 Flying Frost, Inc.	Open	SLE10 Sled, Deluxe	3.00	0.00	3.00
102	1/17/06	FLY01 Flying Frost, Inc.	Open	TOB10 Toboggan, Speeder	2.00	0.00	2.00
103	1/17/06	SLO01 Slope Gear, Inc.	Open	GLO10 Gloves	25.00	0.00	25.00
104	1/17/06	CLI01 Cline Ski Supply	Open	POL10 Ski Poles	12.00	0.00	12.00

Note: This report will default to show only those purchase orders that are open. We can change the parameters to have the report show closed purchase orders as well. Although we do not currently have any closed purchase orders, let us look at the procedures to do this for future reference. You may wish to repeat this after we have closed some of the PO's.
Click the **Options** button at the top of the screen
Click in the **From** column of the **Purchase Order State** row
Using the pull down arrow, select All
Click **OK**. The report would now also show completed purchase orders
Close the report and the **Select a Report** windows

RECEIVING ITEMS ORDERED

Once a purchase order has been created, the next step is to reflect the receipt of the merchandise from the vendor based on the quantities received and the invoice generated by the vendor. In a normal business transaction, a vendor will ship merchandise and mail the invoice on or about the same day. While the invoice and the merchandise are not always received on the same day, the merchandise can still be recorded as received pending receipt of the invoice. When the invoice is received, the purchase order can be reopened and updated with information provided on the invoice.

In addition, we can reflect a partial receipt of inventory leaving the purchase order open until such time as the balance of the merchandise is received. In situations where we no longer can or want to receive the balance due, we can manually close the purchase order to remove it from our open purchase order list. In all of the cases discussed, we will use the Purchases/Receive Inventory to record the receipt of the inventory items. It is the same window used in Chapter 3 to record purchases on account. In this chapter we will also use the Apply to Purchase Order tab that will become active when vendors having open purchase orders are entered into the Vendor ID field. From this tab, we can select the specific purchase order that relates to the inventory received. This will bring up a listing of items ordered against which we can record the specific items received.

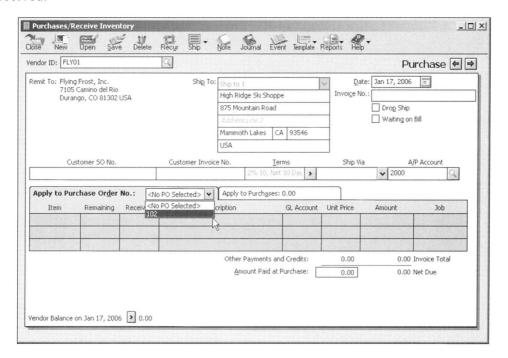

RECORD RECEIPT OF ITEMS NOT ACCOMPANIED BY AN INVOICE

The ability to record inventory items prior to the arrival of the invoice keeps quantities on hand, quantities on order, and the inventory up to date. Items ordered on a purchase order that arrive before the invoice is received are recorded in the same manner as those items received with the invoice. They are marked as received and the purchase order is flagged as waiting for the invoice. When the invoice arrives, it is recorded.

MEMO
DATE: January 19, 2006

> The sleds and toboggans ordered from Flying Frost, Inc., PO Number 102, arrive without an invoice. Record the receipt of the 3 sleds and 2 toboggans.

DO: Receive items as indicated above
Click **Purchases/Receive Inventory** from the **Purchases** button
In the **Vendor ID** field, select Flying Frost, Inc.
Using the drop down arrow in the **Apply to Purchase Order#:** tab, select 102
Click in the **Received** field for the Sled, Deluxe and enter 3.00
Click in the **Received** field for the Toboggan, Speedy and enter 2.00
Click in the box to the left of **Waiting on Bill** to select this option.

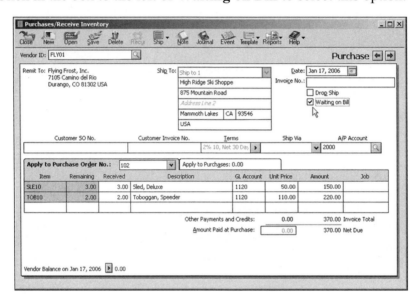

Note: Peachtree® Complete Accounting 2006 has a feature that can enter the Received quantities for all items on the purchase order. It is activated by clicking on the Ship button at the top of the window and then selecting All. Remove the quantities in the Received column and try this feature if you wish

Click **Save** and then **Close**

ENTER RECEIPT OF AN INVOICE FOR ITEMS ALREADY RECEIVED

For items that have been received prior to the bill, the receipt of items is recorded as soon as the items arrive. When the invoice is received, it must be recorded. To do this, we must reopen the Purchase/Receive Inventory form and edit the information to reflect the information contained on the actual invoice. At this time, we can enter the invoice number, remove the Waiting for Bill from Vendor flag and update any prices that may need to be changed.

MEMO

DATE: January 20, 2006

Record the invoice for the sleds and toboggans already received from Flying Frost, Inc. Vendor's Invoice No. 97 dated 01/18/2006, Terms 2% 10 Net 30. Prices remained unchanged.

DO: Receive invoice as indicated above

Click **Purchases/Receive Inventory** from the **Purchases** button

Click on the **Open** button at the top of the screen

Double click on the purchase for Flying Frost, Inc.

Deselect the **Waiting on Bill** flag

Click in the **Invoice #** field, enter 97

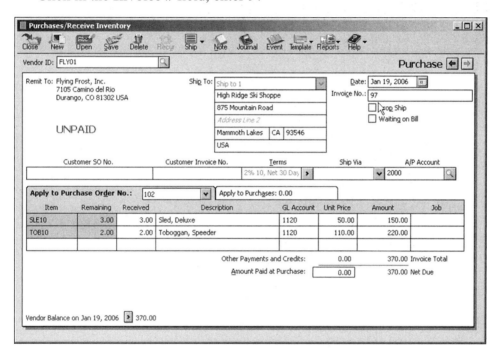

Click **Save** and then **Close**

VERIFY THAT PURCHASE ORDER IS MARKED CLOSED

Once all the items have been marked as received, Peachtree® Complete Accounting 2006 will automatically mark a purchase order as closed.

MEMO

DATE: January 20, 2006

View the original Purchase Order No. 102 to verify that it has been closed.

DO: Verify that Purchase Order No. 102 is marked Closed
Click **Purchase Order** from the **Purchases** button
Click on the **Open** button at the top of the screen
Double click on Purchase Order No. 102 for Flying Frost, Inc.

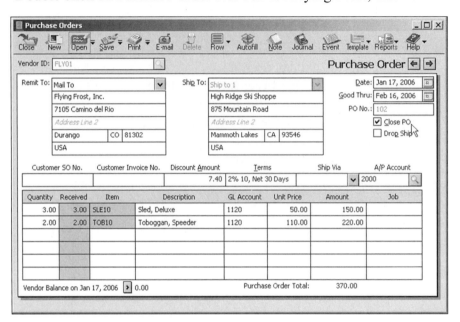

Note: The **Close PO** field has been checked to indicate that this purchase order is closed.

Click **Close**

RECORD RECEIPT OF ITEMS AND AN INVOICE

When ordered items are received and accompanied by an invoice, the receipt of the items is recorded while entering the invoice.

MEMO

DATE: January 20, 2006

Received 15 pairs of snowboard boots and an invoice from Adventurer Boots. Record Invoice No. 0923 dated 01/19/2006 and the receipt of the items assuming no change in pricing.

 DO: Record the receipt of the items and the invoice
Click **Purchases/Receive Inventory** from the **Purchases** button
Using the magnifying glass to the right of the **Vendor ID** field, select Adventurer Boots
Select 101 as the **Apply to Purchase Order#:**

Enter 0923 as the **Invoice No.**

Using the drop down arrow in the **Apply to Purchase Order#:** tab, select 101

Click in the **Received** field for the **Snowboard Boots** and enter 15.00

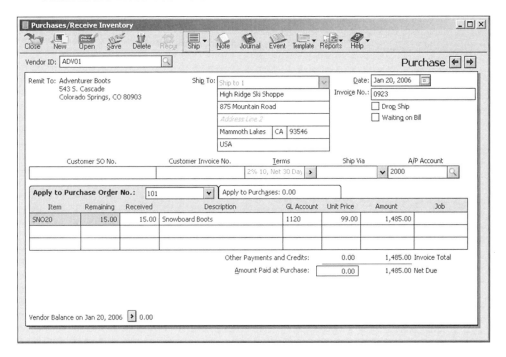

Click **Save** and then **Close**

EDIT A PURCHASE ORDER

As with any other form, purchase orders may be edited once they have been prepared. Purchase orders may be accessed by selecting Purchase Order from the Purchases button, clicking on the Open button and selecting the appropriate purchase order.

MEMO

DATE: January 20, 2006

While reviewing the Purchase Order Report, Matt realized that Purchase Order No. 104 should be for 15 pairs of ski poles. Change the purchase order and reprint.

DO: Change Purchase Order No. 104

Click **Purchase Orders** from the **Purchases** button

Click on the **Open** button at the top of the screen

Double click on Purchase Order No. 104 for Cline Ski Supply

Click in the **Quantity** field, enter 15.00

Reprint the Purchase Order

Close the Purchase Orders window

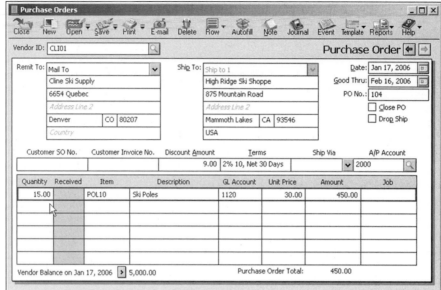

RECORD A PARTIAL RECEIPT OF MERCHANDISE ORDERED

Sometimes when items on order are received, they are not received in full. The remaining items may be delivered as back-ordered items. This will usually occur if an item is out of stock, and you must wait for delivery until more items are manufactured and/or received by the vendor. With Peachtree® Complete Accounting 2006 you record the number of items you actually receive, and the invoice is recorded for that amount.

MEMO

DATE: January 20, 2006

Record Invoice No. A39057 and the receipt of 20 pairs of gloves ordered on Purchase Order No. 103. On the purchase order, 25 pairs of gloves were ordered. Slope Gear, Inc., will no longer be carrying these gloves, so the remaining 5 pairs of gloves on order will not be shipped. Manually close the purchase order. The date of the invoice is 01/19/06.

DO: Record the receipt of the items and the invoice for 20 pairs of gloves from Slope Gear, Inc.

Click **Purchases/Receive Inventory** from the **Purchases** button

In the **Vendor ID** field, select Slope Gear, Inc.

Enter A39057 as the **Invoice No.**

Using the drop down arrow in the **Apply to Purchase Order#:** tab, select 103

Click in the **Received** field for the Gloves, Insulated and enter 20.00

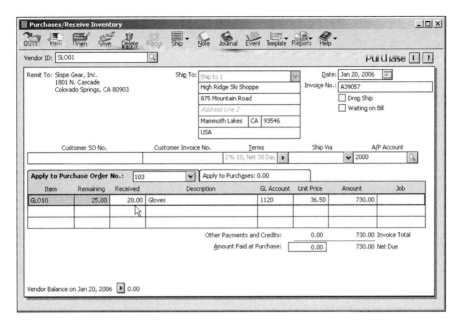

Click **Save** and then **Close**

CLOSE PURCHASE ORDER MANUALLY

Purchase orders are sometimes issued for merchandise that ultimately will not be available for one reason or another. These purchase orders can be closed manually.

DO: Close Purchase Order No. 103 since the item is no longer stocked
Click **Purchase Orders** from the **Purchases** button
Click on the **Open** button at the top of the screen
Double click on Purchase Order No. 103 for Slope Gear, Inc.
Click in the **Close PO** field to close the Purchase Order
Click **Save**
Close the Purchase Orders window

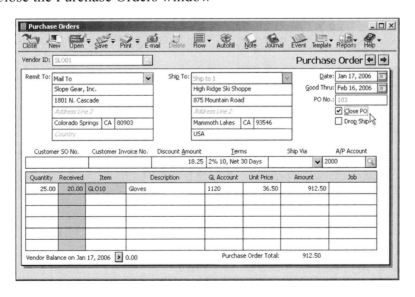

ENTER A CREDIT FROM A VENDOR

Credit memos are prepared to record a reduction to a transaction. With Peachtree® Complete Accounting 2006, you use a Vendor Credit window to record credit memos received from vendors acknowledging a return of or an allowance for a previously recorded bill and/or payment. The amount of a credit memo can be linked to an open invoice and is deducted from the amount owed or it can be left as an open credit to be applied to any vendor payment.

MEMO

DATE: January 21, 2006

Upon further inspection of merchandise received, Renee Squires found that one of the sleds received from Flying Frost, Inc. was cracked. The sled was returned. Received Credit Memo No. 9912 from Flying Frost, Inc. for $50, the full amount on the return of 1 sled.

DO: Prior to recording the above return, check the Inventory Item List to verify how many sleds are on hand.

Click **All Inventory Reports** from the **Inventory** button

Double click Item List and verify that there are 3 in stock

Close the Item List and the Select a Report windows

Click **Credit Memos** from the **Purchases** button.

Click the magnifying glass for **Vendor ID:**

Double click Flying Frost, Inc.

Enter 9912 in the **Credit No.:** field

Tab to or click the **Date** and confirm or type 01/21/06

Select 97 from the **Apply to Invoice No.:** tab pull down arrow

Enter 1.00 in the **Returned** column of the SLE10 row

Click **Save** and then **Close** to record the credit and exit

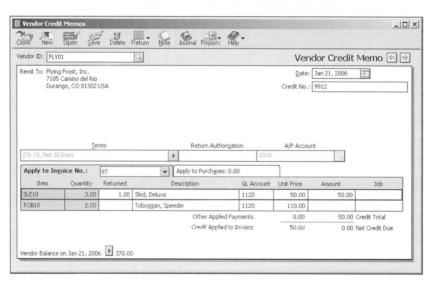

- Peachtree® Complete Accounting 2006 decreases the quantity of sleds on hand and creates a credit in the Vendor account that has been applied to the invoice.
Access the Item List as previously instructed.
- Verify that there are 2 sleds in stock after the return.
Close the Item List and the Select a Report windows

VERIFY VENDOR ACCOUNT BALANCE

To verify that Peachtree® Complete Accounting 2006 has correctly posted the credit memo created above, we can examine a Vendor Ledgers report for Flying Frost, Inc.

 DO: View credit in the Vendor Ledgers Report
Click **All Accounts Payable Reports** in the **Purchases** button
Double click on Vendor Ledgers Report
Click the **Options** icon at the top of the window
Click the drop down list arrow, click in the Type column for the **Vendor ID** field, select Equal To
Click in the **From** field and use the lookup feature (click the magnifying glass) to select Flying Frost, Inc.
Click **OK**
You are presented with a Vendor Ledger Report for just Flying Frost, Inc.:

High Ridge Ski Shoppe
Vendor Ledgers
For the Period From Jan 1, 2006 to Jan 31, 2006
Filter Criteria includes: 1) IDs: FLY01. Report order is by ID.

Vendor ID Vendor	Date	Trans No	Type	Paid	Debit Amt	Credit Amt	Balance
FLY01	1/19/06	97	PJ			370.00	370.00
Flying Frost, Inc.	1/21/06	9912	PJ	*	50.00		320.00
Report Total					50.00	370.00	320.00

As you can see, Peachtree has applied the $50.00 credit memo to our account with Flying Frost, Inc., leaving a balance due of $320.00. When we pay our bills, Peachtree has reduced the amount we must pay to this Vendor.
Close the Vendor Ledgers report and the Select a Report windows.

ENTER A BILL

Peachtree® Complete Accounting 2006 provides accounts payable tracking. Entering bills as soon as they are received is an efficient and correct way to record your liabilities. Once bills have been entered, Peachtree® Complete Accounting 2006 will be able to provide up-to-date cash flow reports, and Peachtree® Complete Accounting 2006 will remind you when it's time to pay your bills. The form used to enter a bill is virtually identical to the form used to enter a sale. Differences include a Vendor ID in place of a Customer ID, the need for a GL expense account and the use of an Apply to Purchases tab in lieu of an Apply to Revenues tab.

MEMO

DATE: January 24, 2006

Took out an ad in the *High Ridge News* announcing our January sale. Received an invoice for $95.00 from *High Ridge News*. Terms Net 30, Invoice No. 381-22. The newspaper is a new vendor, use HIG04 as the Vendor ID. The address is 1450 Main Street, Mammoth Lakes, CA 93546, Contact: Frieda Gustaf, Phone: 619-555-2525, Fax: 619-555-5252. Use a new advertising expense account-6140.

DO: Record the above transaction

Click **Purchases/Receive Inventory** on the **Purchases** button

Click the magnifying glass next to **Vendor**

Click on the **New** button to add this vendor "on the fly"

Enter HIG04 in the **Vendor ID** field

Tab to the **Name** field and enter High Ridge News

Tab to the **Contact** field and enter Frieda Gustaf

Tab to the **Account No.:** field and enter HRSS-2006

Tab to the **Address** field and enter 1450 Main Street

Tab to the **City** field and enter Mammoth Lakes, then tab again and enter CA, tab again and enter 93546

Click in the **Telephone** field and enter 619-555-2525

Tab to the **Fax** field and enter 619-555-5252

Click on the **Purchase Defaults** tab

Click on the magnifying glass to the right of the **Expense Acct:** field. Because the Advertising Expense account does not appear, click **New**

Enter 6140 in the **Account ID** field

Tab to the **Description** field and enter Advertising Expense

Click the drop down list arrow for **Account Type**, select Expenses

Click **Save** and then **Close**

Select account 6140 in the **Purchase Acct** field

Confirm that the Terms are Net 30 Days

Click **Save** and then **Close**

Using the magnifying glass to the right of **Vendor ID**, select High Ridge News

Tab to **Date: ,** confirm or type 01/24/06 as the date

Tab to the **Invoice No.:** field. Type the vendor's invoice number: 381-22

Complete the detail section of the bill in the **Apply to Purchases** tab:

Click in the column for **Description**

Enter Ad for January Sale

Tab to the **GL account** column. Confirm that the GL account is 6140 for Advertising Expense

Tab twice to the **Amount** field. Enter 95.00

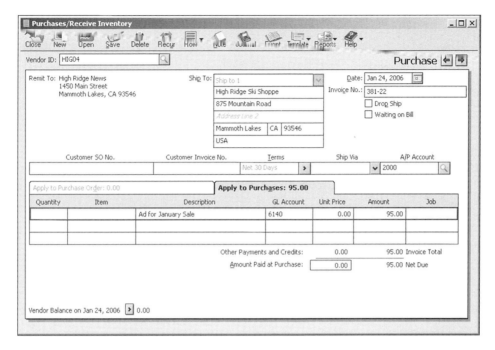

Click **Save** and then **Close**

EDIT EXISTING VENDORS

Once a vendor has been established, changes can be made to the vendors account information. These changes will not affect transactions already recorded for the vendor but will apply to all future transactions entered for this vendor.

MEMO

DATE: January 24, 2006

Renee Squires realized that information was entered incorrectly for High Ridge Power Co., High Ridge Water Co. and High Ridge Telephone Co. when vendor accounts were established. Change the Terms for the three companies to Net 15. Change the default Purchase Accounts as follows: High Ridge Power Co. - 6391, High Ridge Water Co. - 6392 and High Ridge Telephone Co. - 6340.

DO: Change the default Purchase Account and Terms for all of the vendors listed above
Click **Vendors** from the **Purchases** button.
Click the magnifying glass for **Vendor ID:**
Double click High Ridge Power Co.
In the **Purchases Defaults** tab,
Click on the magnifying glass to the right of the **Purchase Acct** field, select 6391
Click on the arrow to the right of **Terms**
Click in the **Net due in** field and enter 15

Click **OK**
Click **Save** and then repeat for the other vendors indicated in the memo above.
Close the Maintain Vendor window when all changes have been made

RECORDING BILLS WITHOUT STEP-BY-STEP INSTRUCTIONS

It is more efficient to record bills in a group or "batch" than it is to record them one at a time. If an error is made while preparing the bill, correct it. High Ridge Ski Shoppe uses the accrual basis of accounting. In the accrual method of accounting the expenses of a period are matched against the revenue of the period. Unless otherwise instructed, use the accrual basis of accounting when recording entries.

MEMO

DATE: January 26, 2006

Record the receipt of the following bills:
High Ridge Power Co. electrical power for January, $359.00, Invoice No. 3510-1023, Net 15.

High Ridge Telephone Co. telephone service for January, $156.40, Invoice No. 7815-21, Net 15.

High Ridge Water Co. water for January, $35.00, Invoice No. 3105, Net 15.

DO: Enter the three transactions in the memo above
  – Refer to the instructions given for previous transactions.
  – To go from one bill to the next, click the **Save** button at the top of the screen.
  – After entering the last bill, click **Save** and then **Close** to record and exit the Purchase/Receive Inventory screen.

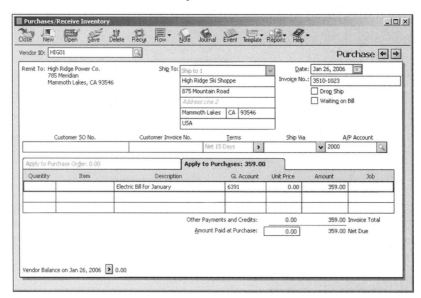

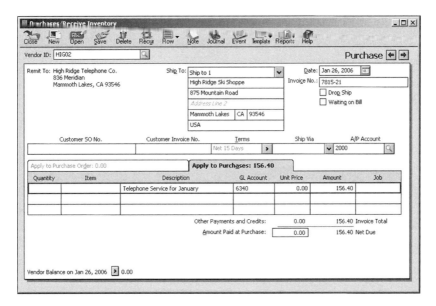

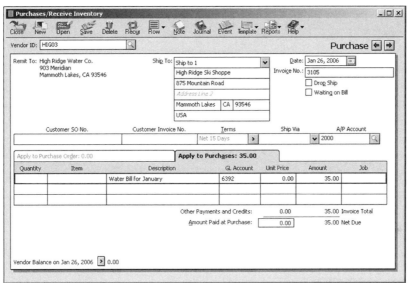

EDIT A TRANSACTION FROM THE PURCHASE JOURNAL

While examining a report an error may be detected. Because Peachtree® Complete Accounting 2006 makes corrections extremely user friendly, a transaction can be edited or changed.

MEMO

DATE: January 26, 2006

Upon examination of a Purchase Journal report, Renee discovers an error. The actual amount of the bill from the water company was **$85.00**, not $35.00. Change the transaction amount for this bill using the drill down feature.

DO: Correct the above transaction from the Purchase Journal
Click on **Purchase Journal** from the **Purchases** button
Click **OK**
Scroll down until you reach High Ridge Water Co.
Double click anywhere in the transaction to go to the transaction
Click in the **Amount** field, enter 85.00
Click **Save** and then **Close**
Verify the change and then close the Purchase Journal

High Ridge Ski Shoppe
Purchase Journal
For the Period From Jan 1, 2006 to Jan 31, 2006
Filter Criteria includes: Report order is by Date. Report is printed in Detail Format.

Date	Account ID Account Description	Invoice/CM #	Line Description	Debit Amount	Credit Amount
1/26/06	6392 Water Expense	3105	Water Bill for January	85.00	
	2000 Accounts Payable		High Ridge Water Co.		85.00

PREPARE AND PRINT CASH REQUIREMENTS REPORT

It is possible to get information regarding the cash needed to pay unpaid bills by simply preparing a report. No more digging through tickler files, recorded invoices, ledgers, or journals. Peachtree® Complete Accounting 2006 prepares a Cash Requirements report listing each unpaid bill grouped and subtotaled by vendor.

MEMO

DATE: January 26, 2006

Renee Squires prepares a Cash Requirements report for Eric and Matt each week. Because High Ridge Ski Shoppe is a small business, the owners like to have a firm control over cash flow so they can determine which bills must be paid by the end of the month.

DO: Prepare and print a Cash Requirements report
Click on **All Accounts Payables Reports** from the **Purchases** button
Double click on Cash Requirements
Print the report
Click **Close**

High Ridge Ski Shoppe
Cash Requirements
As of Jan 31, 2006
Filter Criteria includes: Report order is by ID. Report is printed in Detail Format.

Vendor ID Vendor	Invoice/CM #	Date	Date Due	Amount Due	Disc Amt	Age
ABB01 Abbey's Bindings	766891	12/22/05	1/21/06	2,000.00		10
ABB01 Abbey's Bindings				2,000.00		
CLI01 Cline Ski Supply	889901	12/26/05	1/25/06	5,000.00		6
CLI01 Cline Ski Supply				5,000.00		
ETC01 ETC Accessories	845012	12/27/05	1/26/06	350.00		5
ETC01 ETC Accessories				350.00		
JAC01 Jaclin's Shoes	811231	12/28/05	1/27/06	400.00		4
JAC01 Jaclin's Shoes				400.00		
JAY01 Jay's Office Supply	34461	12/29/05	1/28/06	750.00		3
JAY01 Jay's Office Supply				750.00		
Report Total				8,500.00		

PAYING BILLS WITH SELECT FOR PAYMENT

When using Peachtree® Complete Accounting 2006 to pay your bills, the most efficient method is to use Select for Payment. Use this feature to pay all invoices due on or before a specific date. You may use both the net due date and the discount date in your filter. Bills paid by the discount date earn you cash discounts. Peachtree will combine invoices to the same vendor and will allow for batch check processing. Although we can manually write a check and simply tell Peachtree the check number we used, it is best to let Peachtree write the checks for us.

MEMO

DATE: January 26, 2006

Whenever possible, Renee Squires pays the bills on a weekly basis. Use the Select for Payment window and pay all Invoices due Before or Discounts Lost By February 2, 2006. Use January 26, 2006 as your check date.

DO: Pay bills due before February 2, 2006
Click on **Select for Payment** from the **Purchases** button
Confirm the check date as 1/26/06, which is your system date

In the field labeled **Invoices Due Before**, enter the date 2/2/06
In the field labeled **or Discounts Lost By**, enter the date 2/2/06
Confirm that the radio buttons for **All Invoices** and **All Vendors** are selected
–   Using these filters, we could limit which invoices and/or which vendors to
    include in our criteria for payment.
When filled out correctly, your Select for Payment - Filter Selection window
    should look like this:

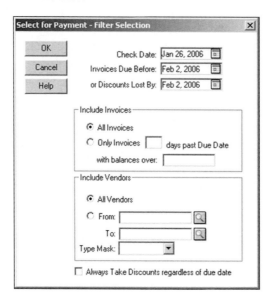

Click **OK**

Note: You are taken to a Select for Payment window that will list all invoices that
        meet the criteria established in the filter selection. The red checkmarks in
        the Pay column indicate the bills that have been selected for payment. A
        flaw in the Peachtree program leaves the discount for Flying Frost at $7.40.
        This does not take into account the return. Manually change this to $6.40.

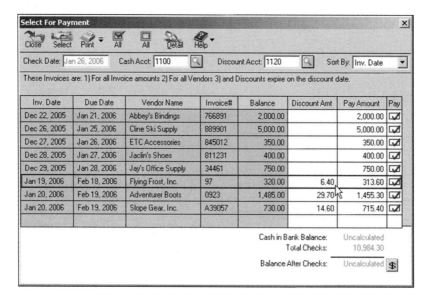

Leave the Select for Payment screen open and continue to the next section.

PRINTING CHECKS FOR BILLS

After the invoices have been marked for payment, you must print them. A company would purchase one of numerous check formats available for the program and print directly on these forms. If for whatever reason, checks were handwritten, you would still need to go through the print process and print the checks on blank paper. This process assigns the check numbers to the payments. If there is more than one amount due for a vendor, Peachtree® Complete Accounting 2006 totals the amounts due to the vendor and prints one check to the vendor. It will include a remittance advice telling the vendor which invoices are being paid with the check. If discounts are available, Peachtree will deduct these amounts when calculating the amount to be paid. It will also show that it has taken these discounts on the remittance advice.

 DO: Print the checks for the bills paid

Click the **Print** icon. We should be continuing with check #1006

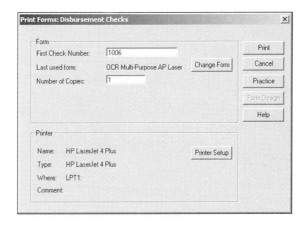

Click **OK**

Because Peachtree would expect you to insert the check forms in your printer, it may pause at this point waiting for you to insert the check forms and tell it to continue. Although we will not be inserting blank checks, we may still tell the printer to continue. See your instructor for these instructions.

After printing the checks, Peachtree will ask you to confirm that they printed properly. It will not assign the check numbers until you have confirmed the printing process. If for some reason the check printing process were interrupted and it became necessary to reprint, the starting check number would change and different check numbers would be used.

Click **Yes**

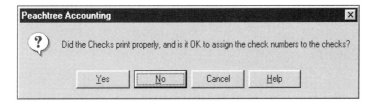

PRINT TAXABLE/EXEMPT SALES REPORT

The Taxable/Exempt Sales report shows your total taxable sales, the total nontaxable sales, and the amount of sales tax owed to each tax agency.

MEMO

DATE: January 26, 2006

Prior to paying the sales tax, Renee prepares the Taxable/Exempt Sales report.

DO: Print the Taxable/Exempt Sales report
Click the **All Accounts Receivables Reports** from the **Sales** button
Double click Taxable/Exempt Sales
Click **Print**
Close the report and the **Select a Report** windows

High Ridge Ski Shoppe
Taxable / Exempt Sales
For the Period From Jan 1, 2006 to Jan 31, 2006
Filter Criteria includes: Report is printed in Summary Format.

Authority ID	Authority Description	Tax Rate	Taxable Sale	Tax Amount	Exempt Sales	Total Sales
CA Sa-1	CA Sales Tax	7.25000	10,607.54	769.05		10,607.54
CA Sa-1	CA Sales Tax				40.00	40.00
CA Sa-1	Total CA Sales Tax		10,607.54	769.05	40.00	10,647.54

PAYING SALES TAX

From the Taxable/Exempt Sales report we can determine there is only one taxing authority, CA Sales Tax. Sales tax dollars that we have collected on behalf of the State of California must be paid to them periodically. The precise frequency is determined using a number of variables. When payments are made, they are made to the Board of Equalization. Regardless of the frequency that a particular firm must use, it is required to pay the Board several times a year. Because of this, it is best to establish the Board of Equalization as a vendor account. This has already been accomplished for High Ridge Ski Shoppe when sales tax defaults were established.

MEMO

DATE: January 26, 2006

Note from Matt: Renee, pay the sales tax owed.

DO: Pay the sales taxes owed
Click the **Write Checks** from the **Purchases** button

Using the magnifying glass to the right of the **Vendor ID** field, select State Board
of Equalization

Tab to the **Date** field, confirm or type 1/26/06

Tab to the **Amount** field, enter 769.05

Click in the **Memo** field, enter Pay Sales Tax for January

Using the magnifying glass next to the **Expense Account** field, select 2200 Sales
Tax Payable. This will force a debit to the sales tax liability account.

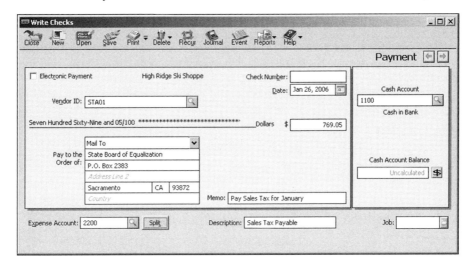

Click **Print** twice

Close the Write Checks window

VOIDING AND DELETING PURCHASE ORDERS, INVOICES AND CHECKS

Peachtree® Complete Accounting 2006 is so user friendly it allows any business forms to be deleted. Some accounting programs do not allow error corrections, except as adjusting entries, once an entry has been posted. Peachtree® Complete Accounting 2006, however, allows a purchase order, invoices or checks to be voided or deleted as the situation may require. If a business form is voided, the form remains as a transaction with a zero amount. This is useful when you wish to retain an audit trail of the entry. This is particularly useful in order to maintain an unbroken series of document numbers, such as check numbers. If the form is deleted, all traces of that form are also deleted. There is a feature in Peachtree® Complete Accounting 2006 called Use Audit Trail, that can be turned on in the Maintain Company Information window. With this feature activated, the program will keep a complete record of all transactions entered. This includes transactions that have been deleted. An audit trail helps to eliminate misconduct such as printing a check and then deleting the check from the company records. Used in conjunction with User Accounts, a very efficient internal security system can be established, a feature missing in many small accounting packages.

The procedures for voiding and deleting business forms are the same for a retail business as for a service business. If you feel the need to refresh your knowledge of voiding and deleting business forms, refer to the relevant portions of Chapters 2, 3 and 5.

VENDOR EVENT LOG

The Vendor Event Log can be accessed to obtain information regarding individual vendors. This log is accessed in the Maintain Vendor window. Once a vendor has been selected, the Log button at the top of the window is clicked.

The Log contains a listing of events relevant to our activities with that vendor. This would include purchase orders, invoices, cash payments and other accounting activities that we are engaged in with this vendor.

DO: View the Vendor Event Log
Click **Vendors** from the **Purchases** button
Using the magnifying glass for **Vendor ID**, select Adventurer Boots
Click on the **Log** button

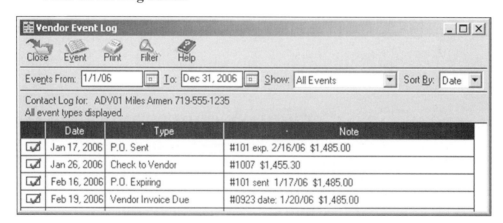

After reviewing, close the Vendor Event Log and the Maintain Vendor windows

VIEW AND PRINT AN AGED PAYABLES REPORT

It is important in a business to maintain a good credit rating by insuring that payments are made on time. In order to avoid overlooking a payment, the Aged Payables report lists the vendors to whom the company owes money and shows how long the money has been owed.

MEMO

DATE: January 31, 2006

Prepare the Aged Payables report for Eric and Matt.

DO: Prepare an **Aged Payables** report
Click **All Accounts Payables Reports** from the **Purchases** button
Double click Aged Payables from the reports listed

High Ridge Ski Shoppe
Aged Payables
As of Jan 31, 2006
Filter Criteria includes: Report order is by ID. Report is printed in Detail Format.

Vendor ID Vendor Contact Telephone 1	Invoice/CM #	0 - 30	31 - 60	61 - 90	Over 90 days	Amount Due
HIG01 High Ridge Power Co. 619-555-3214	3510-1023	359.00				359.00
HIG01 High Ridge Power Co.		359.00				359.00
HIG02 High Ridge Telephone Co. 619-555-8800	7815-21	156.40				156.40
HIG02 High Ridge Telephone Co.		156.40				156.40

Click **Print**
Close the report and the Select a Report windows

BACK UP HIGH RIDGE SKI SHOPPE DATA

Whenever an important work session is complete, you should always back up your data. If your data disk is damaged or an error is discovered at a later time, the backup disk may be restored and the information used for recording transactions. No matter what type of business, the backup procedure remains the same. In addition, it is always wise to make a duplicate of your data disk just in case the disk is damaged in some way.

DO: Follow the instructions given in Chapters 1 and 2 to back up data for High Ridge Ski Shoppe.

SUMMARY

In this chapter, purchase orders were completed, inventory items were received and invoices were recorded. Payments for purchases and invoices were made by check. Sales taxes were paid. Vendors, inventory items and accounts were added while transactions were being recorded. Various reports were prepared to determine the unpaid bills, the sales tax liability and the aging of Accounts Payable accounts.

END-OF-CHAPTER QUESTIONS

TRUE/FALSE

ANSWER THE FOLLOWING QUESTIONS IN THE SPACE PROVIDED BEFORE THE QUESTION NUMBER.

_____ 1. The receipt of purchase order items is never recorded before the bill arrives.

_____ 2. A bill can be paid by handwritten or computer generated check.

_____ 3. A purchase order can be accessed via the Purchase Order Register.

_____ 4. Voiding a purchase order removes all trace of the purchase order from the company records.

_____ 5. You must record the receipt of merchandise on a purchase order line by line even if the entire order is received.

_____ 6. A single purchase order can be prepared and sent to several vendors.

_____ 7. A Sales Tax liability account is required if a company charges sales tax on sales.

_____ 8. A credit received from a vendor for the return of merchandise can be applied to a payment to the vendor.

_____ 9. A new vendor cannot be added while recording a transaction.

_____ 10. A purchase order is closed automatically when a partial receipt of merchandise is recorded.

MULTIPLE CHOICE

WRITE THE LETTER OF THE CORRECT ANSWER IN THE SPACE PROVIDED BEFORE THE QUESTION NUMBER.

_____ 1. If you change the minimum stock for an item, it becomes effective ___.
   A. immediately
   B. the beginning of next month
   C. as soon as outstanding purchase orders are received
   D. the beginning of the next fiscal year

_____ 2. If an order is received with a bill but is incomplete, Peachtree® Complete Accounting 2006 should be used to ___.
   A. record the bill for the full amount ordered
   B. record the bill only for the amount received
   C. not allow the bill to be prepared until all the merchandise is received
   D. close the purchase order

3. The Purchase Order feature must be selected as a preference ___.
   A. when setting up the company
   B. prior to recording the first purchase order
   C. is automatically set when the first purchase order is prepared
   D. does not have to be selected

_____ 4. The proper method of entering bills should be by entering the bills ___.
   A. while writing the checks for payment
   B. in the Payments window
   C. in the Purchases/Receive Inventory window
   D. none of the above

_____ 5. When items ordered are received with a bill, you record the receipt ___.
   A. on an item receipt form
   B. on the bill
   C. against the original purchase order
   D. in the Journal

_____ 6. The sales tax liability is paid by using the ___ window.
   A. Pay Bills
   B. Pay Sales Tax
   C. Write Checks
   D. Credit Card

_____ 7. The amount owed to an individual vendor for Accounts Payable is displayed in the__.
   A. Aged Payable
   B. Purchase Journal
   C. Purchase Order Register
   D. none of the above

_____ 8. Checks to pay bills may be printed ___.
   A. individually
   B. all at once
   C. as the checks are written
   D. all of the above

_____ 9. A credit memo received from a vendor should be _____ .
   A. returned for a cash refund
   B. used to pay other bills
   C. used to reduce your payment to the vendor issuing the credit
   D. none of the above

_____ 10. The ___ matches income for the period against expenses for the period.
   A. cash basis of accounting
   B. credit basis of accounting
   C. accrual basis of accounting
   D. debit/credit basis of accounting

FILL-IN

IN THE SPACE PROVIDED, WRITE THE ANSWER THAT MOST APPROPRIATELY COMPLETES THE SENTENCE.

1. Orders for merchandise are prepared using the _____ form.

2. Information on the amounts owed to our vendors may be displayed in the_____or _____ reports.

3. The _____ Report shows the total taxable sales and the amount of sales tax owed.

4. A purchase order can be closed _____ or _____.

5. Paying a bill by the _____ reduces the amount you must pay.

SHORT ESSAY

Describe the cycle of obtaining merchandise. Include the process beginning with ordering the merchandise through making payment for it. Include information regarding the Peachtree® Complete Accounting 2006 forms prepared for each phase of the cycle, the possible ways in which an item may be received, and the ways in which payment may be made.

_____

_____

_____

_____

_____

_____

_____

_____

_____

_____

_____

_____

NAME _____

TRANSMITTAL

CHAPTER 6: HIGH RIDGE SKI SHOPPE

Attach the following documents and reports:

- ☐ Inventory Reorder Worksheet
- ☐ Purchase Order No. 101: Adventurer Boots
- ☐ Purchase Order No. 102: Flying Frost, Inc.
- ☐ Purchase Order No. 103: Slope Gear, Inc.
- ☐ Purchase Order No. 104: Cline Ski Supply
- ☐ Purchase Order Register
- ☐ Purchase Order Report
- ☐ Purchase Order No. 104: (revised) Cline Ski Supply
- ☐ Cash Requirements Report
- ☐ Check No. 1006: Abbey's Bindings
- ☐ Check No. 1007: Adventurer Boots
- ☐ Check No. 1008: Cline Ski Supply
- ☐ Check No. 1009: ETC Accessories
- ☐ Check No. 1010: Flying Frost, Inc.
- ☐ Check No. 1011: Jaclin's Shoes
- ☐ Check No. 1012: Jay's Office Supply
- ☐ Check No. 1013: Slope Gear
- ☐ Taxable/Exempt Sales Report
- ☐ Check No. 1014: State Board of Equalization
- ☐ Aged Payables Report

END-OF-CHAPTER PROBLEM

ALOHA SUN CLOTHING CO.

Chapter 6 continues with the transactions for purchase orders, merchandise receipts, bills, bill payments, and sales tax payments. Maile prints the checks, purchase orders, and any related reports; and Nalani signs the checks. This procedure establishes cash control procedures and lets both owners know about the checks being processed.

INSTRUCTIONS

Continue to use the copy of Aloha Sun Clothing Co. you used in Chapter 5. Open the company—the file used is **Aloha Sun Clothing Co.** Record the purchase orders, bills, payments, and other purchases as instructed within the chapter. Always read the transactions carefully and review the Chart of Accounts when selecting transaction accounts. Print reports as indicated. Add new vendors, new inventory items and change minimum quantities where indicated. Print all purchase orders and checks issued. The first purchase order used is Purchase Order No. 101. When paying bills, always check for credits that may be applied to the bill, and always check for discounts. Start with Check No. 202.

In addition to the Item List and the Chart of Accounts, you will need to use the Vendor List when ordering merchandise and paying bills.

Aloha Sun Clothing Co.- EFO
Vendor List

Filter Criteria includes: Report order is by ID.

Vendor ID	Vendor	Contact	Telephone 1
ALL01	All About Accessories	All About Assessorie	415-555-1700
APP01	Apparel Supply, Inc.	David Meredith	310-555-7123
MAU01	Maui Clothing	Maui Clothing	808-555-7531
SAN02	Sandals & Such	Michael Kani	
STA01	State Board of Equalization		
WOR01	World of Shades	Alan Basil	310-555-5123

RECORD TRANSACTIONS

January 5, 2006:

Change the minimum stock level for women's sundresses from 20 to 30.

Change the minimum stock level for women's pants to 35.

Display and print an Inventory Reorder Worksheet.

Prepare Purchase Orders for all items on the Inventory Reorder Worksheet. Refer to the Inventory Reorder Worksheet for vendor information. The quantity for each item ordered is indicated in the Reorder Qty column. The cost is $39.50 for sundresses and $15 for pants. Print the purchase orders.

Order a new inventory item, Orchid Print Sundress (use Item ID DRE03), from a new vendor: Clothing Tree, (use CLO01 as the Vendor ID), 9382 Grand Avenue, San Luis Obispo, CA 93407, Contact person is Marshall Rowland, 805-555-5512, Fax is 805-555-2155, Credit terms are 2% 10 Net 30, Credit limit is $5000. The unit cost for the dresses is $41.25, Level 1 pricing is $85.95, GL Sales Acct is 4011, GL Inventory Acct is 1120 and GL Cost of Goods Sold Acct is 5000. Minimum Stock should be 30 and Reorder Quantity should be 50. We will order the Reorder Quantity for our initial order.

Print a Purchase Order Register.

January 7, 2006:

Received pants ordered from Apparel Supply without the bill. Enter the receipt of merchandise. The transaction date is 01/07/2006.

Received dresses from Maui Clothing with Invoice No. 03294, dated 01/07/2006. Enter the receipt of the merchandise and the invoice.

Received 50 dresses from Clothing Tree. Enter the receipt of the merchandise and Invoice No. 77832.

After recording the receipt of merchandise, prepare and print the Purchase Order Report changing the Purchase Order State field to All. Note the PO State column.

January 10, 2006:

Received Invoice No. 872101-27 from Apparel Supply for the pants received on 01/07/06. The bill was dated 01/07/2006.

January 11, 2006:

Discovered unstitched seams in two pairs of women's pants just received from Apparel Supply. Return the pants for credit. Credit Memo No. 023954-CM.

January 14, 2006:

Record bill for January rent of $1150, Invoice No. 762. Vendor is Estate Rental Company (use EST01 as the Vendor ID), 301 Marsh St., San Luis Obispo, CA 93407, Contact person is Marsha Roberts, 805-555-4100, Fax 805-555-0014, Terms Net 30, Purchase Acct 6280.

Record bill for telephone service of $79.85, Invoice No. 643-24. Vendor is SLO Phone Service Company (use SLO01 as the Vendor ID), 8851 Hwy. 58, San Luis Obispo, CA 93407, 805-555-1029. Terms are net 10, Purchase Acct 6340.

January 19, 2006:

Pay all bills that are due or are eligible for a discount as of 1/26/06. Take any discounts for which you are eligible. Pay the bill(s) by check.

January 26, 2006:

Purchase office supplies to have on hand for $250 from Office Source (use OFF01 as the Vendor ID), 8330 Grand Avenue, Arroyo Grande, CA 93420, Contact person is Larry Thomas, 805-555-9915, Fax 805-555-5199 and Purchase Acct 1311. Terms Net 30, Credit limit $1000. Because this is our first order, we are required to pay in cash, use the Write Checks window.

January 31, 2006:

Prepare and print the Taxable/Exempt Sales Report.

Pay Sales Tax due and print the check.

Prepare a Vendor Ledgers Report.

Print a General Ledger Trial Balance.

NAME _____

TRANSMITTAL

CHAPTER 6: ALOHA SUN CLOTHING CO.

Attach the following documents and reports:

- ☐ Inventory Reorder Worksheet
- ☐ Purchase Order No. 101: Maui Clothing
- ☐ Purchase Order No. 102: Apparel Supply, Inc.
- ☐ Purchase Order No. 103: Clothing Tree
- ☐ Purchase Order Register
- ☐ Purchase Order Report
- ☐ Check No. 202: Apparel Supply
- ☐ Check No. 203: Clothing Tree
- ☐ Check No. 204: Maui Clothing
- ☐ Check No. 205: Sandals & Such
- ☐ Check No. 206: SLO Phone Service Company
- ☐ Check No. 207: Office Source
- ☐ Taxable/Exempt Sales Report
- ☐ Check No. 208: State Board of Equalization
- ☐ Vendor Ledgers Report
- ☐ General Ledger Trial Balance

General Accounting and End-Of-Period Procedures: Merchandising Business

7

LEARNING OBJECTIVES

At the completion of this chapter, you will be able to:

1. Complete the end-of-period procedures.
2. Change the name of existing accounts in the Chart of Accounts.
3. Delete an existing account from the Chart of Accounts.
4. Enter the adjusting entries required for accrual-basis accounting.
5. Record depreciation.
6. Understand how to record owners' equity transactions for a partnership.
7. Enter a transaction for owner withdrawals, and transfer owner withdrawals to the owners' capital accounts.
8. Reconcile the bank statement, record bank service charges, and other reconciliation adjustments.
9. Print the General Journal.
10. Print reports such as General Ledger Trial Balance, Income Statement, and Balance Sheet.
11. Export a report to Microsoft® Excel.
12. Perform end-of-period backup and advance the period.

GENERAL ACCOUNTING AND END-OF-PERIOD PROCEDURES

As previously stated, the Peachtree® Complete Accounting 2006 user interface operates from the standpoint of the business document rather than an accounting form, journal, or ledger. While Peachtree® Complete Accounting 2006 does incorporate all of these items into the program, in many instances they operate behind the scenes. Peachtree® Complete Accounting 2006 contains a simple end-of-period closing for both its monthly financial statements and the annual financial statements. At the end of the fiscal year, Peachtree® Complete Accounting 2006 transfers the net income into the Retained Earnings account and automatically prepares the books for the next accounting cycle. Closing the fiscal year will remove transaction details from the system. Since some businesses must still deal with transaction detail well into the next fiscal year, Peachtree® Complete Accounting 2006 does not require you to close the year at the end of the year. Since the program allows you to keep two fiscal years open at the same time, it is generally recommended that you do not officially close the year until near the end of the next fiscal year. In the meantime, all of the transaction detail is maintained and is viewable. Should there be a requirement to view older detail, backup can be restored and detailed information viewed.

A period is ended when we advance Peachtree to the next period. Even though a formal "closing" does not have to be performed within Peachtree® Complete Accounting 2006, when you use accrual-basis accounting, several transactions must be recorded to reflect all expenses and income for the period. For example, bank statements must be reconciled and any charges or bank collections need to be recorded. During the business period, the CPA for the company will review things such as account names, adjusting entries, depreciation schedules, owner's equity adjustments, and so on. Sometimes changes and adjustments will be suggested by your accountant. These changes and adjustments would be entered into the system prior to closing the period.

Once necessary adjustments have been made, reports reflecting the end-of-period results of operations should be prepared. For archive purposes at the end of the fiscal year an additional backup disk is prepared and stored. Ideally, backups will be made and kept at the end of each month as well.

TRAINING TUTORIAL AND PROCEDURES

The following tutorial will once again work with High Ridge Ski Shoppe. As in Chapters 5 and 6, transactions will be recorded for this fictitious company. Refer to the training procedures given in Chapter 5 to maximize training benefits.

OPEN PEACHTREE® COMPLETE ACCOUNTING 2006 AND HIGH RIDGE SKI SHOPPE

DO: Open Peachtree® Complete Accounting 2006 as previously instructed
Open High Ridge Ski Shoppe:
Click **Open an existing company.**
Click the **Browse** button (if High Ridge Ski Shoppe is not already visible)
Click the drop down arrow for **Drives:**
Select the drive where your data files are kept
Locate and double click on High Ridge Ski Shoppe (under the **Company name** text box)
Check the title bar to verify that High Ridge Ski Shoppe-Student's Initials is the open company.

BEGINNING THE TUTORIAL

In this chapter, you will be recording end-of-period adjustments, reconciling bank statements, changing account names, and preparing traditional end-of-period reports. Because Peachtree® Complete Accounting 2006 does not perform a traditional "closing" of the books, you will learn how to advance the period to prepare the books for the next month.

All transactions are listed on memos. The transaction date will be the same as the memo date unless otherwise specified within the transaction. Once a specific type of transaction has been entered in a step-by-step manner, additional transactions of the same or a similar type will be made without instructions being provided. Of course, you may always refer to instructions given for previous transactions for ideas or for steps used to enter those transactions. To determine the account used in the transaction, refer to the Chart of Accounts, which is also the General Ledger.

CHANGE THE NAME OF EXISTING ACCOUNTS IN THE CHART OF ACCOUNTS

Even though transactions have been recorded during the month of January, Peachtree® Complete Accounting 2006 makes it a simple matter to change the name of an existing account. Once the name of an account has been changed, all transactions using the old name are updated and show the new account name.

MEMO

DATE: January 31, 2006

On the recommendation of the company's CPA, Eric and Matt decided to change the account named Freight Income to Delivery Income.

DO: Change the account name of Freight Income
Click on **Chart of Accounts** from the **General Ledger** button
Using the lookup feature, select account number 4020 Freight Income
Peachtree should automatically move to the Description field and highlight the current description. Enter Delivery Income

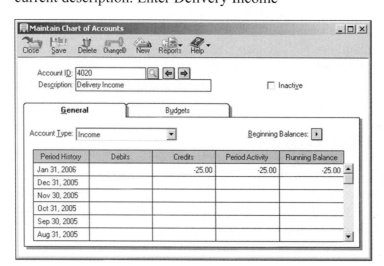

Click **Save**
Do not close the Maintain Chart of Accounts window

MAKE AN ACCOUNT INACTIVE

If you are not using an account and do not have plans to use it in the near future, the account may be made inactive. The account remains visible; however, it may not be used in transactions. After two years of inactivity, the account may be deleted.

MEMO

DATE: January 31, 2006

At this time, High Ridge Ski Shoppe does not plan to rent any equipment. The account Equipment Rental Expense should be made inactive. In addition, Eric and Matt do not plan to use Disability Insurance. Make this account inactive.

  DO: Make the accounts listed above inactive
Click **Chart of Accounts** from the **General Ledger** button
Using the lookup feature, select account number 6170 Equipment Rental Expense
Click in the box next to **Inactive**

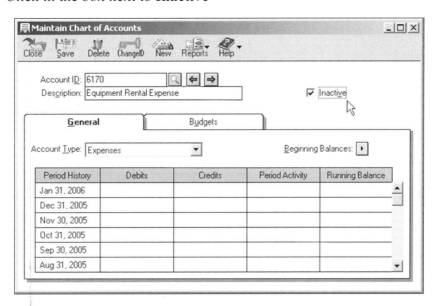

Click **Save**
Follow the steps above to make 6182 Disability Insurance Expense inactive
Click **Save**
Do not close the Chart of Accounts

DELETE AN EXISTING ACCOUNT FROM THE CHART OF ACCOUNTS

If your Chart of Accounts contains an account that you have not used and do not plan to use, making it inactive is not sufficient. Instead, Peachtree® Complete Accounting 2006 allows the account to be deleted. However, as a safeguard, Peachtree® Complete Accounting 2006 does prevent the deletion of an account once it has been used even if it simply contains an opening or an existing balance. As mentioned before, an account that has been used must be made inactive for a period of two years before it can be deleted. An account that has never been used can be deleted at anytime.

MEMO

DATE: January 31, 2006

In addition to previous changes to account names, Eric and Matt find that they do not use nor will they use the expense accounts: Mortgage Expense, Entertainment Expense, Travel Expense and Property Tax Expense. Delete these accounts from the Chart of Accounts.

 DO: Delete the accounts as indicated above

Scroll through accounts until you see Mortgage Expense, click 6213 Mortgage Expense

Click the **Delete** icon at the top of the window

You will be presented with a Delete Confirmation box

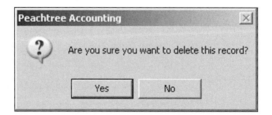

Click **Yes**

Repeat the above steps for the deletion of 6351 Entertainment Expense, 6353 Travel Expense and 6523 Property Tax Expense

Close the Maintain Chart of Accounts window

ADJUSTMENTS FOR ACCRUAL-BASIS ACCOUNTING

As previously stated, the accrual basis of accounting matches expenses to the income they helped earn. This is accomplished in order to arrive at an accurate figure for net income. Thus, the revenue is earned at the time the service is performed or the sale is made no matter when the actual cash is received. The cash basis of accounting records income or revenue at the time cash is received no matter when the sale was made or the service performed. The same holds true when a business buys things or pays bills. In accrual-basis accounting, the expense is recorded at the time the bill is received or the purchase is made regardless of the actual payment date. In cash-basis accounting, the expense is not recorded until it is paid. While Peachtree is capable of performing accounting functions under a cash-basis system, you would have been required to tell Peachtree this when the company was first created. Once accrual or cash-basis accounting is selected, Peachtree® Complete Accounting 2006 will not permit switching the basis of your accounting.

There are several internal transactions that must be recorded when you are using the accrual basis of accounting in order to close the period. These entries are called adjusting entries. For example, equipment does wear out and will eventually need to be replaced. Rather than wait until replacement to record the use of the equipment, one makes an adjusting entry to allocate the use of equipment as an expense for each period of its useful life. This is called depreciation. In addition, a business can pay for expenses in advance. These are recorded as assets and as they are used, they become expenses of the business. For example, insurance for the entire year would be used up month by month and should, therefore, be a monthly expense. Commonly, the insurance is prepaid for the entire year. Until the insurance is used, it is an asset. Each month, the portion of the insurance used becomes an expense for the month.

ADJUSTING ENTRIES—PREPAID EXPENSES

During the operation of a business, companies purchase supplies to have on hand for use in the operation of the business. In accrual-basis accounting, the supplies are considered to be prepaid expenses and are recorded as assets (something the business owns) until they are used in the operation of the business. As the supplies are used, the amount used becomes an expense for the period. The same system applies to other things paid for in advance, such as insurance. At the end of the period, an adjusting entry must be made to allocate the amount of assets used to expenses. These adjustments must be recorded as transactions in the General Journal.

MEMO

DATE: January 31, 2006

NOTE from Matt: Renee, remember to record the monthly adjustment for Prepaid Insurance. The $250 is the amount we paid for two months of liability insurance coverage. Also, we have a balance of $500.00 remaining in office supplies and a balance of $400 remaining in sales supplies. Please adjust accordingly.

   DO: Record the adjusting entries for prepaid insurance, office supplies expense and sales supplies expense in the General Journal.
Click **General Journal Entry** from the **General Ledger** button

Confirm or type Jan 31, 2006 in the **Date** field

In the **Reference field**, enter ADJ01. This is for our reference only and is not
     required.

Tab to or click the **Account No.** column

Click the drop-down list arrow for **Account No.**, double click 6181 Liability
     Insurance Expense

In the **Description** field, enter Adjusting Entry, Insurance

Tab to or click **Debit**

– The $250 given in the memo is the amount for two months; calculate the
     amount of the adjustment for the month:

Enter the amount of the adjustment 125.00 in the **Debit** column

Tab to or click **Account No.**

Click the drop-down list arrow for **Account No.**

Double click 1340 Prepaid Insurance

– The description will be entered automatically.

Tab to or click the **Credit** column

Type 125.00

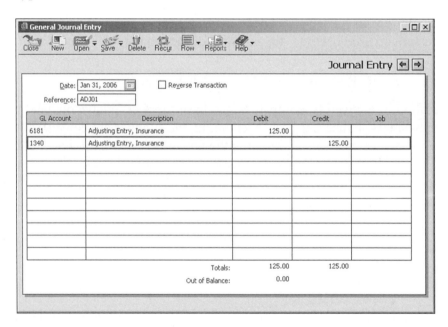

Click **Save**

– Notice that Peachtree brings you to a blank General Journal window and
     automatically changes the Reference to the next number, ADJ02. It will
     continue to do this between entries until the window is closed.

Repeat the above procedures to record the adjustment for the office supplies used

– The amount given in the memo is the amount of the supplies remaining. You
     must calculate the amount used in January by checking a General Ledger Trial
     Balance to see what the current balance is.

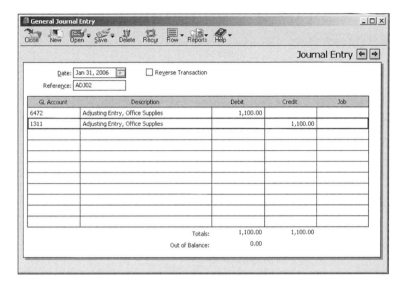

Repeat the above procedures to record the adjustment for the sales supplies used

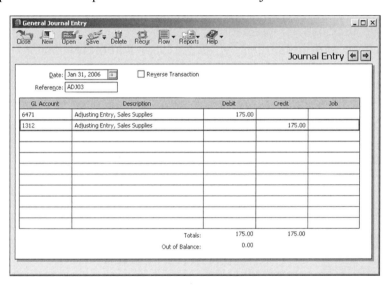

Click **Save**

ADJUSTING ENTRIES—DEPRECIATION

Using the accrual basis of accounting requires companies to record an expense for equipment used in the operation of the business. Unlike supplies—where you can actually see, for example, the paper supply diminishing—it is very difficult to see how much of a computer has been "used up" during the month. To account for the fact that machines do wear out and do need to be replaced, an adjustment is made for depreciation. This adjustment correctly matches the expenses of the period against the revenue of the period. The adjusting entry for depreciation is made in the General Journal.

MEMO

DATE: January 31, 2006

Having received the necessary depreciation schedules, Renee records the adjusting entry for depreciation:

Office Equipment, $85 per month
Store Fixtures, $75 per month

DO: Record a compound adjusting entry for depreciation of the office equipment and the store fixtures in the General Journal:
Confirm or enter 1/31/06 as the **Date**
In the **Reference** field, confirm or enter ADJ04
Tab to or click the **Account No.** column
Click the drop-down list arrow for **Account No.**
Double click 6150 Depreciation Expense
In the **Description** field, enter Record Depreciation for January
Tab to or click **Debit**, enter 160.00
Tab to or click **Account No.**
Click the drop-down list arrow for **Account No.**
Double click 1512 Accum. Depr. Office Equipment
Tab to or click the **Credit** column and type 85.00
Repeat for the credit using 1522 Accum. Depr. Store Fixtures
Tab to or click the **Credit** column and type 75.00

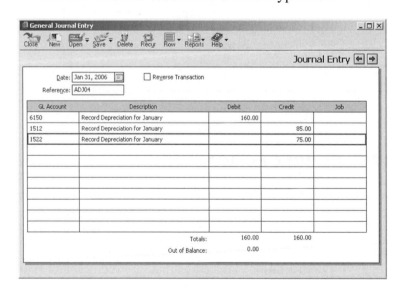

Click **Save** and then **Close** to record the adjustment and close the General Journal Entry window.

PREPARE AND PRINT STANDARD INCOME STATEMENT

MEMO

DATE: January 31, 2006

Print an Income Statement for January 2006.

DO: Print a Standard Income Statement
Click **All Financial Statements** from the **General Ledger** button
Double click on <Standard> Income Statement
You are presented with a <Standard> Income Statement dialog box
Deselect **Show Zero Amounts** and click **OK**

High Ridge Ski Shoppe
Income Statement
For the One Month Ending January 31, 2006

	Current Month			Year to Date	
Revenues					
Clothing & Accessory Sales	$ 1,515.84	14.36	$	1,515.84	14.36
Equipment Sales	9,091.70	86.14		9,091.70	86.14
Sales Discounts	(83.14)	(0.79)		(83.14)	(0.79)
Delivery Income	25.00	0.24		25.00	0.24
Returned Check Revenue	5.00	0.05		5.00	0.05
Total Revenues	10,554.40	100.00		10,554.40	100.00
Cost of Sales					
Cost of Goods Sold	5,546.22	52.55		5,546.22	52.55
Total Cost of Sales	5,546.22	52.55		5,546.22	52.55
Gross Profit	5,008.18	47.45		5,008.18	47.45
Expenses					
Advertising Expense	95.00	0.90		95.00	0.90
Depreciation Expense	160.00	1.52		160.00	1.52
Liability Insurance Expense	125.00	1.18		125.00	1.18
Telephone Expense	156.40	1.48		156.40	1.48
Gas and Electric Expense	359.00	3.40		359.00	3.40
Water Expense	85.00	0.81		85.00	0.81
Sales Supplies Expense	175.00	1.66		175.00	1.66
Office Supplies Expense	1,100.00	10.42		1,100.00	10.42
Total Expenses	2,255.40	21.37		2,255.40	21.37
Net Income	$ 2,752.78	26.08	$	2,752.78	26.08

Click **Print**
Click **Close**

VIEW GENERAL JOURNAL

Once transactions have been entered in the General Journal, it is important to view them. Peachtree® Complete Accounting 2006 maintains a General Journal and allows it to be viewed or printed at any time.

 DO: View the Journal for January
Click **General Journal** in the Reports area of the **General Ledger** button
- Accept the defaults and Click **OK**

High Ridge Ski Shoppe
General Journal
For the Period From Jan 1, 2006 to Jan 31, 2006
Filter Criteria includes: Report order is by Date. Report is printed with Accounts having Zero Amounts and with Truncated Transaction Descriptions and in Detail Format.

Date	Account ID	Reference	Trans Description	Debit Amt	Credit Amt
1/15/06	4040	NSFADJ	Adjust Returned Check Revenue	10.00	
	1100		Adjust Returned Check Revenue		10.00
1/31/06	6181	ADJ01	Adjusting Entry, Insurance	125.00	
	1340		Adjusting Entry, Insurance		125.00
1/31/06	6472	ADJ02	Adjusting Entry, Office Supplies	1,100.00	
	1311		Adjusting Entry, Office Supplies		1,100.00
1/31/06	6471	ADJ03	Adjusting Entry, Sales Supplies	175.00	
	1312		Adjusting Entry, Sales Supplies		175.00
1/31/06	6150	ADJ04	Record Depreciation for January	160.00	
	1512		Record Depreciation for January		85.00
	1522		Record Depreciation for January		75.00
		Total		1,570.00	1,570.00

Close the report without printing

DEFINITION OF A PARTNERSHIP

A partnership is a business owned by two or more individuals. Because it is unincorporated, each partner owns a share of all the assets and liabilities. Each partner receives a portion of the profits based on the percentage of his or her investment in the business or according to any partnership agreement drawn up at the time the business was created. Because the partners are the owners of the business, they do not receive a salary. They are treated the same as a sole proprietor. Any funds obtained by the partners are in the form of withdrawals against their share of the profits. Peachtree® Complete Accounting 2006 makes it easy to set up a partnership and create separate accounts, if desired, for each partner's equity and withdrawals.

OWNER WITHDRAWALS

In a partnership, owners cannot receive a paycheck because they own the business. An owner withdrawing money from a business—even to pay personal expenses—is similar to an owner withdrawing money from a savings account. A withdrawal simply decreases the owners' capital. Peachtree® Complete Accounting 2006 allows you to establish a separate account for owner withdrawals for each owner. If a separate account is not established, owner withdrawals may be subtracted directly from each owner's capital or investment account. Ideally, the owners would be set up as vendors in the Vendor List. This will simplify writing checks to them.

MEMO

DATE: January 31, 2006

Because Eric Boyd and Matthew Wayne are partners in the business, they do not earn a paycheck but rather must make a withdrawal. Prepare checks for Eric's monthly withdrawal of $1,000 and Matt's monthly withdrawal of $1,000. Set up Vendor accounts for each partner using their Drawing account as the default Purchases Account. Use BOY01 for Eric and WAY01 for Matthew.

 DO: Write Check No. 1015 to Eric Boyd for $1,000 withdrawal and Check No. 1016 to Matthew Wayne for $1,000 withdrawal

Click on **Write Checks** from the **Purchases** button

Using the magnifying glass to the right of **Vendor ID**, click the **New** button

Enter BOY01 as the **Vendor ID**

Click to the **Name** field, enter Eric Boyd

Click on the **Purchases Default** tab

Using the magnifying glass to the right of the **Purchase Acct:** field, select 3013 Drawing Eric Boyd

Click **Save** and then **Close**

Using the magnifying glass to the right of **Vendor ID**, select Eric Boyd

Confirm or type Jan 31, 2006 in the **Date:** field

Verify that the cash account used is 1100.

Enter 1,000.00 in the **Dollar** field

Enter January Draw, Eric Boyd in the **Memo:** field

Verify that the expense account is 3013

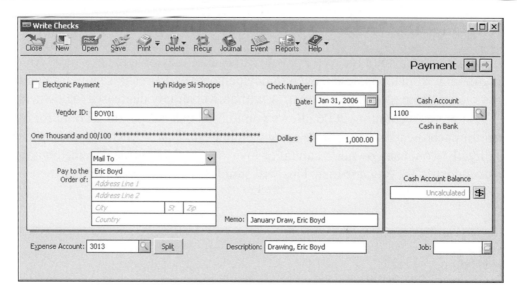

Click **Print** following instructions in previous chapters
Repeat the above procedures to record the withdrawal for Matthew Wayne

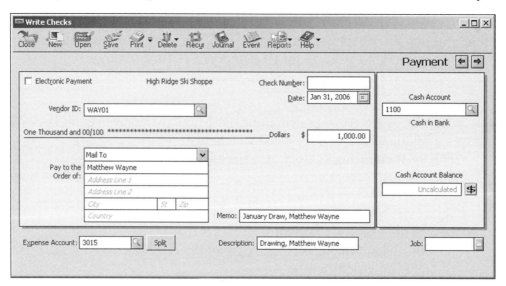

Close the Write Checks window when finished.

A NOTE ABOUT NET INCOME/RETAINED EARNINGS

Net Income will eventually close to Retained Earnings. In Peachtree® Complete Accounting 2006, this is not done monthly but rather will be accomplished when the year is closed. Because High Ridge Ski Shoppe is a partnership, the amount of net income should appear as part of each owner's Capital account rather than be set aside in Retained Earnings. As such, an adjusting entry should be made to move the balance in the Retained Earnings account into the two partners' Capital accounts. In many instances, this is the type of adjustment the CPA would make. The adjustment should be made after the closing has been performed. Because Peachtree® Complete Accounting 2006 automatically transfers the amount in the Net Income account into Retained Earnings, the closing entry for a partnership will transfer the net income into each owner's Capital account. This adjustment is made by debiting Retained Earnings and crediting the owners' individual capital accounts for their portion of the Net Income. In addition, the owners' Withdrawal account would also be closed to their individual Capital Accounts.

Since we will not be doing the year end closing, last year's next income was left in the Retained Earnings account to enable you to practice transferring this amount to the owners' equity accounts. This amount would have normally been transferred at the end of last year. Eric and Matt share profits one-third for Eric and two-thirds for Matt.

MEMO

DATE: January 31, 2006

Transfer the balance in the Retained Earnings account to Eric and Matt's Capital accounts splitting the Retained Earnings one-third for Eric and two-thirds for Matt. Also, close their Drawing accounts to their Capital accounts.

DO: Transfer Retained Earnings and Withdrawals to the Capital Accounts

Access the General Journal as previously instructed

Confirm or enter 1/31/06 as the **Date**

In the **Reference field**, confirm or enter CLOSE01

Tab to or click the **Account No.** column

Click the drop-down list arrow for **Account No.**, double click 3050 Retained
        Earnings

In the **Description** field, enter Close Retained Earnings to Capital

Tab to or click **Debit,** enter 46683.95

Tab to or click **Account No.**

Click the drop-down list arrow for **Account No.**

Double click 3010 Capital, Eric Boyd

Tab to or click the **Credit** column

Type 15561.32 (1/3 of 46683.95)

Tab to or click **Account No.**

Click the drop-down list arrow for **Account No.**

Double click 3012 Capital, Matthew Wayne

Tab to or click the **Credit** column

Type 31122.63 (2/3 of 46683.95)

Tab to or click the **Account No.** column

Click the drop-down list arrow for **Account No.**, double click 3010 Capital, Eric
        Boyd

In the **Description** field, enter Close Eric's Draw to Capital

Tab to or click **Debit,** enter 1000.00

Tab to or click **Account No.**

Click the drop-down list arrow for **Account No.**, double click 3013 Drawing, Eric Boyd

Tab to or click the **Credit** column

Type 1000.00

Tab to or click the **Account No.** column

Click the drop-down list arrow for **Account No.**, double click 3012 Capital, Matthew Wayne

In the **Description** field, enter Close Matt's Draw to Capital

Tab to or click **Debit,** enter 1000.00

Tab to or click **Account No.**

Click the drop-down list arrow for **Account No.**, double click 3015 Drawing, Matthew Wayne

Tab to or click the **Credit** column

Type 1000.00

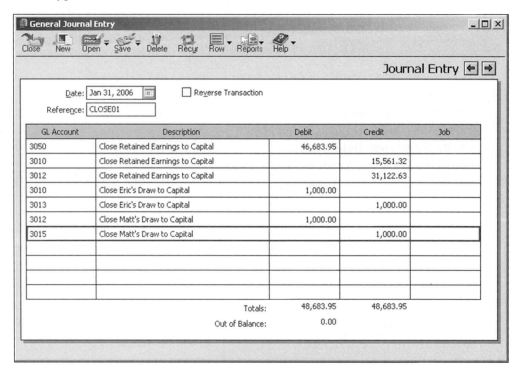

Click **Save** and then **Close** to record the entry and close the General Journal Entry window.

BANK RECONCILIATION

Each month, the checking account should be reconciled with the bank statement to make sure that the balances agree. The bank statement will rarely have an ending balance that matches the balance of the checking account. This is due to several factors: outstanding checks (written by the business but not paid by the bank), deposits in transit (deposits that were made too late to be included on the bank statement), bank service charges, interest earned on checking accounts, collections made by the bank, and errors made in recording checks and/or deposits by the company and/or by the bank.

In order to have an accurate balance in the checking account, it is important that the differences between the bank statement and the checking account be reconciled. If something such as a service charge or a collection made by the bank appears on the bank statement, it needs to be recorded in the checking account.

Reconciling a bank statement is an appropriate time to find any errors that may have been recorded in the checking account. The reconciliation may be out of balance because a transposition was made (recording $94 rather than $49), a transaction was recorded backwards, a transaction was recorded twice, or a transaction was not recorded at all. If a transposition was made, the error may be found by dividing the difference by 9. For example, if $94 was recorded when the actual transaction amount was $49, you would be out of balance by the difference of $45. The number 45 can be evenly divided by 9. This indicates that your error probably was a transposition. If the error can be evenly divided by 2, the transaction may have been entered backwards. For example, if you were out of balance $200, look to see if you had any $100 transactions. Perhaps you recorded a $100 debit, and it should have been a credit (or vice versa).

OPEN ACCOUNT RECONCILIATION

To begin the reconciliation, you need to open the Account Reconciliation window from the General Ledger button. Peachtree allows for reconciliation of any cash account in the General Ledger. We have only one external cash account, 1100 Checking. The reconciliation process will involve comparing the transactions listed on the bank statement with the transactions recorded into or out of this account.

MEMO

DATE: January 31, 2006

Picked up the bank statement from High Ridge Bank. The bank statement is dated January 31, 2006. Renee needs to reconcile the bank statement and print a Reconciliation Report for Eric and Matt.

   DO: Reconcile the bank statement for January
Open the **Account Reconciliation** window from the **General Ledger** button
You are presented with the **Account Reconciliation** window
Using the lookup feature, select account **1100 Checking**

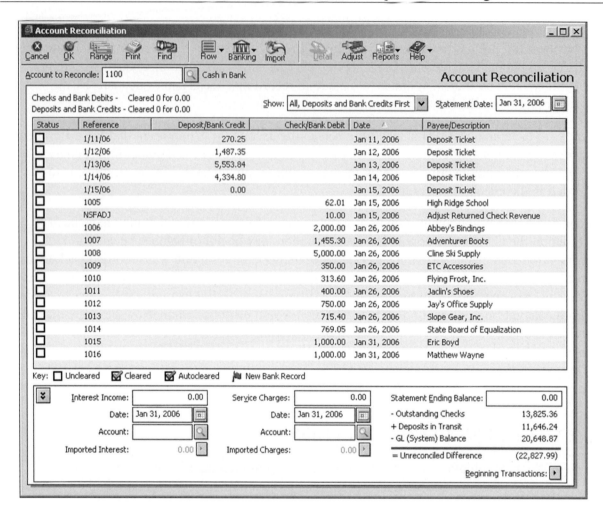

Peachtree has created a list that contains all of the transactions that have decreased the account, typically checks or increased the account, typically deposits. The first column of the list contains a box that can be clicked with the mouse to indicate the item's presence on the bank statement. There are fields for **Interest income** and for **Service charges**. There is also a **Statement Ending Balance** field into which we will enter the ending balance from the bank statement.

ENTER BANK STATEMENT INFORMATION

Information appearing on the bank statement is entered into the Account Reconciliation window as the next step. This information includes bank service charges and interest earned as well as the ending statement balance. Remember, the dates shown for the checks on the bank statement are the dates the checks were processed by the bank, not the dates the checks were written. Deposits will generally appear with the same dates, as they are hand-carried to the bank on the day they are recorded.

HIGH RIDGE BANK
12345 Old Mammoth Road
Mammoth Lakes, CA 93546
(619) 555-3880

BANK STATEMENT FOR:

High Ridge Ski Shoppe
875 Mountain Road
Mammoth Lakes, CA 93546

Acct. # 123-456-7890			January 2006
Beginning Balance 1/1/06			$22,827.99
1/11/06 Deposit	270.25		23,098.24
1/12/06 Deposit	1,487.35		24,585.59
1/13/06 Deposit	5,553.84		30,139.43
1/14/06 Deposit	4,334.80		34,474.23
1/15/06 Deposit	1,087.51		35,561.74
1/15/06 NSF Returned Check 765		1,087.51	34,474.23
1/15/06 NSF Fee		10.00	34,464.23
1/17/06 Check 1005		62.01	34,402.22
1/25/06 Check 1006		2,000.00	32,402.22
1/27/06 Check 1007		1,455.30	30,946.92
1/27/06 Check 1009		350.00	30,596.92
1/28/06 Check 1010		313.60	30,283.32
1/28/06 Check 1011		400.00	29,883.32
1/28/06 Check 1013		715.40	29,167.92
1/29/06 Check 1014		769.05	28,398.87
1/30/06 Office Equip Loan Pmt.: $53.42 Principal, $10.33 Interest		63.75	28,335.12
1/30/06 Store Fixtures Loan Pmt.: $44.51 Principal, $8.61 Interest		53.12	28,282.00
1/31/06 Service Chg.		8.00	28,274.00
1/31/06 Interest	54.05		28,328.05
Ending Balance 1/31/06			$28,328.05

DO: Continue to reconcile the bank statement above with the checking account
In the **Statement Ending Balance** field, enter, 28328.05
Enter the interest earned and the service charge in the appropriate fields selecting
accounts 7010 and 6120 respectively.
Compare the bank statement with the Account Reconciliation window
Click in the Clear column of the items that appear on both statements using the
scroll bars to display additional items. Be sure to clear the blank deposit from

1/15/06 which Peachtree created when we issued and applied the refund check to the Credit Memo as well as the $10.00 NSF fee.
Look at the right side of the Account Reconciliation window
There is an Unreconciled Balance of -116.87 at the bottom of the window
- This is caused by the items on the bank statement that did not appear in the Account Reconciliation window

One issue that requires discussion is the matter of the NSF check (No. 765) that was deposited and then removed from our account. This deposit and removal reflect on the bank statement but does not occur in our Peachtree records. This is due to the fact that Peachtree does not allow us to void a cash receipt but rather only allows us to delete it. This removes all trace of the cash receipt from our records except for the blank deposit. It is obvious from the bank statement that the deposit and subsequent NSF return cancel each other and require no other action on our part. However; should we desire to keep a record of this in Peachtree, we could use the Adjustment feature in the next section to record both the deposit and the withdrawal as adjustments. This would create a permanent record within Peachtree. This process should be used if there were multiple NSF returns. Since we have just the one, we will not record it in this manner.

ADJUSTING AND CORRECTING ENTRIES—BANK RECONCILIATION

As you complete the reconciliation, you may find errors that need to be corrected or transactions that need to be recorded. In our reconciliation, we note that the bank statement contains two electronic loan payments which do not appear in our Account Reconciliation window. Peachtree has included an Adjust icon at the top of the Account Reconciliation window that can be used to record additional transactions in the General Journal as needed. Errors that are noted should be corrected directly on the business form in which they occurred. That is to say, if a manually written check was entered into Peachtree incorrectly, we should bring up the receipt through the Receipts window and make the change directly on the business form. When we enter adjustments using the Adjust feature or make corrections on any business form that affects the cash account, these changes will appear in the Account Reconciliation window. Note too that the Reconciliation window has fields for entering Interest and Bank Service Charges. These can be used in lieu of the general journal although if there are many, the detail provided by the journal entry would be desired.

DO: Enter the electronic loan payments shown on the bank statement
Click on the **Adjust** icon at the top of the window
Enter or confirm 1/31/06 into the **Date** field
In the **Reference** field, enter RECON1
In the **GL Account** column enter 2510
In the **Description** field, enter Loan Pmt. Office Equip.
Click in the **Debit** column, enter 53.42
Click in the **GL Account** field and select account 6212

Tab to the **Debit** column and enter 10.33
Click in the **GL Account** field and select account 1100
Tab to the **Credit** column and enter 63.75
Click in the **GL Account** field and select account 2520
In the **Description** field, enter Loan Pmt. Store Fixtures
Tab to the **Debit** column and enter 44.51
Click in the **GL Account** field and select account 6212
Tab to the **Debit** column and enter 8.61
Click in the **GL Account** field and select account 1100
Tab to the **Credit** column and enter 53.12

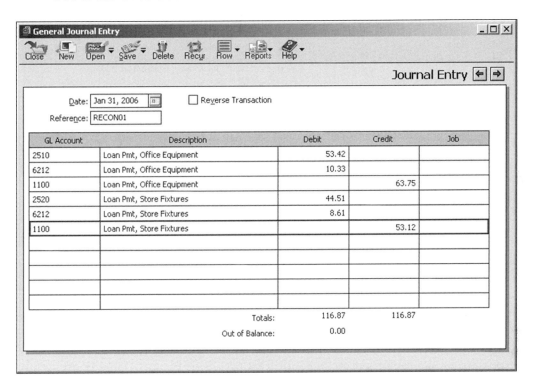

Click **Save** & then **Close**
You are returned to the Account Reconciliation window. Peachtree has added these additional items to the reconciliation item lists.
Scroll through Checks and Credits until you see the adjustments just added. Click the **Clear** column to mark the transactions.
If all has been entered correctly, the Unreconciled Difference should be 0.00. If a balance remains, go back and check to make sure all of the cleared items have a red checkmark in front of them. If they do and you are still out of balance, check each item carefully to make sure the amounts are identical. When you are finished, your Account Reconciliation window should look like this:

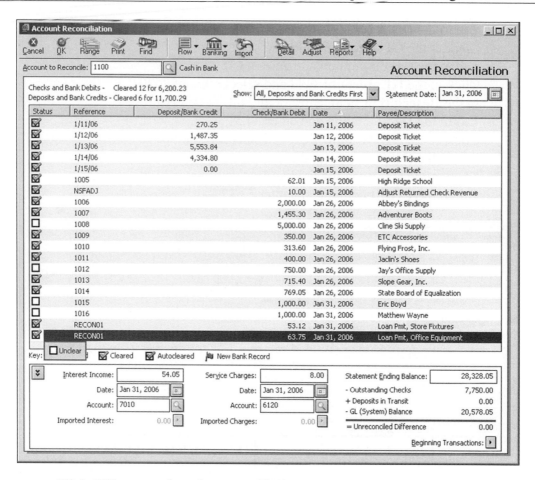

Click **OK** to complete the reconciliation process

PRINT AN ACCOUNT RECONCILIATION REPORT

One of Peachtree's many reports is an Account Reconciliation Report. This report summarizes all of the activity from the account reconciliation process. It is a good idea to print this report and maintain a file copy of it every time you reconcile an account. One of the useful features of the report is to provide a list of uncleared items that will carry over into the next month.

DO: Print an Account Reconciliation Report
Click on the **All Accounts Reconciliation Reports** in the **General Ledger** button
Double click Account Reconciliation from the Select a Report window
Click on the **Print** icon at the top of the window

```
                        High Ridge Ski Shoppe
                      Account Reconciliation
                         As of Jan 31, 2006
                        1100 - Cash in Bank
                  Bank Statement Date: January 31, 2006
Filter Criteria includes: Report is printed in Detail Format.


Beginning GL Balance                                          22,827.99

Add: Cash Receipts                                            11,646.24

Less: Cash Disbursements                                     (13,815.36)

Add (Less) Other                                                (80.82)

Ending GL Balance                                            20,578.05

Ending Bank Balance                                          28,328.05

Add back deposits in transit                         _____

Total deposits in transit

(Less) outstanding checks
                      Jan 26, 2006    1008    (5,000.00)
                      Jan 26, 2006    1012      (750.00)
                      Jan 31, 2006    1015    (1,000.00)
                      Jan 31, 2006    1016    (1,000.00)
                                              _____

Total outstanding checks                                     (7,750.00)

Add (Less) Other                                     _____

Total other

Unreconciled difference                                      _____

Ending GL Balance                                            20,578.05
```

Note: In the event the company has more than one account that has been reconciled, additional reports for these accounts can be obtained by clicking on the Options icon at the top of the window and using the drop down arrow to select the different accounts. Should you desire to see this feature, you can open Bellwether Garden Supply and view this report from within the sample company.

Click **Close**

Close the Select a Report window

VIEW THE ACCOUNT REGISTER FOR CHECKING

Once the bank reconciliation has been completed, it is wise to scroll through the checking account register to view the effect of the reconciliation on the account. You will notice that the adjusting items we entered as RECON1 have been added to the account. This report provides a comprehensive summary of all activity into and out of the checking account. The report is virtually identical to a General Ledger report except the Account Register maintains a running balance after each transaction.

DO: View the Account Register for the Checking account

Click on the **All Accounts Reconciliation Reports** in the **General Ledger** button
Double click on Account Register

High Ridge Ski Shoppe
Account Register
For the Period From Jan 1, 2006 to Jan 31, 2006
1100 - Cash in Bank

Filter Criteria includes: Report order is by Date.

Date	Trans No	Type	Trans Desc	Deposit Amt	Withdrawal Amt	Balance
			Beginning Balance			22,827.99
1/11/06	1/11/06	Deposit	Cash Customer	97.69		22,925.68
		Deposit	Cash Customer	138.35		23,064.03
		Deposit	Cash Customer	34.21		23,098.24
1/12/06	1/12/06	Deposit	Cash Customer	501.88		23,600.12
		Deposit	Cash Customer	889.00		24,489.12
		Deposit	Cash Customer	96.47		24,585.59
1/13/06	1/13/06	Deposit	Vallejo, Martin	975.00		25,560.59
		Deposit	Chang, Melissa	1,085.60		26,646.19
		Deposit	High Ridge Recreation Center	3,493.24		30,139.43
1/14/06	1/14/06	Deposit	Walsh, Victor	919.41		31,058.84
		Deposit	High Ridge School	2,406.91		33,465.75
		Deposit	Eddy, David	500.00		33,965.75
		Deposit	Platter, Susan	408.48		34,374.23
		Deposit	Tanamura, Hideto	100.00		34,474.23
1/15/06	1005	Withdrawal	High Ridge School		62.01	34,412.22
1/15/06	NSFADJ	Other	Adjust Returned Check Reve	10.00		34,402.22
1/26/06	1006	Withdrawal	Abbey's Bindings		2,000.00	32,402.22
1/26/06	1007	Withdrawal	Adventurer Boots		1,455.30	30,946.92
1/26/06	1008	Withdrawal	Cline Ski Supply		5,000.00	25,946.92
1/26/06	1009	Withdrawal	ETC Accessories		350.00	25,596.92
1/26/06	1010	Withdrawal	Flying Frost, Inc.		313.60	25,283.32
1/26/06	1011	Withdrawal	Jaclin's Shoes		400.00	24,883.32
1/26/06	1012	Withdrawal	Jay's Office Supply		750.00	24,133.32
1/26/06	1013	Withdrawal	Slope Gear, Inc.		715.40	23,417.92
1/26/06	1014	Withdrawal	State Board of Equalization		769.05	22,648.87
1/31/06	01/31/06	Other	Interest Income	54.05		22,702.92
1/31/06	01/31/06	Other	Service Charge		8.00	22,694.92
1/31/06	1015	Withdrawal	Eric Boyd		1,000.00	21,694.92
1/31/06	1016	Withdrawal	Matthew Wayne		1,000.00	20,694.92
1/31/06	RECON01	Other	Loan Pmt, Office Equipment		53.12	20,641.80
1/31/06	RECON01	Other	Loan Pmt, Office Equipment		63.75	20,578.05
			Total	11,700.29	13,950.23	

Click **Close**
Close the Select a Report window

VIEW THE GENERAL JOURNAL

After entering several transactions, it is helpful to view the General Journal. In the journal, all transactions entered through the General Journal Entry window or during the reconciliation process will appear in traditional debit/credit format.

DO: View the **General Journal** for January
Click **General Journal** from the Reports area of the **General Ledger** button
You are taken to a General Journal dialog box, accept the default setting, click **OK**
Note: You can easily identify the various types of entries by looking in the Reference column. If you recall, we used ADJ for our adjusting entries and RECON for our reconciliation entries. See how easily you can find these.

High Ridge Ski Shoppe
General Journal
For the Period From Jan 1, 2006 to Jan 31, 2006
Filter Criteria includes: Report order is by Date. Report is printed with Accounts having Zero Amounts and with Truncated Transaction Descriptions and in Detail Format.

Date	Account ID	Reference	Trans Description	Debit Amt	Credit Amt
1/15/06	4040	NSFADJ	Adjust Returned Check Revenue	10.00	
	1100		Adjust Returned Check Revenue		10.00
1/31/06	1100	01/31/06	Interest Income	54.05	
	7010		Interest Income		54.05
	1100		Service Charge		8.00
	6120		Service Charge	8.00	
1/31/06	6181	ADJ01	Adjusting Entry, Insurance	125.00	
	1340		Adjusting Entry, Insurance		125.00
1/31/06	6472	ADJ02	Adjusting Entry, Office Supplies	1,100.00	
	1311		Adjusting Entry, Office Supplies		1,100.00
1/31/06	6471	ADJ03	Adjusting Entry, Sales Supplies	175.00	
	1312		Adjusting Entry, Sales Supplies		175.00
1/31/06	6150	ADJ04	Record Depreciation for January	160.00	
	1512		Record Depreciation for January		85.00
	1522		Record Depreciation for January		75.00
1/31/06	3050	CLOSE01	Close Retained Earnings to Capital	46,683.95	
	3010		Close Retained Earnings to Capital		15,561.32
	3012		Close Retained Earnings to Capital		31,122.63
	3010		Close Eric's Draw to Capital	1,000.00	
	3013		Close Eric's Draw to Capital		1,000.00
	3012		Close Matt's Draw to Capital	1,000.00	
	3015		Close Matt's Draw to Capital		1,000.00
1/31/06	2510	RECON01	Loan Pmt, Office Equipment	53.42	
	6212		Loan Pmt, Office Equipment	10.33	
	1100		Loan Pmt, Office Equipment		63.75
	2520		Loan Pmt, Store Fixtures	44.51	
	6212		Loan Pmt, Store Fixtures	8.61	
	1100		Loan Pmt, Store Fixtures		53.12
		Total		50,432.87	50,432.87

Click **Close**

PRINT THE GENERAL LEDGER TRIAL BALANCE

The Trial Balance, which looks most like that prepared in a manual accounting system, is the General Ledger Trial Balance. It would be prepared after the adjusting entries have been made. It can be used as a final check to insure that all the accounts reflect the desired balances prior to printing the financial statements. If it is determined that an account requires additional adjusting, entries can be made and another Trial Balance can be quickly and easily printed.

DO: Print the General Ledger Trial Balance
Click **All General Ledger Reports** from the Reports area of the **General Ledger** button
Double click on General Ledger Trial Balance

High Ridge Ski Shoppe
General Ledger Trial Balance
As of Jan 31, 2006
Filter Criteria includes: Report order is by ID. Report is printed in Detail Format.

Account ID	Account Description	Debit Amt	Credit Amt
1100	Cash in Bank	20,578.05	
1120	Merchandise Inventory	54,988.35	
1200	Accounts Receivable		250.78
1311	Office Supplies	500.00	
1312	Sales Supplies	400.00	
1340	Prepaid Insurance	125.00	
1511	Office Equipment	5,000.00	
1512	Accum. Depr. Office Equipment		85.00
1521	Store Fixtures	4,500.00	
1522	Accum. Depr. Store Fixtures		75.00
2000	Accounts Payable	7,804.60	
2100	Visa Payable		150.00
2200	Sales Tax Payable		469.31
2510	Office Equipment Loan Payable		2,946.58
2520	Store Fixtures Loan Payable		2,455.49
3010	Capital, Eric Boyd		34,561.32
3012	Capital, Matthew Wayne		50,122.63
4011	Clothing & Accessory Sales		1,515.84
4012	Equipment Sales		9,091.70
4015	Sales Discounts	83.14	
4020	Delivery Income		25.00
4040	Returned Check Revenue		5.00
5000	Cost of Goods Sold	5,546.22	
6120	Bank Service Charges	8.00	
6140	Advertising Expense	95.00	
6150	Depreciation Expense	160.00	
6181	Liability Insurance Expense	125.00	
6212	Loan Interest Expense	18.94	
6340	Telephone Expense	156.40	
6391	Gas and Electric Expense	359.00	
6392	Water Expense	85.00	
6471	Sales Supplies Expense	175.00	
6472	Office Supplies Expense	1,100.00	
7010	Interest Income		54.05
	Total:	101,807.70	101,807.70

Click **Print**
Close the report and the **Select a Report** window

PRINT STANDARD INCOME STATEMENT

Because all revenues and expenses have been recorded, and adjustments have been made for the period, an Income Statement can be prepared. This statement is also known as a Profit and Loss Statement. Peachtree® Complete Accounting 2006 can generate a current period income statement or show a 2-year comparison for analysis purposes. We will print the former.

DO: Print a Standard Income Statement
If necessary, click **Print Financial Statements** from the Reports area of the
  General Ledger button
Double click on <Standard> Income Statement
You are presented with a <Standard> Income Statement dialog box
Deselect **Show Zero Amounts** and click **OK**

High Ridge Ski Shoppe
Income Statement
For the One Month Ending January 31, 2005

	Current Month			Year to Date	
Revenues					
Clothing & Accessory Sales	$ 1,515.84	14.29	$	1,515.84	14.29
Equipment Sales	9,091.70	85.70		9,091.70	85.70
Sales Discounts	(83.14)	(0.78)		(83.14)	(0.78)
Delivery Income	25.00	0.24		25.00	0.24
Returned Check Revenue	5.00	0.05		5.00	0.05
Interest Income	54.05	0.51		54.05	0.51
Total Revenues	10,608.45	100.00		10,608.45	100.00
Cost of Sales					
Cost of Goods Sold	5,546.22	52.28		5,546.22	52.28
Total Cost of Sales	5,546.22	52.28		5,546.22	52.28
Gross Profit	5,062.23	47.72		5,062.23	47.72
Expenses					
Bank Service Charges	8.00	0.08		8.00	0.08
Advertising Expense	95.00	0.90		95.00	0.90
Depreciation Expense	160.00	1.51		160.00	1.51
Liability Insurance Expense	125.00	1.18		125.00	1.18
Loan Interest Expense	18.94	0.18		18.94	0.18
Telephone Expense	156.40	1.47		156.40	1.47
Gas and Electric Expense	359.00	3.38		359.00	3.38
Water Expense	85.00	0.80		85.00	0.80
Sales Supplies Expense	175.00	1.65		175.00	1.65
Office Supplies Expense	1,100.00	10.37		1,100.00	10.37
Total Expenses	2,282.34	21.51		2,282.34	21.51
Net Income	$ 2,779.89	26.20	$	2,779.89	26.20

Click **Print**
Click **Close**

PRINT STANDARD BALANCE SHEET

The Balance Sheet proves the fundamental accounting equation: Assets = Liabilities + Owner's Equity. When all transactions and adjustments for the period have been recorded, a balance sheet should be prepared.

DO: Print a <Standard> Balance Sheet
If necessary, click **All Financial Statements** from the Reports area of the **General Ledger** button
Double click on <Standard> Balance Sheet
You are presented with a <Standard> Balance Sheet Options dialog box
Accept the defaults and click **OK**

```
                        High Ridge Ski Shoppe
                           Balance Sheet
                          January 31, 2006

                              ASSETS

Current Assets
Cash in Bank                          $        20,578.05
Merchandise Inventory                          54,988.35
Accounts Receivable                             (250.78)
Office Supplies                                   500.00
Sales Supplies                                    400.00
Prepaid Insurance                                 125.00
                                             _____
Total Current Assets                                              76,340.62

Property and Equipment
Office Equipment                                5,000.00
Accum. Depr. Office Equipment                     (85.00)
Store Fixtures                                  4,500.00
Accum. Depr. Store Fixtures                       (75.00)
                                             _____
Total Property and Equipment                                      9,340.00

Other Assets
                                             _____
Total Other Assets                                                    0.00
                                                                 _____
Total Assets                          $                          85,680.62
                                                                 ===========


                      LIABILITIES AND CAPITAL

Current Liabilities
Accounts Payable                      $        (7,804.60)
Visa Payable                                      150.00
Sales Tax Payable                                 469.31
                                             _____
Total Current Liabilities                                        (7,185.29)

Long-Term Liabilities
Office Equipment Loan Payable                   2,946.58
Store Fixtures Loan Payable                     2,455.49
                                             _____
Total Long-Term Liabilities                                       5,402.07
                                                                 _____
Total Liabilities                                                (1,783.22)

Capital
Capital, Eric Boyd                             34,561.32
Capital, Matthew Wayne                         50,122.63
Net Income                                      2,779.89
                                             _____
Total Capital                                                    87,463.84
                                                                 _____
Total Liabilities & Capital           $                          85,680.62
                                                                 ===========
```

Click **Print**

Close the report and the Select a Report window

EXPORTING REPORTS TO EXCEL

Many of the reports prepared in Peachtree® Complete Accounting 2006 can be exported to Microsoft® Excel. This allows you to take advantage of extensive filtering options available in Excel, hide detail for some but not all groups of data, combine information from two different reports, change titles of columns, add comments, change the order of columns, and to experiment with "what if" scenarios. Additionally, you can use Excel's charting capabilities to create custom charts and graphs of your accounting data. In order to use this feature of Peachtree® Complete Accounting 2006 you must also have Microsoft Excel 97 or higher.

DO: Optional Exercise: Export a report from Peachtree® Complete Accounting 2006 to
Excel
Click **All General Ledger Reports** from the **General Ledger** button
Double click General Ledger Trial Balance
Click on the **Excel** icon at the top of the screen
You are presented with a Copy Report to Excel dialog box
Peachtree will default to creating a new workbook,

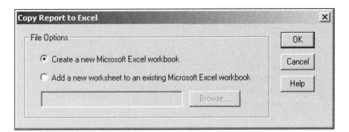

Click **OK** to accept defaults

	A	B	C	D
	Account ID	**Account Description**	**Debit Amt**	**Credit Amt**
1				
2	1100	Cash in Bank	20,578.05	
3	1120	Merchandise Inventory	54,988.35	
4	1200	Accounts Receivable		250.78
5	1311	Office Supplies	500.00	
6	1312	Sales Supplies	400.00	
7	1340	Prepaid Insurance	125.00	
8	1511	Office Equipment	5,000.00	
9	1512	Accum. Depr. Office Equipment		85.00
10	1521	Store Fixtures	4,500.00	
11	1522	Accum. Depr. Store Fixtures		75.00
12	2000	Accounts Payable	7,804.60	
13	2100	Visa Payable		150.00
14	2200	Sales Tax Payable		469.31
15	2510	Office Equipment Loan Payable		2,946.58
16	2520	Store Fixtures Loan Payable		2,455.49
17	3010	Capital, Eric Boyd		34,561.32
18	3012	Capital, Matthew Wayne		50,122.63
19	4011	Clothing & Accessory Sales		1,515.84
20	4012	Equipment Sales		9,091.70
21	4015	Sales Discounts	83.14	
22	4020	Delivery Income		25.00
23	4040	Returned Check Revenue		5.00
24	5000	Cost of Goods Sold	5,546.22	
25	6120	Bank Service Charges	8.00	
26	6140	Advertising Expense	95.00	
27	6150	Depreciation Expense	160.00	
28	6181	Liability Insurance Expense	125.00	
29	6212	Loan Interest Expense	18.94	
30	6340	Telephone Expense	156.40	
31	6391	Gas and Electric Expense	359.00	
32	6392	Water Expense	85.00	
33	6471	Sales Supplies Expense	175.00	
34	6472	Office Supplies Expense	1,100.00	
35	7010	Interest Income		54.05
36				
37		Total:	101,807.70	101,807.70

Click **Print**

High Ridge Ski Shoppe
General Ledger Trial Balance
As of Jan 31, 2006

Account ID	Account Description	Debit Amt	Credit Amt
1100	Cash in Bank	20,578.05	
1120	Merchandise Inventory	54,988.35	
1200	Accounts Receivable		250.78
1311	Office Supplies	500.00	
1312	Sales Supplies	400.00	
1340	Prepaid Insurance	125.00	
1511	Office Equipment	5,000.00	
1512	Accum. Depr. Office Equipment		85.00
1521	Store Fixtures	4,500.00	
1522	Accum. Depr. Store Fixtures		75.00
2000	Accounts Payable	7,804.60	
2100	Visa Payable		150.00
2200	Sales Tax Payable		469.31
2510	Office Equipment Loan Payable		2,946.58
2520	Store Fixtures Loan Payable		2,455.49
3010	Capital, Eric Boyd		34,561.32
3012	Capital, Matthew Wayne		50,122.63
4011	Clothing & Accessory Sales		1,515.84
4012	Equipment Sales		9,091.70
4015	Sales Discounts	83.14	
4020	Delivery Income		25.00
4040	Returned Check Revenue		5.00
5000	Cost of Goods Sold	5,546.22	
6120	Bank Service Charges	8.00	
6140	Advertising Expense	95.00	
6150	Depreciation Expense	160.00	
6181	Liability Insurance Expense	125.00	
6212	Loan Interest Expense	18.94	
6340	Telephone Expense	156.40	
6391	Gas and Electric Expense	359.00	
6392	Water Expense	85.00	
6471	Sales Supplies Expense	175.00	
6472	Office Supplies Expense	1,100.00	
7010	Interest Income		54.05
	Total:	101,807.70	101,807.70

Note: Peachtree® Complete Accounting 2006 created a formal header as well as
the print setting needed to print this report. Any changes that may be needed
can be made directly in the spreadsheet or in the header for the spreadsheet
prior to printing. In the illustration above, a default landscape orientation
was changed to portrait.

Click **Close** button in the top right corner of the Excel title bar to close Excel

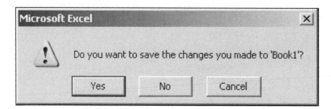

Click **No** to close Book1 without saving
Close the report and the Select a Report window
Close the General Ledger Trial Balance

END-OF-PERIOD BACKUP

Once all end-of-period procedures have been completed, a regular backup and a second backup of the company data should be made and filed as an archive copy. Preferably this copy will be located some place other than on the business premises. The archive or file copy is set aside in case of emergency or in case damage occurs to the original and current backup copies of the company data. There are a number of Internet companies that will provide Internet site-based storage for data backups as well.

 DO: Back up company data and prepare an archive copy of the company data
Insert your backup disk in the A: drive
Click File on the menu bar, click Back Up
In the Back Up Company dialog box, select Include company name in the backup file name by clicking in the blank field to the left of it
Using the Save in drop down arrow, select A:
Click Save
Click OK
Label this disk **Archive, 1-31-2006**

PASSWORDS

Not every employee of a business should have access to all the financial records for the company. In some companies, only the owner will have complete access. In others, one or two key employees will have full access while other employees are provided limited access based on the jobs they perform. Passwords are secret words used to control access to data. Peachtree® Complete Accounting 2006 has several options available when assigning passwords.

In order to assign any passwords at all, you must have an administrator. The administrator has unrestricted access to all Peachtree® Complete Accounting 2006 functions and sets up users and user passwords, and assigns areas of transaction access for each user. Areas of access can be limited to transaction entry for certain types of transactions or a user may have unrestricted access into all areas of Peachtree® Complete Accounting 2006 and company data.

A password should be kept secret at all times. It should be something that is easy for the individual to remember, yet difficult for someone else to guess. Birthdays, names, initials, and similar devices are not good passwords because the information is too readily available. Never write down your password where it can be easily found or seen by someone else.

ADVANCE TO THE NEXT PERIOD

In order for Peachtree® Complete Accounting 2006 to produce interim (monthly) financial statements, it is necessary to inform Peachtree that we are finished with a given period (month) and are ready to begin recording data for the next period. We accomplish this by advancing to the next accounting period.

As part of this process, we will be asked to generate a number of end-of-period reports, primarily the journals that recorded the transactions that occurred during the month. It is always wise to have a printed or "hard copy" of the data. This copy should be kept on file as an additional backup to the data stored on your disk. If your disk becomes damaged, you will still have the paper copy of your transactions available for re-entry into the system.

MEMO

DATE: January 31, 2006

Now that the closing transactions have been performed, advance the system to period - 02 Feb 1, 2006 - Feb 28, 2006 and print the end-of-period reports.

DO: Advance the period and print end-of-period reports
Click on **Change Accounting Period** from the **General Ledger** button
Click on 02 Feb 1, 2006 - Feb 28, 2006

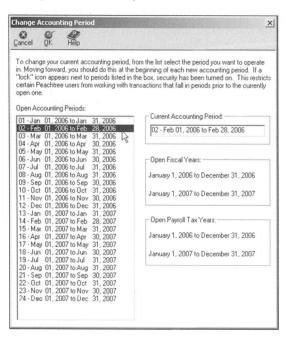

Click **OK**

You are presented with a dialog box asking whether you desire to print end-of-period reports. If these reports had already been printed as part of your end-of-period routine, you would answer no. Since we have not printed these reports, we will do so at this time.

Click **Yes**

You are presented with a Print Reports dialog box. This window lists the reports that will be printed by default. If any of these reports have already been printed, they can be deselected at this time to prevent reprinting them.

Report Name	Reporting Period	Print?
General Journal	1 - Jan 1, 2006 to Jan 31, 2006	☑
Cash Disbursements Journal	1 - Jan 1, 2006 to Jan 31, 2006	☑
Purchase Journal	1 - Jan 1, 2006 to Jan 31, 2006	☑
Purchase Order Journal	1 - Jan 1, 2006 to Jan 31, 2006	☑
General Ledger	1 - Jan 1, 2006 to Jan 31, 2006	☑

Click **OK**

Note: Peachtree® Complete Accounting 2006 will now print the reports that were selected in the Print Report dialog box. Remember that your list may be different. When finished, it will close all windows and take you back to the main Peachtree screen. Note in the lower right-hand corner of your screen, that the system has been moved into Period 2. Your reports may differ from the above list.

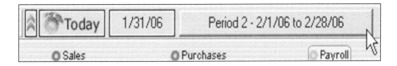

You are now ready to begin recording transactions for the month of February.

ACCESS TRANSACTIONS FROM PREVIOUS PERIOD

Even though the month of January has been "closed," transactions still appear in the account ledgers, the journals, and so on. There will be times when we will need to access an invoice or a cash receipt or some other transaction from a prior accounting period. Peachtree® Complete Accounting 2006 stores this data and keeps it available as we move from period to period. Once a transaction has been completed, the detail will no longer show up in our current reports; however, we can use the Options feature to change the date(s) of the report so that they will reflect the older transactions as well. What this means is that if we wish to see a cash receipt from last month, say the cash receipt from Melissa Chang, we are still able to even though January has been closed.

DO: Access cash receipt from prior period
Click **Cash Receipts Journal** from the Reports section of the **Sales** button
You are presented with an Options window, change the **Date** to This Year and click **OK**
Scroll down until you reach the transaction for Melissa Chang, Invoice No. 107. Position the cursor over one of the lines for the cash receipt for 1/13/06. It will turn into a magnifying glass.

High Ridge Ski Shoppe
Cash Receipts Journal
For the Period From Jan 1, 2006 to Dec 31, 2006
Filter Criteria includes: Report order is by Check Date. Report is printed in Detail Format.

Date	Account ID	Transaction Ref	Line Description	Debit Amnt	Credit Amnt
1/13/06	1200	765	Invoice: 99		975.00
	1100		Vallejo, Martin	975.00	
1/13/06	1200	1026	Invoice: 89		53.63
	1200		Invoice: 107 Ⓩ		1,031.97
	1100		Chang, Melissa	1,085.60	

Double click to view the original cash receipt.
The original cash receipt is brought up on screen for viewing. All of the details can be examined including the deposit ticket ID, the check number and which General Ledger accounts were used in the transaction.
Close the Receipts window
Close the Cash Receipts Journal

EDIT TRANSACTION FROM PREVIOUS PERIOD

If it is determined that an error was made in a previous period, Peachtree® Complete Accounting 2006 does allow a correction to be made. Be aware though, that it is not advisable to change transactions from prior accounting periods. Doing so will alter the financial statements, journals, ledger reports and other reports printed at the end of the accounting period. In most businesses, the accounting manager will decide when an error is significant enough to warrant making the change in the accounting period in which the error took place. It is also important to note that, while Peachtree® Complete Accounting 2006 allows these changes to be made easily, many larger programs do not allow such changes without significant system administrator involvement. Before it will record any changes for previous periods, Peachtree® Complete Accounting 2006 requires that you confirm the change in a dialog box warning you that the change involves a transaction date that is outside the current period for the company.

As an alternative to changing a specific transaction, an error can also be corrected by changing the account that contains the error and using Retained Earnings as the offsetting account. Since any change to the income or loss would have been closed to Retained Earnings anyway, this allows a change to be made without affecting the Income Statement from last period. Errors made in a prior period can also be fixed in the current period by simply shifting money between accounts. This fixes the problem in the current period without the need for changing the financial statements from the previous period.

MEMO

DATE: February 2, 2006

After reviewing the General Journal and reports printed at the end of January, Renee finds that $25 of the Office Supplies should have been recorded as Sales Supplies. Record an entry in the General Journal to transfer $25 from Office Supplies to Sales Supplies.

DO: Move $25 from Office Supplies to Sales Supplies

Click **General Journal Entry** from the **General Ledger** button

Verify or type 2/2/06 in the **Date** field

Tab to the **Reference** field, enter ADJ01

Using the magnifying glass to the right of the **Account No.** field, select 1312 Sales Supplies

In the **Description** field, enter Transfer Office Supplies to Sales Supplies

Tab to the **Debit** field, enter 25.00

Using the magnifying glass to the right of the **Account No.** field, select 1311 Office Supplies

Tab to the **Credit** field, enter 25.00

Click **Save** and then **Close**

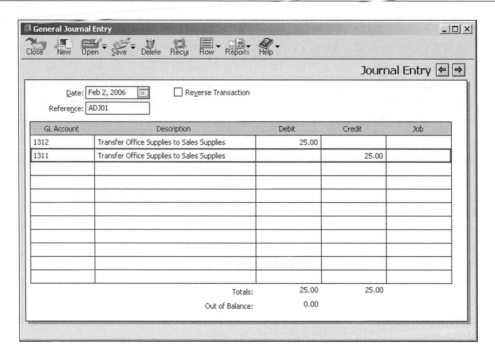

VERIFY THE CORRECTION TO THE SUPPLIES ACCOUNTS

Once the correction has been made, it is important to view the change in the accounts. The transfer of an amount of one asset into another will have no direct effect on the total assets in your reports. The account balances for Office Supplies and Sales Supplies will be changed. To view the change in the account, open the General Ledger Trial Balance and look at the balance of each account. Compare the new numbers for these accounts with the General Ledger Trial Balance printed earlier.

MEMO

DATE: February 2, 2006

Access the General Ledger Trial Balance and view the change in the account balances and the correcting entry for each account.

 DO: View the General Ledger Trial Balance

Click **All General Ledger Reports** from the Reports area of the **General Ledger** button

Double click on General Ledger Trial Balance

High Ridge Ski Shoppe
General Ledger Trial Balance
As of Feb 28, 2006
Filter Criteria includes: Report order is by ID. Report is printed in Detail Format.

Account ID	Account Description	Debit Amt	Credit Amt
1100	Cash in Bank	20,578.05	
1120	Merchandise Inventory	54,988.35	
1200	Accounts Receivable		250.78
1311	Office Supplies	475.00	
1312	Sales Supplies	425.00	
1340	Prepaid Insurance	125.00	

Close the report and the Select a Report window when finished

FOOTNOTE FOR INVENTORY ADJUSTMENTS

As you have worked through this chapter and the last, Peachtree® Complete Accounting 2006 has been maintaining your inventory perpetually. That is to say, as we purchased inventory, our inventory account was increased and as we sold inventory, it was moved into Cost of Goods Sold. At the same time, the Inventory Module kept track of quantities of every item that made up the Merchandise Inventory accounts. Although we have completed a month for a typical business, there are tasks that would be performed at the end of the year that have not been shown. One such task would be to conduct a physical inventory. This entails a physical count of our Merchandise Inventory. Quantities would be counted and recorded and matched with the quantities shown in our Inventory Module. Any discrepancies would be corrected in the program resulting in an increase or decrease in inventory value and a corresponding increase or decrease in Cost of Goods Sold.

DO: Adjust quantity of Ski Bindings, Deluxe from 19 to 17
Click **Inventory Adjustments** from the **Inventory** button
Using the magnifying glass to the right of the **Item ID:** field, select BIN10 Ski Bindings, Deluxe
Click in the **Reference** field, enter INV01
Change the date to Jan 31, 2006
Click in the **Adjust Quantity By:** field, enter -2.00
Click in the **Reason to Adjust:** field, enter Missing from Physical Count

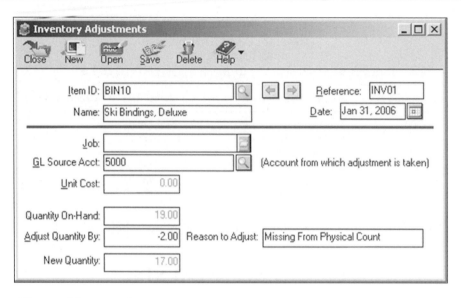

       Close without saving

You can see from the screen capture that Peachtree would have adjusted account 5000, Cost of Goods Sold, as well as the Merchandise Inventory account. In addition, the subsidiary record for this item would now be adjusted. Adjustments would be made prior to initiating closing activities at the end of the period. Any changes made would reflect in the financial statements for the period. In most businesses, this would be accomplished once a year or perhaps even twice.

BACK UP

Whenever an important work session is complete, you should always back up your data. If your data disk is damaged or an error is discovered at a later time, the backup disk may be restored and the information used for recording transactions. No matter what type of business, the backup procedure remains the same. In addition, it is always wise to make a duplicate of your data disk just in case the disk is damaged in some way.

 DO: Follow the instructions given in previous chapters to back up data for High Ridge Ski Shoppe.

SUMMARY

In this chapter, end-of-period adjustments were made, a bank reconciliation was performed, backup and archive disks were prepared, and adjusting entries were made. The use of Drawing and Retained Earnings accounts were explored and interpreted for a partnership. The period was advanced. Account names were changed, and new accounts were created. Even though Peachtree® Complete Accounting 2006 focuses on entering transactions on business forms, journals recording each transaction were kept by Peachtree® Complete Accounting 2006. This chapter presented transaction entry directly into the General Journal. Owner withdrawals and distribution of capital to partners were examined. Many of the different report options available in Peachtree® Complete Accounting 2006 were explored, and a report was exported to Microsoft® Excel. A variety of reports were printed. Correction of errors was analyzed, and corrections were made after the period was closed and inventory adjustments were discussed. The fact that Peachtree® Complete Accounting 2006 does not require an actual closing entry at the end of the period was addressed.

END-OF-CHAPTER QUESTIONS

TRUE/FALSE

ANSWER THE FOLLOWING QUESTIONS IN THE SPACE PROVIDED BEFORE THE QUESTION NUMBER.

_____ 1. The owner's Drawing account should be transferred to capital each month.

_____ 2. Even if entered elsewhere, all transactions are recorded in journals.

_____ 3. You must access Set Up Users in order to close a period.

_____ 4. Inventory adjustments are made directly in the Purchases/Receive Inventory window.

_____ 5. When you reconcile a bank statement, anything entered as a service charge will automatically be entered as a transaction when the reconciliation is complete.

_____ 6. Once an account has been used, the name cannot be changed.

_____ 7. The adjusting entry for depreciation must be made in the General Journal.

_____ 8. At the end of the year, Peachtree® Complete Accounting 2006 transfers the net income into retained earnings.

_____ 9. A withdrawal by an owner in a partnership reduces the owner's capital.

_____ 10. As with other accounting programs, Peachtree® Complete Accounting 2006 requires that a formal closing be performed at the end of each year.

MULTIPLE CHOICE

WRITE THE LETTER OF THE CORRECT ANSWER IN THE SPACE PROVIDED BEFORE THE QUESTION NUMBER.

_____ 1. To perform an account reconciliation you must select ___.
A. nothing
B. the time period
C. the account number
D. the proper business form

_____ 2. The report that proves debits equal credits is the ___.
A. Sales report
B. Balance Sheet
C. Income Statement
D. General Ledger Trial Balance

_____ 3. If reports are prepared as of January 31, net income will appear in the ___.
A. Income Statement
B. Balance Sheet
C. both A and B
D. neither A nor B

_____ 4. In Peachtree® Complete Accounting 2006, you export reports to Microsoft ® Excel in order to ___.
A. print the report
B. explore "what if" scenarios with data from Peachtree® Complete Accounting 2006
C. prepare graphs
D. all of the above

_____ 5. Peachtree® Complete Accounting 2006 automatically records Purchases Discount as _____.
A. income
B. a decrease to merchandise inventory
C. an expense
D. an asset

_____ 6. If a transaction is recorded in the General Journal, its impact may be viewed ___.
A. in the General Journal report
B. in the General Ledgers Report
C. in neither A nor B
D. in both A and B

_____ 7. Entries for bank fund transfers ___.
   A. are automatically recorded at the completion of the bank reconciliation
   B. must be recorded after the bank reconciliation is complete
   C. should be recorded while one is reconciling the bank statement
   D. should be recorded on the first of the month

_____ 8. The accounts that may be reconciled are ___.
   A. Checking
   B. Cash
   C. all accounts
   D. both A and B

_____ 9. The closing entry for drawing transfers the balance of an owner's drawing account into the ___ account.
   A. Retained Earnings
   B. Net Income
   C. Capital
   D. Investment

_____ 10. Any balance in Retained Earnings for a partnership should be allocated to the partners based on ___ .
   A. an equal sharing
   B. the partnership agreement
   C. how much work each partner does
   D. an arm wrestling competition

FILL-IN

IN THE SPACE PROVIDED, WRITE THE ANSWER THAT MOST APPROPRIATELY COMPLETES THE SENTENCE.

1. _____-basis accounting matches income and expenses against a period, and -basis accounting records income when the money is received and expenses when the purchase is made or the bill is paid.

2. The _____ proves that Assets = Liabilities + Owners' Equity.

3. In a partnership, each owner owns a share of all the _____ and _____ based on the percentage of his or her investment in the business or according to any partnership agreements.

4. In order to close an accounting period, the period must be _____ .

5. No matter on what form transactions are recorded, they all appear in a _____.

SHORT ESSAY

Describe the adjustment required for inventory adjustments, and explain why this adjustment should be made.

NAME _____

TRANSMITTAL

CHAPTER 7: HIGH RIDGE SKI SHOPPE

Attach the following documents and reports:

☐   Standard Income Statement

☐   Check No. 1015: Eric Boyd

☐   Check No. 1016: Matthew Wayne

☐   Account Reconciliation Report

☐   General Ledger Trial Balance

☐   Standard Income Statement (Revised)

☐   Balance Sheet

☐   General Ledger Trial Balance from Excel

☐   General Journal

☐   Cash Disbursement Journal

☐   Purchases Journal

☐   Purchase Orders Journal

☐   General Ledgers Report

END-OF-CHAPTER PROBLEM

ALOHA SUN CLOTHING CO.

Chapter 7 continues with the end-of-period adjustments, bank reconciliation, archive disks, and closing the period for Aloha Sun Clothing Co. The company does use a certified professional accountant for guidance and assistance with appropriate accounting procedures. The CPA has provided information for Maile to use for adjusting entries, etc.

INSTRUCTIONS

Continue to use the copy of ALOHA you used in the previous chapters. Open the company—the file used is **Aloha Sun Clothing Co**. Record the adjustments and other transactions as you were instructed in the chapter. Always read the transaction carefully and review the Chart of Accounts when selecting transaction accounts. Print the reports and journals as indicated.

RECORD TRANSACTIONS

January 31—Enter the following:

Change the names of the following accounts:
3011 Nalani Kalaniki, Investment to 3011 Nalani Kalaniki, Capital
3012 Maile Kahala, Investment to 3012 Maile Kahala, Capital
6260 Printing and Repro Expense to 6260 Printing & Duplication Expense

Make the following accounts inactive:
6291 Building Repairs Expense
6351 Entertainment Expense

Delete the following accounts:
3010 Kalaniki & Kahala Capital
3899 Beginning Balance Equity
6182 Disability Insurance Expense
6213 Mortgage Expense
6823 Property Tax Expense

Print the Chart of Accounts

Enter adjusting entries using ADJ01 in the Journal for:

Office supplies used is $35. (Description: Office Supplies Used for January)
Sales supplies used, account balance at the end of the month is $1,400 (Description: Sales Supplies Used for January)
Record a compound entry for depreciation for the month: Office Equipment, $66.67 and Store Fixtures, $79.17 (Description for all accounts used: Depreciation Expense January)

The amount of insurance remaining in the Prepaid Insurance account is for five months of liability insurance. Record the liability insurance expense for the month. (Description: Insurance Expense January)

Enter transactions for Owners' Equity:

Each owner withdrew $500. (Description: Withdrawal for January) Print Check Nos. 209 and 210 for the owners' withdrawals. Add the owners to the Vendors List. (use KAL01 for Nalani Kalaniki and KAH01 for Maile Kahala)

Distribute retained earnings to each owner: divide the balance giving one-third to Nalani Kalaniki and two-thirds to Maile Kahala, use CLOSE01. (Description: Transfer Retained Earnings to Partners Accounts)

Prepare Bank Reconciliation and Enter Adjustments for the Reconciliation:

SAN LUIS OBISPO CENTRAL COAST BANK
1234 Coast Highway
San Luis Obispo, CA 93407
(805) 555-9300

BANK STATEMENT FOR:

Aloha Sun Clothing Co.
784 Marsh Street
San Luis Obispo, CA 93407

Acct. # 987-352-9152			January 2006
Beginning Balance 1/1/06			$38,919.00
1/3/06 Deposit	517.90		39,436.90
1/5/06 Deposit	2,557.99		41,994.89
1/15/06 Deposit	491.02		42,485.91
1/16/06 Deposit	1,338.03		43,823.94
1/16/06 Check No. 201		58.98	43,764.96
1/17/06 NSF Check No. 2311		1,338.03	42,426.93
1/17/06 NSF Fee		10.00	42,416.93
1/20/06 Check No. 202		2,868.00	39,548.93
1/20/06 Check No. 204		3,843.00	35,705.93
1/22/06 Check No. 205		450.00	35,255.93
1/27/06 Check No. 207		250.00	35,005.93
1/28/06 Check 208		168.82	34,837.11
1/31/06 Check 209		500.00	34,337.11
1/31/06 Check 210		500.00	33,837.11
1/30/06 Office Equip Loan Pmt.: $44.51. Principal, $8.61 Interest		53.12	33,783.99
1/30/06 Store Fixtures Loan Pmt.: $53.42 Principal, $10.33 Interest		63.75	33,720.24
1/31/06 Service Chg.		10.00	33,710.24
1/31/06 Interest	73.30		33,783.54
Ending Balance 1/31/06			33,783.54

Print an Account Reconciliation report

Close Drawing accounts into owner's individual Capital accounts

Found one damaged tie. Adjust the quantity of ties on 1/31/06 using the 5000 Cost of Goods Sold account

Print the following for January:
>   General Ledger Trial Balance
>   Standard Income Statement
>   Standard Balance Sheet

Advance the period to 2 - Feb 01, 2006 to Feb 29, 2006. Print all recommended reports

Edit a transaction from a closed period:

Discovered an error in the amount of Office Supplies and Sales Supplies: Transfer $40 from Office Supplies to Sales Supplies on 02/02/06

NAME _____

TRANSMITTAL

CHAPTER 7: ALOHA SUN CLOTHING CO.

Attach the following documents and reports:

- ☐ Chart of Accounts (Revised)
- ☐ Check No. 209: Nalani Kalaniki
- ☐ Check No. 210: Maile Kahala
- ☐ Account Reconciliation Report
- ☐ General Ledger Trial Balance
- ☐ Standard Income Statement
- ☐ Standard Balance Sheet
- ☐ General Journal
- ☐ Cash Receipts Journal
- ☐ Cash Disbursements Journal
- ☐ Sales Journal
- ☐ Purchase Journal
- ☐ Inventory Adjustment Journal
- ☐ Purchase Orders Journal
- ☐ General Ledger

End Of Section 2— Planet Golf Practice Set: Merchandising Business

The following is a comprehensive practice set combining all the elements of Peachtree® Complete Accounting 2006 studied in the second section of the text. In this practice set you will keep the books for a company for the month of January 2006. Entries will be made to record invoices, receipt of payments on invoices, cash sales, credit card sales, receipt and payment of bills, orders and receipts of merchandise, credit memos for invoices and bills and sales tax payments. Account names will be added, changed, deleted, and made inactive. Customer, vendor, and owner names will be added to the appropriate lists. Reports will be prepared to analyze sales, bills, receipts, and items ordered. Formal reports including the General Ledger Trial Balance, Standard Income Statement, and Standard Balance Sheet will be prepared. Adjusting entries for depreciation, supplies used, insurance expense, and automatic payments will be recorded. The bank reconciliation will be prepared. The owners' Drawing accounts will be closed and the period will be advanced.

PLANET GOLF

Located in Palm Springs, California, Planet Golf is a full-service golf shop/course that sells golf equipment and golf clothing. Planet Golf is a partnership owned and operated by Larry Summers and Ann Winters. Each partner contributed an equal amount to the partnership. Larry buys the equipment and manages the store. Ann buys the clothing and accessory items and keeps the books for Planet Golf. Ann and Larry divide the profits evenly.

INSTRUCTIONS

Open Planet Golf. Add your initials to the company name. The company name will be **Planet Golf--Student's Initials**. (Type your actual initials, *not* the words *Student's Initials*.) The following lists are used for all inventory items, customers, and vendors. You will be adding additional customers, vendors and inventory items throughout the practice set. When entering transactions, you are responsible for any descriptions and reference numbers that you wish to include in the transaction. Unless otherwise specified, the terms for each sale or bill will be the default terms specified for each Customer and Vendor.

If a customer's order exceeds the established credit limit, accept the order and process it. If the terms allow a discount for a customer, make sure to apply the discount if payment is made within the discount period. Use 4040 Sales Discounts as the discount account. On occasion, a payment may be made within the discount period but not received within the discount period. Be sure to use the payment date rather than the date received when recording such payments. If a customer has a credit and has a balance on the account, apply the credit to payments received for the customer. If there is no balance for a customer and a return is made, issue a credit memo and a refund check. Always pay bills in time to take advantage of purchase discounts. Remember that the discount due date will be ten days from the date of the bill.

Invoices, purchase orders, and other business forms should be printed as they are entered. Printing Receipts will be at the discretion of your instructor. Back up your work frequently.

Merchandise Inventory:

Planet Golf
Item List

Filter Criteria includes: Report order is by ID.

Item ID	Item Description	Item Class	Active?	Level 1	Level 2	Qty on Hand
BAG01	Bag, Golf Leather	Stock item	Active	129.95	109.95	15.00
BAG02	Bag, Golf, Canvas	Stock item	Active	59.99	49.95	17.00
BAG03	Bag, Golf Vinyl	Stock item	Active	99.95	89.95	18.00
BAL01	Balls, Golf	Stock item	Active	6.95	5.95	60.00
BAL02	Balls, Golf, Spalding	Stock item	Active	8.95	7.95	120.00
BAL03	Balls, Deluxe Golf	Stock item	Active	9.95	8.95	37.00
CLU01	Clubs, Graphite Set	Stock item	Active	750.00	695.00	6.00
CLU02	Clubs, Titanium Woods	Stock item	Active	459.00	395.00	45.00
CLU03	Clubs, Starter	Stock item	Active	159.99	139.00	50.00
CLU04	Clubs, Deluxe Graphite	Stock item	Active	1200.00	1050.00	8.00
CLU05	Clubs, Putter, Iron	Stock item	Active	129.95	109.95	45.00
GIF01	Gift Sets, Golf	Stock item	Active	14.99	12.99	10.00
GLO01	Gloves, Golf	Stock item	Active	39.95	32.95	35.00
HAT01	Golf Hats	Stock item	Active	49.95	39.95	20.00
JAC01	Jacket, Men's Hooded	Stock item	Active	179.95	159.95	12.00
JAC02	Jacket, Women's Wool	Stock item	Active	129.99	109.99	12.00
PAN01	Pants, Men's	Stock item	Active	89.00	79.00	15.00
PAN02	Pants, Women's	Stock item	Active	129.95	109.95	12.00
SHI01	Shirt, Men's Polo	Stock item	Active	59.99	49.99	25.00
SHI02	Shirt, Women's Button Collar	Stock item	Active	59.99	49.99	12.00
SHO01	Shoes, Men's Golf	Stock item	Active	119.99	99.99	18.00
SHO02	Shoes, Women's Golf	Stock item	Active	179.99	159.99	20.00
SHO03	Shoes, Women's Leather	Stock item	Active	149.95	129.95	14.00
SHR01	Shorts, Men's Button Fly	Stock item	Active	49.95	39.95	12.00
SHR02	Shorts, Women's Cotton/Lycra	Stock item	Active	64.99	54.99	15.00
TEE01	Tees, Golf	Stock item	Active	4.95	4.25	30.00
TOW01	Towel, Golf	Stock item	Active	9.95	8.95	10.00

Note: A normal shop may have hundreds if not thousands of individual items for sale. In a real-world scenario, each of these items would exist on the item list for the company. We have included only a fraction of this amount for Planet Golf. The only real difference you will experience is less diversity in purchases and sales.

Vendors:

	Planet Golf		
	Vendor List		
Filter Criteria includes: Report order is by ID.			
Vendor ID	**Vendor**	**Contact**	**Telephone 1**
GOL01	Golfing Clothes, Inc	Chester Milligan	310-555-8800
GOL02	Golf Source	Roger Lewis	619-555-2112
SHO01	Shoe Supplier Corp.	Linda Daruty	310-555-6195
STA011	State Board of Equalization		
TEE01	Tee Club Distributors	Ted Obata	619-555-2929

Customers:

	Planet Golf		
	Customer List		
Filter Criteria includes: 1) Customers only. Report order is by ID.			
Customer ID	**Customer**	**Contact**	**Telephone 1**
ALE01	Alexander, Eric	Eric Alexander	619-555-5587
BRA01	Brandon, Dick	Dick Brandon	619-555-2324
CHA01	Chan, Chioko	Chioko Chan	619-555-6464
CLI01	Cline, Marty	Marty Cline	619-555-4455
DIC01	Dickson, Mark	Mark Dickson	619-555-3595
HIL01	Hill, Fred	Fred Hill	619-555-7412
LOR01	Lorenzo, Juanita	Juanita Lorenzo	619-555-8862
MIL01	Mills, Jan	Jan Mills	619-555-7878
NAT01	Nathon, Jack	Jack Nathon	619-555-5253
OMA01	O'Malley, Donna	Donna O'Malley	619-555-4567
PHI01	Phipps, Rick	Rick Phipps	619-555-1123
REY01	Reyes, Roland	Roland Reyes	619-555-5780
SAN01	Santiago, Sal	Sal Santiago	619-555-3217
SCH01	Schult, Laura	Laura Schult	619-555-4865
SMI01	Smith, Samuel	Samuel Smith	619-555-9511
STA01	Stalker, Stewart	Stewart Stalker	619-555-5796
TOW01	Townsend, Don	Don Townsend	619-555-8523
WAY01	Waylin, Jill	Jill Waylin	619-555-7416

RECORD TRANSACTIONS:

Enter the transactions for Planet Golf and print as indicated.

January 3, 2006:

Change the names and, if necessary, the descriptions of the following accounts:
    6250 Postage and Delivery Expense to 6250 Transportation Out
    6381 Marketing Supplies Expense to 6381 Sales Supplies Expense

Delete the following accounts:
    4100 Freight Income
    6140 Contributions
    6182 Disability Insurance Expense
    6213 Mortgage Expense
    6265 Filing Fees
    6285 Franchise Fees
    6351 Entertainment Expense

Make the following accounts inactive:
   6311 Building Repairs Expense
   6413 Property Tax Expense

Add the following accounts:
   Equity account gets closed: 3025 Ann Winters, Drawing
   Equity account gets closed: 3045 Larry Summers, Drawing

Print the Chart of Accounts. Do *not* show inactive accounts.

Prior to recording any transactions, print a General Ledger Trial Balance.

Print invoices, checks, and other items as they are entered in the transactions. Sales and purchases are on account unless otherwise specified. Assume credit limits can be exceeded unless otherwise stated.

1/3/2006

Sold 2 pairs of women's cotton/lycra shorts @ $64.99 each, 2 women's button collar shirts @ $59.99 each, 1 women's wool jacket @ $129.99, and 1 pair of women's golf shoes @ $179.99 to Jill Waylin. (Start with Print Invoice No. 1)

Having achieved her goal of a handicap under 30, Marty treated herself to the new clubs she had been wanting. Sold 1 set of graphite clubs for $750, 1 leather golf bag for $129.95, and 5 sleeves (packages) of golf balls @ $6.95 each to Marty Cline.

Fred heard that titanium would give him extra yardage with each shot. Sold 4 titanium woods to Fred Hill @ $459.00 each.

Sold 5 canvas golf bags @ $49.95 each and 5 sets of starter clubs @ $139.00 each to Palm Springs Academy (use PAL01 as the Customer ID) for the high school golf team. Palm Springs Academy located at 99-4058 Palm Canyon Drive, Palm Springs, CA 92262 is a nonprofit organization. The telephone number is 619-555-4455, and the contact person is Clare Colburn. The terms are Net 30 and the credit limit is $5,000. Even though this is a nonprofit organization, it does pay California Sales Tax on all purchases. Remember to use Level 2 pricing.

Correct the invoice to Marty Cline. The golf bag was part of a sale and should have been recorded at Level 2 pricing $109.95. Reprint the invoice.

Received Check No. 2285 from Eric Alexander in full payment of his account. (Start with Cash Receipt No. 1)

Received Check No. 102-33 from Sal Santiago, $600, in partial payment of his account.

1/4/2006

Sold 3 golf gift sets @ $14.99 each and 3 sleeves (packages) of Spalding golf balls @ $8.95 each to Laura Schult to be given away as door prizes at an upcoming ladies' club tournament.

Sold 2 pairs of men's button fly shorts @ $49.95 each, 2 men's polo shirts @ $59.99 each, and 1 pair of men's golf shoes @ $119.99 to Stewart Stalker.

Received Check No. 815 from Mark Dickson for $850 in full payment of his account.

Sold 2 golf towels @ $9.95 each to a cash customer, Ted Nishikawa. (Cash is the payment method. Remember to add Cash Customer to the Customer list. All sales will be taxable.)

Sold 1 pair of women's golf shoes @ $179.99 to a new customer: Chris Layton (use LAY01 as the Customer ID), 45-2215 PGA Drive, Rancho Mirage, CA 92270, 619-555-3322, Terms 1% 10 Net 30, Credit Limit $1,000, taxable customer for California Sales Tax.

Received Check No. 2233 for $950 from Rick Phipps in partial payment of his account.

Sold a vinyl golf bag for $99.95 to a cash customer, Yvonne Crane using a Visa card, number 8973-0908-3782-9212, expiration date 08/06.

1/5/2006

Print an Inventory Reorder Worksheet to see if any merchandise needs to be ordered.

Prepare Purchase Orders for all items on the Inventory Reorder Worksheet. Place all orders with the preferred vendors. Prepare only one purchase order per vendor. Order the amount indicated in the Reorder Qty column of the report. (Start with Purchase Order No. 101.) Use the prices in Peachtree unless otherwise instructed.

Order 10 women's golf hats @ $38.00 each from a new vendor: Hats Aplenty (use HAT01 as the Vendor ID), 45980 West Los Angeles Street, Los Angeles, CA 90025, Contact Lisa Griswald, Acct # GW010506, Phone 310-555-8787, Fax 310-555-7878, E-mail hats@la.com, Terms 2% 10 Net 30, Credit Limit $500. Add a new sales item: Hat, Women's Golf (use HAT02 as the Item ID) with Hats Aplenty as the preferred vendor. The purchase and sales description is Hat, Women's Golf. The COGS account is 5000. The Level 1 pricing is $65.50 and Level 2 pricing is $52.00. The hats are taxable. The GL Sales account is 4010-Accessory Sales. The GL Inventory account is 1120-Merchandise Inventory. The reorder quantity is 10. Minimum Stock is 6.

Change the current sales item HAT01 Golf Hats to Hat, Men's Golf. The purchase and sales descriptions should be Men's Golf Hats. Change the Minimum Stock from 15 to 12.

Print a Purchase Order Register.

1/7/2006

Received Check No. 1822 for a cash sale to George Clipper of 2 men's golf hats @ $49.95 each.

Print the Bank Deposits Report.

1/10/2006

Received the order from Hats Aplenty without the bill.

Received the orders from Golf Source, Invoice No. 03835 for the merchandise received. All items were received. Use 01/10/2006 for the bill date for the transaction.

Laura Schult returned 1 of the gift sets purchased on January 3. Issue a credit memo accepting the default number.

Mark Dickson returned 1 pair of men's button fly shorts that had been purchased for $49.95. (The shorts had been purchased previously and were part of his $850 opening balance. Use the next available CM No.) This is a cash refund. Use Check No. 101 and the OCR Multi-Purpose AP Laser format .

Sold 1 complete set of deluxe graphite golf clubs on account to Jack Nathon for $1,200.00.

Sold a graphite set of golf clubs on a special promotional sale (use Level 2 pricing), @ $695 to Patrick Griva using a Visa card. Card number is 2746-3467-0382-2343, expiration date 09/08.

1/12/2006
Received the telephone bill for the month, $85.15 from DST Telephone Co.(Use DST01 as the Vendor ID), Invoice No. 29347, 11-092 Highway 111, Palm Springs, CA 92262, 619-555-9285. The bill has a 10 day net and a credit limit of $500.00.

Purchased $175 of office supplies to have on hand from Serra Office Supply (Use SER01 as the Vendor ID), 3950 46th Avenue, Indio, CA 92201, Contact Cheryl Lockwood, Phone 619-555-1535, Fax 619-555-5351. Use the Write Checks feature for the purchase. Confirm that you are printing Check No. 102. Enter as a vendor for future purchases, 2%/10, N/30; credit limit $1,000.00.

1/14/2006
Received the bill for the order from Hats Aplenty, Invoice No. 87623. Use 01/14/2006 for the bill date.

Received a bill from the West Coast Electric Co. (Use WES01 as the Vendor ID), Invoice No. 3297, 995 Date Palm Drive, Cathedral City, CA 92234, 619-555-4646 for the monthly electric bill. The bill is for $275.00 and has a 15 day net. Credit limit is $1,000.00.

Received the monthly water bill for $500 from Dry Country Water (Use DRY01 as the Vendor ID), Invoice No. 98-786, 84985 Jackson Street, Indio, CA 92202, 619-555-5653. The bill is due upon receipt. Credit limit is $500.00.

Sold a set of deluxe graphite golf clubs on account to Chris Layton for $1200.

Received Check No. 3801 for $1,969.11 from Fred Hill in full payment of his bill.

1/16/2006
Received Check No. 783 for $600.54 from Jill Waylin in full payment of her bill.

1/17/2006
Received Check No. 67-086 for $135.95 from Laura Schult in full payment of her account.

1/18/2006

Pay all bills that are due or eligible to receive a discount if paid by January 25. Print the checks.

Sold 1 leather golf bag @ $129.95, 1 set of deluxe graphite golf clubs @ $1,200.00, 1 putter iron @ $129.95, and 3 sleeves of deluxe golf balls @ $9.95 each to Laura Schult.

Returned 2 men's polo shirts that had poorly stitched seams to Golfing Clothes, Inc. Received Credit Memo No. 8723 from the company. We will keep the credit on our account.

1/21/2006

Sold 1 men's golf hat @ $49.95 and 1 men's hooded jacket at $179.95 to Harry Urich using a MasterCard number 9201-1282-1148-2646, expiration date 12/07.

Sold 1 golf towel @ $9.95, 2 packages of golf tees @ $4.95 each, and 1 sleeve of golf balls at $6.95 to Terry Jamine for cash.

Received Check No. 1256 in full payment of account from Chioko Chan.

Rick Phipps bought a starter set of golf clubs for his son @ $159.99 and a new titanium wood for himself @ $459.

A businessman in town with his wife bought them each a set of deluxe graphite golf clubs @ $1,200.00 per set and a new leather golf bag for each of them @ $129.95 per bag. He purchased a men's hooded jacket for $179.95. His wife purchased a pair of golf shoes for $179.99 and a women's wool jacket for $129.99. He used his Visa to pay for the purchases, Jorge Rodriguez, number 9283-2387-4887-0382, expiration date 7/08.

Print an Inventory Reorder Worksheet. Prepare Purchase Orders to order any inventory items indicated on the report. As with earlier orders, use the preferred vendor, issue only one purchase order per vendor, and use the Reorder Quantity as the amount to order.

Print an Inventory Stock Status Report.

1/24/2006

Laura Schult was declared Club Champion and won a prize of $500. She brought in the $500 cash as a payment to be applied to the amount she owes on her account.

Received the bills and all the items ordered from Golf Source (Invoice No. 85432) and Tee Club Distributors (Invoice No. 0372). The date of the bills is 01/23/2006.

Sold Laura Schult 5 Women's Golf Hats @ $65.50 each to give away as prizes at her next ladies' club tournament.

Received Check No. 5216 from Dick Brandon as payment in full on his account.

Received Check No. 1205 from Marty Cline as payment in full on her account.

1/25/2006

Pay all bills that are due or with discounts lost by February 1. Print the check(s). Do not print the credit.

Received the bill for $3,000 rent (January) from Sahara Rentals, (Use SAH01 as the Vendor ID), Invoice No. 38246-327, 11-2951 Palm Canyon Drive, Palm Springs, CA 92262, Contact Tammi Moreno, Phone 619-555-8368, Fax 619-555-8638. The rent is due in 10 days, credit limit, $3,000.00.

Purchased office supplies to have on hand for $150 from Serra Office Supply. Use the Write Checks feature for the purchase.

Print an Aged Payables report.

1/26/2006

Received payment in full from Sal Santiago, Check No. 102-157.

Received $1,000 from Jack Nathon, Check No. 3716, in partial payment of his account. (Remember to pay off the older invoice first).

Sold 15 sleeves of golf balls @ $6.95 each to a Nancy Walsh, a cash customer to use as prizes in a retirement golf tournament for an employee of her company. Paid with Check No. 2237.

1/31/2006

Print the Taxable/Exempt Sales report for January.

Pay sales tax and print the check.

Print an Items Sold to Customers report for January.

Print a General Ledger Trial Balance.

Enter the following adjusting entries:
    Office Supplies Used for the month is $125.
    The balance of the Sales Supplies is $650 on January 30.
    The amount of Prepaid Insurance represents the liability insurance for 12 months. Record the
        adjusting entry for the month of January.
    Depreciation for the month is: Office Equipment, $83.33, and Store Fixtures, $100.

Record the transactions for owner's equity:
    Each owner's withdrawal for the month of January is $2,000.
    Divide the amount in account 3110-Retained Earnings and transfer one-half the amount into
        each owner's individual Capital account. Larry gives the odd cent to Ann.

Use the following bank statement to prepare a bank reconciliation. Enter any adjustments. Print an Account Reconciliation Report.

DESERT BANK
1234-110 Highway 111
Palm Springs, CA 92270
(619) 555-3300

BANK STATEMENT FOR:

Planet Golf
55-100 PGA Boulevard
Palm Springs, CA 92270

Acct. # 9876-32-922   **January 2006**

Beginning Balance 1/1/06			$48,150.14
1/3/06 Deposit	2,175.00		50,325.14
1/4/06 Deposit	1,928.54		52,253.68
1/7/06 Deposit	107.14		52,360.82
1/10/06 Check 101		53.57	52,307.25
1/10/06 Deposit	745.39		53,052.64
1/12/06 Check 102		175	52,877.64
1/14/06 Deposit	1,969.11		54,846.75
1/15/06 Deposit	600.54		55,447.29
1/17/06 Deposit	135.95		55,583.24
1/18/06 Check 103		500	55,083.24
1/18/06 Check 104		85.15	54,998.09
1/18/06 Check 105		5,000.00	49,998.09
1/21/06 Deposit	5,353.50		55,351.59
1/23/06 Deposit	3,309.57		58,661.16
1/23/06 Check 106		573.5	58,087.66
1/23/06 Check 107		372.4	57,715.26
1/23/06 Check 109		15,000.00	42,715.26
1/23/06 Check 110		275	42,440.26
1/25/06 Check 111		150	42,290.26
1/30/06 Monthly Service Charge		18	42,272.26
1/31/06 Store Fixtures Loan Pmt.: $17.21 Interest, $89.03 Principal		106.24	42,166.02
1/31/06 Office Equip Loan Pmt.: $10.33 Interest, $53.42 Principal		63.75	42,102.27
1/31/06 Interest Earned	76.73		42,179.00
Ending Balance 1/31/06			42,179.00

Close the drawing account for each owner into the owner's individual capital account.

Adjust the number of tees on hand to 24. Reason for adjustment is inventory shrinkage.

Print the following reports for January 2006: General Ledger Trial Balance, Standard Income Statement and Standard Balance Sheet

Advance the period to 02 - Feb 01, 2006 to Feb 28, 2006. Print all reports

NAME _____

TRANSMITTAL

END-OF-SECTION 2: PLANET GOLF

Attach the following documents and reports:

- ☐ Chart of Accounts
- ☐ General Ledger Trial Balance
- ☐ Invoice No. 1: Jill Waylin
- ☐ Invoice No. 2: Marty Cline
- ☐ Invoice No. 3: Fred Hill
- ☐ Invoice No. 4: Palm Springs Academy
- ☐ Invoice No. 2 (Corrected): Marty Cline
- ☐ Invoice No. 5: Laura Schult
- ☐ Invoice No. 6: Stewart Stalker
- ☐ Invoice No. 7: Chris Layton
- ☐ Inventory Reorder Worksheet
- ☐ Purchase Order No. 101: Golf Source
- ☐ Purchase Order No. 102: Hats Aplenty
- ☐ Purchase Order Register
- ☐ Bank Deposit Report
- ☐ Credit Memo No. 10001: Laura Schult
- ☐ Credit Memo No. 10002: Mark Dickson
- ☐ Refund Check No. 101: Mark Dickson
- ☐ Invoice No. 8: Jack Nathon
- ☐ Check No. 102: Serra Office Supply
- ☐ Invoice No. 9: Chris Layton
- ☐ Invoice No. 1 (Revised): Jill Waylin
- ☐ Check No. 103: Dry Country Water
- ☐ Check No. 104: DST Telephone Company
- ☐ Check No. 105: Golfing Clothes, Inc.
- ☐ Check No. 106: Golf Source
- ☐ Check No. 107: Hats Aplenty
- ☐ Check No. 108: Shoe Supplier Corp.
- ☐ Invoice No. 10: Laura Schult
- ☐ Invoice No. 11: Rick Phipps
- ☐ Inventory Reorder Worksheet
- ☐ Purchase Order No. 103: Tee Club Distributors

☐ Purchase Order No. 104: Golf Source
☐ Inventory Stock Status Report
☐ Invoice No. 12: Laura Schult
☐ Check No. 109: Tee Club Distributors
☐ Check No. 110: West Coast Electric Co.
☐ Check No. 111: Serra Office Supply
☐ Aged Payables
☐ Taxable/Exempt Sales
☐ Check No. 112: State Board of Equalization
☐ Items Sold to Customers Report
☐ General Ledger Trial Balance
☐ Check No. 113: Ann Winters, Drawing
☐ Check No. 114: Larry Summers, Drawing
☐ Account Reconciliation Report
☐ General Ledger Trial Balance
☐ Standard Income Statement
☐ Standard Balance Sheet
☐ General Journal
☐ Cash Receipts Journal
☐ Cash Disbursements Journal
☐ Sales Journal
☐ Purchase Journal
☐ Inventory Adjustment Journal
☐ Purchase Orders Journal
☐ General Ledger

Payroll

LEARNING OBJECTIVES

At the completion of this chapter, you will be able to:

1. Create, preview, and print payroll checks.

2. Adjust standard pay parameters.

3. Correct and void paychecks.

4. Edit employee information and add a new employee.

5. Print a payroll Check Register report.

6. Print a Current Earnings report.

7. Prepare a Tax Liability Report and make tax deposits.

8. Prepare and print Forms 941 and 940.

9. Discuss and print W-2 forms for each employee and the W-3 form.

PAYROLL

Many times, a company begins the process of computerizing the accounting system simply to be able to do the payroll using the computer. It is much faster and easier to let Peachtree® Complete Accounting 2006 look at the tax tables and determine how much withholding should be deducted for each employee than to have an individual perform this task manually. Because tax tables change frequently, Peachtree® Complete Accounting 2006 requires its users to enroll in a payroll service plan if they desire the withholding information to be accurate. In order to enroll in a payroll service plan, you must have a company tax identification number and a full, registered copy of Peachtree® Complete Accounting 2006.

The plan allows you to subscribe to the Peachtree® Complete Accounting 2006 Tax Table Service for a small amount per month and receive tax table updates throughout the year by using Peachtree® Complete Accounting 2006 and the Internet to update your tax tables. Once a registered user of Peachtree® Complete Accounting 2006 has subscribed to this plan, he/she will be able to use Peachtree® Complete Accounting 2006 to automatically calculate taxes on paychecks. Without a subscription to the Tax Table Service, Peachtree® Complete Accounting 2006 will continue to provide earnings, additions, and deductions but will not necessarily be accurate. Payroll deductions can be manually entered or changed should the need arise.

Peachtree® Complete Accounting 2006 has provided an educational set of tax tables to be used in the activities in this chapter. These tables are neither complete nor up-to-date and should not be used to perform actual payroll calculations.

Calculations will be made for vacation pay, sick pay, medical and dental insurance deductions, and so on. Paychecks will be created, printed, corrected, and voided. Tax reports, tax payments, and tax forms will be prepared.

TRAINING TUTORIAL

The Brekners Co. is a medical clinic located in Long Beach, California, which is owned and operated by Dr. John Brekner. The business operates as a sole proprietorship. He has a thriving practice and currently employs six people. Francis Henderson is the office manager and is responsible for the smooth operation of the medical clinic and for all the employees. Currently, his salary is $33,800 per year. Wilson Ahmed is also a salaried employee at $29,510 per year. Wilson is responsible for the bookkeeping and the insurance billing. The company is advertising for a part-time billing clerk so that the insurance claims can be processed a little faster. The other employees are the nurse, Julie Meredith; the medical assistant, Tran Ng; the receptionist, Jessica Ruiz; and the lab technician, Heidi Thom. These employees are paid on an hourly basis, and any hours in excess of 80 for the pay period will be paid as overtime. Paychecks for all employees are issued on a bi-weekly basis. The company offers Medical, Dental and Savings deductions for employees. They can choose any or all of these deductions. Pay periods end every other Friday and checks are created the following Monday. Brekners has been set up solely to practice the payroll features of Peachtree Complete 2006.

OPEN PEACHTREE® COMPLETE ACCOUNTING 2006 AND BREKNERS

DO: Open Peachtree® Complete Accounting 2006 as previously instructed
Open Brekners Co.:
Click **Open an existing company.**
Click the **Browse** button (if Brekners Co. is not already visible)
Click the drop down arrow for **Drives:**
Select the drive where your data files are kept
Locate and double click on Brekners Co. (under the **Company name** text box)
Add your initials as in previous chapters
Verify that Brekners Co.-Student's Initials is the open company

CREATE PAYCHECKS

Peachtree® Complete Accounting 2006 has a Payroll Module, which under ideal conditions, can generate a complete payroll in a few short minutes. In order to accomplish this, the employees and all other payroll defaults must be set up correctly. This set up has been accomplished for you in this chapter. Creating paychecks can be accomplished from either the Select for Payroll Entry menu option or Payroll Entry option. The former allows for batch processing of all employees while the latter provides for payment of the employees one at a time.

MEMO

DATE: March 13, 2006

Choose to process the payroll through the Payroll Entry window. This means you will enter the following payroll data for each employee one at a time. Peachtree® Complete Accounting 2006 will automatically calculate required withholding amounts for you. Peachtree® Complete Accounting 2006 will also enter other payroll items such as medical and dental insurance deductions, and it will calculate the total net pay of the checks. Create and print paychecks for the pay period ended March 10, 2006. Use the above date as the check date.

Use the following table of hours to pay the employees for their pay period ended March 10, 2006. Vacation and sick hours are paid hours.

PAYROLL TABLE: MARCH 10, 2006						
	FRANCIS HENDERSON	**HEIDI THOM**	**JULIE MEREDITH**	**JESSICA RUIZ**	**TRAN NG**	**WILSON SPALDING**
HOURS						
REGULAR	80	80	72	40	76	68
OVERTIME		5				
SICK					4	4
VACATION			8			8

 DO: Create checks for the above employees
Set System Date to 03/13/2006 before starting
Click **Payroll Entry** from the **Payroll** button
Using the magnifying glass to the right of **Employee ID**, select Francis Henderson
Change the Pay Period End to March 10, 2006
The data on your check should match the data on the next page.

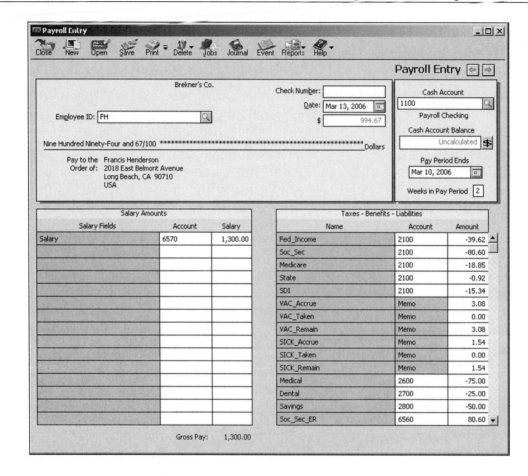

Click the **Print** button at the top of the screen since she needs no other adjustments

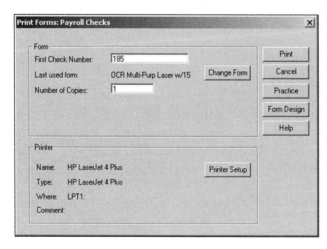

Confirm the check format OCR Multi-Purp Laser w/15
Confirm **First Check Number** 185
Click **Print** You will be brought back to a blank check after the check prints.

The checks would normally be obtained from either Peachtree directly or a company like Nebs specializing in providing checks and other forms for computerized accounting programs. Many different forms are available for Peachtree. We will print ours on plain white paper.

Using the magnifying glass to the right of **Employee ID**, select Heidi Thom

Click in the **Hours** column of the **Overtime** row, enter 5.00 to add her overtime from this pay period. Note that regular hours were filled in by default.

Click **Print**

Verify that the Check No. to be printed is 186

Click **Print** again

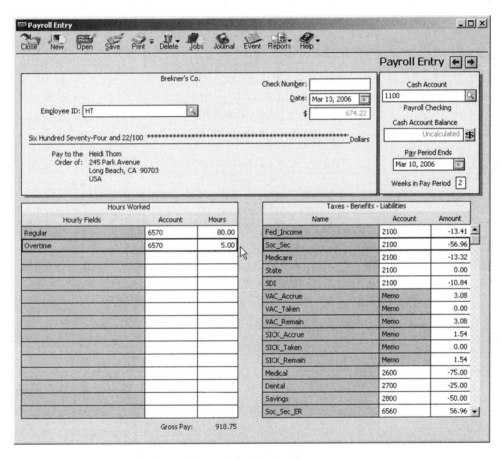

You will be brought back to a blank check.

Using the magnifying glass to the right of **Employee ID**, select Julie Meredith

Click in the **Amount** column of the **VAC_Taken** row, enter 8.00.

Note: Peachtree maintains vacation time as a memo only. That is, it tracks the hours but does not use them to calculate pay. For this reason, we must still pay the employee for 80 regular hours. Sick Leave works in a similar manner. To Peachtree, a vacation hour is the same as a sick hour and that is the same as a regular hour with regards to the paycheck amount. Peachtree will also not reflect total accumulated hours in the on-screen check stub but rather shows only the effect within the current pay cycle. Note that the vacation remaining (**VAC_Remain**) for Julie is a -4.92, which is the 3.08 hours accrued minus the 8.00 hours taken. Her correct balance will show on subsequent payroll reports as well as in the Year To Date column of the paycheck itself. If for some reason this calculation is not made, you will be required to enter the balance in the **VAC_Remain** field. It should always reflect the **VAC_Accrue** minus the **VAC_Taken** fields. The same applies for sick leave.

Click **Print**

Verify that the Check No. to be printed is 187

Click **Print** again

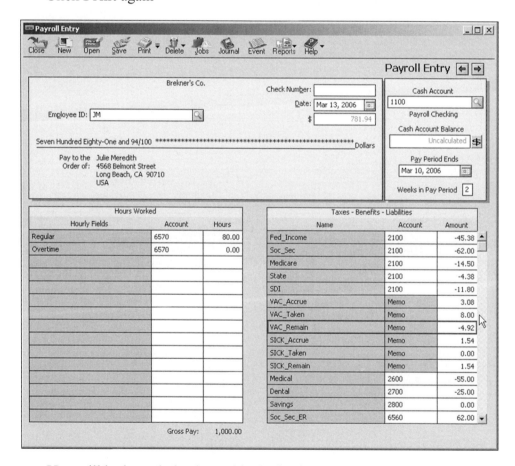

You will be brought back to a blank check.

Using the magnifying glass to the right of Employee ID, select Jessica Ruiz

Click in the **Hours** column of the **Regular** row, enter 40.00.

Note: Since Jessica only worked 40 hours this pay period, it necessitated changing her normal 80 hours to 40 hours. Note that this simple and easy to accomplish change initiates substantial change in her check. All of her deduction amounts instantly change to the corrected amounts based on her new gross pay.

Click **Print**

Verify that the Check No. to be printed is 188

Click **Print**

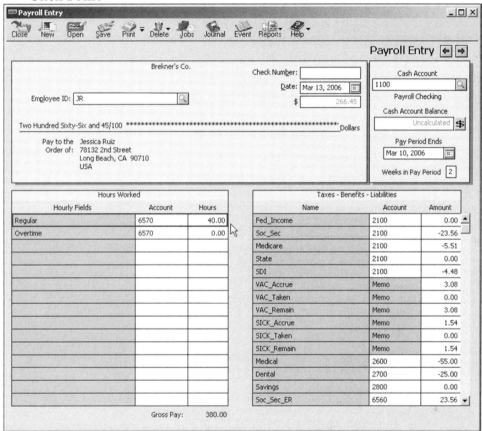

You will be brought back to a blank check.

Using the magnifying glass to the right of Employee ID, select Tran Ng

Click in the **Amount** column of the **SICK_Taken** row, enter 4.00.

Note: Peachtree maintains sick leave time as a memo only. That is, it tracks the hours but does not use them to calculate pay. For this reason, we must still pay Tran for 80 regular hours. Vacation Leave works in a similar manner. To Peachtree, a vacation hour is the same as a sick hour and that is the same as a regular hour with regards to the paycheck amount. Peachtree will also not reflect total accumulated hours in the on-screen check stub but rather shows only the effect within the current pay cycle. Note that the sick time remaining (**SICK_Remain**) for Tran is a -2.46, which is the 1.54 hours accrued minus the 4.00 hours taken. His correct balance will show on subsequent payroll reports as well as in the Year To Date column of the paycheck itself. If for some reason this calculation is not made, you will be required to enter the balance in the **SICK_Remain** field. It should always reflect the **SICK_Accrue** minus the **SICK_Taken** fields. The same applies for vacation leave.

Click **Print**

Verify that the Check No. to be printed is 189

Click **Print**

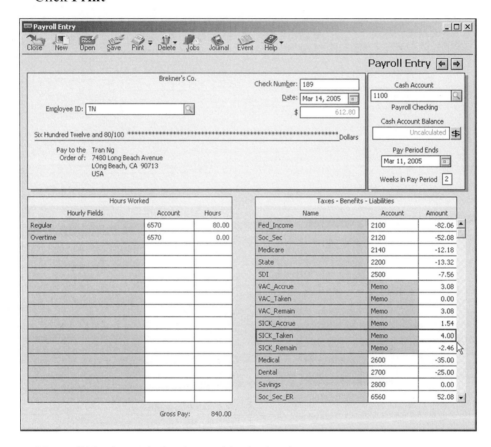

You will be brought back to a blank check.

Using the magnifying glass to the right of Employee ID, select Wilson Spalding

Click in the **Amount** column of the **VAC_Taken** row, enter 8.00.

Click in the **Amount** column of the **SICK_Taken** row, enter 4.00.

Note: Since Wilson is salaried, we must enter only his vacation and sick leave hours in the appropriate memo fields to allow Peachtree to accurately maintain the balances. In the event a salaried employee must be docked pay, it would be necessary to calculate a new salary amount and change that entry in the Payroll Entry form just as we changed hours for an hourly employee.

Click **Print**

Verify that the Check No. to be printed is 190

Click **Print**

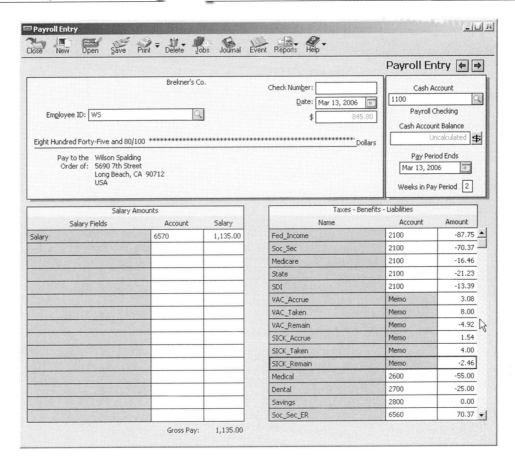

PRINTING PAYCHECKS

Paychecks may be printed one at a time or all at once; however, they must be printed separately from other checks. In the previous activity we printed the checks one at a time. We just as easily could have clicked on Save rather than Print and batch printed the checks at a later time. Batch printing payroll checks is accomplished through the Reports menu. Typically when batch printing payroll checks, they are set up through the Select for Payroll Entry option rather than Payroll Entry. Since we will be running our next payroll with this option.

CHANGE EMPLOYEE INFORMATION

Whenever a change occurs for an employee, it may be entered at any time.

MEMO

DATE: March 13, 2006

Effective today, Francis Henderson will receive a pay raise to $35,000 annually.

DO: Change the salary for Francis
Click **Employees** from the **Payroll** button
Using the magnifying glass to the right of **Employee ID**, select Francis Henderson
Select March 13, 2006 in the **Last Raise:** field
Click on the **Pay Info** tab
Click on his old salary to highlight it and enter 1,346.15, (35,000 ÷ 26)
Click **Save**

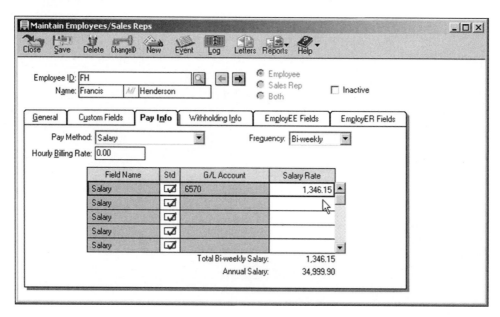

Do *not* close the Maintain Employees/Sales Reps window

ADD A NEW EMPLOYEE

As new employees are hired, they should be added.

MEMO

DATE: March 20, 2006

Hired a part-time employee to help process insurance claims. Ms. Elizabeth Hill, 102 Bayshore Drive, Long Beach, CA 90713, SS No. 111-55-6936, phone number 562-555-9874. Paid hourly rate of $7.00 regular and $10.50 overtime, bi-weekly frequency. Federal and state withholding: Married, 1 Allowance. No local taxes, dental insurance, medical insurance, sick time, or vacation time. It is anticipated she will work 40 hours per pay period. She would like $20.00 taken out of each paycheck for her savings account.

DO: Add Elizabeth Hill

From the **Maintain Employees/Sales Reps** window, click on the **New** button at
  the top of the screen

Enter EH in the **Employee ID** field

Tab to or click in the **Name** field, enter Elizabeth Hill

Click on the **General** tab, if necessary and click in the Address field. Enter 102
  Bayshore Drive.

Tab to the **City** field, enter Long Beach, tab to the **State** field, enter CA, tab again
  and enter 90713

Click in the **Social Security #:** field, enter 100-55-6936

Click in the **Telephone 1:** field, enter 562-555-9874

Using the calendar to the right of the **Hired:** field, select March 20, 2006

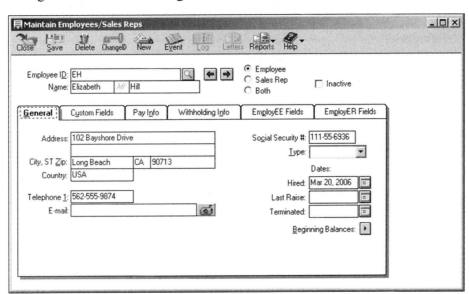

Click on the **Pay Info** tab

In the **Pay Method** field, select Hourly- Hours per Pay Period

In the **Frequency** field, select Bi-weekly

Click in the **Hours per Pay Period** field, enter 40.00

Click in the **Hourly Rate** column of the **Regular** row, enter 7.00

Click in the **Hourly Rate** column of the **Overtime** row, enter 10.50

We will not use the **Hourly Billing Rate** field since this is to establish a rate at
  which to bill the employees time to customers. This is not a feature we will
  be using.

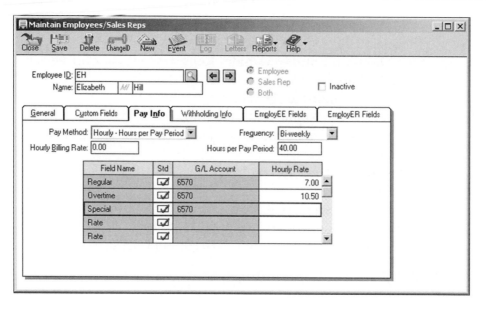

Click on the **Withholding Info** tab

Click in the **Filing Status** column of the **Federal** row of the Withholding
 Information section of the window. Using the drop down arrow, select
 Married.

Tab to the **Allow** column, enter 1

Click in the **Filing Status** column of the **State** row of the Withholding Information
 section of the window. Select Married.

Tab to the **Allow** column, enter 1

Click in the **Filing Status** column of the **Local** row of the Withholding
 Information section of the window. Select Married.

Tab to the **Allow** column, enter 1

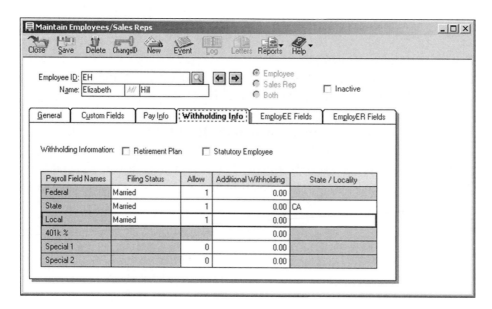

Click on the **EmployEE Fields** tab
Scroll to the fields as needed for the following instructions
Deselect **Savings**, **VAC_Accrued**, **VAC_Taken**, **VAC_Remain**,
    SICK_Accrued, **SICK_Taken** and **SICK_Remain** by clicking on the red
    checkmarks in the **Std** and/or **Calc** columns
Click in the **Amount** column for the **Savings** row and enter -20.00.

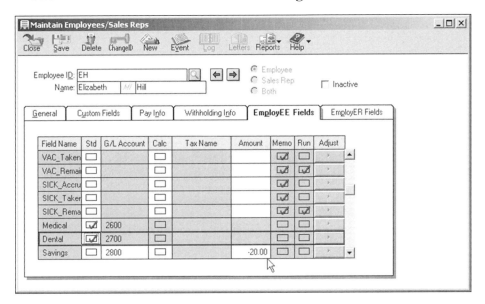

Click **Save** and then **Close**

CREATE AND PRINT PAYCHECKS FOR THE NEXT PAY PERIOD

A second method of generating payroll within Peachtree® Complete Accounting 2006 is to use the Select for Payroll Entry window. This window pays all employees who meet a set of criteria rather than requiring you to pay them one by one. It is similar to the Select for Payment window used in paying Accounts Payable. It is particularly useful when payroll information does not change from pay period to pay period. When used it will automatically pay employees based on their default information. It does allow this information to be changed on an employee by employee basis. Checks are printed in a batch process rather than one by one.

MEMO

DATE: March 27, 2006

Enter the payroll for the pay period ended 03/24/06. All employees get 80 hours except Elizabeth Hill, our new part-time employee hired last week, who worked only 20 hours. Accept all other defaults when generating the payroll.

PAYROLL TABLE: MARCH 24, 2006							
	ELIZABETH HILL	**FRANCIS HENDERSON**	**HEIDI THOM**	**JULIE MEREDITH**	**JESSICA RUIZ**	**TRAN NG**	**WILSON AHMED**
HOURS							
REGULAR	20	80	80	72	80	80	80
SICK				8			

DO: Process the payroll for March 24
Set System Date to 03/27/2006 before starting
Click **Select for Payroll Entry** from the **Payroll** button
You are presented with a Select Employees - Filter Selection window
Change the **Pay End Date** to 3/24/2006, the end of the pay period

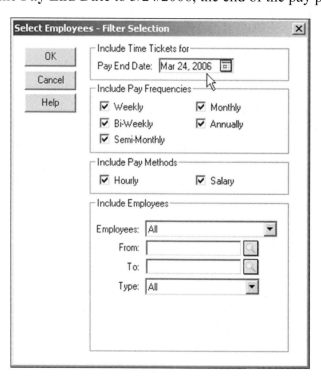

Note: This dialog box allows us to tell Peachtree which employees to pay. In it we establish the date, the pay frequency, the pay methods and the range of employees to include. As you can see, Peachtree will default to pay all categories unless told otherwise. We could pay just Salary or just Hourly employees if we desired or perhaps even just one employee.

Click **OK**

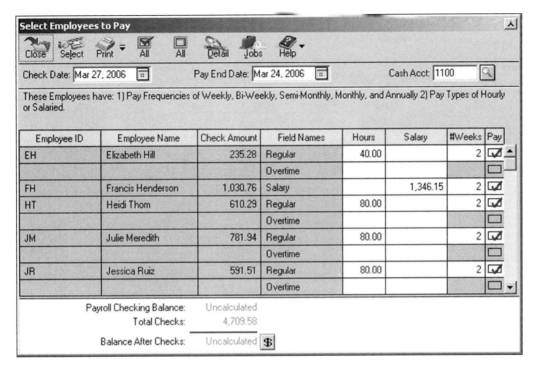

Note: All employees meeting the criteria from the filter are now displayed with their defaults selected. All full-time employees are shown with 80 hours while salaried employees are shown with their full bi-weekly salary. No sick leave or vacation leave hours are used and all required deductions for dental, medical or credit union have been made. Any employee can be highlighted and the **Detail** button clicked to see the details of that employee's paycheck. At this time, any changes can be made. For example, Elizabeth Hill worked only 20 hours this pay period but she has defaulted to 40 hours.

Additionally, Julie Meredith had 8 hours sick leave that needs to be entered.

Highlight Julie Meredith by clicking on her row.

Click the **Detail** button

All the details of Julie's paycheck can be observed here

Using the scroll bar, scroll to the **Sick_Taken** row

Click in the **Amount** column of this row, enter 8.00

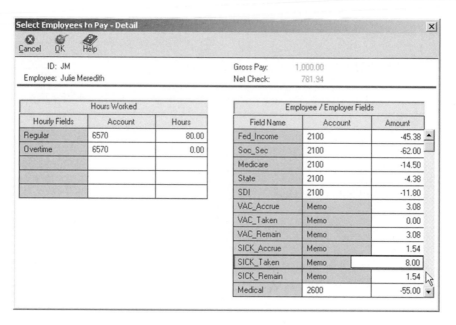

Click **OK**

We can change Elizabeth Hill's 40 hours to 20 hours in the same manner or can
 shorten the process by clicking in the **Hours** column of Elizabeth Hill's row
 to highlight the 40 hours.

Enter 20.00

Press the **Enter** key to recalculate the payroll

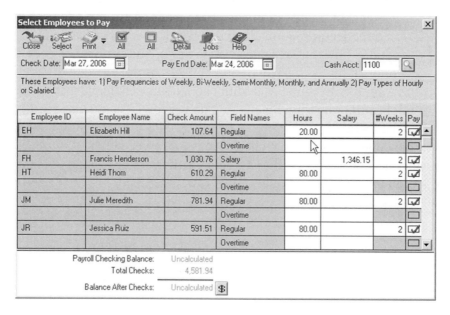

Note: At the bottom of the screen you might see that your payroll checking balance
 is uncalculated at this point. To determine whether you have sufficient funds
 for this payroll, you may click on the **$** sign to force a recalculation.

Click the **$** sign at the bottom of the screen

Payroll Checking Balance:	305,750.75
Total Checks:	4,581.94
Balance After Checks:	301,168.81

At this point we can print the checks or there are tasks we can perform to verify the payroll prior to printing. Click on the arrow to the right of the **Print** button and select **Preview**.

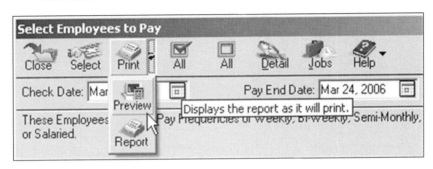

Click **Preview** to accept the check form and a starting Check number of 191
You can page through the checks to view them. Click **Close** when finished.
Another option prior to printing the checks is to generate a preview report that is a printed record of what will be generated when checks are printed.
Click on the arrow to the right of the **Print** button and select **Report**.

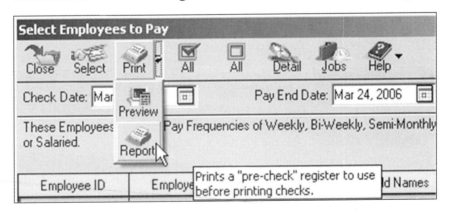

Click **OK** to print the report
Note: In a larger organization with many employees, it would be wise to preview the payroll prior to printing in one of these two ways. Any errors noted can be corrected prior to generating the actual payroll.
Click **Print** to print the actual checks
Confirm that the run will start with Check No. 191
Click **Print**

VOIDING AND DELETING CHECKS

As with regular checks, paychecks may be voided or deleted. A voided check still remains as a zero amount check. If a check is deleted, it is completely removed from the company records. The only way to have a record of the deleted check would be if audit trail had been selected as a company preference. If you have pre-numbered checks and the original check is misprinted, lost, or stolen, you should void the check. If an employee's check is lost or stolen and needs to be replaced and you are not using pre-numbered checks, it may be deleted and reissued. For security reasons, it is better to void a check than to delete it. Although Peachtree would allow a printed check to be brought up on screen and edited for reprinting, checks are typically printed on pre-numbered forms making it easier to simply void the old check and issue a new check.

MEMO

DATE: March 31, 2006

Jessica Ruiz lost her paycheck for the March 10 pay period. Void Check No. 188, issue and print a new one. Remember that she worked 40 hours.

 DO: Void Jessica's paycheck dated March 13 and issue a new one
Click **Void Check** from the **Payroll** button
Using the magnifying glass to the right of **Account ID:**, select 1100 Payroll
      Checking
Highlight Check Number 188 for Jessica Ruiz

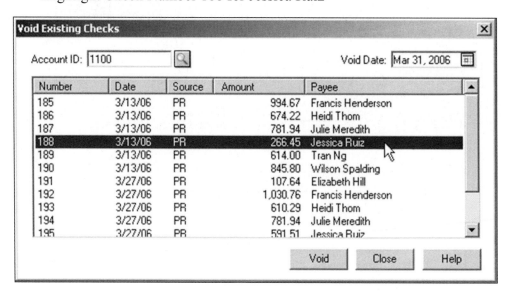

Click on the **Void** button

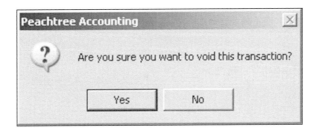

Click **Yes**, the check is no longer on the list
Click **Close**
Click **Payroll Entry** from the **Payroll** button
Using the magnifying glass to the right of **Employee ID**, select **Jessica Ruiz**
Using the calendar to the right of the **Pay Period End** field, select Mar 10 2006
Confirm in the **Weeks in Pay Period** field, 2
Click in the **Hours** column of the **Regular** row, enter 40.00

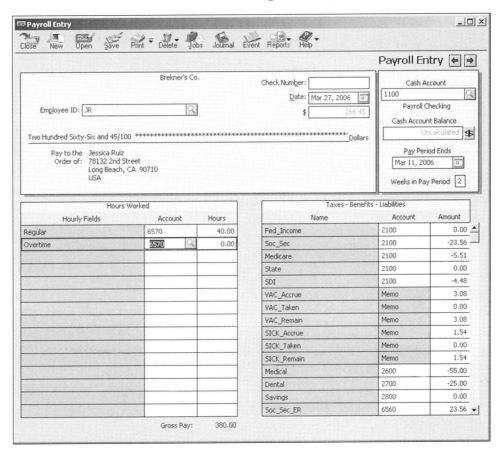

Click the **Print** button at the top of the screen
Confirm that you will be using Check No. 198
Click **Print** and then **Close**

PAYROLL REPORTS

There are a number of payroll reports available within Peachtree® Complete Accounting 2006. These can range from a simple Payroll Check Register to a very detailed Current Earnings Report that shows the following detail:

Employee ID	Date	Amount	Gross	Fed_Income	Soc_Sec	Medicare
Employee	Reference		State	SDI	VAC_Accrue	VAC_Taken
SS No			VAC_Remain	SICK_Accrue	SICK_Taken	SICK_Remain
			Medical	Dental	Savings	Soc_Sec_ER
			Medicare_ER	FUTA_ER	SUI_ER	SETT_ER

Reports can also be generated for the various federal and state filing requirements such as the 940, 941, DE-88 and W-2's.

MEMO

DATE: March 31, 2006

Dr. John Brekners has Wilson print a payroll Check Register.

DO: Print the payroll Check Register
Click **All Payroll Reports** from the **Payroll** button
Double click on **Payroll Check Register**

Brekner's Co.
Payroll Check Register
For the Period From Mar 1, 2006 to Mar 31, 2006
Filter Criteria includes: Report order is by Check Date. Report is printed in Detail Format.

Reference	Date	Employee	Amount
185	3/13/06	Francis Henderson	994.67
186	3/13/06	Heidi Thom	674.22
187	3/13/06	Julie Meredith	781.94
188	3/13/06	Jessica Ruiz	266.45
189	3/13/06	Tran Ng	614.00
190	3/13/06	Wilson Spalding	845.80
191	3/27/06	Elizabeth Hill	107.64
192	3/27/06	Francis Henderson	1,030.76
193	3/27/06	Heidi Thom	610.29
194	3/27/06	Julie Meredith	781.94

Click **Print**

Close the report. Do not close the **Select a Report** window.

PRINT CURRENT EARNINGS REPORT

MEMO

DATE: March 31, 2006

Prepare the Current Earnings Report.

DO: Print the payroll Current Earnings Report

Double click on **Current Earnings Report**

Brekner's Co.						
Current Earnings Report						
For the Period From Mar 1, 2006 to Mar 31, 2006						
Filter Criteria includes: Report order is by Employee ID. Report is printed in Detail Format.						

Employee ID Employee SS No	Date Reference	Amount	Gross State VAC_Remain Medical Medicare_ER	Fed_Income SDI SICK_Accrue Dental FUTA_ER	Soc_Sec VAC_Accrue SICK_Taken Savings SUI_ER	Medicare VAC_Taken SICK_Remain Soc_Sec_ER SETT_ER
EH	3/27/06	107.64	140.00		-8.68	-2.03
Elizabeth Hill	191			-1.65	3.08	
111-55-6936						
					-20.00	-8.68
			-2.03	-1.12	-5.39	-0.14
		107.64	140.00		-8.68	-2.03
Total 3/1/06 thru 3/31/06				-1.65	3.08	
					-20.00	-8.68
			-2.03	-1.12	-5.39	-0.14
Report Date Total for		107.64	140.00		-8.68	-2.03
Elizabeth Hill				-1.65	3.08	
					-20.00	-8.68
			-2.03	-1.12	-5.39	-0.14
YTD Total for		107.64	140.00		-8.68	-2.03
Elizabeth Hill				-1.65	3.08	
					-20.00	-8.68
			-2.03	-1.12	-5.39	-0.14

Click **Print**

Close the report. Do not close the **Select a Report** window.

PAYROLL TAX LIABILITY REPORT

A third payroll report is the payroll Tax Liability Report. This report lists the company's payroll liabilities categorized by filing type. That is to say, it will group the liabilities by type, such as, 940, 941, and CA State. It will also include subtotals for the various withholding and tax items such as FIT, FICA EE, FICA ER, etc. This information can be used to make deposits of payroll taxes due. These deposits can be made by issuing a check or by direct electronic funds transfer at your bank. When a funds transfer is made, only a general journal entry is needed to reflect this.

MEMO

DATE: March 31, 2006

Prior to paying taxes, the doctor will have Wilson print the payroll Tax Liability Report.

 DO: Prepare and print the Tax Liability Report
Double click on **Tax Liability Report**
Click on the **Options** button
Click on the **Fields** tab
Click on the box in the **Column Break** column of the **Employee ID** row

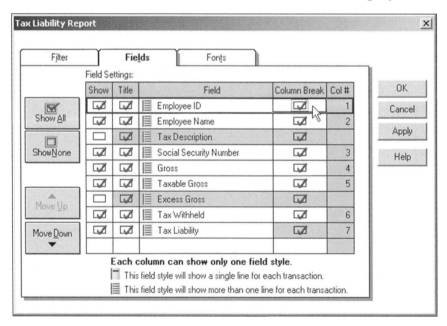

Note: Although this step is not required, it will make the report much more user
friendly by condensing the vertical space.
Click **OK**

Brekner's Co.
Tax Liability Report
For the Period From Mar 1, 2006 to Mar 31, 2006
Filter Criteria includes: Report order is by Employee ID. Report is printed in Detail Format.

Employee ID	Employee	SS No	Gross	Taxable Gross	Tax Withheld	Tax Liability
FUTA						
EH	Elizabeth Hill	111-55-6936	140.00	140.00		1.12
FH	Francis Henderson	199-55-5570	2,646.15	2,646.15		21.17
HT	Heidi Thom	100-45-5698	1,758.75	1,758.75		14.07
JM	Julie Meredith	333-44-8113	2,000.00	2,000.00		16.00
JR	Jessica Ruiz	345-76-8906	1,140.00	1,140.00		9.12
TN	Tran Ng	555-12-5678	1,680.00	1,680.00		13.44
WS	Wilson Spalding	099-56-6942	2,270.00	2,270.00		18.16
			11,634.90	11,634.90		93.08
940 Total						93.08
FIT						
EH	Elizabeth Hill	111-55-6936	140.00	140.00		
FH	Francis Henderson	199-55-5570	2,646.15	2,646.15	83.85	83.85
HT	Heidi Thom	100-45-5698	1,758.75	1,758.75	18.95	18.95
JM	Julie Meredith	333-44-8113	2,000.00	2,000.00	90.76	90.76
JR	Jessica Ruiz	345-76-8906	1,140.00	1,140.00	21.38	21.38
TN	Tran Ng	555-12-5678	1,680.00	1,680.00	158.54	158.54
WS	Wilson Spalding	099-56-6942	2,270.00	2,270.00	175.50	175.50
			11,634.90	11,634.90	548.98	548.98
FICA EE						
EH	Elizabeth Hill	111-55-6936	140.00	140.00	8.68	8.68
FH	Francis Henderson	199-55-5570	2,646.15	2,646.15	164.06	164.06
HT	Heidi Thom	100-45-5698	1,758.75	1,758.75	109.04	109.04
JM	Julie Meredith	333-44-8113	2,000.00	2,000.00	124.00	124.00
JR	Jessica Ruiz	345-76-8906	1,140.00	1,140.00	70.68	70.68
TN	Tran Ng	555-12-5678	1,680.00	1,680.00	104.16	104.16
WS	Wilson Spalding	099-56-6942	2,270.00	2,270.00	140.74	140.74
			11,634.90	11,634.90	721.36	721.36

Click **Print**

Close the report and the **Select a Report** windows

PAY TAX LIABILITIES

All of the withholdings from employee's paychecks as well as payroll taxes calculated on each payroll must at some point be sent to the appropriate agency. These payments follow different frequencies depending on type. As an example, the 940 FUTA payroll tax must be submitted quarterly although the report is produced annually. Since we have just completed the end of a quarter, a deposit is due at the end of March (presuming a liability of $100 or more). The 941 requires monthly deposits and a quarterly report. The 941 report would be due at the end of March and a deposit of 941 taxes and withholdings (FIT, FICA EE, FICA ER, Medicare EE, Medicare ER) would be due no later than the 15th of April. All of these payments follow a similar pattern in terms of how they are paid. They simply have different payees. Deposits can be made by writing a check or as is more frequently the case, by a transfer of funds at our bank. This transfer eliminates the need to write a check and requires only a journal entry to debit the liabilities and credit the cash account that will be used. We will take this easier approach.

MEMO

DATE: March 31, 2006

Based on the information in the payroll Tax Liability Report, Wilson has been instructed to make the 941 deposit using an electronic funds transfer from the business checking account.

DO: Make the 941 deposit

Click **General Journal Entry** from the **General Ledger** button

Confirm or type Mar 31, 2006 in the **Date** field

In the **Reference field**, enter 941DEP. This is for our reference only and is not required

Tab to or click the **Account No.** column

Click the drop-down list arrow for **Account No.**, double click 2100 FIT Payable

In the **Description** field, enter 941 Deposit for March

Tab to or click in the **Debit** column

Using your Tax Liability Report, find the total FIT liability and enter the amount of the liability 548.98

FIT						
EH	Elizabeth Hill	111-55-6936	140.00	140.00		
FH	Francis Henderson	199-55-5570	2,646.15	2,646.15	83.85	83.85
HT	Heidi Thom	100-45-5698	1,758.75	1,758.75	18.95	18.95
JM	Julie Meredith	333-44-8113	2,000.00	2,000.00	90.76	90.76
JR	Jessica Ruiz	345-76-8906	1,140.00	1,140.00	21.38	21.38
TN	Tran Ng	555-12-5678	1,680.00	1,680.00	158.54	158.54
WS	Wilson Spalding	099-56-6942	2,270.00	2,270.00	175.50	175.50
			11,634.90	11,634.90	548.98	548.98
FICA EE						

Tab to or click **Account No.**

Select 2120 FICA-OASDI Payable

Tab to or click the **Debit** column, enter the total FICA-OASDI liability

Note: you will need to add the FICA EE and FICA ER totals to arrive at the total FICA liability of 1442.72.

Enter 1442.72

Tab to or click **Account No.**

Select 2140 FICA-HI Payable

Tab to or click the **Debit** column, enter the total FICA-HI liability

Note: you will need to add the Medicare EE and Medicare ER totals to arrive at the total Medicare liability of 337.42

Enter 337.42

Tab to or click **Account No.**

Click the drop-down list arrow for Account No.
Double click 1100 Payroll Checking
Tab to the **Credit** column, enter the 941 Total tax liability from the report, 2329.12

Click **Save** and then **Close**

PAY OTHER PAYROLL LIABILITIES

A number of other liabilities are generated as a result of payroll that are not related to federal, state and local taxes. In our sample company, Brekners Co., the employees have deductions made to pay for medical and dental insurance as well as optional withholdings for a savings account at the local Medical Credit Union. Since Brekners' does not have a cafeteria plan in effect, all of these deductions are from the net pay. That is, payroll taxes are calculated based on the total gross rather than gross less medical and dental payments. These other deductions must eventually be paid to the appropriate entity. The medical and dental withholdings must be paid to the insurance company while the savings withholdings must be paid to the credit union. In order to sum these amounts, we must modify one of the reports used previously. Prior to paying these other liabilities we will generate a modified Check Register report.

MEMO

DATE: March 31, 2006

Modify the Check Register report to include non-tax payroll liabilities and pay them.

DO: Modify the Check Register report and pay liabilities
          Click **Payroll Reports** from the **Payroll** button
          Highlight the **Payroll Check Register** and click the **Options** button
          Click on the **Fields** tab
          Using the scroll bar, locate the fields called **Medical**, **Dental** and **Savings**
          Click in the box in the **Show** column for each

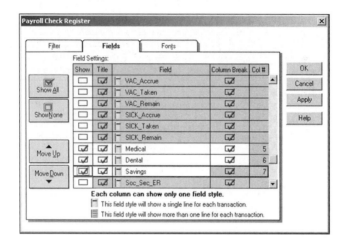

Click **OK**
Click the **Design** button and adjust the width of the **Employee** column to fit the
    report on one page
Click **Print**

Brekner's Co.
Payroll Check Register
For the Period From Mar 1, 2006 to Mar 31, 2006
Filter Criteria includes: Report order is by Check Date. Report is printed in Detail Format.

Reference	Date	Employee	Amount	Medical	Dental	Savings
185	3/13/06	Francis Henderson	994.67	-75.00	-25.00	-50.00
186	3/13/06	Heidi Thom	674.22	-75.00	-25.00	-50.00
187	3/13/06	Julie Meredith	781.94	-55.00	-25.00	
188	3/13/06	Jessica Ruiz	266.45	-55.00	-25.00	
189	3/13/06	Tran Ng	614.00	-35.00	-25.00	
190	3/13/06	Wilson Spalding	845.80	-55.00	-25.00	
191	3/27/06	Elizabeth Hill	107.64			-20.00
192	3/27/06	Francis Henderson	1,030.76	-75.00	-25.00	-50.00
193	3/27/06	Heidi Thom	610.29	-75.00	-25.00	-50.00
194	3/27/06	Julie Meredith	781.94	-55.00	-25.00	
195	3/27/06	Jessica Ruiz	591.51	-55.00	-25.00	
196	3/27/06	Tran Ng	614.00	-35.00	-25.00	
197	3/27/06	Wilson Spalding	845.80	-55.00	-25.00	
198	3/27/06	Jessica Ruiz	266.45	-55.00	-25.00	
188V	3/31/06	Jessica Ruiz	-266.45	55.00	25.00	
		3/1/06 thru 3/31/06	8,759.02	-700.00	-300.00	-220.00
		3/1/06 thru 3/31/06	8,759.02	-700.00	-300.00	-220.00

Note: Peachtree has now included columns for the Dental, Medical and Savings deductions that we have made throughout the month. It is these totals that we must submit to the insurance company and credit union.

Click **Close**, do not save the modified report

Close the Select a Report window

Click **Payments** from the **Purchases** button

Using the magnifying glass to the right of **Vendor ID**, select Medical and Dental Insurance, Inc.

Confirm or type Mar 31, 2006 in the **Date** field

Click in the **Memo** field, enter Pay Medical and Dental Premiums

Click in the **Description** field, enter Pay Medical Premium

Tab to the **GL Account** field, accept 2600 Medical Insurance Payable

Tab to the **Amount** field, enter 700.00

Tab to the **Description** field, enter Pay Dental Premium

Tab to the **GL Acco**unt field, using the magnifying glass, select 2700 Dental Insurance Payable

Tab to the **Amount** field, enter 300.00

Click **Print**

Use **Change Form** to select OCR Multi-Purpose AP Laser

Use **First Check No.** 501

Click **Print**

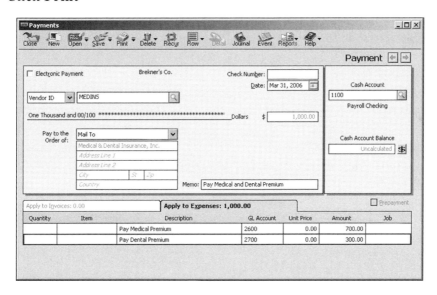

Using the magnifying glass to the right of **Vendor ID**, select Medical Credit Union Assoc.

Confirm or type Mar 31, 2006 in the **Date** field

Click in the **Memo** field, enter Pay Savings Withholdings

Click in the **Description** field, enter Pay Savings Withholdings

Tab to the **GL Account** field, accept 2800 Credit Union Payable

Tab to the **Amount** field, enter 220.00

Click **Print**
Enter or confirm Check No. 502
Click **Print** and close the **Payments** window

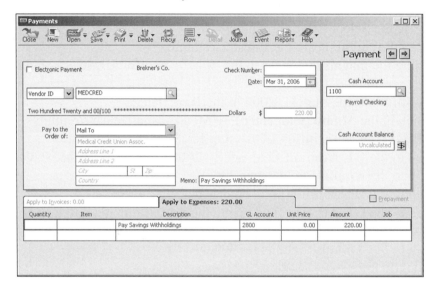

FILING PAYROLL TAX FORMS

Peachtree® Complete Accounting 2006 creates and will print a variety of Federal and State required forms. The program does not create the report form but rather prints it on a blank report form. Reports include Form 941—Employer's Quarterly Federal Tax Return and Form 940—Employer's Annual Federal Unemployment Tax Return. These formats are accurate and updated by the payroll subscription service. The program will also create the California State forms DD-88 and DE-6. You may also create a custom tax form that may be submitted in conjunction with any state or federal taxes paid. Even though the form 940 is for the year, we will prepare it for the month of March just to provide experience in the preparation of this item. We will also prepare a form 941, albeit with our incomplete data, for the same reason. What we create will not be accurate nor cover the correct time period. We are performing this task only to provide you with experience using the process.

PREPARE AND PRINT FORM 941

Peachtree® Complete Accounting 2006 can print the report directly on a blank form 941 or can print a 941 worksheet that resembles the 941 report. Since we do not have a blank Form 941 on which to print, we will print the 941 worksheet instead. This will resemble an actual 941 form but is not an acceptable substitute for one. The report is for the Employer's Federal Tax Return and is prepared to report federal income tax withheld, Social Security tax, and Medicare tax. The taxes are based on the total wages paid. All of these reports can only be printed and cannot be viewed on screen.

MEMO

DATE: March 31, 2006

Prepare and print Form 941 Worksheet for March.

DO: Prepare and print Form 941 Worksheet for March
Click **Payroll Reports** from the **Payroll** button
Click on the Federal Form 941 button in the Report List: of the Select a Report
    window
Double click on Form 941 Worksheet - 2005

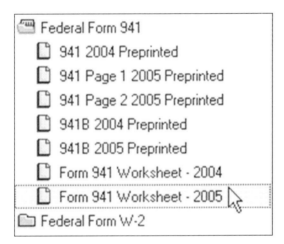

You are brought to a Form 941 Worksheet filter

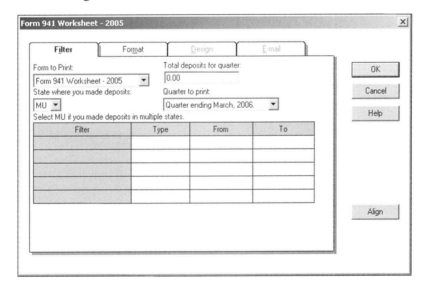

Note: In normal usage you would insert the total deposits for the quarter in the
appropriate field. Because we have only March's data, we will not get
accurate results. We will omit entering deposits we have made thus far.

Click **OK**

Click **OK** in the Print dialog box to print the worksheet

Do not close the Select a Report window

PREPARE AND PRINT FORM 940

The preparation of Form 940 for the Employer's Annual Federal Unemployment Tax Return
(FUTA) is similar to the preparation of Form 941. As with the 941, Peachtree® Complete
Accounting 2006 expects you to print this report on a blank 940 form. We will print the report on
blank paper to illustrate the process.

MEMO

DATE: March 31, 2006

Prepare and print Form 940 for March.

DO: Prepare and print Form 940 for March

Click on the **Federal Form 940** button in the **Report List:** of the **Select a Report**
window

Double click on **Form 940-EZ**

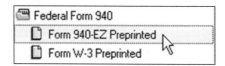

You are brought to a Form 940 EZ Worksheet filter similar to the 941 filter

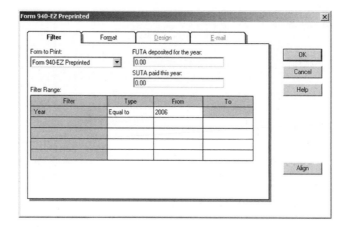

> *Note:* In normal usage you would insert the total deposits for the year in the
> appropriate fields. Because it is not the end of the year, we have not made all
> our deposits and will not get an accurate report. We will therefore, omit
> entering deposits we have made thus far.

Click **OK**

Click **OK** in the Print dialog box

Do not close the **Select a Report** window

PREPARE AND PRINT EMPLOYEES' W-2 FORMS

The W-2 form is prepared at the end of the year, mailed to each employee, and mailed to the required government agencies. The wages earned and taxes withheld for the individual employee for the year are shown on the form. A W-3 form is a summary of all the W-2 forms you are submitting to the government. Peachtree® Complete Accounting 2006 is set up to fill in this information on blank W-2 and W-3 forms. Electronic filing of W-2s for companies employing 250 or more is required. Peachtree® Complete Accounting 2006 does not support electronic filing of W-2s. W-2s and the corresponding W-3 are prepared at the end of the year. However, for experience with this procedure, you will prepare and review the W-2s for each employee. In addition, a W-3 will be prepared to summarize the information on the W-2s. Since we do not have the blank forms, we will print them on blank paper.

MEMO

DATE: March 31, 2006

Prepare W-2s for each employee as well as the W-3 transmittal.

DO: Prepare the W-2s and W-3 for Brekners Co.

Click on the Federal Form W-2 button in the Report List: of the Select a Report
window

Double click on W-2 2004 Standard

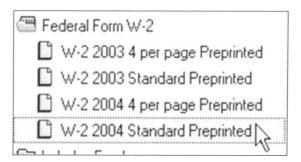

You are brought to a W-2 2004 Standard filter

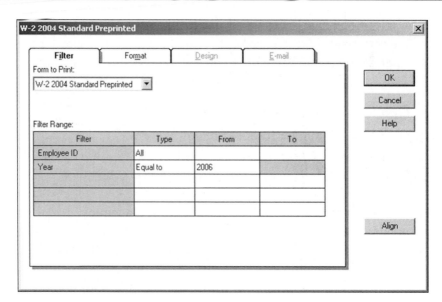

Click **OK** to accept all the defaults

Click **OK** in the **Print** dialog box and any other warning box you may receive

Do not close the **Select a Report** window

Double click on the **Federal Form 940** button in the **Report List:** of the **Select a Report** window

Double click on **Form W-3**

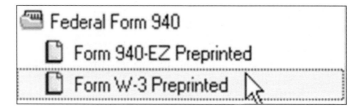

You are brought to a Form W-3 filter

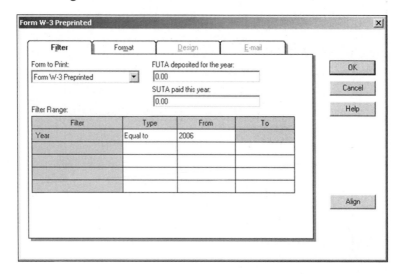

Click **OK** to accept all the defaults
Click **OK** in the **Print** dialog box
Close the **Select a Report** window

BACK UP

Whenever an important work session is complete, you should always back up your data. If your data disk is damaged or an error is discovered at a later time, the backup disk may be restored and the information used for recording transactions. No matter what type of business, the backup procedure remains the same. In addition, it is always wise to make a duplicate of your data disk just in case the disk is damaged in some way.

 DO: Follow the instructions given in previous chapters to back up data for Brekners Co.

SUMMARY

In this chapter, paychecks were generated for employees who worked their standard number of hours, who took vacation time, who took sick time, and who were just hired. Peachtree® Complete Accounting 2006 calculated the amount of payroll deductions and generated the pay checks automatically. Changes to employee information were made, and a new employee was added. Payroll reports were printed and/or viewed, payroll liabilities were paid, and 941, 940, W-2 and W-3 forms were printed.

END-OF-CHAPTER QUESTIONS

TRUE/FALSE

ANSWER THE FOLLOWING QUESTIONS IN THE SPACE PROVIDED BEFORE THE QUESTION NUMBER.

_____ 1. You cannot enter payroll deductions manually on paychecks.

_____ 2. Once a paycheck has been printed, you may not edit it.

_____ 3. Paychecks and regular checks may be printed at the same time.

_____ 4. A W-3 is printed and mailed to all employees at the end of the year.

_____ 5. Checks may be created and previewed or created without previewing.

_____ 6. Peachtree® Complete Accounting 2006 can print an accurate up-to-date Form 941 and Form 940.

_____ 7. When several taxes are owed to a single agency, Peachtree® Complete Accounting 2006 automatically generates a single check to the agency for all tax liability items.

_____ 8. If a salaried employee uses vacation time, Peachtree® Complete Accounting 2006 will automatically calculate the remaining balance on the Current Earnings Report.

_____ 9. Processing the Tax Liability Report also generates the checks for payment of the liabilities.

_____ 10. A W-3 summarizes all W-2s.

MULTIPLE CHOICE

WRITE THE LETTER OF THE CORRECT ANSWER IN THE SPACE PROVIDED BEFORE THE QUESTION NUMBER.

_____ 1. When completing paychecks manually, ___.
   A. you must confirm the information about hours worked
   B. Peachtree® Complete Accounting 2006 will use the same hours as the last paycheck
   C. you must preview all checks
   D. all of the above

_____ 2. The form sent to the government as a summary of the earning statements sent to all the individual employees of the company is the ___ form.
   A. W-2
   B. 940

     C. W-3

     D. 941

_____ 3. When paying tax liabilities, you ___.

     A. must pay all liabilities at one time

     B. may select individual tax liabilities and pay them automatically

     C. are generating checks manually

     D. all of the above

_____ 4. A new employee may be added ___.

     A. at any time

     B. only at the end of the week

     C. only at the end of the pay period

     D. only when current paychecks have been printed

_____ 5. Pay stub information is printed ___.

     A. as part of a payroll check

     B. separate from the payroll check

     C. only as an individual employee report

     D. both A and B

_____ 6. The Peachtree Complete Select for Payroll Entry window is accessed _____.

     A. from the Task menu

     B   from the Payroll navigation aid button

     C. using the hot key Ctrl-Shift-P

     D. both A and B

_____ 7. A voided check ___.

     A. shows a negative amount

     B. has a V after the check number

     C. remains as part of the company records

     D. all of the above

_____ 8. When employees to be paid have been selected, Peachtree® Complete Accounting 2006 will ___.

     A. create a separate check for each employee

     B. consolidate pay amounts and create one check for all the employees

     C. automatically pay the liabilities in a Tax Liability Report

     D. none of the above

_____ 9. You must obtain blank ___ forms, and Peachtree® Complete Accounting 2006 will fill them in when printing.

     A. 940

     B. 941

     C. W-2

     D. all the above

_____ 10. Changes made to an employee's pay rate will become effective ___.
   A. immediately
   B. at the end of the next payroll period
   C. at the end of the quarter
   D. after a W-2 has been prepared for the employee

FILL-IN

IN THE SPACE PROVIDED, WRITE THE ANSWER THAT MOST APPROPRIATELY
COMPLETES THE SENTENCE.

1. The form created for the Employer's Quarterly Federal Tax Return is Form _____.

2. Information regarding hours worked must be reviewed before the employees' _____ can be printed.

3. The report that show an employee's gross pay, federal and state withholdings, sick and vacation hours, miscellaneous deductions, and other details is _____ .

4. To add a new employee, _____ must be selected from the Payroll button.

5. The report listing the check numbers issued, the date issued, the employee name and the amount of the check is the _____.

SHORT ESSAY

What is the difference between voiding a paycheck and deleting a paycheck? Why should a business prefer to void paychecks rather than delete them?

_____

_____

_____

_____

_____

_____

_____

_____

NAME

TRANSMITTAL

CHAPTER 8: BREKNERS CO.

Attach the following documents and reports:

- ☐ Check No. 185: Francis Henderson, 03/14/06
- ☐ Check No. 186: Heidi Thom, 03/14/06
- ☐ Check No. 187: Julie Meredith, 03/14/06
- ☐ Check No. 188: Jessica Ruiz, 03/14/06
- ☐ Check No. 189: Tran Ng, 03/14/06
- ☐ Check No. 190: Wilson Spalding, 03/14/06
- ☐ Select Employees to Pay Preview Report
- ☐ Check No. 191: Elizabeth Hill, 03/28/06
- ☐ Check No. 192: Francis Henderson 03/28/06
- ☐ Check No. 193: Heidi Thom, 03/28/06
- ☐ Check No. 194: Julie Meredith, 03/28/06
- ☐ Check No. 195: Jessica Ruiz, 03/28/06
- ☐ Check No. 196: Tran Ng, 03/28/06
- ☐ Check No. 197: Wilson Spalding, 03/28/06
- ☐ Check No. 198: Jessica Ruiz (reissued from 03/14/06 pay period)
- ☐ Payroll Check Register
- ☐ Current Earnings Report
- ☐ Tax Liability Report
- ☐ Payroll Check Register (with Dental, Medical and Savings added)
- ☐ Check No. 501: Medical and Dental Ins., Inc.
- ☐ Check No. 502: Medical Credit Union Assoc.
- ☐ Employer's Quarterly Federal Tax Return, Form 941
- ☐ Employer's Annual Federal Unemployment (FUTA) Tax Return, Form 940
- ☐ W-2's for all current employees w/W-3 Transmittal

END-OF-CHAPTER PROBLEM

AQUA SKI MANUFACTURING

Aqua Ski Manufacturing is a water ski manufacturing company located in Newport Beach, California. The company is owned by Keith Bermudez. Keith handles all the sales and marketing for the company. Business is booming, and Aqua Ski Manufacturing currently has several advertisements for factory workers in the local newspapers.

Wilma Anderson is the office manager and is responsible for the smooth operation of the company and for all the employees. Wilma's salary is $37,700 per year. The assistant manager is responsible for the bookkeeping, ordering, delivery schedules, and so on. Janet Marquez is the assistant manager and earns $32,500 per year. Jack Ryder is the lead line person and supervisor in the factory and earns $15.00 per hour. The senior line assistant is Harriet Thomas. She earns $12.50 per hour. Regular line personnel earn $9.50 per hour. Currently, Frances Helga and Tien Nguyen are regular line personnel. The employees typically work 80 hours within a biweekly pay period. Any hourly employee working more than 80 hours will be paid overtime for extra hours.

INSTRUCTIONS

Open **Aqua Ski Manufacturing** and add your initials to the company name. The title bar for the company name will be **Aqua Ski Manufacturing-Student's Initials**.

RECORD TRANSACTIONS:

March 13, 2006

Use the following Payroll Table to prepare and print checks for the biweekly pay period ended March 10, 2006 using the Payroll Entry window. Checks will begin with number 179. Use the OCR Multi-Purp Laser w/15 check form. It is important to remember that you must add overtime, vacation and sick hours into the regular hours to insure they are paid properly.

PAYROLL TABLE: MARCH 10, 2006						
	Wilma Anderson	Janet Marquez	Jack Ryder	Harriet Thomas	Frances Helga	Tien Nguyen
HOURS						
Regular	80	72	80	76	80	80
Overtime			20		8	8
Sick				4		
Vacation		8				

March 13, 2006

Wilma hired two new employees who start today as line trainees at $6.50 per hour and time-and-a-half overtime at $9.75 per hour: <u>Russ Timothy</u> (use RT as the Employee ID), 230 Coast Way, Newport Beach, CA 92660; 714-555-2323; Social Security No. 100-55-2145; Federal and State withholding: Single, 0; no dental, medical, sick, credit union or vacation time. <u>Victor Strauss</u> (use VS as the Employee ID), 7821 Laguna Canyon Drive, Newport Beach, CA 92660; 714-555-3257; Social Security No. 678-54-8487; Federal and State withholding: Married, 2; no dental, medical, sick, or vacation time. Victor will have $10.00 taken out of each paycheck for savings.

March 20, 2006

Hired an additional person to work in the office taking orders and answering telephones: Leo Lyons; $7.50 per hour and time-and-a-half overtime (calculate); 890 Cove Lane, Newport Beach, CA 92660; 714-555-2233; Social Security No. 587-87-1147; Federal and State withholding: Married, 1; dental $25; medical $50; no credit union savings, but standard sick/vacation time.

Jack Ryder received a raise to $16.00 per hour for his regular hourly rate. Enter the new rate. Calculate the new rate for time-and-a-half overtime rate.

Harriet's telephone number changed to 714-555-5111.

March 27, 2006

Prepare and print checks for the biweekly pay period ended March 24, 2006 using the Select for Payroll Entry window.

PAYROLL TABLE: MARCH 24, 2006									
	Wilma Anderson	Janet Marquez	Jack Ryder	Harriet Thomas	Frances Helga	Tien Nguyen	Russ Timothy	Victor Strauss	Leo Lyons
HOURS									
Regular	72	80	80	75	80	78	80	80	40
Overtime			10						
Sick				5					
Vacation	8								

March 31, 2006:

Victor spilled coffee on his check. Void his check for March 27 (Check No. 192), reissue the paycheck, and print it using Check No. 194.

Victor and Russ have completed their first two weeks of training. Because both are doing well, change their regular pay to $7.00 per hour. In addition, calculate and enter their time-and-a-half overtime rate.

Prepare and print a payroll Check Register for March.

Prepare and print the Current Earnings Report for March.

Prepare and print the payroll Tax Liability Report for March.

Using the Tax Liability Report make the 941 deposit electronically.

Create a modified Check Register and pay the medical, dental and credit union liabilities. Start with Check No. 301. (HEALTHINS is the vendor ID for the Medical/Dental payment and HEALTHCRED for the savings)

Prepare and print Forms 941 and 940 Worksheet on plain paper. Do not make adjustments to either of the reports.

NAME _____

TRANSMITTAL

CHAPTER 8: AQUA SKI MANUFACTURING

Attach the following documents and reports:

☐ Check No. 179: Frances Helga   *Note: numbers 179-184 may be assigned differently.*

☐ Check No. 180: Harriet Thomas

☐ Check No. 181: Janet Marquez

☐ Check No. 182: Jack Ryder

☐ Check No. 183: Tien Nguyen

☐ Check No. 184: Wilma Anderson

☐ Check No. 185: Frances Helga

☐ Check No. 186: Harriet Thomas

☐ Check No. 187: Janet Marquez

☐ Check No. 188: Jack Ryder

☐ Check No. 189: Leo Lyons

☐ Check No. 190: Russ Timothy

☐ Check No. 191: Tien Nguyen

☐ Check No. 192: Victor Strauss

☐ Check No. 193: Wilma Anderson

☐ Check No. 194: (Reissued) Victor Strauss

☐ Check Register

☐ Current Earnings Report

☐ Tax Liability Report

☐ Check Register (Modified)

☐ Check No. 301: HealthCare Insurance, Inc.

☐ Check No. 302: HealthyCare Credit Union Assoc.

☐ Employer's Quarterly Federal Tax Return, Form 941

☐ Employer's Annual Federal Unemployment (FUTA) Tax Return, Form 940 Worksheet

Computerizing a Manual Accounting System

9

LEARNING OBJECTIVES

At the completion of this chapter, you will be able to:

1. Set up a company using the Create a New Company feature
2. Modify a Chart of Accounts for the new company.
3. Create lists for customers, vendors, inventory items and enter beginning balances.
4. Create payroll defaults and enter employees.
5. Print lists and reports.

COMPUTERIZING A MANUAL SYSTEM

In previous chapters, Peachtree® Complete Accounting 2006 was used to record transactions for businesses that were already set up. In this chapter, you will actually set up a business based on a sample company, modify the chart of accounts, create vendor and customer accounts, add inventory items and create various defaults. Peachtree® Complete Accounting 2006 makes setting up the records for a business user friendly by going through the process using Peachtree's New Company Setup Guide. Once the basic structure of the company has been established based on input provided to Peachtree, further refinement will be made to individualize the company to our specific needs.

TRAINING TUTORIAL

The following tutorial is a step-by-step guide to setting up the fictitious company Ike's Bikes. The Create a New Company feature will be used to set up the basic company structure. Once created, modifications to the company data will be made following a Setup Guide. Information for the company setup will be provided in tables.

COMPANY PROFILE: IKE'S BIKES

Ike's Bikes is a fictitious company that sells bicycles. In addition, Ike's Bikes has a service department that cleans, conditions, and repairs bicycles. Ike's Bikes is located in Fairfield, California, and it is a sole proprietorship owned by Daniel Lee. Mr. Lee is involved in all aspects of the business. Ike's Bikes has four full-time employees: Mark Canfield, a salaried employee who manages the store and is responsible for supervising all of the other employees, Carrie Bernstein, a salaried employee whose duties include all the ordering, managing the office, and keeping the books. There are two full-time hourly employees: Jimmy Hernandez, who works in the service/repair department, and Sally Richards, who works in the store selling bicycles.

CREATE A NEW COMPANY

Since Ike's Bike is a new company, it would not appear as a company file if you were to select Open an existing company on the Peachtree opening screen as in previous chapters. Instead, a new company may be created by selecting Set up a new company from this screen.

MEMO

DATE: January 1, 2006

Because this is the beginning of the fiscal year for Ike's Bikes, it is an appropriate time to set up the company books in Peachtree® Complete Accounting 2006. Use the Create a New Company feature.

 DO: Open Peachtree® Complete Accounting 2006 as previously instructed

Click on **Set up a new company**
You are presented with an introduction window that provides information but requires no information to be input.

Click **Next**
You are presented with a blank Company Information form

MEMO

DATE: January 1, 2006

In preparation for setting up Ike's Bikes company records, the following information is provided to Carrie by Mr. Lee. The business is a sole proprietorship:

Company: Ike's Bikes-Student's Initials
Address: 2398 Taylor Avenue, Fairfield, CA 94533
Telephone: 707-555-8273
Fax: 707-555-6362
Business Type: Sole Proprietorship
Federal Employer ID: 94-9487376
State Employer ID: 382-23847-2
E-mail address: Ikes@bike.com

DO: Enter the above information in the New Company Setup - Company Information window. Be sure to indicate the Business Type of Sole Proprietorship.

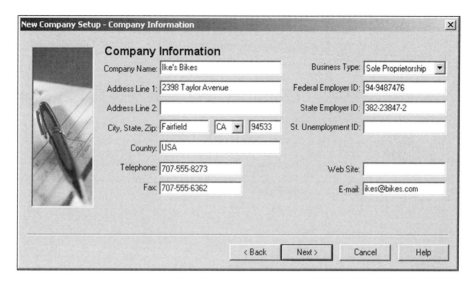

Click **Next**

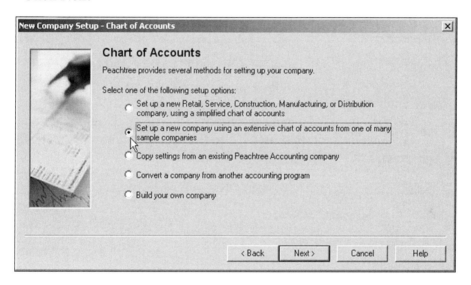

Note: At this point Peachtree provides you with five options for the creation of a
Chart of Accounts. The first option is the default option and will allow you
to select one of Peachtree's built-in sample companies as the template for
your company. This option provides for a simple, basic chart of accounts
based on your business type that you would subsequently modify. The
second option provides the same thing except you would choose from many
sample companies built into Peachtree and you would have a more extensive
chart of accounts. The third option allows you to copy the basic structure,
including the Chart of Accounts, of a company that already exists in
Peachtree. The fourth option allows you to convert data from Quicken,
QuickBooks or an earlier version of Peachtree. The final option allows you
to manually create a Chart of Accounts from scratch. We will select the

second option and allow Peachtree to create an extensive Chart of Accounts from one of its sample companies.

Click **Next**

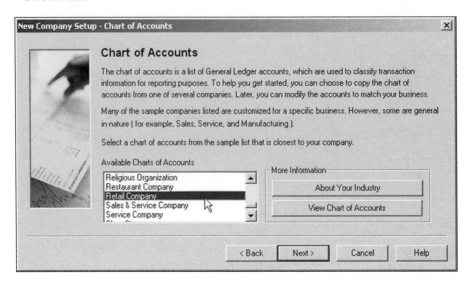

Using the down arrow, scroll through the list of **Available Charts of Accounts** and select Retail Company

Note: Should you desire to see what Chart of Accounts would be created with any of the sample company selections, you can click on the button View Chart of Accounts to bring up a list of the accounts that will be created.

Click **Next**

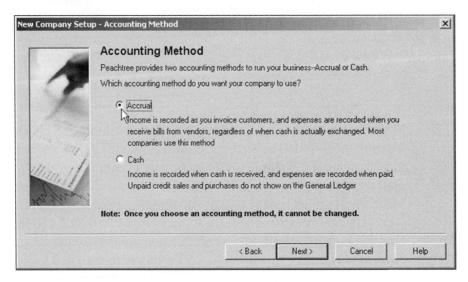

Peachtree will now ask whether we wish to use Accrual basis or Cash basis accounting. The program will default to accrual basis, which we will accept.

Click **Next**

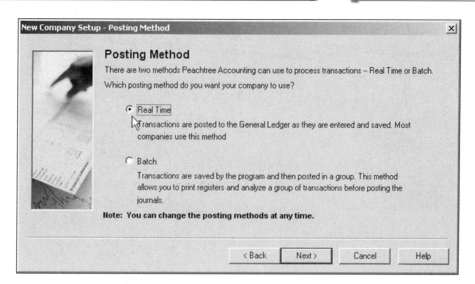

Peachtree will now need to know what posting method you would like to use. Peachtree can post transactions as we enter them (Real Time) or it can accumulate transactions and post them all at once upon command (Batch). In a real life, controlled situation, batch posting may be used to prevent lower level employees from posting information to the General Ledger. Accept the default of **Real Time**.

Click **Next**

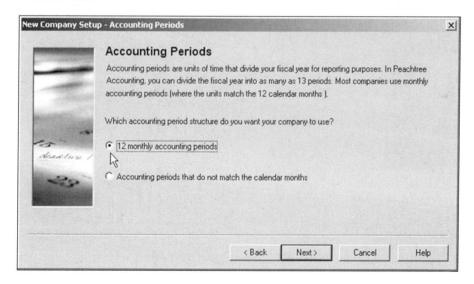

Peachtree now offers us the option of using standard monthly periods or using periods other than the calendar months. We will accept the default **12 monthly accounting periods**.

Click **Next**

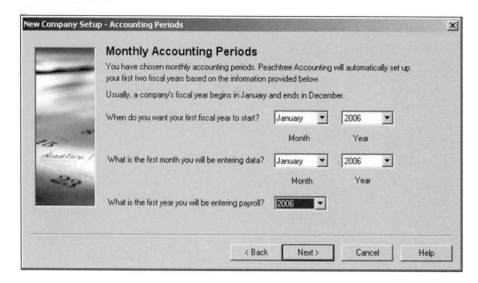

In order to set up our accounting periods, Peachtree requires information about our
fiscal and payroll years as well as when we will begin entering data. We will
use January 2006 as our start date. Change the first two options to **January
2006** and the third option to **2006**.

Click **Next**

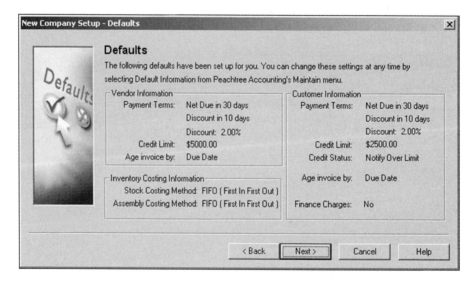

Peachtree presents you with a Defaults information screen that specifies the
various defaults Peachtree has selected for you concerning your vendors,
your customers and your inventory. Even though Peachtree is creating your
company with these defaults, you will be given the option to changing any of
these defaults using a Setup Guide presented later.

Click **Next**

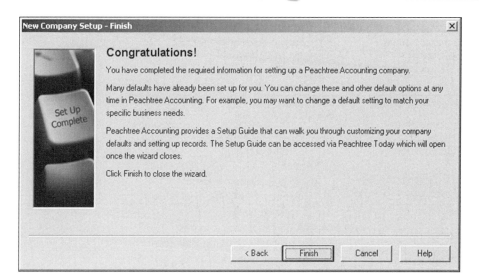

Peachtree now has sufficient information to create the basic structure for your
company. In this final screen, you are informed about the Set-Up Guide that
will allow you to further customize your company. It will appear in the
Peachtree Today screen that will open once we click on Finnish.

Click **Finish**

After a few moments of file creation, Peachtree will bring you to the Peachtree
Today screen with the Setup Guide Option:

Click on **Setup Guide** if it is not already selected.

You are brought to an area that contains a six-page task for setting up your new
company. These are:

Area	Contents
General Ledger	Chart of Accounts
	Bank Accounts
	General Ledger Defaults
	Account Beginning Balances
Accounts Payable	Vendor Defaults
	Vendor Records
	Vendor Beginning Balances
Accounts Receivable	Customer Defaults
	Statement and Invoice Defaults
	Set up Customer Records
	Customer Beginning Balances
Payroll	Employee Defaults
	Set up Employee Records
	Employee Beginning Balances
Inventory	Inventory Defaults
	Set up Inventory Items
	Inventory Beginning Balances
Jobs	Job Defaults
	Set up Job Records
	Job Beginning Balances

Peachtree has completed a number of these items for us in the initial setup process. You will see it has marked these items complete by placing a checkmark next to them. The checkmarks can be removed by clicking on them. Even though these items are marked complete, we are still able to click on them and make changes to the choices that were made. We will now proceed through the Setup Guide making minor changes to some of the items already marked as complete and entering the data to complete those that are not marked complete. Not all areas will require input. We will look only at those that require changes or input. Click on **Set up General Ledger**.

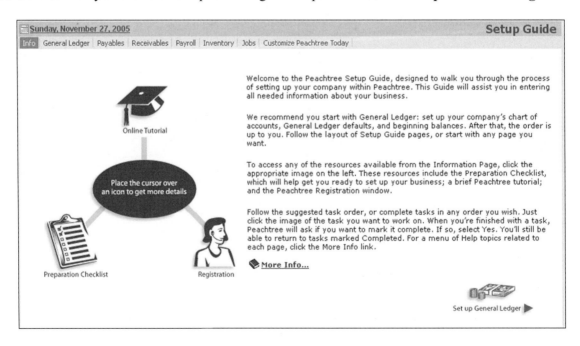

GENERAL LEDGER SETUP

The most important item in the General Ledger setup is the Chart of Accounts. As you recall, we created our company based on a sample company within Peachtree. As such, Peachtree created a generic Chart of Accounts for us. It will contain accounts that we do not need, but will also be missing accounts that we do need. Some accounts, such as the capital accounts, may require simple modification to suit our needs. It is not necessary to delete every account whose use is not anticipated at this time. Only accounts that you are reasonably sure will not be used should be deleted. It does not affect our records to keep accounts with zero balances. It is also in this section that we will enter the Trial Balance amounts from our manual accounting records.

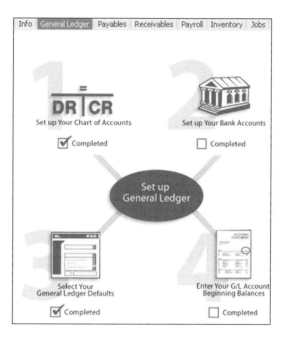

MEMO

DATE: January 1, 2006

An evaluation of Ike's Bikes needs the following deletions and changes to the Chart of Accounts.

Delete the following accounts:
   11100 Accounts Receivable Service
   15500 Building
   15600 Building Improvements
   16900 Land

17500 Accum. Depreciation - Building

17600 Accum. Depreciation - Bldg Imp.
19100 Organization Costs
19150 Accum. Amortiz. - Org. Cost
24900 Suspense-Clearing Account
40400 Sales-Clearance
60500 Amortization Expense

Change the following accounts:
  12000 Product Inventory to 12000 Merchandise Inventory
  23000 Accrued Expenses to 23000 Accrued Expenses Payable
  39006 Owner's Contribution to 39006 Daniel Lee, Capital
  39007 Owner's Draw to 39007 Daniel Lee, Drawing

DO: Using the Setup Guide, make the above modifications to the Chart of Accounts
From the Setup Guide, click on **Set up Your Chart of Accounts** in the **General Ledger** area
Note: If you have closed the Setup Guide, you may retrieve it by clicking Setup Guide from the Peachtree Today screen
Delete and modify accounts as previously instructed.

MEMO

DATE: January 1, 2006

Enter the following beginning General Ledger Balances into Peachtree® Complete Accounting 2006.

Account ID	Account Description	Debit	Credit
10000	Petty Cash	$50.00	
10100	Cash on Hand	$500.00	
10200	Regular Checking Account	$2,000.00	
10400	Savings Account	$10,000.00	
11000	Accounts Receivable	$1,913.91	
11500	Allowance for Doubtful Account		$400.00
12000	Merchandise Inventory	$8,450.47	
12050	Cleaning Supplies Inventory	$396.00	
12100	Office Supplies Inventory	$852.00	
14700	Other Current Assets	$750.00	
15000	Furniture and Fixtures	$3,800.00	
15100	Equipment	$1,200.00	

Account ID	Account Description	Debit	Credit
17000	Accum. Depreciation - Furniture		$800.00
17100	Accum. Depreciation - Equipment		$250.00
20000	Accounts Payable		$11,672.96
23100	Sales Tax Payable		$426.00
23400	Federal Payroll Taxes Payable		$1,292.00
23500	FUTA Tax Payable		$87.00
23600	State Payroll Taxes Payable		$429.00
23700	SUTA Payable		$328.00
39006	Daniel Lee, Capital		$14,227.42

DO: Using the Setup Guide, add the above beginning balances to the Chart of Accounts

From the **Setup Guide**, click on **GL Account Beginning Balances** in the **General Ledger** area

Using the scroll bar, select From 12/1/05 through 12/31/05

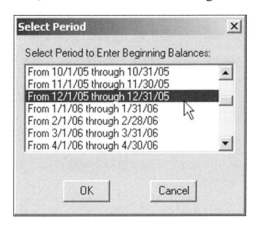

Click **OK**

Click in the white **Assets, Expenses** column in the row for the first item in our trial balance, **10000 Petty Cash**, enter 50.00

Tab to the second item, **10100 Cash on Hand**, enter 500.00

Continue tabbing to the fields needed to enter the rest of the balances.

Note: In most cases, a Credit account will show the white entry column on the Credit side (liabilities, income, equity) while a Debit account will show the white entry column on the Debit side (assets, expenses). An exception to this will be the Allowance for Doubtful Accounts. Because this is a Contra Asset, the amount must be entered as a negative number.

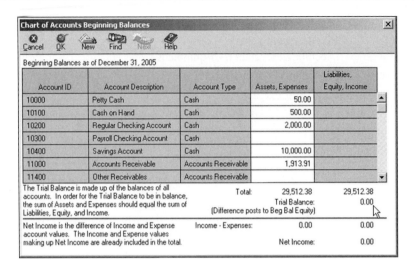

When all entries are complete, click **OK.** You will know they are accurate and complete when the Trial Balance row equals 0.00 as illustrated.
You are presented with the following confirmation window

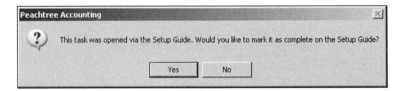

Click **Yes** to mark this item as complete and click on **Set up Payables**

ACCOUNTS PAYABLE SETUP

The Accounts Payable section allows us to establish our vendor defaults as well as enter our current vendors and their beginning balances. When we set up defaults for vendors, we are telling Peachtree what information to enter into various fields in the Vendor Setup screen when we add new vendors. It would be impossible to have defaults that would work with every vendor. As such, we are able to change the default information in the Maintain Vendor window when we are adding a vendor. The defaults merely serve as a time saving tool when they can be used.

MEMO
DATE: January 1, 2006

Change the Vendor Default Credit Limit to 1,000.00. Change the aging default to Invoice Date instead of Due Date. Add a new custom field called Comments.

  DO: Using the Setup Guide, make the above modifications to the Vendor Defaults

From the **Setup Guide**, click on **Vendor Defaults** in the **Payables** area
Click in the **Credit Limit** field, enter **1,000.00**

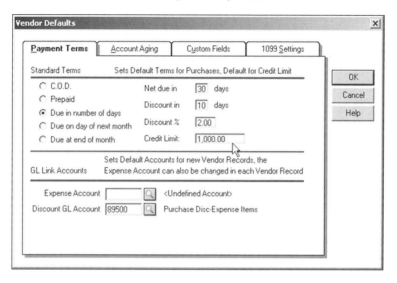

Click on the **Account Aging** tab
Click on the **Invoice date** radio button in the **Age Invoices by:** section

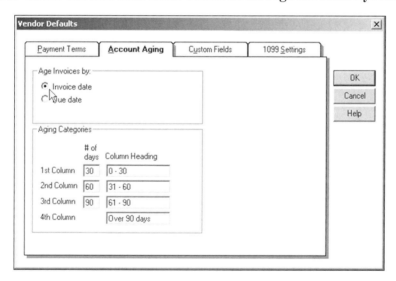

Click on the **Custom Fields** tab
Click in the **Enabled** box for Field Label row 4 to place a checkmark in that field
Click in **Field Label 4** and enter Comments

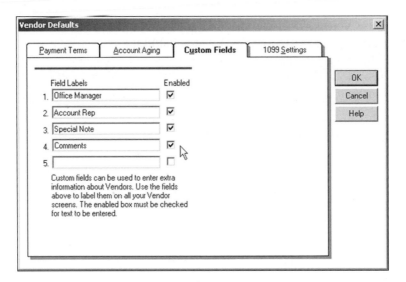

Click **OK**

MEMO

DATE: January 1, 2006

Add our current vendors to Peachtree based on the enclosed list.

Vendor ID	Vendor Name	Address	Telephone	Expense Default	Vendor Terms	Ship Via
POW01	Power & Water Co.	P.O. Box 02838 Fairfield, CA 94533	707-555-3929	78000	Net 10 days	Best Way
CLE01	CleanSweep Janitorial	23948 Main Street Suisun, CA 94585	707-555-3805	68000	Net 10 days	Best Way
SCH01	Schwinn Dealer, Inc.	93248 Texas Street Marysville, CA 95723	508-555-8390	12000	2% 10 Net 30	Best Way
YEL01	Yellow Pages	2934 Union Drive Fairfield, CA 94533	707-555-2746	60100	Net 15 days	Best Way
NAN01	Nantucket Property Mngmt.	92348 West Marina Fairfield, CA 94533	707-555-1827	74000	Net 30 days	Best Way
MIS01	Mission Uniforms	8387 Riker Vacaville, CA 95383	707-555-2763	68000	Net 10 days	Hand Deliver
BIK01	Bike Parts, Inc.	2473 Pajaro Street Suisun, CA 94585	707-555-0324	12000	1% 15 Net 30	UPS Ground
TEL01	TeleCom Company	P.O. Box 23873 Fairfield, CA 94533	707-555-2375	76000	Net 10 days	Best Way
BMX01	BMX Wholesale Distribution	2387 Lerner Lane Modesto, CA 94823	508-555-2772	12000	2% 15 Net 30	Best Way
UNI01	UNIX Insurance	9382 Mercer Street Vacaville, CA 95383	707-555-8382	67000	Net 30 days	Best Way

DO: Using the Setup Guide, add the above vendors

From the **Setup Guide**, click on **Set up Your Vendors** in the **Accounts Payable** area

Enter the vendors from the above list using the information provided and accepting defaults for any other items in the Setup window. Refer to Chapter 3 should you require a refresher in this process

Click **Close** after the last vendor has been entered

Click **Yes** to mark this item as complete

MEMO

DATE: January 1, 2006

At the time of our conversion to Peachtree, there were still three unpaid invoices in our Accounts Payable. Enter these invoices using the data in the attached list.

Vendor Name	Invoice No.	Invoice Date	Amount
Bike Parts, Inc.	0398-837	12/15/05	$ 398.62
BMX Wholesale Distribution	34-234-5	12/27/05	$ 4,892.15
Schwinn Dealer, Inc.	00-26464	12/31/05	$ 6,382.19

DO: Using the Setup Guide, add the invoices using the data provided

From the **Setup Guide**, click on **Vendor Beginning Balances** in the **Payables** area. You are presented with a list of vendors

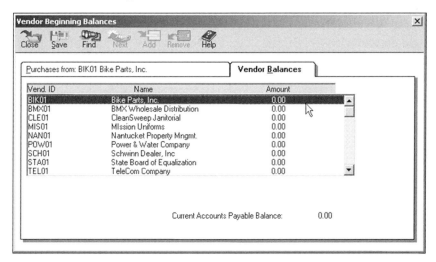

Double click on Bike Parts, Inc.

Click in the first row of the **Invoice Number** column, enter 0398-837

Tab to the **Date** column, enter Dec 15, 2005

Tab to the **Amount** column, enter 398.62

Click **Save**

Click on the **Vendor Balances** tab to return to the vendor list

Add the remaining two invoices following the same steps

Click **Close** when finished adding the three invoices

Click **Yes** to mark this item complete

TAX TABLES SETUP

Peachtree® Complete Accounting 2006 will automatically calculate sales tax on our taxable customers but will do so only if the proper sales tax codes have been set up in advance. This is a two step process that involves setting up the Sales Tax Authority and then the Sales Tax Code itself. The Authority is a component of the sales tax code for which sales tax is collected. This might include the general sales tax for the state as well as special taxes for transit districts and disaster funds such as earthquakes. The Sales Tax Code is the collection of authorities that apply to a given customer and may include state taxes, city taxes, county taxes and other special assessments. Each of these components must be set up as a Sales Tax Authority before it can be included in a Sales Tax Code.

MEMO

DATE: January 1, 2006

Set up a standard Sales Tax of 7.25% to be collected for the Board of Equalization. You will need to set up a new vendor STA01 State Board of Equalization, P.O. Box 3822, Sacramento, CA 95814, Purchase Default 23100 Sales Tax Payable. This will also be your Sales Tax Payable G/L account. The State does not offer a discount on the payment of sales tax so change the terms to Net 30.

DO: Set up a Sales Tax Code to use with our customers

Close the Setup Guide

Select **Sales Tax Authorities** from the **Sales** button

In the **ID** field, enter CA-Sales

Tab to the **Description** field, enter California Sales Tax

Tab to the **Tax Payable To** field and using the magnifying glass, select New

In the **Vendor ID** field, enter STA01

Tab to the **Name** field, enter State Board of Equalization

Tab to or click in the **Address** field, **enter P.O. Box 3822**

Tab to the **City** field, enter Sacramento, tab again and enter CA, tab again and
    enter 95814

Click on the **Purchases Defaults** tab

Using the magnifying glass to the right of the **Purchase Acct:** field, select 23100
    Sales Tax Payable

Click **Save** and then **Close**

Using the magnifying glass to the right of the **Tax Payable to:** field, select STA01
    State Board of Equalization

Tab to the **Sales Tax Payable G/L Account:** field, select 23100 Sales Tax Payable

Tab to the **Single Tax Rate:** field, enter 7.25

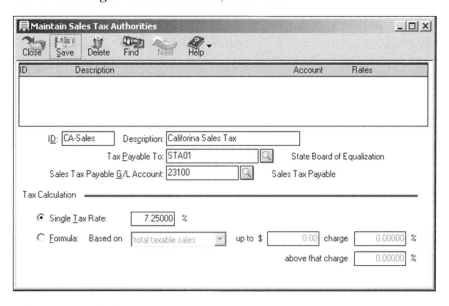

Click **Save** and then **Close**

Select **Sales Tax Codes** from the **Sales** button

In the **Sales Tax Code** field, enter CA Sa-1

Tab to the **Description** field, enter CA Sales Tax

Tab to the **ID** field, type C which will cause a list of all available authorities to be
    displayed (any letter would result in this list). Hit **Enter** to accept the
    highlighted authority. The rest of the row will fill in automatically.

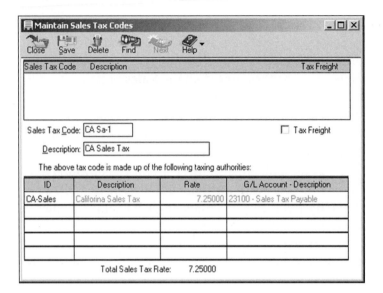

Click **Save** and then **Close**

ACCOUNTS RECEIVABLE SETUP

The Accounts Receivable section allows us to establish our customer defaults as well as enter our current customers and their beginning balances. When we set up defaults for customers, we are telling Peachtree what information to enter into various fields in the Customer Setup screen when we add new customers. It would be impossible to have defaults that would work with every customer. As such, we are able to change the default information in the Maintain Customer window when we are adding a customer. The defaults merely serve as a time saving tool when they can be used. In addition, Peachtree allows us to change defaults that have been set up regarding statements and invoices. This includes information on which customers to print invoices for and what messages to include on statements.

MEMO

DATE: January 1, 2006

Change the method of aging invoices to Invoice Date and the method of assigning deposit ID's to In Receipts.

DO: Using the Setup Guide, make the above modifications to the Customer Defaults
Select **Setup Guide** from the **Peachtree Today** window
Click on **Receivables** at the top of the window
Click on **Select Your Customers Defaults**
Click on the **Account Aging** tab

In the **Age Invoices by**: area, click the radio button for **Invoice date**

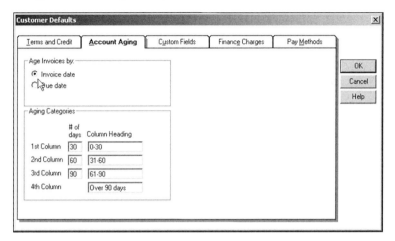

Click on the **Pay Methods** tab
In the **Assign Deposit Ticket ID** area, click the radio button for **In Receipts**

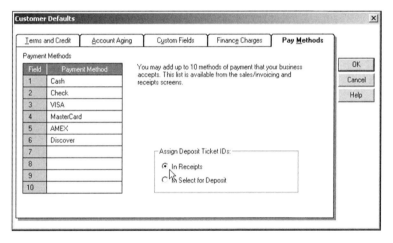

Click **OK**

MEMO

DATE: January 1, 2006

Add our current customers to Peachtree based on the attached list. All customers are taxable. Accept defaults for all information not given.

Customer ID	Customer Name	Address	Telephone
GOL01	Goldman, Barney	1980 A Street, Fairfield, CA 94533	707-555-3694
MIR01	Mirovich, Randolph	719 4th Street, Fairfield, CA 94533	707-555-5478
ROB01	Robinson, Yolanda	37601 State Street, Vacaville, CA 95383	707-555-2235
THA01	Thatcher, Rafael	2210 Columbia Street, Suisun, CA 94585	707-555-7632

DO: Using the Setup Guide, add the above customers

From the **Setup Guide**, click on **Set up Your Customers**

Enter the customers from the above list using the information provided and accepting defaults for any other items in the Setup window. Refer to Chapter 2 should you require a refresher in this process

Click **Close** after the last customer has been entered

Click **Yes** to mark this item as complete

MEMO

DATE: January 1, 2006

Add the following beginning balances to our current customers.

Customer Name	Invoice No.	Invoice Date	Amount
Goldman, Barney	4800	12/15/05	$ 563.27
Mirovich, Randolph	4907	12/27/05	$ 492.35
Robinson, Yolanda	5110	12/30/05	$234.89
Thatcher, Rafael	5112	12/31/05	$623.40

DO: Using the Setup Guide, add the invoices using the data provided

From the **Setup Guide**, click on **Enter Your Customer Beginning Balances**. You are presented with a list of customers

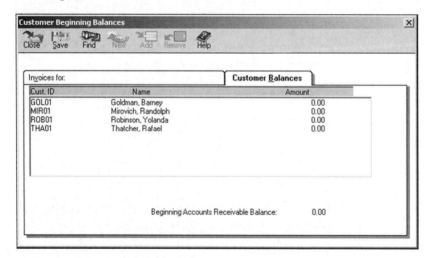

Double click on Goldman, Barney

Click in the first row of the **Invoice Number** column, enter 4800

Tab to the **Date** column, enter Dec 15, 2005

Tab to the **Amount** column, enter 563.27

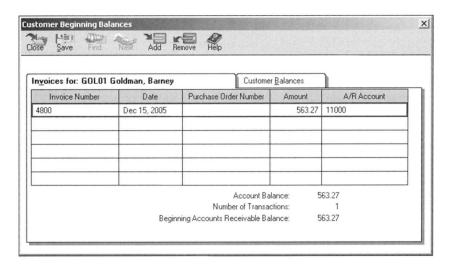

Click **Save**
Click on the **Customer Balances** tab to return to the customer list
Add the remaining three invoices following the same steps
Click **Close**
Click **Yes** to mark this item complete

PAYROLL SETUP

Setting up Payroll is the most complicated part of establishing a new company. Payroll must be flexible enough to accommodate a variety of needs and situations. In Peachtree® Complete Accounting 2006 the majority of the set up required for Payroll is accomplished through the use of a Payroll Setup Wizard. Selecting Employee Defaults from the Setup Guide will activate a Payroll Setup Wizard that will step you through the majority of items necessary to begin processing payroll. In addition, employees must be added and information adjusted from the defaults established in the Wizard. In addition, any existing Y-T-D balances as well as any carryovers for sick or vacation leave must be input prior to processing the first payroll.

MEMO

DATE: January 1, 2006

Setup Payroll Defaults. Use 3.5% as the Unemployment Percent for the Company. The company offers 80 hours per year vacation leave and 80 hours per year sick leave accrued each payroll period. Ike's Bikes offers Medical and Dental insurance to employees. Add these items to the Employee Defaults $75 for Medical and $35 for Dental. These amounts will accrue in account 24100 Employee Benefits Payable.

DO: Using the Setup Guide, set up the payroll
From the **Setup Guide**, click on the **Set Up Payroll** in the lower right hand corner.
Click on **Select Your Employee Defaults**.
You are presented with the **Initial Payroll Setup** opening screen

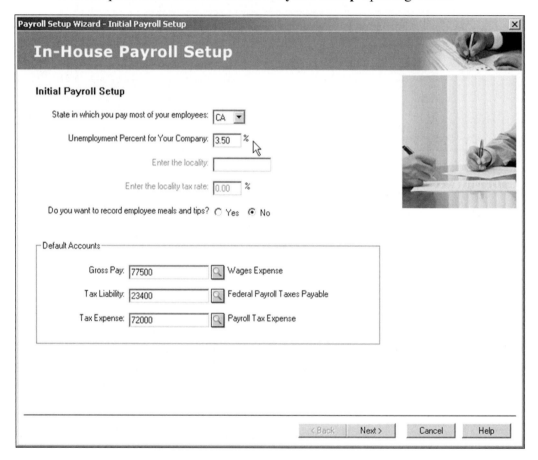

Confirm that the state is California (CA)
Enter 3.5 in the **Unemployment Percent for Your Company**
Note: The program has made certain assumptions regarding our **Default Accounts**
for payroll. Confirm that your defaults are as listed in the screenshot above.
Note that the program only allows us to choose one liability account for all of
our payroll liabilities. We could change the account for each payroll liability
when we set up the Payroll defaults in the next section however, the sample
company we have chosen does not have the same liability accounts that we
had with Brekners in chapter 8. Instead, we will allow all our liabilities to
accrue in account 23400 and determine the payment amount for each from
the Tax Liability report.
Click **Next**
You are presented with the **401(k) Setup** screen

Note: This screen allows us to set up the accounts for a 401(k) Retirement Plan
should the company offer one. It can accommodate both an employee
contribution only plan or a plan involving an employer match of employee
contributions. We will not be offering our employees a 401(k) plan and will
accept the default which is to not offer such a plan.

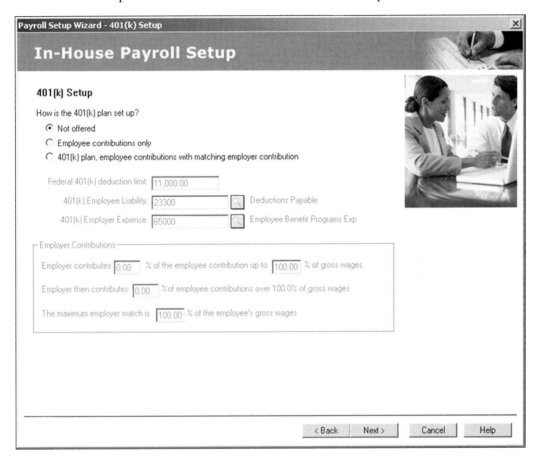

Click **Next**
You are presented with the **Vacation and Sick Time Tracking** screen
Click the radio button in Vacation Time Tracking **Accrues 0.00 hours each year**
Click in the **Number of hours to be accrued each year** field and enter 80.00
Click in the box next to **Remaining vacation hours carry over to the new year**
Click the radio button in Sick Time Tracking **Accrues 0.00 hours each year**
Click in the **Number of hours to be accrued each year** field and enter 80.00
Click in the box next to **Remaining sick hours carry over to the new year**

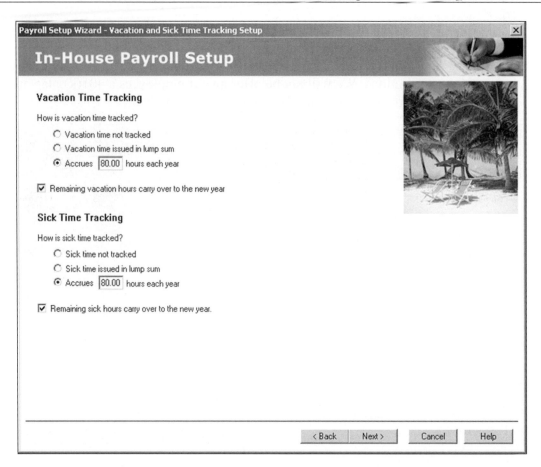

Note: Even though we have made the assumption that every employee is entitled to 80 hours of vacation each year, we can change that amount with each employee individually when he or she is entered. This holds true for Sick Leave as well.

Click **Next**

You are presented with the **Payroll Setup Complete** screen

Note: No input is required. This screen provides information on making changes after the process is completed if they are needed. It also contains a link to set up payroll direct deposit if your company so chooses.

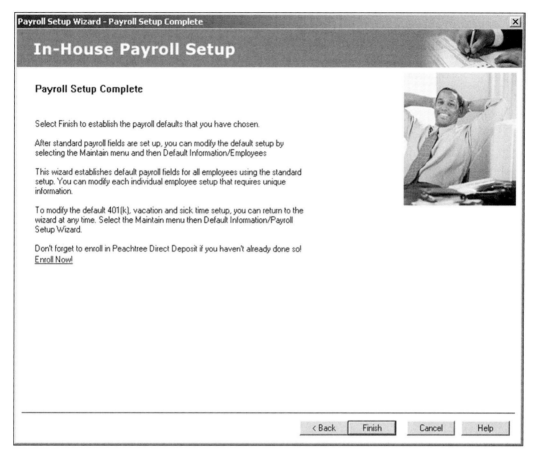

Click **Finish**

Click **Select Your Employee Defaults**

Note: All of the fields have been filled in automatically based on the information
furnished in the Payroll Wizard. Additional entries can be made in things
like Custom Fields for additional information or special withholdings that
were not set up during the Payroll Wizard process. We will need to add
deductions for our Medical and Dental insurance.

Click on the tab for **EmployEE Fields**

Using the scroll bar, move the cursor to the first available **Field Name** row, which
should be the row immediately following the **Sick_Rema** field and enter
Medical

Tab to the **G/L Account** column

Using the magnifying glass, select 24100 Employee Benefits Payable

Tab to the **Amount** column and enter -75.00

Click in the next available **Field Name** row and enter Dental

Tab to the **G/L Account** column

Using the magnifying glass, select 24100 Employee Benefits Payable

Tab to the **Amount** column and enter -35.00

Note: Even though we have set up default amounts for the Medical insurance and Dental insurance, most plans use different amounts depending on the employee's individual circumstances. These amounts can be changed individually in the Employee Setup screen. Note also that the sample company is using a single employee benefits liability account to maintain both the dental and the medical. As with the payroll tax liabilities discussed earlier, Peachtree uses reports to keep track of the amounts spent in each area rather than using a General Ledger account for this purpose. Be sure to enter the numbers as a negative value since this is a deduction. Note too that had we wished to use different liability accounts for our various taxes, we would change them here and in the **EmployER** Fields tab.

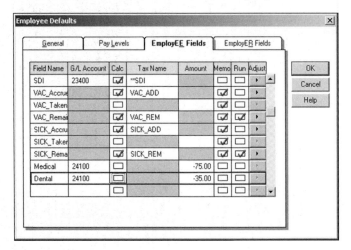

Click **OK** and then **Yes** to mark this item complete

MEMO

DATE: January 1, 2006

Add our existing employees to the Payroll Module. Employees will be paid weekly. All hourly employees work a standard 40-hour work week. Use their initials as their employee ID. Accept defaults for all fields that do not have specific information given.

Employee Name, Address and Telephone	Social Security #	Hire Date	Wages	Deductions and Insurance	
Mark Canfield 1077 Columbia Street Fairfield, CA 94533 Tel: 707-555-1232	100-55-2525	3/17/02	$39,000 Annual Salary, paid weekly	Medical $75 Dental $35	State and Federal: Married 4 allowances

Carrie Bernstein 751 7th Street Fairfield, CA 94533 Tel: 707-555-3654	100-55-3274	4/23/01	$26,000 Annual Salary, paid weekly	Medical $50 Dental $25	State and Federal: Single 0 allowances
Jimmy Hernandez 2985 A Street Vacaville, CA 94383 Tel: 707-555-9874	100-55-6961	6/30/03	$16.00 Hourly $24.00 Overtime	Medical $40 Dental $20	State and Federal: Married 2 allowances
Sally Richards 159 Ketter Drive Suisun, CA 94585 Tel: 707-555-8591	100-55-8723	5/2/01	$10.00 Hourly $15.00 Overtime		State and Federal: Married 1 allowance

DO: Using the Setup Guide, add the above employees

From the **Setup Guide** click on **Set up Your Employees**

Enter the employees from the above list using the information provided and accepting defaults for any other items in the Setup window. Refer to Chapter 8 should you require a refresher in this process

Note: Remember that to change Medical and Dental deduction amounts, you must first uncheck the Std column for that row.

Click **Close** after the last employee has been entered

Click **Yes** to mark this item complete

MEMO

DATE: January 1, 2006

Because we are converting to Peachtree at the start of a new payroll year, there are no Y-T-D balances to bring forward. There are however, accrued hours for sick and vacation leave that will carry over into the new year. Enter these balances furnished on the attached table.

Employee Name	Vacation Accrued	Sick Accrued
Mark Canfield	40	40
Carrie Bernstein	20	20
Jimmy Hernandez	50	40
Sally Richards	0	0

DO: Using the Setup Guide, add accrued Vacation/Sick hours using the data provided

From the **Setup Guide**, click on **Enter Your Employee Beginning Balances**.

You are presented with the Employee Beginning Balances window

In the **Employee ID** field, select MC Mark Canfield

Click in the **Dates:** row of column 1, and enter 1/1/06

Using the scroll bar, locate the **VAC_Accrue** and enter 40.00 in the first column

Using the scroll bar, locate the **SICK_Accrue** and enter 40.00 in the first column

Employee Beginning Balances							

Employee ID MC01   Mark Canfield

		1	2	3	4	5	
	Dates:	Jan 1, 2005					
	Payroll Field						Total
6	SDI	0.00	0.00	0.00	0.00	0.00	
7	VAC_Accrue	40.00	0.00	0.00	0.00	0.00	40.00
8	VAC_Taken	0.00	0.00	0.00	0.00	0.00	
9	VAC_Remain	0.00	0.00	0.00	0.00	0.00	
10	SICK_Accrue	40.00	0.00	0.00	0.00	0.00	40.00
11	SICK_Taken	0.00	0.00	0.00	0.00	0.00	

Net Check: 0.00   0.00   0.00   0.00   0.00

Click **Save**
Enter the balances for the remaining employees in the same manner
Click **Close** after the last employee balances have been entered
Click **Yes** to mark this item complete

INVENTORY ITEMS SETUP

The Inventory Items section allows us to set the defaults for our inventory item management as well as enter our current inventory. As with previous sections, we not only create the item list but we also enter the beginning balances. The first item in this section is the Inventory Defaults.

MEMO

DATE: January 1, 2006

Change the costing method for our Stock Item to Average and change our GL Sales account for our Non-stock Item to 40200 Sales-Services. Because the majority of our bikes will be picked up by the customers, switch Shipping fields 1 and 4 with each other so that field 1 reflects Cust. Pickup and field 4 reflects Airborne. Add "Comments" to Custom field 5. Change the name for Price Level 1 to Regular Price and Price Level 2 to Sale Price.

DO: Using the Setup Guide, make the above modifications to the Inventory Defaults
From the **Setup Guide**, click on the **Set up Inventory** in the lower right hand corner.
Click on **Select Your Inventory Defaults**
Click on the **GL Accts/Costing** tab

In the rows for **Stock Item** and **Master Stock Item**, click in the **Costing** column. Using the drop down arrow, select Average

In the row **Non-stock item**, click in the **GL Sales/Inc** column. Using the magnifying glass, select 40200 Sales-Services

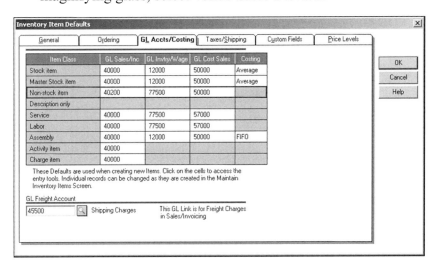

Click on the **Taxes/Shipping** tab

Click on **Field 1** in the **Ship Methods** area and enter Cust. Pickup

Click in **Field 4** in the **Ship Methods** area and enter Airborne

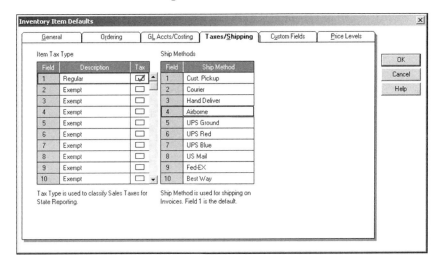

Click on the **Custom Fields** tab

Confirm that there is a checkmark in the **Enabled** box for **Field 4**

Click in **Field Label 4** and enter Comments

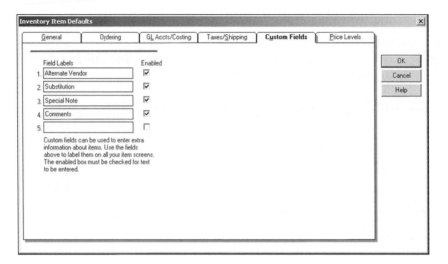

Click on the **Price Levels** tab

Click in the **Level Name** column for **Price Level 1** and enter Regular Price

Click in the **Level Name** column for **Price Level 2** and enter Sale Price

Note: Each level field has available to it a default calculation. This would enable us, as an example, to have the Sale Price calculated as 20% less than the Regular Price. If no formula is entered, Peachtree will expect us to enter the prices manually when we enter the inventory items.

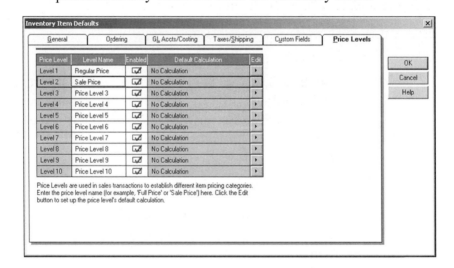

Click **OK**

MEMO

DATE: January 1, 2006

Add our current inventory balances to Peachtree based on the attached list.

Item ID	Description	Item Class	Regular Price	Sale Price	Unit	Min. Stock	Reorder Quantity	Preferred Vendor ID
BIK01	Bike, BMX 4400	Stock	$ 212.00	$ 169.60	EA	6	3	BMX01
BIK02	Bike, BMX Cross Country	Stock	$ 262.00	$ 209.60	EA	8	4	BMX01
BIK03	Bike, Schwinn 2034	Stock	$ 198.00	$ 158.40	EA	6	3	SCH01
BIK04	Bike, Schwinn Dirt	Stock	$ 238.00	$ 190.40	EA	8	4	SCH01
BIK05	Bike, Schwinn Competition	Stock	$ 462.00	$ 369.60	EA	4	2	SCH01
HEL01	Helmet, BMX Bike	Stock	$ 25.95	$ 20.76	EA	16	12	BIK01
HEL02	Helmet, CRU Deluxe	Stock	$ 45.95	$ 36.76	EA	24	12	BIK01
TIR01	Tire, Wilson 25"	Stock	$ 28.95	$ 23.16	EA	12	6	BIK01
TIR02	Tire, Wilson 30"	Stock	$ 35.95	$ 28.76	EA	12	6	BIK01
SEA01	Seat, ComfortSeat 45	Stock	$ 56.95	$ 45.56	EA	8	4	BIK01
GEA01	Gears, TrueShift	Stock	$ 53.00	$ 42.40	EA	6	3	BIK01
REP01	Repair, First Hour	Non-stock	$ 35.00	--	--	--	--	--
REP02	Repair, Additional Hour	Non-stock	$ 25.00	--	--	--	--	--
SER01	Service, Assemble Bike	Non-stock	$ 50.00	--	--	--	--	--
SER02	Service, PM	Non-stock	$ 75.00	--	--	--	--	--

DO: Using the Setup Guide, add the inventory from the information provided
From the **Setup Guide**, click on **Set up Your Inventory Items**
You are presented with the Maintain Inventory Items window. Enter the above inventory as previously instructed. Accept Peachtree defaults for information not furnished.
When the inventory items have bee added, click **Close** and mark the Guide complete

Item ID	Quantity	Cost
BIK01	9	95.40
BIK02	12	117.90
BIK03	16	89.10
BIK04	12	107.10
BIK05	7	207.90
GEA01	18	23.85
HEL01	36	11.68
HEL02	18	20.68
SEA01	19	25.63
TIR01	12	13.03
TIR02	9	16.18

DO: Using the Setup Guide, add the items using the data provided in the table from the previous page

From the **Setup Guide**, click on **Enter Your Inventory Beginning Balances**. You are presented with a list of items

Click on the first item, BIK01

Click in the **Quantity** field and enter 9.00

Tab to the **Unit Cost** field, enter 95.40

Tab twice and you are brought to the next item

Note: At the same time, Peachtree is calculating the total for that particular item and enters it for you.

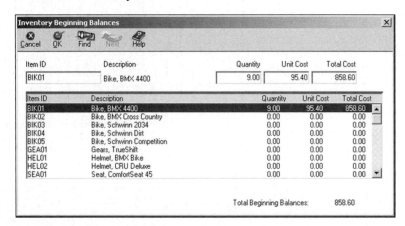

Tab again to be brought to the **Quantity** field and enter 12.00

Tab to the **Unit Cost** field, enter 117.90

Repeat for all items in the inventory list provided

Click **OK**

Click **Yes** to mark this item complete

JOBS SETUP

Since we will not be using the Job Costing Module there is no need to set up the defaults in this area. As such, we are finished setting up our company.

PRINT LISTS AND REPORTS

From the Reports feature, print the following lists and reports:

Chart of Accounts

Customer List

Vendor List

Employee List

Inventory Item List

General Ledger Trial Balance

Inventory Valuation Report

BACKUP

Whenever an important work session is complete, you should always back up your data. If your data disk is damaged or an error is discovered at a later time, the backup disk may be restored and the information used for recording transactions. No matter what type of business, the backup procedure remains the same. In addition, it is always wise to make a duplicate of your data disk just in case the disk is damaged in some way.

 DO: Follow the instructions given in previous chapters to back up data for Ike's Bikes.

SUMMARY

In this chapter a new company was created using the Set up a new company feature provided by Peachtree® Complete Accounting 2006. Once the automatic portion of the process was complete, the rest of the required information was entered through a company Setup Guide. The company Chart of Accounts/General Ledger was customized. Detailed information was given for customers and vendors. Employee defaults were created, and employees were added. Employee sick and vacation balances were brought forward. Inventory items were set up and beginning balances entered. Lists and reports were printed.

END-OF-CHAPTER QUESTIONS

TRUE/FALSE

ANSWER THE FOLLOWING QUESTIONS IN THE SPACE PROVIDED BEFORE THE QUESTION NUMBER.

_____ 1. You must return to the Setup Guide to add additional customers, and vendors.

_____ 2. A company may be created without using the Set up a new company feature.

_____ 3. Vacation leave and Sick leave can be carried over from one year to the next.

_____ 4. Default setups tell Peachtree how to fill in fields in the absence of specific input.

_____ 5. Companies should be started or converted to Peachtree at the start of a fiscal year.

_____ 6. The Setup process allows you to input only the balances for all asset accounts.

_____ 7. Peachtree® Complete Accounting 2006 has sales tax tables built into it and requires only that you specify in what state you live.

_____ 8. When using one of Peachtree's sample companies, a typical and workable Chart of Accounts is created automatically.

_____ 9. Once defaults for Accounts Receivable have been established, you may not change this information for individual customers.

_____ 10. A Payroll Wizard assists the user in setting up Payroll Defaults.

MULTIPLE CHOICE

WRITE THE LETTER OF THE CORRECT ANSWER IN THE SPACE PROVIDED BEFORE THE QUESTION NUMBER.

_____ 1. When setting up each area of Peachtree, one must first set up the ___ .
   A. beginning balances
   B. items
   C. defaults
   D. total value

_____ 2. To assist you in setting up a new company, Peachtree provides a ___ .
   A. Preference List
   B. Menu
   C. Setup Guide
   D. Details List

_____ 3. Once Vendor Defaults have been established, the next step would be to ___.
   A. enter the vendors
   B. enter the beginning balances
   C. reenter each vendor invoice separately
   D. pay off all vendors to avoid entering them in the system

_____ 4. The correct sequence in establishing a new tax code is ___.
   A. Sales Tax Vendor, Sales Tax Code, Sales Tax Authority
   B. Sales Tax Code, Sales Tax Authority, Sales Tax Vendor
   C. Sales Tax Authority, Sales Tax Vendor, Sales Tax Code
   D. none of the above

_____ 5. When setting up payroll defaults, sick and vacation leave can be set up to accrue ___ .
   A. one lump sum each year
   B. each pay cycle
   C. both of the above
   D. neither of the above

_____ 6. The mechanism for Peachtree to calculate Payroll taxes for the employer is established in the ___ tab.
   A. Custom Fields
   B. Pay Info
   C. EmployEE Fields
   D. EmployER Fields

_____ 7. Inventory costing options in Peachtree consist of ___ .
  A. Standard, FIFO and Average
  B. FIFO, LIFO and Average
  C. FIFO, Average and WACM
  D. none of the above

_____ 8. Peachtree Complete will allow you to set up ___ shipping methods.
  A. one
  B. six
  C. ten
  D. as many as you need

_____ 9. The unemployment percent for the company is entered through the ___.
  A. Employee Default window
  B. Maintain Employees/Sales Reps window
  C. Payroll Entry window
  D. Payroll Setup Wizard

_____ 10. The Setup Guide is broken into ___ major areas.
  A. four
  B. six
  C. eight
  D. nineteen

FILL-IN

IN THE SPACE PROVIDED, WRITE THE ANSWER THAT MOST APPROPRIATELY COMPLETES THE SENTENCE.

1. After the Inventory defaults and the Inventory Items List have been established, all existing balances are placed into the _____ .

2. Year-to-date information is inserted into the _____ area of the Setup Guide.

3. Information which is used for the majority of our accounts, customers, vendors, employees is entered through the _____ section of each major area.

4. Different names for multiple prices on Inventory Items can be entered through the _____ tab of the Inventory Item Default window.

5. The Chart of Accounts forms the basis for the _____.

SHORT ESSAY

List the six sections in the Setup Guide. Describe the portion of the company setup completed in each section.

_____

_____

_____

_____

_____

_____

NAME _____

TRANSMITTAL

CHAPTER 9: IKE'S BIKES

Attach the following documents and reports:

- ☐ Chart of Accounts
- ☐ Customer List
- ☐ Vendor List
- ☐ Employee List
- ☐ Item List
- ☐ General Ledger Trial Balance
- ☐ Inventory Valuation Report

END-OF-CHAPTER PROBLEM

GOTTA DANCE

Gotta Dance is a fictitious company that sells dance shoes, clothing and accessories. Gotta Dance is located in San Francisco, California, and is a sole proprietorship owned by Heather Nicolae. Ms. Nicolae is involved in all aspects of the business. Gotta Dance has a full-time employee who is paid a salary—Ms. Rebecca Lacy, who manages the store, is responsible for the all the employees, and keeps the books. There is one full-time hourly employee, who works in the shop, Ms. Justine Plauski.

CREATE A NEW COMPANY

Use the Set up a new company feature to create a new company.

Gotta Dance--Your Initials is used for the Company Name, address: 550 Geary Street, San Francisco, CA 94102, telephone number 415-555-1212, fax number 415-555-1213, email address gottadance@abs.com. Federal Employer ID 94-2837205, State Employer ID 456-22-1346, tax year and fiscal year both begin in January 2006. The business type is a sole proprietorship.

The following includes information that will help you answer some of the Setup questions: Gotta Dance is a retail business. It does have an inventory. The file for the company should be **Gotta Dance–Your Initials**. Create the company using the extensive Chart of Accounts for the sample Retail Company, the Accrual method of accounting, and Real Time posting. The company start date is 01/01/06 and will use 12 monthly accounting periods. The company does collect sales tax for California at the rate of 7.25%. The California sales tax is payable to the State Board of Equalization. As previously stated, there are two employees. The Peachtree® Complete Accounting 2006 payroll feature will be used. The company will not be using Job Costing. Gotta Dance does not have any service items, non-inventory part items, or other charge items. It uses Average Costing for its inventory management. Accept the defaults provided by Peachtree for vendor and customer terms and credit limits.

CHART OF ACCOUNTS

Use the Chart of Accounts that was automatically created during the Set up process and make the following deletions and changes:

Delete the following accounts:
  11100 Accounts Receivable Service
  15500 Building

15600 Building Improvements

16900 Land

17500 Accum. Depreciation - Building

17600 Accum. Depreciation - Bldg Imp.

19100 Organization Costs

19150 Accum. Amortiz. - Org. Cost

24900 Suspense-Clearing Account

40200 Sales Service

40400 Sales-Clearance

60500 Amortization Expense

Change the following accounts:

12000 Product Inventory to 12000 Merchandise Inventory

23000 Accrued Expenses to 23000 Accrued Expenses Payable

39006 Owner's Contribution to 39006 Heather Nicolae, Capital

39007 Owner's Draw to 39007 Heather Nicolae, Drawing

GENERAL LEDGER

Enter the following beginning General Ledger Balances from 12/1/05 to 12/31/05 into Peachtree® Complete Accounting 2006.

Account ID	Account Description	Debit	Credit
10000	Petty Cash	$75.00	
10100	Cash on Hand	$3,619.00	
10200	Regular Checking Account	$487.00	
10400	Savings Account	$15,000.00	
11000	Accounts Receivable	$922.60	
11500	Allowance for Doubtful Account		$79.00
12000	Merchandise Inventory	$9,015.02	
12050	Cleaning Supplies Inventory	$418.00	
12100	Office Supplies Inventory	$623.00	
14700	Other Current Assets	$987.00	
15000	Furniture and Fixtures	$4,200.00	
15100	Equipment	$1,600.00	
17000	Accum. Depreciation - Furniture		$1,360.00
17100	Accum. Depreciation - Equipment		$485.00
20000	Accounts Payable		$1,316.24
23100	Sales Tax Payable		$219.00
23400	Federal Payroll Taxes Payable		$316.00
23500	FUTA Tax Payable		$52.00
23600	State Payroll Taxes Payable		$113.00
23700	SUTA Payable		$48.00
39006	Heather Nicolae, Capital		$32,958.38

VENDOR LIST

Using the Setup Guide, enter the following Vendor List and balances. Confirm the Vendor Default Credit Limit as 5,000.00. Change the aging default to Invoice Date instead of Due Date. Add a new custom field called Special Terms.

Vendor ID	Vendor Name	Address	Telephone/ Fax	Purchase Default	Vendor Terms	Ship Via
SHO01	Shoes for Dance	123 7th Street San Francisco, CA 94104	415-555-2788	12000	2% 10 Net 30	Best Way
DAN01	DanceWear	785 Market Street San Francisco, CA 94103	415-555-3184 415-555-4813	12000	2% 10 Net 30	Best Way
TEL01	TeleComm	1095 8th Street San Francisco, CA 94103	415-555-5759	76000	Net 15 days	Best Way
BAY01	Bay Properties	20854 Oak Drive Marin, CA 95212	415-555-8877 415-555-8879	74000	Net 30 days	Best Way
POW01	PowerTech Co.	302 Second Street San Francisco, CA 94104	415-555-8722	78000	Net 30 days	Best Way
WAT01	WaterWorks	P.O. Box 2390 San Francisco, CA 94103	415-555-4238	78000	Net 10 days	Best Way

Vendor Name	Invoice No.	Invoice Date	Amount
Shoes for Dance	00-93912	12/15/05	$ 563.89
DanceWear	IN-9874	12/28/05	$ 752.35

TAX TABLES

Set up a standard Sales Tax of 7.25% to be collected for the Board of Equalization. You will need to set up a new vendor for the Tax Payable to STA01 State Board of Equalization, P.O. Box 3822, Sacramento, CA 95814, Purchase Default 23100 Sales Tax Payable. This will also be your Sales Tax Payable G/L account.

ACCOUNT RECEIVABLE

Using the Setup Guide, change the method of aging invoices to Invoice Date and the method of assigning deposit ID's to In Receipts. Add our current customers and their balances to Peachtree based on the tables below. All customers are taxable. Accept defaults for all information not given. Note that Franciscan Recreation is a non-profit organization. They will get level 2 pricing (Sales Price) but will still pay California sales tax.

Customer ID	Customer Name	Address	Telephone
MAR01	Market Street Dance	725 Market Street, San Francisco, CA 94102	415-555-8762
STU01	Studio 59	203A 59th Street, San Francisco, CA 94102	415-555-8283
FRA01	Franciscan Recreation	892 Alameda Aveune, San Francisco, CA 94104	415-555-0281

Customer ID	Invoice No.	Invoice Date	Amount
Market Street Dance	83738	12/14/05	$ 95.65
Studio 59	2382-392	12/20/05	$ 236.95
Franciscan Recreation	IN-208472	12/30/05	$ 590.00

PAYROLL

Using the Setup Guide, set up Payroll Defaults. Use 3.5% as the Unemployment Percent for the Company. The company offers 80 hours per year vacation leave and 40 hours per year sick leave accrued each payroll period. Gotta Dance offers Medical and Dental insurance to employees. Add these items to the Employee Defaults $55 for Medical and $25 for Dental. These amounts will accrue in account 24100 Employee Benefits Payable.

Add our existing employees to the Payroll Module. Employees will be paid weekly. All hourly employees work a standard 40-hour work-week. Use their initials as their employee ID. Accept defaults for all fields that do not have specific information given.

Employee Name, Address and Telephone	Social Security #	Hire Date	Wages	Deductions and Insurance	
Rebecca Lacy 177 Post Street San Francisco, CA 94101 Tel: 415-555-1222	100-55-5259	2/17/02	$32,500 Annual Salary, paid weekly	Medical $40 Dental $15	State and Federal: Single 1 allowances
Justine Plauski 833 Pine Street San Francisco, CA 94102 Tel: 415-555-7862	555-10-6456	4/3/03	$10.00 Hourly $15.00 Overtime	Medical $55 Dental $25	State and Federal: Married 3 allowances

Employee Name	Vacation Accrued	Sick Accrued
Rebecca Lacy	40	40
Justine Plauski	20	20

ITEMS LIST

Using the Setup Guide, enter the following Inventory Items List and balances. Change the costing method for our Stock Item to Average. Because the majority of our business is from walk in customers purchasing merchandise that will leave with them, switch Shipping fields 1 and 4 with each other so that field 1 reflects Cust. Pickup and field 4 reflects Airborne. Add "Comments" to Custom field 5. Change the name for Price Level 1 to Regular Price and Price Level 2 to Sale Price.

Item ID	Description	Regular Price	Sale Price	Unit	Minimum Stock	Reorder Quantity	Preferred Vendor
BAL01	Ballet Shoes, Grishko	$35.00	$32.31	PAIR	10	25	SHO01
BAL02	Ballet Shoes, Gaynor Minden	$30.00	$27.69	PAIR	10	25	SHO01
BAL03	Ballet Shoes, Capezio	$24.50	$22.62	PAIR	15	35	SHO01
CHA01	Character Shoes, Capezio	$39.99	$36.91	PAIR	8	20	SHO01

Item ID	Description	Regular Price	Sale Price	Unit	Minimum Stock	Reorder Quantity	Preferred Vendor
CHA02	Character Shoes, Gaynor Minden	$36.99	$34.14	PAIR	10	25	SHO01
ELA01	Elastic, Ballet Pink	$3.50	$3.23	PAIR	25	50	SHO01
JAZ01	Jazz Shoes, Capezio	$39.99	$36.91	PAIR	10	20	SHO01
JAZ02	Jazz Shoes, Capezio Sneakers	$42.00	$38.77	PAIR	10	20	SHO01
JAZ03	Jazz Shoes, Botch	$34.50	$31.85	PAIR	18	30	SHO01
LEG01	Leggings, Warm Ups	$25.00	$23.08	PAIR	12	25	DAN01
LEO01	Leotard, Long Sleeve	$30.00	$27.69	EACH	12	25	DAN01
LEO02	Leotard, Tank Top	$28.00	$25.85	EACH	12	25	DAN01
LEO03	Leotard, Spaghetti Strap	$25.00	$23.08	EACH	7	15	DAN01
POI01	Pointe Shoes, Grishko	$65.00	$60.00	PAIR	12	25	SHO01
POI02	Pointe Shoes, Botch	$63.00	$58.15	PAIR	7	15	SHO01
POI03	Pointe Shoes, Gaynor Minden	$60.00	$55.38	PAIR	12	25	SHO01
RIB01	Ribbon, Ballet Pink	$5.00	$4.62	PAIR	25	50	SHO01
TAP01	Tap Shoes, Capezio	$35.00	$32.31	PAIR	10	20	SHO01
TAP02	Tap Shoes, Botch	$29.99	$27.68	PAIR	7	15	SHO01
TIG01	Tights, Footed	$10.50	$9.69	PAIR	15	30	DAN01
TIG02	Tights, Stirrup	$12.00	$11.08	PAIR	15	30	DAN01
TOE01	Toe Pads, Lambswool	$12.00	$11.08	PAIR	10	20	DAN01
TOE02	Toe Pads, Ouch Pouch	$19.99	$18.45	PAIR	10	20	DAN01

Item ID	Quantity	Cost
BAL01	12	$26.92
BAL02	10	$23.08
BAL03	8	$18.85
CHA01	15	$30.76
CHA02	20	$28.45
ELA01	42	$2.69
JAZ01	15	$30.76
JAZ02	12	$32.31
JAZ03	20	$26.54
LEG01	20	$19.23
LEO01	18	$23.08
LEO02	14	$21.54
LEO03	12	$19.23
POI01	18	$50.00
POI02	13	$48.46
POI03	20	$46.15
RIB01	40	$3.85
TAP01	28	$26.92
TAP02	21	$23.07
TIG01	17	$8.08
TIG02	25	$9.23
TOE01	12	$9.23
TOE02	18	$15.38

PRINT LISTS AND REPORTS

Print the following reports:
    Chart of Accounts
    Customer List
    Vendor List
    Employee List
    Item List
    General Ledger Trial Balance
    Inventory Valuation Report

NAME _____

TRANSMITTAL

CHAPTER 9: GOTTA DANCE

Attach the following documents and reports:

- ☐ Chart of Accounts
- ☐ Customer List
- ☐ Vendor List
- ☐ Employee List
- ☐ Inventory Item List
- ☐ General Ledger Trial Balance
- ☐ Inventory Valuation Report

End Of Section 3—
The Paint Can Practice Set:
Merchandising Business

The following is a comprehensive practice set combining all the elements of Peachtree® Complete Accounting 2006 studied in the second section of the text. In this practice set you will keep the books for a company for the month of January 2006. Entries will be made to record invoices, receipt of payments on account, cash sales, credit card sales, receipt and payment of bills, orders and receipts of merchandise, credit memos for invoices and bills, payment of employees and sales tax payments. Account names will be added, changed, deleted, and made inactive. Customer, vendor, and employee names will be added to the appropriate lists. Reports will be prepared to analyze accounts receivables, sales, accounts payable, cash receipts, and inventory items ordered. Formal reports including the General Ledger Trial Balance, Standard Income Statement, and Standard Balance Sheet will be prepared. Adjusting entries for depreciation, supplies used, insurance expired, and automatic payments will be recorded. The bank reconciliation will be prepared. The owner's Drawing account will be closed and the period will be advanced.

THE PAINT CAN

Located in Sacramento, California, The Paint Can is a specialty paint store that sells paints and painting supplies. Paint is sold in a base color by type and size. After purchasing the desired type and size, colorant is added to achieve the customer's desired color. The Paint Can is a sole proprietorship owned by Edward Kramer. Mr. Kramer does all the purchasing and is involved in all aspects of the business. The Paint Can has a full-time employee, Mr. Alan Tremain, who is paid a salary and manages the store. The store is currently advertising for a part-time stock clerk who will maintain the stock room and store shelves.

CREATE A NEW COMAPANY

Use the Set up a new company feature to create a new company.

The Paint Can--Your Initials is used for the Company Name, Address: 1055 Front Street, Sacramento, CA 95814; Telephone Number: 916-555-8272, Fax Number: 916-555-8274; Business Type: Sole Proprietorship; Federal Employer ID: 84-2837436, State Employer ID: 466-52-1446; tax year and fiscal year both begin in January 2006.

The following includes information that will help you answer some of the Setup questions: The Paint Can is a retail business requiring an extensive Chart of Accounts. It does have an inventory. The file for the company should be **The Paint Can–Your Initials**. Base the company of a sample company using the Accrual method of accounting and Real Time posting. The company does collect sales tax for California at the rate of 7.25%. The California sales tax is payable to the State Board of Equalization. As previously stated, there is one employee. The Peachtree® Complete Accounting 2006 payroll feature will be used. The company will not be using Job Costing. The company start date is 01/01/06 and will use 12 monthly accounting periods. The Paint Can does not have any service items, non-inventory part items, or other charge items. Accept the defaults provided by Peachtree for vendor and customer terms and credit limits.

CHART OF ACCOUNTS

Use the Chart of Accounts that was automatically created during the Set up process and make the following deletions and changes:

Delete the following accounts:

  10300 Payroll Checking Account
  11100 Accounts Receivable Service
  15500 Building
  15600 Building Improvements
  16900 Land
  17500 Accum. Depreciation - Building
  17600 Accum. Depreciation - Bldg Imp.
  19100 Organization Costs
  19150 Accum. Amortiz. - Org. Cost
  24900 Suspense-Clearing Account
  40200 Sales Service
  40400 Sales-Clearance
  60500 Amortization Expense

Change the following accounts:

  10100 Cash on Hand to Payroll Checking Account
  12000 Product Inventory to 12000 Merchandise Inventory
  23000 Accrued Expenses to 23000 Accrued Expenses Payable
  39006 Owner's Contribution to 39006 Edward Kramer, Capital
  39007 Owner's Draw to 39007 Edward Kramer, Drawing

GENERAL LEDGER

Enter the following beginning General Ledger Balances into Peachtree® Complete Accounting 2006.

Account ID	Account Description	Debit	Credit
10000	Petty Cash	$50.00	
10200	Regular Checking Account	$15,298.00	
10400	Savings Account	$26,450.00	
11000	Accounts Receivable	$923.30	

Account ID	Account Description	Debit	Credit
11500	Allowance for Doubtful Account		$64.35
12000	Merchandise Inventory	$3,702.01	
12050	Cleaning Supplies Inventory	$250.00	
12100	Office Supplies Inventory	$459.23	
14700	Other Current Assets	$892.00	
15000	Furniture and Fixtures	$3,500.00	
15100	Equipment	$1,200.00	
17000	Accum. Depreciation - Furniture		$623.00
17100	Accum. Depreciation - Equipment		$253.00
20000	Accounts Payable		$922.60
39005	Retained Earnings		$50,861.59

As previously discussed in Chapter 7, Peachtree closes expenses and revenues to the Retained Earnings account at year's end. In order to allow you practice in transferring this balance to the Capital account, we have left the year 2005's net income in the retained earnings account instead of moving it to the Capital account. You will be accomplishing this later in the practice set.

VENDOR LIST

Using the Setup Checklist, enter the following Vendor List and balances. Change the Vendor Default Credit Limit to 10,000.00. Change the aging default to Invoice Date instead of Due Date. Add a new custom field called Holiday Terms.

Vendor ID	Vendor Name	Address	Telephone/ Fax	Expense Default	Vendor Terms	Ship Via
BES01	BestBrand Manufacturing	559 4th Street, Sacramento, CA 95814	916-555-2788	12000	2% 10 Net 30	Best Way
SUP01	Supply King	3908 Sutter Mill Road Sacramento, CA 95814	916-555-3827 916-555-3828	12000	2% 10 Net 30	Best Way
TEL01	TelCom Services	P.O. Box 20842 Sacramento, CA 95814	916-555-4949	76000	Net 15 days	Best Way
JAC01	Jackson Realty	2348 8th Street Sacramento, CA 95814	916-555-3224 916-555-7932	74000	Net 30 days	Best Way
GAS01	Gas & Electric Co.	2785 Market Street Sacramento, CA 95814	916-555-6523	78000	Net 10 days	Best Way
CAW01	CA Water Co.	P.O. Box 38282 Sacramento, CA 95814	916-555-2726	78000	Net 10 days	Best Way

Vendor Name	Invoice No.	Invoice Date	Amount
BestBrand Manufacturing	64325	12/22/05	$ 398.85
Supply King	72-643-3	12/30/05	$ 523.75

TAX TABLES

Set up a standard Sales Tax of 7.25% to be collected for the Board of Equalization. You will need to set up a new vendor STA01 State Board of Equalization, P.O. Box 3822, Sacramento, CA 95814, Expense Default 23100 Sales Tax Payable. This will also be your Sales Tax Payable G/L account.

ACCOUNT RECEIVABLE

Using the Setup Checklist, change the method of aging invoices to Invoice Date and the method of assigning deposit ID's to In Receipts. Additionally, change the Payment Method list to the following:

> Cash/Check
> VISA
> Mastercard
> AMEX
> Discover

Add our current customers and their balances to Peachtree based on the tables below. All customers are taxable. Accept defaults for all information not given. Note that Harold's Construction is in the trade and is entitled to a trade discount. They will get level 2 pricing but will still pay California sales tax. All customers will pick up their own paint.

Customer ID	Customer Name	Address	Telephone
ARN01	Arnold's Custom Painting	785 Harvard Street, Sacramento, CA 95814	916-555-8752
NEL01	Nelson, Loreen	8025 Richmond Avenue, Sacramento, CA 95814	916-555-2264
STE01	Stein, Victor	6784 16th Street, Sacramento, CA 95814	916-555-6482
HAR01	Harold's Construction	239 Sutter Mill Road, Sacramento, CA 95814	916-555-8328

Customer ID	Invoice No.	Invoice Date	Amount
Arnold's Custom Painting	950	12/18/05	$ 85.35
Stein, Victor	8764	12/29/05	$ 252.95
Harold's Construction	00-2397	12/30/05	$ 585.00

PAYROLL

Using the Setup Checklist, set up Payroll Defaults. Use 4.1% as the Unemployment Percent for the Company. The company offers 80 hours per year vacation leave and 40 hours per year sick leave accrued each payroll period and carried over annually. The Paint Can offers Medical and Dental insurance to its employees. Add these items to the Employee Defaults $95 for Medical and $45 for Dental. These amounts will accrue in account 24100 Employee Benefits Payable. The Paint Can also chooses to use the payroll liability accounts available to it in its chart of accounts. Make the following changes to account numbers in both the **EmployEE** and the **EmployER** tabs.

EmployEE tab Account Name	From	To
State	23400	23600
SDI	23400	23700
EmployER tab Account Name	From	To
FUTA_ER	23400	23500
SUI_ER	23400	23700
SETT_ER	23400	23700

Add our existing employees to the Payroll Module. Employees will be paid bi-weekly. All employees work a standard 40-hour work-week. Use their initials as their employee ID. Accept defaults for all fields that do not have specific information given.

Employee Name, Address and Telephone	Social Security #	Hire Date	Wages	Deductions and Insurance	
Alan Tremain 1777 Watt Avenue Sacramento, CA 95814 916-555-1382	100-55-5244	2/15/03	$26,000 Annual Salary	Dental $45 Medical $95	State and Federal: Married 1 allowances

Employee Name	Vacation Accrued	Sick Accrued
Alan Tremain	40	30

ITEMS LIST

Using the Setup Checklist, enter the following Inventory Items List and balances. Change the costing method for our Stock Item to Average. Because the majority of our business is from walk in customers purchasing merchandise that will leave with them, switch Shipping fields 1 and 4 with each other so that field 1 reflects Cust. Pickup and field 4 reflects Airborne. Add "Comments" to Custom field 5. Change the name for Price Level 1 to Regular Price and Price Level 2 to Sale Price.

Item ID	Description	Regular Price	Sale Price	Unit	Minimum Stock	Reorder Quantity	Preferred Vendor
DRO01	Dropcloth	$4.20	$3.40	EACH	25	50	SUP01
FLA01	Flat, BestBrand Int - Gal	$26.30	$21.10	GALLON	7	15	BES01
FLA02	Flat, BestBrand Int - Qt	$12.00	$9.60	QUART	7	15	BES01
FLA03	Flat, BestBrand Int - Pt	$7.80	$6.30	PINT	5	10	BES01
FLA04	Flat, BestBrand Ext - Gal	$27.50	$22.00	GALLON	7	15	BES01
FLA05	Flat, BestBrand Ext - Qt	$11.40	$9.20	QUART	7	15	BES01
GLO01	Gloss, BestBrand Int - Gal	$31.00	$24.80	GALLON	8	20	BES01
GLO02	Gloss, BestBrand Int - Qt	$12.00	$9.60	QUART	8	20	BES01
GLO03	Gloss, BestBrand Int - Pt	$7.20	$5.80	PINT	6	12	BES01
GLO04	Gloss, BestBrand Ext - Gal	$33.40	$26.80	GALLON	8	20	BES01
GLO05	Gloss, BestBrand Ext - Qt	$15.50	$12.40	QUART	8	20	BES01

Item ID	Description	Regular Price	Sale Price	Unit	Minimum Stock	Reorder Quantity	Preferred Vendor
PAI01	Paintbrush, 4"	$10.20	$8.20	EACH	12	25	SUP01
PAI02	Paintbrush, 3"	$5.40	$4.40	EACH	12	25	SUP01
PAI03	Paintbrush, 2"	$5.40	$4.40	EACH	7	15	SUP01
PAI04	Paintbrush, 1"	$3.60	$2.90	EACH	7	15	SUP01
ROL01	Roller, Heavy Nap 8"	$4.80	$3.90	EACH	12	25	SUP01
ROL02	Roller, Medium Nap 8"	$4.70	$3.80	EACH	12	25	SUP01
ROL03	Roller, Low Nap 8"	$4.60	$3.70	EACH	7	15	SUP01
ROL04	Roller, Medium Nap 4"	$2.30	$1.90	EACH	7	15	SUP01
ROL05	Roller, Low Nap 4"	$2.20	$1.80	EACH	7	15	SUP01
ROL06	Roller, Corner and Edge Set	$7.50	$6.00	SET	10	20	SUP01
ROL07	Roller Handle, for 8" Roller	$6.00	$4.80	EACH	15	30	SUP01
SEM01	Semigloss, BestBrand Int - Gal	$27.50	$22.00	GALLON	10	25	BES01
SEM02	Semigloss, BestBrand Int - Qt	$13.10	$10.50	QUART	10	25	BES01
SEM03	Semigloss, BestBrand Int - Pt	$6.00	$4.80	PINT	7	15	BES01
SEM04	Semigloss, BestBrand Ext - Gal	$29.80	$23.90	GALLON	10	25	BES01
SEM05	Semigloss, BestBrand Ext - Qt	$14.30	$11.50	QUART	10	25	BES01
TAP01	Tape, Painters 2"	$1.80	$1.50	EACH	25	50	SUP01
TAP02	Tape, Painters 1"	$1.50	$1.20	EACH	12	25	SUP01
TRA01	Tray, Painters, Plastic	$3.00	$2.40	EACH	15	30	SUP01
TRA02	Tray, Painters, Aluminum	$3.60	$2.90	EACH	20	40	SUP01

Item ID	Quantity	Cost
DRO01	62	$1.35
FLA01	42	$8.46
FLA02	11	$3.98
FLA03	16	$2.50
FLA04	48	$8.84
FLA05	8	$3.65
GLO01	48	$9.99
GLO02	10	$3.85
GLO03	14	$2.31
GLO04	59	$10.25
GLO05	20	$4.98
PAI01	17	$3.27
PAI02	14	$2.69
PAI03	20	$1.73
PAI04	12	$1.15
ROL01	19	$1.54

Item ID	Quantity	Cost
ROL02	22	$1.50
ROL03	17	$1.46
ROL04	19	$0.73
ROL05	18	$0.69
ROL06	29	$2.41
ROL07	45	$1.92
SEM01	40	$8.84
SEM02	10	$4.23
SEM03	8	$1.92
SEM04	48	$9.61
SEM05	14	$4.61
TAP01	35	$0.63
TAP02	74	$0.48
TRA01	27	$0.96
TRA02	34	$1.15

PRINT LISTS AND REPORTS

Print the following reports:

    Chart of Accounts
    Customer List

Vendor List
Employee List
Item List
General Ledger Trial Balance
Inventory Valuation Report
Current Earnings Report

ENTER TRANSACTIONS

Print invoices, sales receipts, purchase orders, checks, and other items as they are entered in the system. Use payroll checks for payroll and standard checks for all other checks. Create new items, accounts, customers, vendors, etc., as necessary. Refer to information given at the beginning of the problem for additional transaction details and information.

Prepare an Inventory Reorder Worksheet every Friday as the last transaction of the day to see if anything needs to be ordered. If anything is indicated, order the reorder quantity.

Full-time employees usually work 80 hours during a payroll period. Hourly employees working in excess of 80 hours in a pay period are paid overtime. There is a separate Payroll Checking account used when paying employees. These checks are different than our regular business checks. Start them with Check No. 129. Change the default check format to OCR – Multi-Purp Laser w/15 Flds for payroll checks.

Pay Accounts Payable every Friday paying all invoices due or eligible for discount by the following Friday.

January 1, 2006:

Cash sale to Laura Tibbets, of five gallons Semi-gloss BestBrand Interior paint at $27.50 (use 10200 Regular Checking Account as the cash account. Remember to set up a Cash Customer in the Customer List, start with Cash Receipt No. 101. Be sure to charge sales tax).

Harold's Construction purchased ten gallons of Semi-gloss BestBrand Exterior paint at $23.90 and ten gallons of Flat BestBrand Interior paint at $21.10 on account (start with Invoice No. 589).

Sold seven pints of Gloss BestBrand Interior paint at $7.20 each to, Jacob Still, Check No. 2398, Mr. Still is a cash customer.

Received Check No. 1096 from Arnold's Custom Painting for $85.35 as payment in full on his account.

Sold eight 4" paintbrushes $10.20 to Loreen Nelson on account.

Sold four 4" paintbrush, $10.20, three 8" heavy nap roller at $4.80 and six gallons of Semi-gloss BestBrand Interior paint at $27.50 to Terry Brown using a Visa card, number 8321-2382-2387-3722, expiration date 02/07.

January 3:

Received Check No. 915 for $252.95 from Victor Stein for the full amount due on his account.

Received the bill from Gas & Electric Co. for $135.82, Invoice No. 87-987-2.

Sold twelve rolls of 2" painter's tape at $1.80 each to Loreen Nelson on account.

Received payment of $585 from Harold's Construction, Check No. 7824.

January 4:

Kristen Urich purchased three Corner and Edge Roller sets at $7.50 and seven drop cloths at $4.20, this is a cash sale.

Received the bill from CA Water Co. for $24.38, Invoice No. 09876.

Sold six 8" Low Nap Rollers at $4.60 and six Roller Handles at $6.00 to a new customer: Ben Schultz (ID: SCH01), 478 Front Street, Sacramento, CA 95814, Phone: 916-555-6841, E-mail: bschultz@email.com, taxable.

January 5:

Sold eight quarts of BestBrand Gloss Interior paint at $12.00 each to a cash customer Victoria Norton.

Sold four pints of BestBrand Gloss Interior paint at $7.20 and six gallons of BestBrand Flat Interior paint at $26.30 to Arnold's Custom Painting on account.

Prepare and print an Inventory Reorder Worksheet to see if anything needs to be ordered (change the Options to Display Item Description). Prepare and print Purchase Orders for any merchandise that needs to be ordered (start with Purchase Order No. 201). No price increases have occurred since the last order.

Obtained a new vendor, PaintBoy Suppliers (ID: PAI01), 9824 Taylor Road, Sacramento, CA 95814, telephone number 916-555-1215, term are 2%/5, Net 15. Expense account is 12000. Purchased the following new items, use the Reorder Quantity for the initial order. Confirm that Average Costing Method will be used.

Item ID	Description	Cost	Regular Price	Sale Price	Unit	Minimum Stock	Reorder Quantity
TAP03	Tape, Craft Edge 3"	$0.84	$1.95	$1.75	EACH	15	30
COV01	Coveralls, Tyvex	$4.29	$15.99	$12.99	EACH	10	25
HAT01	Hat, Painters	$2.50	$7.50	$6.00	EACH	7	20
MAS01	Mask, Dust, 10 pk	$0.82	$2.95	$2.35	10 PK	7	25

January 8:

The nonprofit organization Homes for Habitat bought seven gallons of BestBrand Flat Exterior paint at $22.00, five quarts BestBrand Semi-gloss Exterior paint at $11.50 and six 8" Medium Nap Rollers at $3.80. Add the new customer: Homes for Habitat (ID HOM01), 451 State Street,

Sacramento, CA 95814, Contact Allison Hernandez, 916-555-8787, Fax 916-555-7878, Terms Net 30, Credit Limit $2000, use Level 2 (Sale Price) pricing, taxable.

Sold four Aluminum Painters Tray at $3.60 and twelve rolls of 1" Painters Tape at $1.50 to Victor Stein on account.

Add the contact name to Jackson Realty, Jeanette Thompson.

January 9:

Received Check No. 1525 from Harold's Construction, $472.98 for payment in full on his account.

Homes for Habitat returned two 8" Medium Nap Rollers purchased on January 8 (Use CM594 for the Credit No. field).

Received paint order in full from BestBrand Manufacturing (Purchase Order 201) with the bill, Invoice No. 8329-90.

January 10:

Sold eight gallons of BestBrand Semi-gloss Interior paint for $27.50, seven rolls of 2" Painters Tape at $1.80, two Plastic Painters Tray at $3.00, five Drop cloths at $4.20 and three 8" Low Nap Rollers at $4.60 to Arnold's Custom Painting.

Received bill from TelCom Services for $50.50, Invoice No. 34234.

Received Check No. 825 as payment from Loreen Nelson, for Invoice No. 590, discount was taken.

January 11:

Received order in full from Supply King (Purchase Order 202), Invoice No. 72123.

Received order in full from PaintBoy Suppliers (Purchase Order 203), Invoice No. 82762.

January 12:

Sold seven gallons BestBrand Gloss Interior Paint at $31.00 and four Drop cloths at $4.20 to a cash customer, Theresa Adesso.

Victor Stein purchased seven Drop cloths at $4.20, four 3" Paintbrush at $5.40 and ten gallons of BestBrand Semi-gloss Interior paint at $27.50 on account.

Sold five gallons BestBrand Flat Exterior Paint at $22.00, four quarts BestBrand Flat Exterior Paint at $9.20, eight gallons BestBrand Gloss Interior Paint at $24.80, three quarts BestBrand Gloss Interior Paint at $9.60, four 3" Paintbrushes at $4.40, four quarts BestBrand Semi-gloss Interior Paint at $10.50 and two pints BestBrand Semi-gloss Interior Paint at $4.80 to Harold's Construction on account.

Pay all bills due on or before or discounts lost by January 19 (start with Check No. 567).

Prepare and print an Inventory Reorder Worksheet to see if anything needs to be ordered (include Item Description in the report). Prepare and print Purchase Orders for any merchandise that needs to be ordered.

Prepare payroll using the following table, start Payroll Checks with Check No. 129.

PAYROLL TABLE: JANUARY 12, 2006		
	ALAN TREMAIN	
HOURS		
REGULAR	80	
OVERTIME		
SICK		
VACATION		

In order to cover the payroll check just written, transfer $691.84 from 10200 Regular Checking Account into 10100 Payroll Checking Account.

January 13:

Received Check No. 1265 from Loreen Nelson in payment for full amount due, $22.71.

Received Check No. 8722 from Homes for Habitat for $243.14 as payment in full on their account (note that the credit has been applied).

January 15:

Received Check No. 10-283 for $68.21 from Ben Schultz in payment of Invoice No. 592.

January 16:

Received merchandise from BestBrand Manufacturing on Purchase Order No. 204 in full, Invoice No. 8932-00.

Received merchandise from Supply King on Purchase Order No. 205 in full, Invoice No. 71235.

Sold ten packs of Dust Masks at $2.95 and fifteen Painter's Hats at $7.50 to Arnold's Custom Painting on account.

January 19:

Sold four quarts BestBrand Flat Interior Paint at $12.00, two quarts of BestBrand Flat Exterior Paint at $11.40, three pints of BestBrand Gloss Interior Paint at $ 7.20 and three quarts of BestBrand Semi-gloss Exterior Paint at $14.30 to Mary Turrey for cash.

Pay all bills due on or before or discounts lost by January 26.

Prepare and print an Inventory Reorder Worksheet to see if anything needs to be ordered. Prepare and print Purchase Orders for any merchandise that needs to be ordered.

January 20:

Sold ten gallons of BestBrand Flat Interior Paint at $21.10, ten gallons of BestBrand Gloss Interior Paint at $24.80 and seven gallons of BestBrand Semi-gloss Interior Paint at $22.00 to Harold's Construction on account.

Sold twelve gallons of BestBrand Semi-gloss Exterior Paint at $23.90, eight quarts of BestBrand Gloss Exterior Paint at $12.40, five Drop cloths at $3.40, five packs of Dust Masks at $2.35, three Aluminum Paint Trays at $2.90 and ten rolls of 1" Painter's Tape at $1.20 to Homes for Habitat on account.

Hired a new employee to help out part-time in the stock room, Kristen Kriton, 1177 Florin Road, Sacramento, CA 95814, 916-555-7766, Social Security Number 100-55-3699, Hourly rate $6.50, Overtime rate $9.75, 40 hours per bi-weekly pay period, Federal and State: Single, 0 Allowance, no Medical or Dental, no Sick or Vacation.

January 22:

Sold six rolls of 3" Craft Edge Tape at $1.95, three Corner and Edge Roller sets at $7.50, three pairs of Tyvex Coveralls at $15.99 and four 8" Heavy Nap Rollers at $4.80 to Victor Stein on account.

Sold five quarts of BestBrand Semigloss Exterior Paint at $14.30, seven gallons of BestBrand Flat Exterior Paint at $27.50, four 8" Low Nap Rollers at $4.60, four Roller Handles at $6.00, 10 rolls of 2" Painter's Tape at $1.80 and ten rolls of 1" Painter's Tape at $1.50 to a cash customer, Gail Totman.

Received merchandise from PaintBoy Suppliers on Purchase Order No. 206 in full, Invoice No. 89620.

Sold three 8" Medium Nap Rollers at $4.70, three Roller Handles at $6.00, 10 rolls of 3" Craft Edge Tape at $1.95, six pairs of Tyvex Coveralls at $15.99, six 4" Paintbrushes at $10.20, six 3" Paintbrushes at $5.40 and ten 1" Paintbrushes at $3.60 to Loreen Nelson on account.

Received $642.60 from Arnold's Custom Painting, Check No. 1192, payment in full on his account.

Received $1,110.11 from Harold's Construction, Check No. 1625, payment in full on his account.

January 23:

Received Check No. 9203 from Homes for Habitat for payment on Invoice No. 601 for $467.02.

Received $384.39 from Victor Stein for payment on Invoice Nos. 595 and 597, Check No. 9823.

Sold fifteen quarts BestBrand Semi-gloss Exterior Paint at $14.30, three Plastic Painter's Trays at $3.00, eight quarts of BestBrand Gloss Exterior Paint at $15.50, five packs of Dust Masks at $2.95 and ten Painter's Hats at $7.50 to Ben Schultz for cash.

Sold six Drop cloths at $4.20, four gallons BestBrand Gloss Exterior Paint at $33.40 and four 3" Paintbrushes at $5.40 to a cash customer, Glenn Mayford.

January 24:

Sold nine pints of BestBrand Flat Interior Paint at $7.80, nine pints of BestBrand Gloss Interior Paint at $7.20, five Aluminum Painter's Tray at $3.60, two Corner and Edge Roller sets at $7.50 and three packs of Dust Masks at $2.95 to Arnold's Custom Painting on account.

Sold twelve quarts of BestBrand Flat Exterior Paint at $9.20, seven quarts of Semi-gloss Interior Paint at $10.50, ten Drop cloths at $3.40 and twenty rolls of 2" Painter's Tape at $1.50 to Homes for Habitat on account.

January 25:

Sold six pairs of Tyvex Coveralls at $15.99, eight gallons of BestBrand Flat Exterior Paint at $27.50, four gallons of BestBrand Gloss Exterior Paint at $ 33.40, four quarts of BestBrand Semi-gloss Exterior Paint at $14.30 and eight 4" Medium Nap Rollers at $2.30 to a cash customer, James Jones.

Sold ten rolls of 2" Painter's Tape at $1.80, ten rolls of 1" Painter's Tape at $1.50, seven 2" Paintbrushes at $5.40, six Painter's Hats at $7.50 and four 8" Low Nap Rollers at $4.60 to Victor Stein on account.

January 26:

Pay all bills due on or before or discounts lost by February 2.

Prepare and print an Inventory Reorder Worksheet to see if anything needs to be ordered. Prepare and print Purchase Orders for any merchandise that needs to be ordered.

Prepare payroll using the following table.

PAYROLL TABLE: JANUARY 26, 2006		
	ALAN TREMAIN	KRISTEN KRITON
HOURS		
REGULAR	72	20
OVERTIME		
SICK	8	
VACATION		

In order to cover the payroll checks just written, transfer $807.91 from 10200 Regular Checking Account into 10100 Payroll Checking Account. Note that Kristen works only one week this pay period.

January 29:

Received Check No. 8325 for $265.87 from Homes for Habitat, payment in full on their account.

Jeanette Thompson, from Jackson Realty stopped by for the month's rent. Issued a check for $900.

Received merchandise from Supply King for Purchase Order No. 208 with Invoice No. 72324, order received in full.

Sold four gallons of BestBrand Gloss Exterior Paint at $33.40, two quarts of BestBrand Semi-gloss Interior Paint at $13.10, two packs of Dust Masks at $2.95, three Drop cloths at $4.20, three Tyvex Coveralls at $15.99 and three Painter's Hats at 7.50 to Arnold's Custom Painting on account.

Received merchandise from BestBrand Manufacturing, Purchase Order No. 207 without the invoice.

January 30:

Received Check No. 906 from Loreen Nelson in full payment of her account.

Received Check No. 12030 from Victor Stein in full payment of his account.

Sold twelve rolls of 3" Craft Edge Tape at $1.95, two Aluminum Paint Trays at $3.60, four gallons of BestBrand Flat Interior Paint at $26.30 and three 4" Paintbrushes at $10.20 to a cash customer, Helen Katz.

Sold three 4" Medium Nap Rollers at $2.30, six quarts BestBrand Flat Exterior Paint at $11.40 and five 1" Paintbrushes at $3.60 to Ben Schultz on account.

Sold seven gallons BestBrand Semi-gloss Interior Paint at $27.50, four gallons of BestBrand Gloss Interior Paint at $31.00 and four Drop cloths at $4.20 to Patrick Forest using his MasterCard, number 9822-0202-7263-3726, expiration date 01/07.

January 31:

Print the Tax Liability Report (payroll taxes) for January.

Make the 941 payroll tax deposit using an electronic funds transfer from the regular checking account. Remember from Chapter 9 that both the Social Security and the Federal Income Tax liabilities are kept in the same liability account 23400.

Prepare and print a Payroll Check Register for January. Include the fields of Reference, Date, Employees, Amount, Medical and Dental.

Use the Payroll Check Register to determine the appropriate amounts and pay the Medical and Dental liabilities. The Medical and Dental liabilities will be paid to our new insurance company, MediDent Corp. (MED01), P.O. Box 92873, Sacramento, CA 95814, 916-555-1020. Remember from Chapter 9 that both withholdings are kept in a single benefits liability account 24100.

Print the Taxable/Exempt Sales report and pay Sales Tax to the State Board of Equalization.

Print a Working Trial Balance.

Enter adjusting entries: Depreciation—Equipment $33.00, Furniture and Fixtures $99.00. Supplies used—Office Supplies $125, Cleaning Supplies $75.

Transfer the balance in the Retained Earnings account to Edward Kramer's Capital account.

Record the owner withdrawal for the month $500. Set up a Vendor account for Edward Kramer (ID: KRA01).

Prepare a bank reconciliation for Acct. # 97-1130-07824 Payroll Checking Account. Use the bank statement on this page. Print an Account Reconciliation Report.

STATE BANK
102 8th Street
Sacramento, CA 95814
(619) 555-9889

BANK STATEMENT FOR:

The Paint Can
1055 Front Street
Sacramento, CA 95814

Acct. # 97-1130-07824			January 2006
Beginning Balance 1/1/06			$0.00
1/12/06 Deposit	703.34		703.34
1/12/06 Check 129		703.34	0.00
1/26/06 Deposit	819.05		819.05
1/26/06 Check 130		703.34	115.71
1/26/06 Check 131		115.71	0.00
Ending Balance 1/31/06			$0.00

Prepare a bank reconciliation for Acct. # 97-1132-07992 Regular Checking Account and record any adjustments. Use the bank statement on the next page. Print an Account Reconciliation Report.

STATE BANK
102 8th Street • Sacramento, CA 95814 • (619) 555-9889
BANK STATEMENT FOR:

The Paint Can
1055 Front Street
Sacramento, CA 95814
Acct. # 97-1132-07992   **January 2006**

Beginning Balance 1/1/06			$15,298.00
1/1/06 Deposit	523.03		15,821.03
1/3/06 Deposit	837.95		16,658.98
1/4/06 Deposit	55.66		16,714.64
1/5/06 Deposit	102.96		16,817.60
1/9/06 Deposit	472.98		17,290.58
1/10/06 Deposit	85.77		17,376.35
1/12/06 Deposit	250.75		17,627.10
1/12/06 Check 567		102.63	17,524.47
1/12/06 Check 568		24.38	17,500.09
1/12/06 Check 569		135.82	17,364.27
1/12/06 EFT		703.34	16,660.93
1/13/06 Deposit	265.85		16,926.78
1/15/06 Deposit	68.21		16,994.99
1/19/06 Deposit	145.11		17,140.10
1/19/06 Check 570		697.31	16,442.79
1/19/06 Check 571		202.95	16,239.84
1/20/06 Check 572		176.88	16,062.96
1/20/06 Check 573		50.50	16,012.46
1/22/06 Deposit	2,116.72		18,129.18
1/23/06 Deposit	1,513.84		19,643.02
1/25/06 Deposit	563.21		20,206.23
1/26/06 Check 574		49.00	20,157.23
1/26/06 EFT		819.05	19,338.18
1/29/06 Deposit	265.87		19,604.05
1/29/06 Check 575		523.75	19,080.30
1/30/06 Deposit	1,074.81		20,155.11
1/31/06 EFT		445.63	19,709.48
1/31/06 Fire Insurance Pmt.: $26.00		26.00	19,683.48
1/31/06 Liability Insurance Pmt: $79.00		79.00	19,604.48
1/31/06 Service Chg.		8.00	19,596.48
1/31/06 Interest	54.05		19,650.53
Ending Balance 1/31/06			$19,650.53

CONTINUE WITH PROBLEM

Print a Standard Income Statement and a Standard Balance Sheet for January.

Print the following for January: General Ledger Trial Balance

Print Standard Cash Flow for January

Advance the period to 02 - Feb 01, 2006 to Feb 28, 2006 and print the reports recommended by Peachtree.

> General Journal
> Cash Receipts Journal
> Cash Disbursements Journal
> Sales Journal
> Purchase Journal
> Payroll Journal
> Purchase Order Journal
> General Ledger

Do not run an Internal Accounting Review.

NAME _____

TRANSMITTAL

PRACTICE SET: THE PAINT CAN

Attach the following documents and reports:

- ❑ Chart of Accounts
- ❑ Customer List
- ❑ Vendor List
- ❑ Employee List
- ❑ Item List
- ❑ General Ledger Trial Balance
- ❑ Inventory Valuation Report
- ❑ Current Earnings Report
- ❑ Cash Receipt 101: Cash Customer
- ❑ Invoice No. 589: Harold's Construction
- ❑ Cash Receipt No. 102: Cash Customer
- ❑ Cash Receipt No. 103: Arnold's Custom Painting
- ❑ Invoice No. 590: Loreen Nelson
- ❑ Cash Receipt No. 104: Cash Customer
- ❑ Cash Receipt No. 105: Victor Stein
- ❑ Invoice No. 591: Loreen Nelson
- ❑ Cash Receipt No. 106: Harold's Construction
- ❑ Cash Receipt No. 107: Cash Customer
- ❑ Invoice No. 592: Ben Schultz
- ❑ Cash Receipt No. 108: Cash Customer
- ❑ Invoice No. 593: Arnold's Custom Painting
- ❑ Inventory Reorder Worksheet as of January 5, 2006
- ❑ Purchase Order No. 201: BestBrand Manufacturing
- ❑ Purchase Order No. 202: Supply King
- ❑ Purchase Order No. 203: PaintBoy Suppliers
- ❑ Invoice No. 594: Homes for Habitat
- ❑ Invoice No. 595: Victor Stein
- ❑ Cash Receipt No. 109: Harold's Construction
- ❑ Credit Memo No. 596: Homes for Habitat
- ❑ Invoice No. 596: Arnold's Custom Painting
- ❑ Cash Receipt No. 110: Loreen Nelson

❑ Cash Receipt No. 111: Cash Customer
❑ Invoice No. 597: Victor Stein
❑ Invoice No. 598: Harold's Construction
❑ Check No. 567: BestBrand Manufacturing
❑ Check No. 568: CA Water Co.
❑ Check No. 569: Gas & Electric Co.
❑ Inventory Reorder Worksheet as of January 12, 2006
❑ Purchase Order No. 204: BestBrand Manufacturing
❑ Purchase Order No. 205: Supply King
❑ Payroll Check No. 129: Alan Tremain
❑ Cash Receipt No. 112: Loreen Nelson
❑ Cash Receipt No. 113: Homes for Habitat
❑ Cash Receipt No. 114: Ben Schultz
❑ Invoice No. 599: Arnold's Custom Painting
❑ Cash Receipt No. 115: Cash Customer
❑ Check No. 570: BestBrand Manufacturing
❑ Check No. 571: PaintBoy Suppliers
❑ Check No. 572: Supply King
❑ Check No. 573: TelCom Services
❑ Inventory Reorder Worksheet as of January 19, 2006
❑ Purchase Order No. 206: PaintBoy Suppliers
❑ Invoice No. 600: Harold's Construction
❑ Invoice No. 601: Homes for Habitat
❑ Invoice No. 602: Victor Stein
❑ Cash Receipt No. 116: Cash Customer
❑ Invoice No. 603: Loreen Nelson
❑ Cash Receipt No. 117: Ben Schultz
❑ Cash Receipt No. 118: Arnold's Custom Painting
❑ Cash Receipt No. 119: Harold's Construction
❑ Cash Receipt No. 120: Homes for Habitat
❑ Cash Receipt No. 121: Victor Stein
❑ Cash Receipt No. 122: Ben Schultz
❑ Cash Receipt No. 123: Cash Customer
❑ Invoice No. 604: Arnold's Custom Painting
❑ Invoice No. 605: Homes for Habitat
❑ Cash Receipt No. 124: Cash Customer
❑ Invoice No. 606: Victor Stein
❑ Check No. 574: PaintBoy Suppliers
❑ Check No. 575: Supply King
❑ Inventory Reorder Worksheet as of January 26, 2006
❑ Purchase Order No. 207: BestBrand Manufacturing
❑ Purchase Order No. 208: Supply King
❑ Purchase Order No. 209: PaintBoy Suppliers

❑   Payroll Check No. 130: Alan Tremain
❑   Payroll Check No. 131: Kristen Kriton
❑   Cash Receipt No. 124: Homes for Habitat
❑   Check No. 576: Jackson Realty
❑   Invoice No. 607: Arnold's Custom Painting
❑   Cash Receipt No. 125: Loreen Nelson
❑   Cash Receipt No. 126: Victor Stein
❑   Cash Receipt No. 127: Cash Customer
❑   Invoice No. 608: Ben Schultz
❑   Cash Receipt No. 128: Cash Customer
❑   Tax Liability Report
❑   Check No. 577: MediDent Corp.
❑   Payroll Check Register (modified)
❑   Taxable/Exempt Sales report
❑   Check No. 578: State Board of Equalization
❑   Working Trial Balance
❑   Check No. 579: Edward Kramer, Drawing
❑   Account Reconciliation (Regular Checking Account)
❑   Account Reconciliation (Payroll Checking Account)
❑   Standard Income Statement
❑   Standard Balance Sheet
❑   General Ledger Trial Balance
❑   Standard Cash Flow
❑   General Journal
❑   Cash Receipts Journal
❑   Cash Disbursements Journal
❑   Sales Journal
❑   Purchase Journal
❑   Payroll Journal
❑   Purchase Order Journal
❑   General Ledger

Introduction to Windows®— Screens, Terminology, and Disk Duplication

INTRODUCTION TO WINDOWS®

When you turn on the computer, Windows will automatically be in use and icons will be visible on the desktop. (Some computer laboratories require the use of passwords in order to access Windows and the various application programs available. Check with your instructor regarding the configuration of your classroom computers.) There is very little difference visually between Windows 95 and 98 and only minor differences with Windows 2000. Windows XP can have a similar look or a completely different look depending on how it was configured. This appendix will show only one set of screen shots from Windows XP Professional. Your version of Windows may be slightly different not only due to version but due to configuration.

    DO: If needed, turn on your computer and monitor
Windows will begin running, and the desktop will be displayed on the screen

In order to use Windows effectively, it is helpful to understand the terminology used in describing the various Windows elements.

Desktop	The primary work area and covers the entire screen.
Icons	Pictorial representations of objects. Some icons on the desktop are "shortcuts" used to access programs and/or documents. Other icons are used to access information regarding your computer or to delete files/programs from the computer.
Taskbar	The major focal point of Windows. It usually appears at the bottom of your screen. The taskbar contains the Start button, which is used to launch (open) programs, access documents, alter the appearance of the desktop, and shut down the computer when you are finished working.
Taskbar buttons	Indicate the names of any programs/files that are currently open.
Status area	Programs can place information or notification of events in the status area. Windows places information in the status area: the time and (if available on your computer) a sound icon, which is used to control the volume of the computer's sound system. Shortcuts to access programs may also be displayed on the taskbar. In Windows 95, these program icons are located on the right side of the taskbar. In Windows 98, 2000 and XP, they can be located next to the Start button or the tray on the far right side of the taskbar.
ToolTip	is a definition, instruction, or information that pops up when you point to something. For example, pointing to the time in the status area of the taskbar gives you a ToolTip that displays the full date; pointing to the Start button gives you the ToolTip "Click here to begin."

Start button	Used to access the primary menu in Windows. This menu lists the main functions available.
Programs	A menu listing the application programs available on your system. Frequently, you must make selections from several menus to access a program. For example, to access Calculator, which is a Windows Accessory Program, you point to the **Program** menu, then point to the **Accessories** menu, and finally point to and click on **Calculator**.
Documents	Lists the names of documents recently in use on the computer. (In a classroom environment, the documents listed may not be your documents; they may have been in use by another student.)
Settings	Allows you to alter the Windows environment.
Search	Allows you to locate files, folders, computers, or a network.
Help	Takes you to a program to obtain online help for Windows.
Run	Allows you to execute a program by name.
Shut Down	*Always* used to exit Windows or restart the computer.

Once you have opened a program and are ready to work, Windows will provide several items that are similar to those shown in the following Peachtree® Complete Accounting 2006 window.

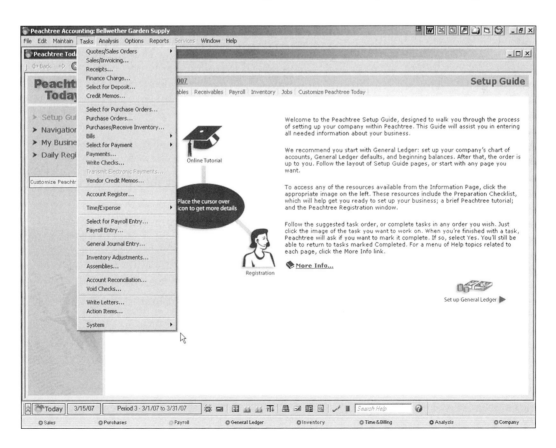

Control menu icon	Always in the upper left corner of every window. Clicking on this allows you to access a drop-down menu, which is used for resizing, moving, maximizing, minimizing, closing, or switching a window.
Title bar	A bar at the top of the window that indicates the name of the program and the file in use.
Minimize button	Located on the upper right side of the screen. It appears as a button with a minus sign. Clicking on this allows you to shrink or minimize a window into a button, which appears on the taskbar. When a window is minimized, the program/document is still open and usable; it is just placed on the taskbar as a button so it is out of the way.
Maximize button	A button with a single window as the icon. This is the middle button on the Right side of the title bar. Clicking on this allows you to fill the entire screen with the contents of the active window. This is not shown on the Peachtree window above.
Restore button	Appears when a window is maximized, the maximize button changes into a button with two windows. This is shown in the Peachtree window above. Clicking on this restores the window to its previous size.
Close button	On the far right side of the title bar. This button has an **X** on it. Clicking on this button closes both the document and/or the program. (The document window may also have its own minimize, maximize, and close buttons to be used only with the active document. If so, these buttons will usually appear below the program minimize, maximize, and close buttons.)
Windows borders	The borders around the outside of open windows. You may point to a border, display a double arrow, then hold down the primary mouse button and drag the border to resize a window.
Menu bar	Will drop down a menu when clicked. These different menus allow you to access most of the commands within a program. The Peachtree window on the previous page shows the Task menu item selected and its options displayed.
Dialog box	A box that appears in the middle of your screen and presents information to you or requests information from you.
Message box	A type of dialog box that informs you of a condition—a question, information, a critical error. Most message boxes require you to confirm, cancel, or retry an action by clicking on a command button.
Command button	A button used to answer the questions within a dialog box.

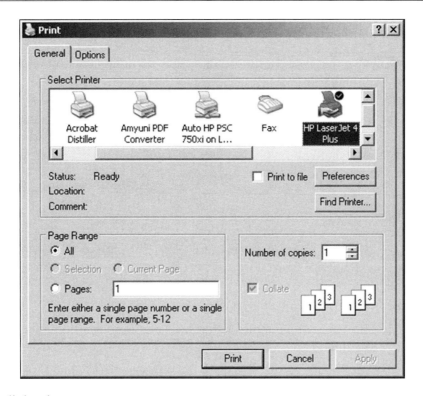

Other items in dialog boxes are:

Drop-down list or box	Contains the default choice. If you wish to make another selection, click the arrow next to the drop-down list box. If your choice is displayed, simply click on the desired item.
Option buttons	Present more than one choice; however, only one item may be chosen. The selected option contains a black dot. Options that are unavailable are dimmed. (Look at the section for "Page Range" in the "Print" dialog box.)
Text box	Allows you to key in information. (Look at the box next to "Pages:" item.)
Check box	Provides a choice that may be enabled or disabled. More than one item may be selected. If an option is unavailable, it is dimmed. (Look at the check box for "Print to file".)
Spin box	allows you to key in a number or to click on up or down arrows to increase or decrease a number. (Look at the "Number of copies:" item.)

BEGIN USING THE COMPUTER

At this point you will begin to use the computer. If you are not able to finish the appendix in one session, refer to the section later in this appendix on How to Close or Shut Down Windows.

HOW TO USE A MOUSE

A mouse is an input device that is primarily used to issue commands within a software program. When working in a graphical user interface environment such as Windows, the user sends instructions to programs by simply using the mouse to position the mouse pointer and clicking either the right or left mouse button. A mouse pointer is an arrow that can be used to point to an icon. When you are in a document or a dialog box that requires typing, the mouse pointer turns into an I-beam so it may be positioned more easily.

MOUSE TERMINOLOGY

When using a mouse, terms such as "click," "double-click," "right-click," "drag," and "drag and drop" will be used.

Mouse pointer	The arrow used when pointing to icons.
I-beam	The shape of the mouse pointer when being positioned within a document or a dialog box requiring typing.
Click	Pressing the primary (usually left) mouse button one time.
Right-click	Pressing the secondary (usually right) mouse button one time.
Double-click	To press the primary (usually left) mouse button two times very quickly.
Drag	To hold down the primary mouse button while dragging the mouse pointer through something (usually text) to highlight.
Drag and drop	To reposition something. This is achieved by pointing to an object or highlighted text with the mouse pointer, holding down the primary mouse button, and moving the mouse pointer/object by moving the mouse. When the item is repositioned, release the mouse button to "drop" the item into the new position.

PRACTICE USING A MOUSE

DO: Turn on the computer and monitor, if not already on
             You should see the taskbar at the bottom of the screen and several icons on the desktop
             –   If you are working in a laboratory environment, the steps you follow to start the computer and access Windows may be different. Check with your instructor for directions.
             Point to the **Time** in the lower right corner of your screen
             You will see the full date as a ToolTip
             Point to the **Start** button

–   Notice ToolTip: Click Here to Begin. You may need to point for several seconds before the ToolTip will appear.

Open the **Notepad** program:

Click the **Start** button

Point to **Programs**

Point to **Accessories**

Point to **Notepad**, click the primary mouse button

–   If you need to click the primary mouse button to activate a command, future instructions will not tell you to point to the item first or to click the primary mouse button. The above instruction will be given as: Click Notepad.

Click the **Control menu icon** in the upper left corner of the Notepad title bar

Click **Minimize** on the menu

–   Notepad appears as a button on the taskbar.

–   Click the **Notepad button** on the taskbar

–   This opens the same Notepad window.

–   A button for Notepad remains on the taskbar.

–   Notice the difference in the button's appearance when the program is in use.

Click the **Maximize** button in the upper right corner of the Notepad window

–   Notepad covers the entire screen.

Click the **Restore** button

–   The Notepad window is restored to its former size.

Resize the window:

Point to the **right border** of the Notepad window

–   The mouse pointer will turn into a double arrow.

Hold down the primary mouse button

Drag the window border to the right

–   Notice the dotted line indicating the new size.

Release the primary mouse button

Move the window:

Point to the **Title bar**

Hold down the primary mouse button

Drag the window to a new location on the desktop

–   Notice the dotted window outline indicating the new position.

Release the primary mouse button

Click the **Close** button to close Notepad

DUPLICATING A DISK

When working with any computer program, it is essential to make a backup disk of your work. In Peachtree you regularly make a backup file of the company on a floppy disk or other storage device. This does not backup the program but rather it is a backup of the company data that must be restored if lost. If something happens to your hard drive, you may lose all of your work. There may be times when a duplicate of this backup disk should be maintained such as allowing a manager in the company to take a duplicate disk home each night for safety purposes. Rather than backing up the files twice, we can use Disk Copy feature to make the duplicate disk.

DO: Turn on the computer and monitor, if not already on
You should see the taskbar and several icons on the desktop
Insert the disk containing your company file in the A: drive
Point to the **Start** button and right-click on the **Start** button

Click **Explore**

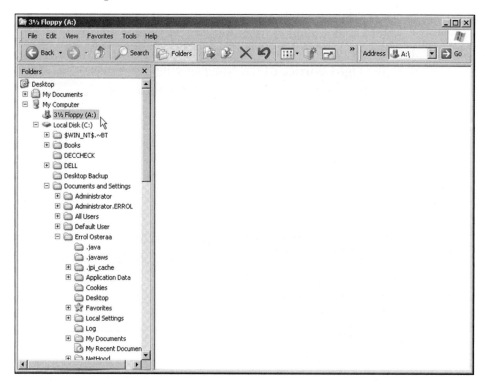

Right-click **3½ Floppy (A:)**

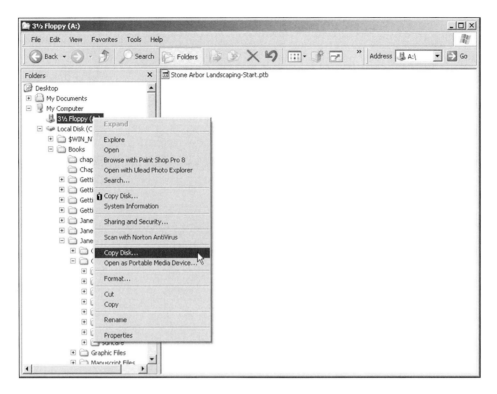

Click **Copy Disk**

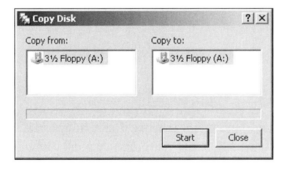

Click on **Start**

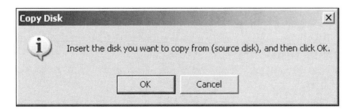

Insert the disk to be copied in Drive A:
Click **OK**

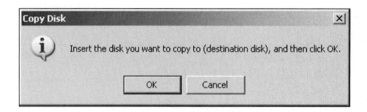

Remove your disk from A: and insert a new disk into A:
–   The disks must be the same storage size. For example if your original disk
      is a high-density disk, the disk you copy to must also be a high-density disk.
Click **OK**

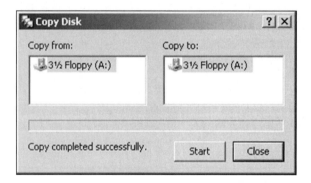

Once the disk has been copied successfully, click **Close**
Label this disk as Duplicate Company Backup Disk

HOW TO CLOSE OR SHUT DOWN WINDOWS®

When you have exited your application program and are ready to close Windows, you need to
follow proper exit/closing procedures. Simply turning off the machine is *not* the method to
follow when exiting Windows. This might corrupt files that are needed to make the program
work properly. When you close or shut down, Windows must close certain files and write
information to disk so it will be ready for use the next time the computer is needed. Always be
sure to follow the appropriate steps for closing/shutting down Windows.

DO: Click **Start**
            Click **Shut Down**

Select **Shut Down**

–   Unless you are instructed to follow a different procedure by your instructor. In some computer labs you may be required only to log off rather than shut down. In other situations, you may need to restart Windows using the Restart option.

Click **OK**

Remove the disk from drive A:

Index

A

About Peachtree® Accounting, 17
Accessories (Windows®) menu, 490
Account balance, 303
Account ID, 64
Account reconciliation
    adjusting/correcting entries, 170–172
    bank statement information,
        169–170, 340–342
    opening of, 167–168, 339–340
    printing report, 173–174, 344–345
    unreconciled difference, 170–171
Account Register for Checking, 174–175,
345–346
Accounting, 324–325; *See also* General
accounting; Merchandising business; Service
business
    accrual method, 107, 152, 306,
        325, 428
    adjustments for, 152–153, 157–158, 325,
        328–332
    advancing to next period, 185–187
    cash basis, 157–158, 329, 428
    computerizing a manual system,
        424–457
    fundamental accounting equation, 181,
        349
    manual vs. computerized, 5
Accounting periods, 429–430
Accounts. *See also* Chart of Accounts
    adding new, 68–69, 227
    changing name of existing, 154–155, 326–
        327
    deleting existing account, 156–157, 328
    drawing, 165
    making inactive, 155–156, 327
Accounts Payable, 99
    new company setup, 429–432,
        436–440
Accounts Payable Ledger, 99–100
Accounts Payable Subsidiary Ledger, 283
Accounts payable tracking, 102
Accounts Receivable, 49
    new company setup, 432, 442–445
    printing A/R reports, 56–58

Accounts Receivable Ledger, 44, 214
Accounts Receivable Register, 225
Accrual method of accounting, 107, 152, 306,
        325, 428
    adjustments for, 157–158, 325,
        328–332
Activity keyboard shortcuts, 14
Additional Products and Services, 17
Adjusting entries, 152–153, 158, 329
    bank reconciliation, 170–172, 342–344
    depreciation, 160–161, 331–332
    prepaid expenses, 158–160, 329–331
Administrator, 185, 353
Advancing to next period, 185–187,
        354–355
Aged Payables report, 140–141, 314–315
Aged Receivables report, 238–239, 260
All Accounts Payable Reports, 106, 125, 135,
        139, 303
All Accounts Receivables Reports, 56–58,
        229, 248, 270
All Accounts Reconciliation Reports, 174,
        261, 346
All Financial Statements, 165, 333
Allowance for Doubtful Accounts, 435
Alt key, 15
ALU (Arithmetic/Logic Unit), 2
American Express credit cards, 241
Analysis command, 13
Analysis Graphs, 26–27
Analysis Navigation Aids, 11
Apple Computers, 4
Application software, 4–5
Apply to Invoices tab, 83, 85
Apply to Purchase Order # tab, 296, 298, 300
Apply to Revenue tab, 77
Apply to Sales tab, 49
Archive copy, 184, 353
Audit trail, 225, 265
Available Charts of Accounts, 428

B

Back-ordered items, 300

Backing up work, 89–90, 143, 271, 315, 360, 415, 457
    duplicating a disk, 30–31, 495–498
    end-of-period backup, 184
Backup file, 30–31, 495–498
Balance Sheet, 24, 165–166, 181–182, 349–350
Bank fees, 241
Bank reconciliation, 167, 338–339
    adjusting/correcting entries, 170–172, 342–344
Bank statements, 167, 338–339; *See also* Account reconciliation
    entering information, 169–170, 340–342
Bills
    adding new vendor while recording, 115–118
    Cash Requirements Report, 112
    deleting, 114–115
    entering of, 102–103, 303–305
    items received prior to bill, 296
    more than one expense account, 104–105
    paying with Payment window, 130–132
    paying with select for payment, 121–124, 309–310
    printing checks for, 124–125, 311
    reviewing paid bills, 125–126
    waiting on bill flag, 296
Bits (binary digits), 2
Bounced checks, 262–265, 342
Brought Forward Balances, 5
Browse button, 40
Business transactions, documents received/send/give, 19
Bytes, 2–3

C

Calculator, 28, 491
Capital Accounts, 162, 337–338
Cash. *See* Petty cash
Cash basis accounting, 157–158, 329, 428
Cash Disbursement Journal, 142–143
Cash Flow Forecast, preparing and printing, 178–179
Cash flow management, 99, 303
Cash investment by owner, 163–164
Cash Manager, 11

Cash purchases, 99
Cash receipt, correcting and printing, 249–250
Cash Receipts Journal, 37, 75–77, 239, 267–268
Cash Requirements Report, 112, 308–309
Cash sales, 37, 211, 239, 241–243
    receipts, 19
    recording of, 75–77, 239–241
    sales tax and, 239–240
    transactions, 77–78
Central processing unit (CPU), 2
Change System Date window, 46
Chart of Accounts, 11, 44, 100, 214, 326
    adding new account to, 68–69, 227
    Available Charts of Accounts, 428
    changing name of account, 154–155, 326–327
    deleting an account, 156–157, 328
    new company/new company setup, 426–428, 433–436
    petty cash account added to, 127
Check(s), 19; *See also* Account reconciliation
    Account Register for Checking, 174–175, 345–346
    Check Register report, 134–135
        insufficient funds returns, 262–265
        paychecks, voiding/deleting, 400–401
        printing, 136–137
        printing checks for bills, 124–125, 311
        printing paychecks, 391
        printing post printing check register, 138–139
        refund checks, 265–267
        sales paid by, 244–247
        voiding, 138, 313
        ways to generate, 121–122
Check box (Windows®), 493
Check Register Report, 134–135, 138–139
    Payroll Check Register, 402–403
Click, 494
Close button (Windows®), 20, 492
Closing the books, 187, 324–325, 336–337, 356
Closing a company, 28–29, 89–90, 143
Closing a purchase order manually, 301
Closing Today screen, 41–42
Collection Manager, 11
Command button (Windows®), 492

Company(ies)
    closing a, 28–29, 89–90, 143
    creating new, 424–432
    opening a, 39–41, 212–213
    personalizing company name, 42
    tax identification number, 383
    verifying, 8, 41, 213
Company button, 43
Company Information, 426–427
Company Navigation Aids, 11
Company profile, 39
Computer hardware
    input devices, 2
    output devices, 3
    processing devices, 2
    storage devices, 3
Computerizing a manual system
    accounting method, 428
    accounting periods, 429–430
    Accounts Payable setup, 432, 436–440
    Accounts Receivable, 442–445
    Chart of Accounts, 426–428
    Company Information form, 426–427
    creating, 424–432
    General Ledger setup, 433–436
    Inventory Items, 452–456
    payroll setup, 445–452
    posting method, 429
    print lists and reports, 456
    Setup Guide, 424–432
    tax tables setups, 440–442
Computers
    beginning use of, 493–494
    hardware, 1–3
    input devices, 2
    introduction to, 1–3
    output devices, 3
    processing devices, 2
    software, 3–5
    storage devices, 3
    as way of life, 1
Contents and Index, 16
Contra Asset, 435
Control menu (Windows®), 492
Copy command, 9
Copying a file, 29–30
Correcting. *See* Errors, editing/correcting
Cost of Goods Sold, 359

Credit card charge receipts, 19
Credit cards, 241–244
Credit Limit, 72, 117, 231, 234, 289
    transaction exceeding, 222–224
Credit memos, 19, 119, 265–267, 302
    preparation of, 65–67, 236–238
    refund checks and, 265–267
Credit sales transactions, 211
Credits, 88, 90, 119, 211, 268, 330, 405, 407
    credit from a vendor, 19, 119–120,
        302–303
    payment on account with credit, 253–254
    Vendor Ledgers Report, 120–121
Current Earnings Report, 402–403
Custom toolbar, 12, 43
Customer(s)
    adding new, 69–70, 230–232
    analysis of, 270
    credit limit, 222–224
    early-payment discount, 254–255
    Event Log, 44, 269–270
    Items Sold to Customers report, 247–249
    partial payments on account, 84–85
    payments on account, 83–84, 251–253
    sale to new customer, 232–233
Customer analysis, 270
Customer Event Log, 44, 269–270
Customer ID, 71, 74–75, 102, 240, 269
Customer Ledgers, 57–58, 65–67
Customer Ledgers Report, 65, 86–87,
        224–225, 229–230
    Drilldown feature, 225
    viewing and printing, 259–260
Customer List, 37, 44
Customer Log, 44
Customer payments on account, 251–253
Customer purchase order (PO), 49
Customer records, modifying of, 74–77,
        233–234
Customer Sales History report, 270
Customer Support and Service, 16
Customer/Prospects List, 214
Customer, Vendor, or Employee ID filter, 64

D

Dates, 14, 46, 49, 215
DE-88 form, 402

Debits, 88, 90, 107, 120, 211, 268, 330, 405–406
Default settings, 21–24
Delete, 20
Deleting
    invoice, 60, 62–64, 235–236, 313
    paychecks, 400–401
    payment transaction, 135–136
Dental insurance, 407, 449–450
Deposit slips, 19
Deposit ticket ID, 75, 83, 240, 261
Deposits in Transit Report, 261
Depreciation, 158, 160, 329
    adjusting entries for, 160–161, 331–332
Description field, 49
Desktop features (Windows®), 9–10, 490
Dialog box (Windows®), 492–493
Disbursement Checks, 125–126
Discount pricing, 228–229
Discounts
    early-payment discount, 254–255
    loss of discount, 258–259
Discounts Lost By, 122, 310
Discover cards, 241
Disks, 3, 495–498
Documents, 491
Documents received/ to send/give, 19
DOS (Disk Operating System), 4
Dot matrix printer, 3
Double-click, 494
Drag and drop, 494
Drag (mouse), 494
Drawing account, 165
Drilldown feature, 25–26, 58
    payables and purchases, 106–107
    sales and receivables, 58, 225
Drop-down list or box, 20, 493
Duplicating a disk, 495–498

E

E-mail, 20
Early-payment discount, 254–255
    loss of discount, 258–259
Edit command, 13
Editing. See Errors, editing/correcting
Editing keyboard shortcuts, 14

Employee information, 391–392
    adding a new employee, 392–395
Employees' W-2 Forms, 413–415
End-of-period backup, 184, 353
End-of-period procedures, 152–153, 324–325;
    See also Merchandising business; Service business
    Account Reconciliation, 167–168, 173–174, 344–345
    accrual-basis accounting adjustments, 157–158, 328–332
    bank reconciliation, 167, 338–345
    Cash Flow Forecast, 178–179
    exporting to Excel, 182–184, 350–352
    General Ledger Trial Balance, 177, 347–348
    interim financial statements, 354
    making account inactive, 155–156
    noncash investment by owner, 164–165
    prepaid expenses adjustments, 158–160, 329–331
    Statement of Cash Flow, 179–180
    transactions for previous period, 187–189, 356–358
    Trial Balance, 175–176, 191
Ending work session, 31–32
Entering transactions, two sales items, 52–53
Entry Windows, 18–21
Errors, editing/correcting, 49–50
    bank reconciliation, 170–172, 342–344
    cash receipt, 249–250
    discount pricing and, 228–229
    existing vendors, 305–306
    invoice information, 217–218, 225–227
    payables and purchases, 103–104
    payment transaction, 133–134
    previous period transactions, 187–189, 356–358
    purchase orders, invoices, and checks, 299–300, 313
    sales and receivables, 49–50
    supplies accounts, 358–359
    Vendor Ledger Report, 109–110
Esc key, 15
Event, 20
Excel, 6
    exporting reports to, 182–184, 350–352

Exempt sales report, 251, 312
Exiting company, 28–29
Exiting program, 31–32
Expense account, preparing bills from,
    104–105, 303

F

Favorites, 18
Federal Income Tax, 410
Field, 19
File (archive) copy, 184, 353
File command, 13
Filters, 64
    Account ID, 64
    Customer, Vendor or Employee ID, 64
    Item ID, 64
    Job ID, 64
    Reference Number, 64
    Transaction Amount, 64
    Transaction Type, 64
Financial Manager, 11
Financial statements, 354
Financing Activities, 179
Find Transactions, 62–63, 80, 234–235
Floppy disk, 3
Form 940 (Employer's Annual Federal
Unemployment Tax Return) (FUTA), 402,
404, 412–413
Form 941 (Employer's Quarterly Federal Tax
Return), 402, 404, 410–412
401(k) setup screen, 447
Functions keyboard shortcuts, 14
Fundamental accounting equation, 181, 349

G

General accounting
    accrual-basis accounting adjustments,
        157–158, 328–332
    Balance Sheet, 165–166, 181–182,
        349–350
    cash investment (additional) by owner,
        163–164
    deleting accounts, 156–157, 328
    depreciation, 160–161, 331–332
    General Journal, 161–162, 175, 334,
        346–347

General Ledger Trial Balance, 177,
        347–348
    inactive accounts, 327
    Income Statement, 180–181, 333,
        348–349
    inventory adjustments, 359–360
    net income/retained earnings, 336–338
    noncash investment by owner, 164–165
    owner withdrawals, 162–163, 335–336
    partnerships, 334
    prepaid expenses, 158–160, 329–331
    previous period transactions, 356–358
    supplies accounts, 358–359
General Journal, 12, 158, 267, 329–332
    viewing, 161–162, 175, 334, 346–347
General Ledger, 37, 44, 81, 100, 102, 211, 326,
        339
    new company setup, 432–436
General Ledger Navigation Aids, 11
General Ledger Trial Balance, 177, 268–269,
        347–348
Gigabyte (GB), 3
Graphical user interface (GUI), 4
Graphs, 26–27, 179

H

Hard copy, 3
Hard disk, 3
Hardware. *See* Computer hardware
Headers, 184, 352
Health insurance, 407, 449–450
Help, 21, 491
Help command, 13
Help Window keyboard shortcuts, 14

I

I-beam, 494
IBM, 4
Icons (Windows®), 2, 4, 489–490, 492
Inactive accounts, 155–156, 327
Income Statement, 180–181, 189, 333,
        348–349, 357
Index, 18
Ink jet printer, 3
Input devices, 2
Installation of default settings, 21–24
Insufficient funds, 262–265

Insurance, medical/dental insurance, 407, 449–452
Interest income, 340, 342
Interim financial statements, 354
Inventory, 283, 359
    adjustments, 359–360
    items already received, 296–297
    items not accompanied by invoice, 295–296
    minimum stock level/reorder quantity, 292–293
    new company setup, 432
    partial receipt of, 300–301
    purchase order marked closed, 297–298
    receiving items ordered, 294–295
    recording receipt of items/invoice, 298–299
Inventory Items, 44, 69–70, 212, 214, 227
    new company setup, 452–456
Inventory Navigation Aids, 11
Inventory Reorder Worksheet, 285–286
Investing Activities, 179
Invoice(s). See also Sales/invoicing
    adding note to, 54
    correcting of, 58–60, 225–227
    deleting of, 60, 62–64, 235–236, 313
    discount pricing, 228–229
    items already received, 296–297
    items received without invoice, 295–296
    printing of, 50–52, 58–60, 218, 225–227
    receipt of items/invoice, 298–299
    voiding of, 60–61, 234–236, 313
Invoice Due Before, 122, 310
Invoice number, 49, 105
Invoice Register, 37
Item field, 49
Item ID filter, 64
Item List, 45
    adding new items to, 69–70, 227–229
    verifying additions on, 70
Items Sold to Customers report, 78–79, 247–249

J

Job costing system, 11
Job ID filter, 64

Jobs setup, 456
    new company setup, 432
Journal, 20

K

Keyboard, 2
Keyboard commands, 43
Keyboard conventions, 15
Keyboard shortcuts, 14
Kilobyte (K), 3

L

Laser printer, 3
Ledger accounts, 5
License Agreement, 17
Lists, 24

M

Maintain Chart of Accounts feature, 227
Maintain command, 13
Maintain Customer window, 37, 222, 230–233
Maintain Employees/Sales Reps window, 393
Maintain Inventory Item, 227
Maintain Vendor window, 314
Manual accounting, 5
    Computerizing. See Computerizing a manual system
Master file, 29
Master Stock Item, 453
MasterCard, 241
        Maximize/restore button (Windows®), 20, 492
Medical/dental insurance, 407–408, 449–452
Medicare tax, 410
Megabyte (MB), 2
Memos, 38
    Credit Memos, 65–67
Menu bar, 43, 492
Menu Commands, 13–14
Merchandising business
    general accounting and end-of-period procedures
        Account Reconciliation Report, 344–345
        accrual-basis accounting adjustments, 328–332
        advance to next period, 354–355

Balance Sheet, 349–350
bank reconciliation, 338–345
checking account register,
    345–346
deleting accounts, 328
depreciation, 331–332
exporting reports to Excel,
    350–352
General Journal, 334, 346–347
General Ledger Trial Balance,
    347–348
inactive accounts, 327
Income Statement, 330, 348–349
inventory adjustments, 359–360
name change of existing accounts,
    326–327
net income/retained earnings,
    336–338
owner withdrawals, 335–336
partnerships, 334
prepaid expenses, 329–331
previous period transactions,
    356–358
supplies accounts, 358–359
payables and purchases
    accounting for, 283–284
    aged payables report, 314–315
    bills, 303–305
    cash requirements report, 308–309
    checks for bills, 311
    closing purchase order manually,
        301
    credit from vendor, 302–303
    deleting/editing POs, invoices,
        and checks, 299–300
    deleting/editing Pos, invoices, and
        checks, 313
    Inventory Reorder Worksheet,
        285–286
    items already received, 296–297
    items not accompanied by invoice,
        295–296
    minimum stock level/reorder
        quantity, 292–293
    partial receipt of merchandise
        ordered, 300–301
    paying bills, 309–310
    Purchase Journal editing, 307–308

purchase order, 286–290
purchase order marked closed,
    297–298
purchase order register, 292
Purchase Order Report, 293–294
receipt of items/invoice, 298–299
receiving items ordered, 294–295
sales tax, 312–313
taxable/exempt sales report, 312
vendor account balance, 303
vendor event log, 314
vendors, 305–306
sales and receivables
    accounting for, 211–212
    Aged Receivables report, 238–239,
        260
    cash sales with sales tax, 239–241
    Chart of Accounts, 227
    checks/cash sales, 244–247,
        249–250
    correct/print an invoice, 225–227
    credit cards, 241–244
    credit memo, 236–238
    credit memo and refund check,
        265–267
    customer analysis, 270
    Customer Event Log, 269–270
    Customer Ledgers Report,
        224–225, 229–230, 259–260
    customer payments on account,
        251–253
    customer records, 233–234
    customer's credit limit, 222–224
    Deposits in Transit Report, 261
    discount pricing, 228–229
    Drilldown feature, 225
    early-payment discount, 254–255
    editing/correcting errors, 217–218
    General Ledger Trial Balance,
        268–269
    Inventory Items, 227
    items sold to customers report,
        247–249
    more than one sales item and sales
        tax, 219–220
    new customers, 230–232
    nonsufficient funds returns,
        262–265

printing an invoice, 218
sale to new customer, 232–233
sales on account, 216–217
sales forms, 234–236
Sales Journals, 267–268
taxable/exempt sales report, 251
Message box (Windows®), 492
Microsoft Excel, 6
exporting reports to, 182–184, 350–352
Microsoft Internet Explorer, 6
Minimize button (Windows®), 20, 492
Minimum stock level, 292–293
Monitor, 3
Monthly (interim) financial statements, 354
Mouse terminology, 494
Mouse/mouse pointer, 2, 494–495
Moving around a window, 14
MS-DOS, 4

N

Name change of existing accounts, 154–155
Navigation Aids, 10–11, 14, 23–24, 43
Analysis, 11
Company, 11
General Ledger, 11
Inventory, 11
Payroll, 10
Purchases, 10
Sales, 10
Time & Billing, 11
Net Due, 72
Net income, 152, 165–166, 324, 336–338
New, 20
New company setup
accounting method, 428
accounting periods, 429–430
Accounts Payable setup, 432, 436–440
Accounts Receivable, 442–445
Chart of Accounts, 426–428
Company Information form, 426–427
creating, 424–432
General Ledger setup, 433–436
Inventory Items, 452–456
payroll setup, 445–452
posting method, 429
print lists and reports, 456
Setup Guide, 424–432

tax tables setups, 440–442
Non-stock item, 453
Noncash investment by owner, 164–165
Nonsufficient funds (NSF), 262–265, 342
Note, 20
adding to invoice, 54
private note, 54
Note window, 54

O

On-line credit card service, 241
On-screen help, 16–18
Open, 20
Opening a company, 39–41, 212–213
dialog box, 7–8
Opening program, 6–7, 39, 100–101, 384, 425
Operating Activities, 179
Operating system software, 3–4
Option buttons, 493
Options command, 13
Out of stock items, 300
Output devices, 3
Owner(s)
additional cash investment, 163–164
capital account, 162, 337–338
noncash investment by, 164–165
owners withdrawals, 162–163, 335–336

P

Partial payments on account, 84–85
Partial receipt of merchandise ordered, 300–301
Partnership, definition of, 334
Passwords, 184–185, 353, 489
Paste command, 9
Payables and purchases
accounting for, 99–100, 283–284
merchandising business. *See* Merchandising business
service business. *See* Service business
Paychecks
creating, 384–391
next pay period, 395–399
printing, 391
voiding/deleting, 400–401
Payment Manager, 11

Payment method
    credit cards, 241–244
    payments, 122
    select for payment, 122
    write checks, 122
Payment transaction
    deleting a payment, 135–136
    editing of, 133–134
Payments windows, 99, 122
    pay bills using, 130–132
Payroll, 383–384
    creating paychecks, 384–391
    Current Earnings Report, 403
    employee information, 391–392
    filing tax forms, 410
    Form 940, 412–413
    Form 941, 410–412
    medical, dental, and savings plans,
        449–452
    medical, dental, and savings plans,
        407–410
    new company setup, 432
    new employee, 392–395
    other payroll liabilities, 407–410
    paychecks for next pay period, 395–399
    paying taxes, 405–407
    payroll reports, 402–403
    printing paychecks, 391
    Tax Liability Report, 404–405
    vacation/sick time, 385–391
    voiding/deleting checks, 400–401
    W-2s/W-3s, 413–415
Payroll Check Register, 402
Payroll deductions, 383
Payroll Navigation Aids, 10
Payroll setup, new company setup, 445–452
Payroll Tax Liability Report, 404–405
Payroll taxes
    filing tax forms, 410
    payment of, 405–407
PC-DOS, 4
PDF (Portable Document Format), 182
Peachtree® Accounting Guided Tour, 16
Peachtree® Accounting Help, 16–18
Peachtree® Complete
    desktop features, 9–10
    how to start program, 6–7
    introduction to, 9–10

open a company, 7–8
    overview of, 5–6
    system requirements for, 5–6
Peachtree® Registration, 17
Peachtree® Today screen, 41–42
Peachtree® on the Web, 17
Personalizing company name, 42, 213
Petty cash, 126–127
    adding account to Chart of Accounts, 127
    establishing by writing checks, 127–128
    record replenishments of, 129–130
Post-Closing Trial Balance, 191
Posted transaction, 109–110, 138–139
Posting method, 429
Prepaid assets, 107
Prepaid expenses, adjusting entries for,
        158–160, 329–331
Previewing
    Customer Ledgers Report, 229–230
    Purchases Journal Report, 111
Print icon, 20
Printers, 3
Printing
    Account Reconciliation Report, 173–174,
        344–345
    Accounts Receivables (A/R reports),
        56–58
    Aged Payables Report, 140–141, 314–315
    Aged Receivables Report, 238–239, 260
    Balance Sheet, 181–182, 349–350
    Cash Disbursement Journal, 142–143
    Cash Requirements Report, 308–309
    checks, 136–137
    checks for bills, 124–125, 311
    Current Earnings Report, 403
    Customers Ledgers Report, 259–260
    Deposits in Transit Report, 261
    Form 940, 412–413
    Form 941, 410
    General Ledger Trial Balance, 177,
        268–269, 347–348
    Income Statement, 180–181, 333,
        348–349
    Inventory Reorder Worksheet, 285–286
    invoices, 50–52, 218, 225–227
    Items Sold to Customers report, 78–79,
        247–249
    Journal reports, 267–268

paychecks, 391
paychecks for next pay period, 395–399
post printing check register, 138–139
Purchase Order Register, 292
Purchase Order Report, 293–294
Purchases Journal, 111
Sales Journal, 87–88
sales receipt, 79–81
taxable/exempt sales report, 251
trial balance, 89
Vendor Ledger Report, 105–106, 141–142
W-2 forms, 413–415
Processing devices, 2
Profit and Loss Statement, 180, 189, 333, 348–349
Program menu, 491
Programs, 491
.Ptb extension, 30
Purchase Journal
editing a transaction from, 307–308
previewing and printing, 111
Purchase order(s), 20, 286
closing manually, 301
editing of, 299–300
for new items, 288–290
partial receipt of merchandise ordered, 300–301
preparing orders, 286–287
printing report, 293–294
receiving items ordered, 294–295
verifying marked closed, 297–298
voiding and deleting, 313
Purchase Order Register, 292
Purchases Navigation Aids, 10
Purchases/Receive Inventory, 99, 104, 283, 295, 298, 300, 302

Q

Quantity field, 49

R

Random access memory (RAM), 2
Real time default, 429
Recalculation, 398–399
Receipt Number field, 75, 83
Receipts, 75
correcting cash receipt, 249–250

Receipts module, 37, 211
Receivables. *See* Merchandising business; Service business
Recording cash sales, 75–77
Recur, 20
Reference field, 83
Reference Number filter, 64
Refund checks, 265–267
Reorder points, 212, 285, 289, 292–293
Report options, 113–114
Reports, 20, 25
Reports command, 13
Reports menu, 25
Restore button, 492
Retail business, 212
Retained Earnings account, 152, 189, 324, 336–338, 356
Right-click, 494
Row, 20
Run, 491

S

Sales. *See also* Sales/Invoicing
analyzing, 81–82
merchandising business. *See* Merchandising business
paid by check, 244–247
sale to new customer, 232–233
service business. *See* Service business
taxable/exempt sales report, 251, 312
transactions using two items, 52–53
Sales on Account, 47–49, 216–217
Sales Defaults tab, 72
Sales forms, voiding/deleting of, 60–65, 234–236
Sales invoices, 20
Sales Journal, 37–38, 47, 75, 211, 239
view and print, 87–88, 267–268
Sales Navigation Aids, 10
Sales Navigation button, 47, 216
Sales Receipt, correcting and printing, 79–81
Sales Rep, 49
Sales report, taxable/exempt report, 251
Sales tax, 219–220, 239–240, 312–313
new company setup, 440–442
Sales Tax Authority, 440–442
Sales Tax Code, 440–442

Sales/Invoicing
    adding note to invoice, 54
    cash sales, 75–77, 239–240
    correcting/printing an invoice, 58–60
    discount pricing, 228–229
    entering transactions, 52–53
    multiple items and sales tax, 219–220
    new customer, 232–233
    print A/R reports, 56–58
    printing an invoice, 50–52
    sales on account, 216–217
Sales/Invoicing module, 37, 211
Sales/Invoicing option, 48
Sales/invoicing window, 19–20
Save, 20
Savings plans, 407–409
Scanner, 2
Scroll Bar, 18
Search, 18, 491
Select for Payment, 99, 121–124, 309–310
Select for Payroll Entry window, 395–399
Service business
    general accounting and end-of-period
      procedures, 152–153
        account name change in Chart of
          Accounts, 154–155
        Account Reconciliation, 167–168,
          173–174
        Account Register for checking,
          174–175
        accrual-basis accounting
          adjustments, 157–158
        balance sheet, 165–166, 181–182
        bank reconciliation, 167
        bank statement information,
          169–170
        Cash Flow Forecast, 178–179
        cash investment (additional) by
          owner, 163–164
        deleting existing account, 156–157
        depreciation adjustments, 160–161
        exporting to Excel, 182–184
        General Journal, 161–162, 175
        General Ledger Trial Balance, 177
        Income Statement, 180–181
        making account inactive, 155–156
        noncash investment by owner,
          164–165

        owner withdrawals, 162–163
        prepaid expenses adjustments,
          158–160
        Statement of Cash Flow, 179–180
        transactions for previous period,
          187–189
        Trial Balance, 175–176, 191
payables and purchases
    accounting for, 99–100
    adding vendor while recording bill,
      115–118
    aged payables report, 140–141
    bills using multiple expense
      accounts, 104–105
    Cash Disbursements Journal, 142–
      143
    Cash Requirements Report, 112
    check register report, 134–135
    credit from a vendor, 119–120
    deleting a bill, 114–115
    deleting payment transaction,
      135–136
    drilldown feature, 106–107
    edit payment transaction, 133–134
    editing posted transaction,
      109–110
    editing/correcting errors, 103–104
    entering a bill, 102–103
    modifying vendor records,
      118–119
    paying bills, 121–124, 130–132
    petty cash, 126–130
    previewing/printing Purchases
      Journal, 111
    print post printing check register,
      138–139
    print vendor ledger report,
      105–106
    printing checks, 124–125, 136–137
    reviewing bills paid, 125–126
    training tutorial/procedures,
      100–101
    Vendor Ledgers Report, 120–121,
      141–142
    voiding checks, 138
sales and receivables, 37–38
    accounting for, 37–38
    adding note to invoice, 54

analyzing sales, 81–82

cash sales, 75–77

Chart of Accounts, adding new, 68–69

correcting an invoice, 58–60

Customer Ledgers Report, 86–87

customer records, modifying, 74–77

customers, adding new, 68–73

editing/correcting errors, 49–50

Item List, adding new/verifying, 69–70

Items Sold to Customer report, 78–79

partial payments, 84–85

payments on account, 83–84

preparing credit memos, 65–67

printing A/R reports, 56–58

printing an invoice, 50–52, 58–60

sales on account, 47–49

Sales Journal, 87–88

sales receipt, 79–81

training tutorial/procedures, 38, 43–47

trial balance, 89

two sales items transactions, 52–53

viewing customer ledgers report, 67

voiding/deleting sales forms, 60–65

Service charges, 340, 342

Services command, 13

Services menu, 13–14

Settings, 491

Setup Guide, 429–432

Setup new company. *See* New company

Shift+Tab key combination, 15

Ship Date, 49

Ship Via, 49

Show Me How To, 16

Shut Down, 491

Sick leave, 385–390

Social Security tax, 410

Software, 3–5

application software, 3–5

computerized accounting, 5

introduction to, 3–5

operating system software, 4

Sole proprietorship, 162

Spin box (Windows®), 493

Split Transaction window, 129

Start button (Windows®), 491

Start program, 6–7

Startup Screen, 13

Statement of Cash Flow, 179–180

Statement Ending Balance, 168, 340–341

Statement of Owner's Equity, 165

Status area (Windows®), 490

Status Bar, 13

Stock Item, 453

Storage devices, 3

Subsidiary Accounts Receivable ledger, 37, 211

Supplies Accounts, 358–359

System date, 46

System requirements, 5–6

T

Tab key, 15, 19

Taskbar buttons (Windows®), 490

Taskbar (Windows®), 490

Tasks command, 13

Tax forms

Form 940, 402, 405, 412–413

Form 941, 402, 405, 410–412

W-2 Forms, 402, 413–415

Tax Liability Report, 404–405

Tax Service Registration, 17

Tax Table Service, 383

Tax tables setup, new company, 440–442

Taxable/exempt sales report, 251, 312

Template, 20

Terms, 49, 117, 215

Terms and Credit tab, 72, 231

Text box, 20, 493

Time & Billing Navigation Aids, 11

Title bar, 9, 20, 40–41, 492

Today button, 9

Today screen, 41

Toolbar, 20

custom toolbar, 12

Toolbar Components, 12

ToolTip (Windows®), 490

Training procedures, 38

Training tutorial, 38
    beginning the tutorial, 43–47
    computerizing manual accounting system, 424
    merchandising business
        general accounting and end-of-
            period procedures, 325–326
        payables and purchases, 283–284
        sales and receivables, 212–215
    payroll, 384
    service business
        general accounting and end-of-
            period procedures, 152–153
        payables and purchases, 100–101
        sales and receivables, 38, 43–47
Transaction(s)
    customer's credit limit, 222–224
    editing previous period, 189–191, 356–358
    entering, using two sales items, 52–53, 219–220
    previous period transactions, 187–189, 356
    sales tax and, 219–220
Transaction Amount filter, 64
Transaction date, 215, 285
Transaction entry, 44
Transaction Type filter, 64
Trial balance, 89, 175–176, 433
    post-closing trial balance, 191
Tutorial. *See* Training tutorial

U
Unemployment percentage, 446
Unit Price, 233, 290
Unreconciled difference, 170–171
USB Flash Memory, 3
User Manuals, 16

V
Vacation time, 385–390
Vacation/sick time, 447–448
Vendor(s)
    adding new, 115–118
    editing existing vendors, 305–306
    entering credit from, 19, 119–120, 302–303
    modifying vendor records, 118–119
    new company setup, 436–440
    paying sales tax, 312–313
    verifying account balance, 303
Vendor Event Log, 314
Vendor ID, 102, 303
Vendor Ledgers Report
    edit a posted transaction from, 109–110
    printing, 105–106, 141
    view credit in, 120–121
    view single Vendor Ledger, 142
Vendor List, 99–100, 283–285, 335
Verifying an open company, 8, 41, 213
Visa card, 241
Voiding an invoice, 60–61, 234–235, 313
Voiding checks, 138, 400–401

W
W-2 Forms, 402, 413–415
Waiting on Bill flag, 296–297
What's This?, 16
Windows®, 4, 13
    closing/shutting down, 498–499
    introduction to, 489–493
    mouse terminology, 494
    terminology of, 490
Windows Accessory Program, 491
Windows borders, 492
Windows Calculator, 28
Working Trial Balance, 175–176
Write Checks option, 122, 127–128

Z
Zip disk drives, 3